The Jersey Shore

The Jersey Shore

The Past, Present, and Future of a National Treasure

Dominick Mazzagetti

RUTGERS UNIVERSITY PRESS
NEW BRUNSWICK, CAMDEN, AND NEWARK,
NEW JERSEY, AND LONDON

978-0-8135-9374-6
978-0-8135-9375-3
978-0-8135-9377-7

A Cataloging-in-Publication record for this book is available from the Library of Congress.

A British Cataloging-in-Publication record for this book is available from the British Library.

♾ The paper used in this publication meets the requirements of the American National Standard for Information Sciences—Permanence of Paper for Printed Library Materials, ANSI Z39.48-1992.

www.rutgersuniversitypress.org

Manufactured in the United States of America

To Zachary and Alexander,
in the hope that their days at the Jersey Shore will be filled with
as much beauty, wonder, and fun as mine

Map of New Jersey, 1795. This map shows Sandy Hook as an island, the Shrewbury and Navesink Rivers outletting into the Atlantic Ocean, the "Cranberry New Inlet" at the current border between Seaside Park and Seaside Heights, and the Turtle Gut Inlet and Cold Spring Inlet in Cape May County. Courtesy of David Rumsey Map Collection, www.davidrumsey.com.

The Atlantic from Sandy Hook to Cape May beats upon a coast full of changing beauty. The long, quiet reaches of the southern New Jersey shore, broad highways of hard sand, seem ever complacent in the sunlight; which glitters upon the shining pebbles and small seashells, and streams full upon undulating sand-dunes. As you pass northward, the beaches are more and more pronounced in contrast against the sand-hills, marked here and there by rugged, ragged, unfriendly sand cedars,—those knarled and twisted trees that refuse to be civilized, and die rather than live in the care of man. The sand-dunes become sand-hills, and finally along the northern half of the coast are lost in bluffs, against which the sea beats with ever-increasing appetite. . . .

The invaders, whose advance guards reach the coast by May-day, work a great transformation. The summer cities are invested with life, light, and color. Everything is in motion; everywhere is animation, youth, and beauty; flowers, music, laughter, are the rule. The great hotels are crowded with people from all over—a thousand beneath a single roof; the sidewalks, the summer arbors, the long piers jutting out into the sea, are covered with fugitives from the inland towns. They are chatting, reading, smoking, lounging, strolling, riding about, bathing, sleeping, and eating, with no cares but for the shadow-side of the porch, and the sound of the dinner gong, if one there be. . . . Here is Utopia. Here, the education of the winds and the sun is free to both sexes alike. . . . And the inhabitants are very merry, having nothing to fear but flood-tide; sleeping as honest toilers only can; knowing that tomorrow's sun shall find no trace of to-day's misdoings. They will be obliterated, and the friendly Atlantic will make everything smooth again. The days grow hotter inland; the dust of July begins to settle in the streets of the great cities; the nights become more and more insufferable. Here on the coast the breezes are more even-tempered; the sea seems more blue; there is a greater charm than before.

. . .

In this way—or rather in these words—the reader is invited to the Jersey Coast. Is it asked to what the invitation leads? The coastline of the State comprises parts of Monmouth, Ocean, Burlington, Atlantic, and Cape May counties, and is a little over one hundred and twenty-seven miles in length from Sandy Hook to Cape May. . . . The bays and sounds along the coast afford a livelihood for quite a little world of people, whose commerce is comprised in fish, oysters, clams, lobsters, crabs, and wild fowl. These bays and sounds are about 117,000 acres in extent. The development of the coast into what it is, in the summer of 1883, has been largely brought about by the railroads. The facilities by them afforded have prompted the formation of companies and organizations, of which there are twenty-nine in operation upon the beaches of the five counties named. These companies have founded a string of cities that in time will so extend that there will be both rail and carriage way along the ocean front from the drive, at Long Branch, to the signal station, at Cape May Point. Every summer adds to the thousands who are already dwellers by the sea; every winter, to the householders in the towns and cities.

—Pennsylvania Railroad Company,
Cape May to Atlantic City, A Summer Note Book, 1883

Contents

      The Public Trust Doctrine and Eminent Domain   277
      State Action, Federal Funding, and University
          Support   286
      Revival: Cape May, Long Branch, Asbury Park,
          and Atlantic City   293
      Superstorm Sandy   298

      THE FUTURE OF THE JERSEY SHORE   303

      Acknowledgments   311
      Notes   313
      Index   333

The Jersey Shore

Introduction

I come to the subject of the Jersey Shore with a personal bias. For the millions of us who grew up in New Jersey, the Jersey Shore has a pervasive hold. We may not remember the first time we were dipped in the ocean by our parents, but the Jersey Shore has become part of who we are. Whether our experience as a child was day trips to the beach anxiously awaited, week-long vacations in a cramped bungalow with family and friends, or long summers spent at a family beach house, the shore evokes compelling memories. As teenagers it may have been the freedom of being on our own on the boardwalk for the first time, learning to sail in the bay, or lifeguarding on the beach. As adults, we continue to be drawn to the shore to give our own children and grandchildren the experiences we so enjoyed.

I grew up in Newark in the 1950s. We had few opportunities for vacations except for several days each summer spent at Long Branch, Seaside Heights, or Asbury Park. The thrills of riding the waves at the beach and the rides on the boardwalk lasted twelve months until we returned. As a teenager, especially with the availability of a car, the shore was the go-to trip in the summer on a hot day, or overnight if we could find a friend whose family had a summer home or was renting a house for a week or two. The ride might be hours on the Parkway in stop-and-go traffic with no air-conditioning; the accommodations might be a spot on the floor

in a crowded summer home. Whatever, we could sleep on the beach
the next day. Later on, one of my most memorable trips to the shore was
a July weekend spent at the home of the Commandant of the National
Guard at Sea Girt (a friend's father). We raised the flag the next morning
after a night hopping the local bars. Another was hitting a long-shot
Daily Double at Monmouth Park on the way to the shore (never since
repeated).

As an adult, I have visited the shore every summer since getting married in the fall of 1974, for one or two weeks at various beaches—from the
Dover beaches in Toms River to Avalon—and at various Long Beach
Island (LBI) communities. Eventually, we returned each year to LBI and
purchased a seasonal home in Harvey Cedars in 1999. We have entertained at the shore, learned to sail, visited the casinos at Atlantic City, and
simply enjoyed lazy days lying on the beach relaxing by the water. I am
hopeful that my retelling of the story of the Jersey Shore demonstrates my
appreciation of seasons and vacations lovingly enjoyed.

The story of the Jersey Shore is a story of change, constant change, right
up through today, which is not obvious to those who return each year to
the same resort looking for the same simple pleasures. The first chapter of
this book describes the physical elements of that change: geography and
climate. The final chapters describe the political and cultural changes currently shaping the Jersey Shore. New Jersey's geology provides a coastline
naturally suited for summer pleasures and adventures. But will it last? The
coastline shifts, sands attrite and recede with little regard to human
desires, and storms take buildings and livelihoods on a regular basis. Changing societal norms dealing with beach access and a heightened awareness
about our environment have already and will continue to impact the way
we see and enjoy the shore.

The story of the Jersey Shore is a story about transportation. The development of the Jersey Shore as a national resort parallels the growth and
development of transportation. The widespread popularity of the Jersey
Shore begins with the coming of railroads. Without clean, cheap, and

convenient access, the shore might still be largely uninhabited, the pur-view of hermits and fishermen. The individual (and mostly tiny) com-munities that dot the shore came about through the efforts of local businessmen eager to bring a train to wasteland areas that could be divided into lots and sold at a profit. The automobile eclipsed the trains in the 1900s and made the development of these communities even easier. As a result, each shore community offers its own unique amenities, allow-ing day-trippers, weekenders, and week-long visitors, as well as summer residents and year-round residents, to choose from a variety of beaches, home styles, fashions, and entertainments. And at all price levels. Could Atlantic City, Spring Lake, and the Wildwoods be any different? Over the last fifty years the availability of cheap and easy airplane service to dis-tant and exotic destinations has impacted the economics of the Jersey Shore's largest resorts, most notably Atlantic City.

The story of the Jersey Shore is a story of individuals driving develop-ment and taking control of beachfront properties. Beachfront devel-opment was a local issue in the not too distant past, as was beachfront protection. How the locals dealt with these issues contrasts with con-temporary approaches. The state government became a major player only in the past seventy-five years and still struggles at times with local poli-tics and "home rule." The federal government became a factor at about the same time through its ability to focus resources on issues of erosion, beach nourishment, and disaster recovery. Federal funding in the past fifty years has provided the impetus for the beach nourishment efforts that now dominate our approach to beach protection. But will that funding continue?

The story of the Jersey Shore today is a story of ideas and ideals. The laws defining who can access the beach have evolved since the civil rights movement of the 1950s and 1960s. The nature of the debate about who should be allowed to enjoy the beaches has changed from an economic issue to a civil rights issue. And even more recently, the focus on global warming puts the Jersey Shore at the crossroads of the debate about rising sea levels and what, if any, measures should be taken to deal with the issue both in the short and the long term (depending on each person's definition of short term versus long term). These issues have highlighted and exacerbated the tension between beach access and private property rights and the result can be seen in the post-Sandy efforts to protect all the state's beaches with dunes. The difference between historic and modern attitudes and efforts in regard to civil rights and climate change may be startling for the modern reader. All of these themes are present throughout the history of the Jersey Shore. They intersect and overlap.

One of the surprises of my initial research as I began this history of New Jersey's beach communities, was the realization that so much has already been written about the Jersey Shore. In the second half of the nineteenth century, during the development and rise of multiple summer resort locations, three books of substance appeared. First, Gustav Kobbé authored a well-written, gazetteer-like volume in 1889, *The New Jersey Coast and Pines*, detailing the stories of the shore and providing a history of the few established communities. The next year Edwin Salter covered some of the same ground in *Salter's History of Monmouth and Ocean Counties*. And in 1902 William Nelson produced a more elaborate and tastefully presented work in two volumes, *The New Jersey Coast in Three Centuries*. Although details and style differ in these three works, the story of the blossoming of New Jersey's beach communities is told well, albeit with emphasis on the leading resorts of the day, Long Branch and Atlantic City. Add to these the beautifully produced *Historical and Biographical Atlas of the New Jersey Coast* by T. F. Rose and T. T. Price (1878), which includes local, county, and statewide maps to go along with a history of the shore to that date.

By 1900, local writers and local boosters produced many additional volumes dealing with individual communities or groups of destinations. Some of these are simply resort guides that are fun to read both for the descriptions of the hotels, beaches, and amenities that could be found in each location and for the advertisements that paid for their publication.

In 1914 and 1936, two local businessmen on LBI (George B. Somerville and Charles Edgar Nash, respectively) each produced a volume about its glories under the same title, "The Lure of Long Beach." The railroads, ever aware of the need for advertising, produced their own versions including one or two that are unabashed attempts to sell lots at or near the station stops for each resort.

A full and comprehensive history, *The Jersey Shore* (1953, three volumes), covered the four counties on the coast: Monmouth, Ocean, Atlantic, and Cape May. In this work, Harold F. Wilson does a fine job bringing the history of the shore up to date and ties into the history of the interior sections of each county. John Cunningham, the author of more than twenty books on New Jersey history, joined the group in 1958 with *The New Jersey Shore* and Wilson authored *The History of the Jersey Shore* as part of New Jersey's tercentennial celebration in 1964. A simple search on Amazon.com for "Jersey Shore" will bring up sixteen thousand titles on every conceivable aspect of Jersey Shore history and lore, from the seasonal migrations of Native Americans to the seasonal migrations of Snooki and her friends of the *Jersey Shore* reality TV show.

This volume has been written for the state's sesquarcentennial (350th anniversary) and takes us back to the arrival of the English in 1664, but as with all histories, the story of the shore started long before. The book covers earlier stirrings, including the migrations of Native Americans, the appearance of whalers, and the sovereignty of Dutch traders. Soon thereafter pirates and smugglers took advantage of the shore's geology to plague the English authorities who came after the Dutch. Further drama occurred after 1800, when a few desirable beach resorts arose to draw the rich and sophisticated in nearby Philadelphia and New York City away from the heat and smells of their cramped cities each summer. Cape May and Long Branch attracted beachgoers of high station, including successive presidents now honored at Seven Presidents Park at the north side of Long Branch. When the first train pulled into Absecon in 1854 with passengers for Atlantic City the shore began its transformation from a

wasteland to a continuous stretch of beach communities from Sandy
Hook to Cape May fashioned to suit all lifestyles and all pocketbooks.
Trains brought the middle class to the shore in the second half of the
nineteenth century and the working class in the twentieth century.
Modern visitors to the Jersey Shore still enjoy sights and pleasures created
a hundred years ago to lure vacationers and to keep them coming back:
the boardwalks, amusement rides, saltwater taffy, Victorian architecture,
and more. Revelers in the Wildwoods and Bradley Beach might wonder
what all the fuss was about Atlantic City before gambling, and about
Asbury Park before Bruce Springsteen. Habitués of New Jersey's modern-
day seashore resorts, filled with McMansions and Starbucks, might appreciate learning how the shore's culture changed in the last one hundred
years from the fashionable big-city, big-hotel resorts into fashionable
single-family second homes in exclusive tiny boroughs. Homeowners who
suffered from Superstorm Sandy in 2012 might find a shared experience
in terror and loss with those who lived through the storms of 1944 and 1962,
the latter still within the memory of many senior citizens.

This volume presents a modern retelling of the history of New Jersey's
coast and its colorful stories. Readers may see their preferred stretch of
beach in a new light once they know how it developed. Bringing the story
of the Jersey Shore up to date also makes it clearer than ever that the one
constant at the beach is change and that the story line has shifted (like the
beachfront) in the last seventy-five years. Transportation, local developers, and local leaders no longer dominate our discussions of the Jersey
Shore. The coastline is fully developed; local communities need the state
and federal governments to preserve what they have; economics may continue exclusivity, but discrimination can no longer; environmental issues
now impact every aspect of shore activity. Natural forces, political forces,
and cultural forces have coincided to make us sit up and take notice of
what we have, who can enjoy it, and how we might lose it.

Today, more than forty communities line the 127 miles from Sandy
Hook to Cape May Point. Each beach community has its own history and

I have tried to cover many of these local stories. For the sake of space and breadth, I have deliberately avoided a history of the inland communities in the beach counties and the Raritan Bay resorts that do not front the Atlantic Ocean. Nor is this journey "down the Shore" meant to be a travel guide for today's beachgoers looking for the best beach, the best accommodations, the best rides, the best surfing, or the best pizza—there are more than enough guides to fill the bookshelves. Rather, I aim to provide a short history of each resort's development and quirks.

Everyone who visits the Jersey Shore has his or her favorite beach. For adults, this usually comes after years of beach hopping that leads to a gradual settling in to one particular beach. One of the shore's intriguing mysteries is how each person comes to truly believe that his or her favorite beach is the best beach at the shore.

Everyone who visits the Jersey Shore has his or her favorite moments. For some it's the thrills, for others the serenity.

Our spot is Harvey Cedars and our moment is the warmth and solitude of the beach in early evening: just us, the birds, the breeze, and the beauty of the ocean.

CHAPTER 1

The Ever-Changing Shore

Then the Sunne arose, and we steered away North againe, and saw the Land from the West by North, to the North-west by North, all like broken Ilands, and our soundings were eleuen and ten fathoms. . . . The course along the Land we found to be North-east by North. From the Land which we had first sight of, vntill we came to a great Lake of water, as wee could judge it to be, being drowned Land, which made it rise like Ilands, which was in length ten leagues. The mouth of the Lake had many shoalds, and the Sea breaketh on them as it cast out of the mouth of it. And from that Lake or Bay, the Land lyeth North by East, and wee had a great streame out of the Bay; . . . This is very good Land to fall with, and a pleasant land to see.

—Journal of Robert Juet, first mate, *Halve Maen*, September 2, 1609

The first written account of the Jersey coast comes from Robert Juet, first mate on Henry Hudson's *Halve Maen* (Half Moon) in 1609. Probing the coast of the New World north from Virginia, Hudson brought the ship into a shallow bay (the Delaware Bay) where it struck ground on the shoals. Lucky to be released, the captain would not risk his ship in this shallow water and left the bay, sailing south and east around a sandy-beached cape. Out in open water again, the ship continued north. At first, the coast visible on the lee side of the ship seemed hardly inviting: "all I lands to our sight and great stormes from them, and are shoald three leagues off." As they sailed further they found what appears to be Barnegat Bay ("a great Lake of water") and one of its inlets ("The mouth of that Lake hath many shoalds, and the Sea breaketh on them as it is cast out of the mouth of it"). It does not appear that the ship dared to enter the

"Lake," but anchored offshore for the night. Here Juet made his most famous pronouncement about the Jersey Shore: "This is very good Land to fall with, and a pleasant Land to see."[1] The ship continued north the next day and soon rounded Sandy Hook and anchored in what is now Raritan Bay. There the crew interacted with natives on the shore and later explored the river that now carries the name of the ship's captain before returning home.

The New Jersey shoreline that Henry Hudson and his crew viewed from seaward in 1609 may have looked much the same as it does today, absent the buildings. The sandy beaches of Cape May County, the tidal basins of Atlantic County, the barrier islands of Ocean County, and the coastal beaches of Monmouth County led up to the sandy peninsula that is appropriately named "Sandy Hook." Numerous inlets allowed access to the inner bays, the rivers, and the mainland. Many of the plentiful fish and game these and later explorers catalogued still inhabit these areas, feeding travelers and inhabitants alike, and many varieties of the birds they saw still grace the landscape with seasonal migrations. And yet, the geology and the climate of the New Jersey coastline have conspired to change the details of Hudson's panorama of four hundred years ago. The pounding waves on the beaches and the currents at the inlets change the contours of the shoreline every day, every month, and every year. The shoreline today would have been thousands of feet seaward in 1609; the contours of the islands have surely changed; the location and access to the inlets cannot be the same. Only in the past hundred years have the constant efforts of humans to discipline the forces of nature lessened the impact of the relentless reworking of the Jersey Shore. And yet, despite these efforts, powerful storms would still create new inlets and wipe away beaches if not for immediate and long-term responses.

Geology makes the Jersey Shore a unique natural treasure. The low sloping beaches of fine sand and shallow bays filled with wildlife attract millions each year. The beaches are the result of Ice Age phenomena, marking the boundary of the ice flows and shaping the land to the south of those boundaries with receding and rising waters. The impact of a rising sea level traceable to the Ice Age continues to be felt. Subtle differences in the beaches can be attributed to their facing angle to the sea, the materials that compose their sand, and their relation to the mainland. New Jersey's shoreline remains a changing mix of mainland, barrier islands, inlets, and bays, from north to south.

The Jersey Shore is part of the Coastal Plain, one of four parallel geological strata running through the state from the southwest to the northeast. The three northerly geological strata, each about twenty miles wide, contain mountains, valleys, dense forests, and arable farmland. The northernmost stratum, sometimes referred to as the "ridge and valley complex," encompasses the Appalachians, the mountain region running from New York to Alabama and cutting through the top of New Jersey (Sussex and Warren counties). The next southerly stratum is the Highlands, a southwest to northeast line of rock running about 600 feet high, with valleys interspersed (parts of Passaic, Morris, and Hunterdon counties). The southernmost of these three strata, the Piedmont strata, begins at Trenton in the southwest and runs northeast to Carteret just north of the Raritan Bay. The foothills in this stratum contain sedimentary rock, tumbling rivers and streams, and considerable arable land. These three geological areas cover about 40 percent of the state and represent the farthest extent of the glacial advance during the last ice age, 20,000 years ago.

The remaining southern part of the state is the beginning of a vast coastal plain that runs as far south as Georgia. These lands were at one time submerged beneath the sea. With the coming of the Ice Age, the waters receded, drying the land and dragging the coast eighty to ninety miles out to the Continental Shelf. As the ice melted, this process reversed as the flat land to the west of the Continental Shelf became sea bottom once again under a rising ocean. The coast moved westward and firm land now meets the Atlantic Ocean at the Jersey Shore. The Coastal Plain reaches further west, however, to the Delaware River, which remains saltwater as far north as Trenton (where the Piedmont stratum begins). The natural phenomenon of the fresh waters from New Jersey's highlands meeting the salt water from the Delaware Bay is called the "Trenton Falls."

During this latest warming period, the ocean has risen perhaps as much as 350 to 400 feet, although not at a steady pace throughout. The annual rise slowed about 2,500 years ago but modern science suggests that the pace has accelerated in the twentieth century.[2] Some geologists believe that Barnegat Bay, which now runs from Bay Head to Little Egg Harbor, may have reached further north and that the beaches at Long Branch and Asbury Park may have once been barrier islands like those today at Long Beach Island; that the constant action of the waves and the rising sea not only moved the shoreline westward but also merged these barrier islands with the mainland. In the 350 years of recorded New Jersey history, the coastland has moved steadily inland so the beaches viewed by Henry Hudson's crew are now far out to sea.[3]

The changes to the shoreline over the past 350 years can be seen by studying historic maps. Inlets have come and gone and islands have changed shape. Sandy Hook has alternately been an island and a peninsula on maps from 1614 to the present. The ocean has breached the beaches protecting the bays to the west on numerous occasions during our state's recorded history, including at a location somewhat north of Mantoloking near the outlet of the Metedeconk River, prior to the 1750s (the Herring Inlet); at Seaside Heights in the 1750s (the Cranberry Inlet); on and off, at the mouth of the Shrewsbury River sometime prior to 1778 and again in the winter of 1830; at Holgate and Harvey Cedars in 1962; and, as recently as 2012, at Mantoloking during Superstorm Sandy (just south of the earlier Herring Inlet). Most of the early incursions reversed themselves naturally, some quickly and others slowly, such as the Cranberry Inlet, which remained open for more than forty years but eventually closed on its own despite strenuous human efforts to keep it open and then to reopen it. In recent decades, in an effort to maintain the status quo, breaches like those at Harvey Cedars and at Mantoloking were quickly resealed.

Much of the change to the shore occurs during storms, but geologists can demonstrate that other, more constant, forces are at work as well. Part of this is pure geology. The three northeastern geological strata of New Jersey, like most of the coastline north of New Jersey and into in New England, were impacted by the glaciers and consist of bedrock that makes the shoreline resistant to erosion. The Coastal Plain south of the glacial advance, on the other hand, contains sediments that erode with the steady pounding of the waves. All the wave action on the Monmouth County beaches is from the east or southeast because Long Island and New England act as a shield against waves from the north and northeast.[4] The ocean face at Long Branch consists of sediments that presented an imposing bluff 350 years ago. The bluff has continuously released eroded sand northward to feed the beaches of Sea Bright and Monmouth Beach and on Sandy Hook (this is called littoral movement). Sandy Hook consists entirely of sand washed north by the littoral action of the waves pounding the beaches at Long Branch.

The littoral action on the Long Branch bluff also moves sand south, funding the barrier islands from Long Beach Island down to Cape May. But these beaches receive sand from the ocean floor as well. Without the protection of Long Island and New England, the waves in Ocean, Atlantic, and Cape May counties come more from the east and northeast. The mix of sand on these beaches suggests that a goodly portion of the sand comes directly from offshore and not from the eroding bluff to the north. Only the movement of currents at the inlets keep this constant process from overwhelming the barrier island beaches; the low sloping coastal plain below Atlantic City does the same for Cape May. Geologists have discovered that the size of each grain of sand on the southern beaches is considerably smaller (by half) of that on the northern beaches and that the mineral composition differs significantly. The northern beaches tend to be steeper and the southern beaches flatter due to these geological variations.[5]

In the past one hundred years, in an effort to understand the shore and its changes, geologists have identified five distinct regions[6]:

the Northern Barrier Spit (from Sandy Hook to Long Branch)
the Northern Headlands (from Long Branch to the Manasquan Inlet)
the Northern Barrier Islands Complex (from Manasquan Inlet to
    Little Egg Inlet)
the Southern Barrier Islands Complex (from Little Egg Inlet to the
    Cape May Inlet)
the Southern Headlands (from the Cape May Inlet to Cape May Point)

This scientific approach to New Jersey's coastline may distract from the allure of the beach on a sunny day, but it helps us understand the changes that have taken place in the past 350 years and explains some of the differences in the beach communities from north to south.

The Northern Barrier Spit includes Sandy Hook, Sea Bright, and Monmouth Beach. Today, Sea Bright and Monmouth Beach are characterized by a scarcity of sand, which is due, in part, to the erosion of the Long Branch bluff and the efforts of the population to keep out the ocean by building barriers like the seawall in Sea Bright. This 1914 monument to man's fight with the ocean has protected the houses and businesses on the other side but has also steepened the beach and stripped the beach of sand. One response to Superstorm Sandy in 2012 was the almost immediate announcement of funding to repair and rebuild the seawall. Although environmental issues have delayed the seawall project, the state acted quickly to replace the sand on these beaches, allowing sunbathers to return to Sea Bright and neighboring Monmouth Beach for the summer of 2013 despite the devastation caused by Superstorm Sandy. Sandy Hook has also been affected. Its contours continually change. The 1764 lighthouse built at the northern tip of the peninsula just 500 feet from the water, now sits one-and-a-half miles from the water. On the other hand, the narrow southern end of the peninsula breached several times in the

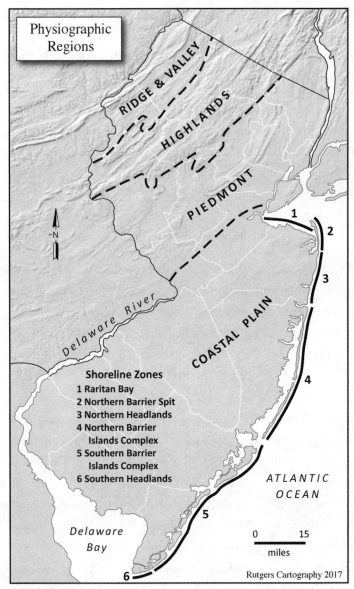

Map 1. Geological and Ecological Map of New Jersey. Geologically, the Jersey Shore is located within the coastal plain that begins at the Atlantic Ocean and continues to the Delaware River in New Jersey. The shoreline zones, as they have been identified by ecologists in the last seventy-five years, organize the beach communities into regions for tracking erosion and accretion. Map designed by Michael Siegel, Rutgers University.

last 350 years and threatened to breach during storms as recent as 1950 and 1978.

The Northern Barrier Spit and the Northern Headlands are unique because these are the only portions of mainland New Jersey exposed to the ocean. The Northern Headlands includes what is left of the bluff, which is at its highest (22 feet) between Long Branch and Deal. This area includes some of the most popular beaches at the shore and efforts to protect individual beaches with groins, jetties, breakwaters and the like have been ongoing for decades. Several of these beaches have also been replenished with transported sand.

The Northern Barrier Islands Complex includes the beaches from Point Pleasant Beach to Island Beach State Park (the barrier peninsula), all of the beaches on Long Beach Island, and the northern portion of the Edwin B. Forsythe National Wildlife Refuge. Perhaps the most dramatic impact of Superstorm Sandy occurred in this region: the breach at Mantoloking that linked the ocean to the bay and threatened the stability of the bridge from the mainland to the beach. Island Beach State Park, at the southern end of the peninsula, remains undeveloped and provides the best example of what the barrier peninsula and barrier islands looked like 200 years ago. The contours of the Barnegat Inlet at its tip have varied significantly, moving south by more than 3,500 feet as measured from 1866 to 1932 when jetties were first introduced to stabilize it. This inlet separates Island Beach State Park from Barnegat Light on Long Beach Island and remains a treacherous access for mariners.

The Jersey Shore begins a decided southwest turn at the Barnegat Inlet and is characterized by barrier islands thereafter. Long Beach Island runs eighteen miles from northeast to southwest and is defined by its inlets, Barnegat Inlet at the north end and Little Egg Harbor/Beach Haven Inlet to the south. Barnegat Bay runs behind the beaches from Bay Head to Holgate, providing a tranquil water park. Every major storm threatens Long Beach Island and the island has breached numerous times at different locations. Nonetheless, Long Beach Island has thousands of structures—houses, restaurants, businesses, and docks—and welcomes hundreds of thousands of people to its beautiful beaches every summer. One of its earliest attractions was the belief that it was free from pollen because of its distance from the mainland, and therefore a haven for allergy sufferers.

The Southern Barrier Islands Complex begins at the Edwin B. Forsythe National Wildlife Refuge and runs to the Cape May Inlet. The islands in this area are shorter than Long Beach Island and the areas to the west are salt marsh and sedge islands. The islands in this section, including Absecon Island, which contains Atlantic City, Ventnor, Margate, and Longport, have a unique "drumstick" shape, wide at the north end and narrow to the south. Seven inlets separate the islands and the original names of the islands reflect their geography: Seven Mile Island (home to Avalon and Stone Harbor), Five Mile Island (home to the Wildwoods), and Two Mile Island and Cape Island (once separate islands but now connected at the end of the county). The Southern Headlands runs from the Cape May Inlet to Cape May Point and includes the city of Cape May and the U.S. Coast Guard Base at the southern tip of New Jersey.

The inlets separating the barrier islands and peninsulas have played an important part in New Jersey's history as they allow boats to travel from the Atlantic Ocean to the New Jersey mainland through inland bays, estuaries, and rivers. The number and the locations of the inlets have changed from time to time and not all of New Jersey's inlets are friendly. From north to south, twelve inlets interrupt the shoreline today and several of these inlets (and several that have since disappeared) have colorful histories.

The Shrewsbury Inlet leads north to the Raritan Bay. This has not always been the case, especially over the period 1750 to 1850. Prior to 1778 (the date of the earliest reliable maps), both the Shrewsbury River and its neighbor just north, the Navesink River, flowed directly into the Atlantic Ocean, north of what is now Sea Bright. Sandy Hook was separated from the beaches to its south by this opening, which was as much as three miles wide, but Sandy Hook remained connected to the mainland by an isthmus that blocked a water route from the rivers to the bay. A storm in the winter of 1777 breached the isthmus. Slowly but surely, the resulting tidal flows filled in the opening to the sea. By 1810 the rivers' outlet to the sea was closed leaving only the passage north to Sandy Hook Bay. But another storm in late 1830 reversed the process, creating a new outlet to the sea further south and beginning the reestablishment of the isthmus. Human engineering took a hand in the process at this point. The isthmus was dug out to secure the opening to the bay, which allowed both outlets to coexist for a while, but by 1848 the currents closed the sea outlet. A number of years later, railroad engineers built bulkheads on the narrow strip of land along the oceanfront to protect their investment when they laid track for a train from Sandy Hook to Long Branch. This and subsequent man-made structures have prevented any new reopenings, despite several close calls.[7]

The Manasquan Inlet, which is a favorite spot for surfing, was a shallow inlet that was severely impacted by the digging of the Point Pleasant Canal in 1925. The canal connects the Manasquan River to Barnegat Bay and serves as the northern entry to the Intracoastal Waterway, which provides an inland passage to Florida for smaller boats. The idea for such a canal was originally raised in the 1830s, but it did not become a reality for almost one hundred years. When it opened, the river's waters flowed into the bay. An unintended consequence was the silting of the inlet. The state worked for five years to reopen the inlet and finally succeeded in 1931 by using high pressure hoses manned by National Guardsmen. This proved only of temporary help and the job had to be finished with rock jetties built by the Army Corps of Engineers. The jetties also stabilized the location of the inlet, which had been slowly moving south.

The Barnegat Inlet also moved south in the 1800s, erosion taking away the first lighthouse, built in 1835 at the tip of Long Beach Island, and threatening the second, the current "Old Barney" built in 1859. Bulwarking in 1940 and as late as 1988 saved this beautiful structure. The Barnegat Inlet, notoriously treacherous, has taken hundreds of ships to the bottom. Barnegat or "Barende-gat" is Dutch for "Breakers Inlet," a name supposedly given this nautical menace in the 1600s by the Dutch explorer Cornelius Mey, after whom Cape May was named.

The land mass and the inlets at the south end of Long Beach Island also have shifted several times in the last 200 years. At one point an island existed to the southwest of Long Beach Island across from Tuckerton, called Tucker's Island. Over time, the bottom third of this island was breached by an inlet, creating "Little Beach" as an island to its south. Little Beach continued to drift south and is currently an uninhabited island within the Edwin B. Forsythe National Wildlife Refuge. Eventually part of Tucker's Island became attached to Long Beach Island as a new inlet appeared and widened to become Beach Haven Inlet. The remainder of Tucker's Island slowly shoaled over, its lighthouse (built in 1848) fell into the sea in 1927, and the rest of the buildings and all of the island completely disappeared in the early 1950s.

Shifting inlets also account for some unusual county and municipal alignments. A boundary dispute lingered for decades between Atlantic County and Burlington County because the exact location of the inlet established in 1710 as the southern boundary of Burlington County could not be ascertained in the mid-1800s. The original county line separated Burlington County from Gloucester County; Atlantic County, created in 1837, succeeded to Gloucester's claim. A commission established by the New Jersey Supreme Court in 1885 took days of testimony as to the location of the current inlets and all prior inlets. Burlington County argued that the boundary line was the Brigantine Inlet; Atlantic County argued that the referenced inlet had been further north. Atlantic County prevailed and the Galloway Township sedge islands that front on the Atlantic Ocean (just east of the Edwin B. Forsythe National Wildlife Refuge) became part of Atlantic County.[8] Along these same lines, Atlantic City was the entirety of Absecon Island when the city was incorporated in 1854, separated from an island to its south by a shallow inlet. The inlet slowly silted until it became known as the "Dry Inlet" and then disappeared, becoming Jackson Avenue. Hence, the independent municipalities of Ventnor, Margate, and Longport now share Absecon Island with Atlantic City.[9]

Further south, Turtle Gut Inlet led from the Delaware Bay to the Atlantic Ocean where the Wildwood Crest beach exists today (at Toledo Avenue). The inlet separated Five Mile Beach and Two Mile Beach and was the site of one of the first naval battles of the Revolutionary War in June 1776 (see chapter 2). Cape May County filled in the narrow inlet in 1922 but the U.S. government reconnected the Atlantic Ocean and Delaware Bay in 1942 with a canal built as part of the Intracoastal Waterway.

Perhaps the most important transitory inlet in New Jersey history was the Cranberry Inlet. At some point in the mid-1700s a storm opened an inlet at the mouth of the Toms River near today's dividing line between Seaside Park and Seaside Heights. This inlet was deep enough for a square-rigged ship and immediately became important because it saved merchant ships the time, effort, and danger of sailing ten miles south to pass through the treacherous Barnegat Inlet. Toms River became a thriving port as a result, shipping pig iron and lumber to New York City. With the coming of the Revolutionary War, this inlet also served as a means for privateers (discussed in chapter 2) to slip in and out of the bay to smuggle goods to the Continental Army and attack British ships offshore. This inlet was of such significance that a British raiding party burned the town of Toms River to the ground in March 1782 to stop the depravations on its shipping. But natural forces give and take. A storm in 1812 began a slow process that eventually closed the Cranberry Inlet. Its economic importance caused the community to attempt to dig it out in 1821 and again in 1847. Two hundred and fifty men succeeded on the second attempt to get the channel open for a July 4 celebration, but the Atlantic Ocean would not let it be and sanded it over again almost immediately.

Natural phenomena and human activity continue to impact the face of the Jersey Shore, often at cross purposes, as efforts over the past 150 years to maintain the status quo have been more successful. The availability of heavy equipment and new energy sources has allowed individuals, entrepreneurs, local and state governments, and the federal government to build bulkheads and seawalls to hold the ocean back. Groins and jetties have also been built to retain inlet access to the ocean and to stop erosion before it takes structures close to the sea. Tons of sand have been brought from the ocean floor to replenish beaches lost to storms and waves. So, now that a great portion of the New Jersey shoreline has been developed (76 percent)[10] and modern technology affords man-made solutions, the men and women living and working along the shore no longer seek to adapt, but to fashion the shoreline to their needs and liking, maintaining the status quo or attempting to improve it.

Man-made solutions, however, often have unintended or unexpected consequences. The seawall protecting Sea Bright and Monmouth Beach, for example, has contributed to the loss of sandy beaches in those communities. The modern-day response to erosion is the nourishment of the beaches with sand from other locations and an emphasis on dune building, which has also been criticized. It is an expensive solution and some experts believe that the offshore sources of replenishing sand may be at the point of exhaustion or present other environmental difficulties. Over much of the last 350 years, local economics dictated these efforts. Only in the past seventy-five years have the state and the federal government intervened, as planning and funding for extensive and expensive projects require more than local resources. Only recently, as well, have environmental concerns been seriously considered in decision making as the changing mores of our society and the perceived impact of global warming and sea rise have altered traditional attitudes.

Anyone who witnessed the fury of Superstorm Sandy in October 2012 recognizes the fragility of New Jersey's beaches. Can we develop the shore further or even continue to maintain it? Over the next fifty years, the varying and diverse interests of federal, state, and local governments, homeowners, fishermen, business owners, and tourists will compete with the growing influence of environmentalists to determine how we react to the changing shoreline. Can this geological treasure be saved?

TABLE 1

INLETS ALONG THE NEW JERSEY SHORE, 2017

Shrewsbury Inlet: This inlet does not reach the Atlantic Ocean but instead runs north from the mouth of the Shrewsbury River to Sandy Hook Bay.

Shark River Inlet: The mouth of the Shark River enters the Atlantic Ocean between Avon-by-the-Sea on the north and Belmar on the south

Manasquan Inlet: This is the mouth of the Manasquan River between Manasquan and Point Pleasant.

Barnegat Inlet: This inlet separates the southern tip of Island Beach State Park from Barnegat Light at the northern tip of Long Beach Island.

Little Egg Inlet/Beach Haven Inlet: These two inlets have shifted considerably over the last 200 years, providing access to Barnegat Bay behind and the Great Bay/Mullica River at the southern tip of Long Beach Island.

Brigantine Inlet: This inlet separates Brigantine Island from Pullen Island to its north.

Absecon Inlet: This inlet separates Atlantic City on Absecon Island from Brigantine Island to its north.

Great Egg Harbor Inlet: This inlet is at Longport and separates the southern tip of Absecon Island from the northern end of the island of Ocean City.

Corson's Inlet: This inlet separates the island of Ocean City from Strathmere on the northern end of Ludlam's Island.

Townsend's Inlet: This inlet separates Sea Isle City on Ludlam's Island from Avalon on the northern end of Seven Mile Island.

Hereford Inlet: This inlet separates Stone Harbor on the southern end of Seven Mile Island from North Wildwood at the northern end of Five Mile Island.

Cape May Inlet ("Cold Springs"): This inlet is the man-made entrance to the Cape May Canal that runs from the Atlantic Ocean to Delaware Bay.

FURTHER READING

As mentioned in the introduction, numerous books detailing the history of New Jersey's beach communities have been written since the 1880s and I have drawn on them throughout this book for background and colorful stories, particularly as to how contemporaries saw and related events. Most particularly, I relied

on the following: Gustav Kobbé, *New Jersey Coast and Pines, An
Illustrated Book with Roadmaps* (Short Hills, NJ: DeLeeuw and
Oppenheimer, 1889); William Nelson, *The New Jersey Coast in
Three Centuries* (New York: The Lewis Publishing Company, 1902);
T. T. Price and T. F. Rose, *Atlas of the New Jersey Coast* (New York:
Woolman and Rose, 1878); Edwin Salter, *Salter's History of Monmouth
and Ocean Counties*, 1890); Edwin Salter and George C. Beekman,
Old Times in Old Monmouth (Baltimore, MD: Genealogical
Publishing Co., 1980); Harold F. Wilson, *Social and Economic
History of the Counties of Atlantic, Cape May, Monmouth and
Ocean* (New York: Lewis Historical Publishing Co., Inc., 1953);
National Park Service, *An Historic Theme Study of the New Jersey
Heritage Trail,* http://www.nps.gov/parkhistory/online_books/nj1
/chap1a.htm.

CHAPTER 2

1664–1764

A FEW DESOLATE BEACHES

Be it further enacted by the authorities aforesaid, that all commission offi-cers in their several precincts, within this Province, are hereby required and impowered upon his or their knowledge or notice given, that any pri-vateers, pirates, or other persons, suspected to be upon any unlawful design, are in any place within their respective precincts, to raise and levy such a number of well arm'd men, as he or they shall think needful for the seizing, apprehending and carrying to gaol, all and every such person or persons.

—An Act for the restraining and punishing Privateers
and Pirates, 1698

The Native Americans who enjoyed the beaches and the bays along the New Jersey coast were few, perhaps, but they recognized as we do today the richness of the fauna and flora, the waters teeming with life, and the wonders of the pristine beaches. The Dutch arrived in what is now New York and New Jersey in the 1600s, claiming the land based on Henry Hudson's 1609 voyage. They established New Netherland, an area that included present-day New York and New Jersey and lands to the north and south. But the Dutch claim did not stick. The English followed the Dutch, staking their claim on John Cabot's explorations of North Amer-ica in 1497 and well to the north of New Jersey. The English threw out the Dutch landlords in 1664 and so began the 350-year history of New Jersey. The English did not fully control the coast. It remained mostly unin-habited. They went about colonizing the mainland and for the most part left the coast to whalers, pirates, smugglers, and privateers who had the ability to make a living in these waters.

Native Americans at the Shore

The number of Native Americans living in the area now covered by New Jersey in 1492 has been estimated at about 20,000, but the population fell by three-quarters in the next hundred years as the European diseases brought by Columbus and those following behind him swept through the Americas. The 6,000 or so natives remaining when the first Europeans arrived after 1600 were scattered throughout the area. The Native American name for the entire area was "Scheyichbi," or "land of long water." New Jersey's Native Americans were the Lenape (referred to by the English as the Delaware) and are identified in three groups: the Minsi, the Unamee, and the Unalatchtigo. The Minsi kept mostly to the northwest, away from the coast. The Unamee filled in the center, including the shoreline from what is now Sandy Hook to the mouth of the Mullica River. The Unalatchtigo lived in the most southern section, around the cape and along the Delaware Bay. None of these tribes maintained permanent settlements on the Jersey coast. The oceanfront did not allow for comfortable year-round living.

During the summer months the Unalatchtigo along Delaware Bay would move the tribe from its permanent settlements to the tidal islands that are now Atlantic City and its surroundings. A loose translation of Unalatchtigo is "the people who live by the ocean." All three tribes of the Lenape visited the shore, however. Specific trails have been identified from Trenton southeast to Little Egg Harbor (using today's designations) and from Camden due east to Long Beach Island, and south and east, paralleling Delaware Bay to Cape May. Two northern trails began in Minsi territory at spots along the Delaware River, as high up as the Delaware River Gap, and led through Unamee territory to Sandy Hook. It was most likely the Unamees that Henry Hudson's men encountered in September 1609 while anchored in Sandy Hook Bay. There may have been Unalatchtigo natives along the southern shore in summer lodgings as the *Halve Maen* passed by in August and September, but the ship's log does not record any sightings. It is probable that the first European contact with the Unalatchtigo was made by the Swedes, who settled along the Delaware River in 1637.

On the coast in the summers, the Native Americans used reeds from the marshlands to build temporary lodgings. They fished the rivers and streams, the bays, and the ocean, and, like the Europeans after them, took oysters from wherever they could find them. They also ate clams and mussels. Historians and archaeologists evidence their life along the shore by the shell piles ("middens") found at Tuckerton and Barnegat. Shellfish provided a plentiful supply of food and certain shells were kept and worked into wampum, or currency, for trading and decoration. As much as we like to believe that New Jersey's first peoples enjoyed the beaches and the surf, the evidence suggests that they kept on the mainland for the most part and fished in the bays and estuaries, only occasionally making their way across to the ocean beaches. They were generally peaceable tribes eager to trade pelts to the Dutch for practical goods. The journal kept by first mate Robert Juet describes numerous contacts, including meetings on board the *Halve Maen* and on land for trading. Even so, on at least one occasion their interactions turned violent, leaving one crewman and many natives dead. And so it was to continue for the fifty years following Hudson's passage, after Dutch traders established a trading post on Manhattan Island to accommodate the demand in the Netherlands for furs. Schoolchildren were once taught that Peter Minuet "purchased" Manhattan Island in 1624 from the Native Americans for twenty-four dollars-worth of beads. Whatever the truth of this legend, the location provided the Dutch with an entrée to the fur trade to the north and west, a deepwater port, and a protecting bay with easy access to the Atlantic

Ocean. The Native Americans and the Dutch proprietors interposed decades of peaceful coexistence with short periods of violent clashes, particularly in 1643 and 1655, in the northeastern part of the mainland (what is now Bergen County), well away from the shore.

The Dutch tolerated the natives, exchanging cloth, metal utensils, guns and gunpowder, and alcohol for the furs of bears, deer, elks, beavers, otters, and foxes. The Dutch were not otherwise accommodating to the natives and had no interest in the expense of colonization. The Dutch population never grew beyond 1,000 inhabitants in all of Manhattan, Long Island, and northern New Jersey and never ventured far into the interior of what is now New Jersey. The Native Americans and the dense forests of elm, oak, dogwood, ash, chestnut, and maple discouraged permanent settlements. The Dutch did not settle along the Jersey Shore. The coastal shoreline proved hazardous for trading vessels and the rivers accessible through the inlets led to uninhabited areas. Except for the possibility of a few early whalers at Cape May and a few fishermen, the shore remained barren. Far to the southwest, along the Delaware River, Swedes and Finns started villages in 1638, but these encroachments were limited and depended on good relations with the Dutch as well as the natives. The Lenape, for their part, changed their way of life to accommodate the demand for furs, hunting well beyond their needs for subsistence. They had no workable concept of land ownership and over the next hundred years were moved out of the state.

The English Replace the Dutch

The ultimate departure of New Jersey's Native American population began with the coming of the English. In August 1664 a British fleet arrived in New York Harbor and demanded the Dutch territory for the British Crown. The outgunned directors turned it over. Thus begins the history of New Jersey 350 years ago, a tale of conquest, real estate development, and settlement. The most immediate impact was felt by the

Lenape. The English were interested in settling and sought to purchase the land from the natives and move them into distinct enclaves or out of the area entirely. By 1700 there were only 500 Native Americans still in New Jersey and in 1758 they agreed to accept a "permanent home" of 3,284 acres in Burlington County. Even this proved futile and the remaining tribe members, fewer than one hundred by 1796, moved to New York to join the Oneida.

As soon as the English gained possession of New Netherland in 1664, a portion—the province of New Jersey—was awarded by the English Crown in equal undivided shares to two English lords as a reward for their loyalty to the royal cause in the English Civil War. The land grants were of questionable value, however, being in an uncharted land inhabited by indigenous people 3,000 miles from England. Neither proprietor, Lord John Berkeley for West Jersey nor Sir George Carteret of East Jersey, ever made it to the New World to survey their prize. And prior and subsequent events made the Berkeley and Carteret land grants even more nebulous. Richard Nicholls, as governor of both New York and New Jersey, was busy granting property rights in New Jersey, including the Monmouth (Navesink) Patent in April 1665 that included land from Sandy Hook to Barnegat Bay and up the Raritan River. This patent led to early settlements of Middletown and Shrewsbury. When Sir George Carteret's cousin, Philip Carteret, arrived in the New World several months later to serve as governor, land disputes erupted that led to the dissolution of the Nicholls patents in 1672. To add to the confusion, the Dutch returned to New York in August 1673 and successfully reclaimed their former possession. The Dutch held title for twelve months until the Treaty of Westminster returned it to the English. The brief lapse in English ownership technically voided the grants to Berkeley and Carteret. Berkeley reacted quickly and sold his undivided claim to a group of Quakers in a complex transaction that featured bankruptcies, trustees, and phantom owners. Carteret waited on the benevolence of his friends to reinstate his claim, which came in 1676 through a famous five-party contract known as the

Quintipartite Deed, an effort to settle the overlapping and complex land disputes.[1] The proprietorships were divided and became known as East Jersey and West Jersey. The dividing line was less than clear (as were all contemporary maps), but ran approximately northwest/southeast from Little Egg Harbor on the shore to a point near the northerly beginning of the Delaware River. The government of East Jersey met in Perth Amboy and West Jersey's was based in Burlington. Carteret retained East Jersey; Quakers, headed by William Penn, achieved control of West Jersey.[2]

In the final event, New Jersey as we now know it began as these two English proprietorships. Legal and political machinations created land title disputes for more than a century thereafter along the dividing line, which moved with each survey and was not resolved until after the unification of the province in 1702. Vestiges of the line can still be seen today as the northwest/southeast borders of Burlington, Ocean, Monmouth, and Mercer Counties. Some observers explain the New York affiliation by half of New Jersey's residents and the Philadelphia affiliation by the other half as a remnant of this historical anomaly. The road name "Province Line Road" still exists throughout the state, notably in Princeton, Hopewell, and Allentown. The greater part of the Jersey Shore fell within East Jersey, from Sandy Hook to Little Egg Harbor at the end of Long Beach Island. The remaining third of the Jersey Shore fell within West Jersey, from Tuckerton to Cape May. The area around Raritan Bay was considered of significant importance due to its entrée to Manhattan and the Hudson River. The coastal beaches remained uncharted and uninhabited territory. Settlements along the water in West Jersey were maintained north from Cape May along the Delaware River, but not north along the ocean.

Once English dominion over the "Jerseys" became a settled fact, immigration began and settlements arose, but not along the shore for decades after 1664. Farmers and businessmen located near the beach but on the mainland, at Tuckerton, Toms River, Deal, and "Squan." The first permanent settlement along the beach was probably the whaling village at the southern tip of Cape May in the late 1600s when several families relocated from Long Island. In the next hundred years, Tucker's Island (at the southern tip of Long Beach Island) was visited occasionally by the Quakers in Tuckerton for retreats and enjoyment; the few whaling families at Cape May developed their settlements into a viable community; and other whalers set up shop at various spots along the beach, notably at Long Beach. But other than that, the shore was quiet and desolate.

WHALING

Whaling has an ancient history that goes back in Europe 1,000 years. European whalers pursued these huge animals in the English Channel, the North Sea, and in the waters around Iceland and Greenland for their blubber, their internal structure, the baleen found in some whales, and even the detritus in their stomachs, or ambergris. Whaling was difficult and dangerous work. A whale could weigh as much as eighty tons and would fight capture and death. Even though the loss of whalers and whaling ships was a constant threat, whaling was pursued vigorously to fulfill the demand of growing civilized populations for lighting oil. The oil was made by boiling down the blubber, and a single whale could produce forty to fifty barrels. The baleen could be used for umbrellas, corset stays, canes, and whips. The ambergris was used to make sponges and perfume. Enterprising whalers were able to sell the entirety of their take, not just the oil.

The first whaling enterprises in the British North America colonies were located on Long Island and in New England as early as 1640. Whales were plentiful in the Atlantic Ocean near the northern colonies and almost all early visitors to the Jersey Shore could envision whaling enterprises because of the abundance of whales spotted close in to shore. The first accounts of whaling in New Jersey describe "drift whaling," that is, the salvaging of dead whales washing ashore. Such a find could bring financial benefits to those lucky enough to be nearby and capable of processing the blubber into oil and extracting the baleen. (Spermaceti Cove on the western shore of Sandy Hook was named for a beached whale in 1688.) The importance of whaling in the colony can be seen from the interest of the proprietors, the assemblies, and the royal governors of the colonies: as early as 1678, licenses were given to a chosen few to take "great fish" from Barnegat Bay to Sandy Hook and for the processing of blubber; instructions to the Governor of East Jersey in 1683 included the recommendation that he "take particular inspection into the conveniency of fishing . . . and especially as to the Whale fishing, which we desire may be encouraged"; in 1692 agents were directed *not* to sell any lands "convenient for whale fishing"; an act of the West Jersey Assembly in 1693 required that poachers from out of the area taking whales from Delaware Bay pay a 10 percent share of "all the Oyl and Bone made out of said Whale or Whales."[3]

Court records and newspaper accounts from these early days also attest to the abundance of whales in the Jersey waters and the value of a beached whale despite the work involved in extracting the oil and baleen. The *Boston Newsletter* told of six whales taken in February 1718 at Cape May and Egg Harbour; the *Pennsylvania Gazette* reported that two whales, yielding forty barrels of oil apiece, were killed in March 1718 at Cape May and that "a Whale came ashore dead" near Cape May on March 5, 1730. The *American Weekly Mercury* reported that one whale washed ashore at Cape May and another, with several harpoons still in it, at "Absecun" in April 1740.[4] One early New Jersey story (1686) recounts that Caleb Carmen claimed ownership of a drift whale found by Native Americans along the beach in Burlington County and sold to Evan Davis. While there is scant evidence of Native Americans taking to the sea after whales, they understood the uses and value of whale blubber and baleen and claimed carcasses that would occasionally wash up on the beaches. Carmen based his claim on the markings on the harpoon found in the whale. A court ruled in Carmen's favor when Davis failed to appear.[5]

As early as the 1630s, two Dutch entrepreneurs, David Pietersen DeVries and Samuel Godyn, arranged for the purchase of land at the tip

of Cape May from the local Native Americans[6] to replace the whaling village across the bay at Lewes that had been wiped out by Native Americans
several years earlier. Despite their interest, the enterprise was abandoned quickly and decades passed with little activity at the cape. After
the English partitioned the Jerseys, Quakers associated with William
Penn and English businessmen, notably among them Daniel Coxe, began
to purchase land from the Native Americans in what is now Cape May
County. In 1683 Penn wrote that "Mighty whales roll upon the Coast, near
the Mouth of the Bay of Delaware, Eleven caught and worked into Oyl in
one season. We justly hope a considerable profit by a Whalery; they being
so numerous and the Shore so suitable."[7] Coxe clearly intended to establish a whaling community and advanced 3,000 pounds for the purpose.[8]
He arranged for French Huguenots to settle at Cape May to bolster both
whaling and wine-making enterprises. Even though his efforts proved a
success, Coxe ran into political problems and had to sell his holdings in
1692. Nevertheless, these early families brought to Cape May County
settled the area, and by 1698 one observer declared that "The Commodities of Capemay-County, are Oyl and Whale-Bone of which they make
prodigious, nay vast, quantities every year."[9]

The original whaling families, about thirty-five of them, dominated
Cape May through politics and intermarriage for as long as three generations
from 1700, even after whaling ceased to be their major enterprise. During
this period, the families—Carmen, Corson, Creese, Eldredge, Foster, Goff,
Goldin, Hand, Hewitt, Hildreth, Hoskins, Howell, Hughes, Leamings, Ludlam, Mason, Osborn, Reeves, Richarson, Shaw, Shelink, Stillwell, Stites,
Swain, Taylor, Townsend, Willets, Whildren, and Young—owned almost
three-quarters of the settled land in Cape May, three-quarters of all businesses in the county, and held most of the political offices in the county.
Interestingly, many of these families were descended from pilgrims who
arrived on the *Mayflower* in 1620.[10] The location of their settlement was
known as Town Bank, all of which was lost to the sea more than a hundred years ago. Similarly, a whaler named Soper established the first settlement on Long Beach Island at the "Great Swamp" (near Surf City and

Harvey Cedars) for the express purpose of chasing and capturing whales. He was followed by Aaron Inman and his sons. The borough of Harvey Cedars on Long Beach Island, where the Inmans continued the business through the 1700s and into the first half of the 1800s, was once known as Harvey's Whaling Quarters.[11]

Whaling was a strenuous and dangerous business. Taking to the sea in a small, open boat in the winter took courage, but it contributed to the income and livelihood of those daring enough to partake in it. For just a few months each year, generally February and March, watchers in towers erected at the beach would scour the ocean horizon for the spout of a whale. Once a whale was spotted, six men would run to the beach and launch a whaleboat. The pursuit was often for naught, but if the boat could get close to the whale a harpooner would hurl his spear at the beast. If the harpoon landed effectively, the whale would take the boat for a furious ride as it tried to escape. If the men did not let out their rope quickly or efficiently, the whale could easily capsize the boat; if successful, the whalers held onto their catch until the whale eventually tired. Then, they would pull the boat close, finish the job with a lance, and row the boat and the catch back to shore. The stripping of the blubber, in the early years on the beach and later at "try-outs" designed for the purpose, could take days. It was difficult and malodorous work as the animal decayed in the process. The oil distilled from the blubber and the baleen taken from the whale's innards were sold for cash and goods. One or two whales each season could prove a boon for the whaling families, bringing in $3,000 to $4,000 in Philadelphia for the product rendered from each one. Even so, the whaling families relied on farming and lumber and other enterprises to sustain themselves continuously through the years.

The whaling life of Cape May residents effectively came to an end in the late 1600s as the number of whales close to shore dwindled. By the early 1700s, the whaling business shifted to larger boats that could go farther out and stay out to sea for extended periods. An influenza-type epidemic devastated the Cape May community in 1713–1714 and politics and war before and during the American Revolution impaired the country's whaling industry even further. The British Parliament passed an act in 1775 prohibiting New England whalers from fishing the North Atlantic Coast and the Newfoundland areas. During the Revolutionary War, the British Navy effectively destroyed the New England whaling villages.

Whaling as a way of life did not necessarily leave the Jersey Shore with its disappearance in Cape May, however. After the war, when commercial whaling was restored, the geographic focus shifted to the Pacific Ocean and the North Sea, made famous in the nineteenth-century through accounts like Herman Melville's *Moby Dick*. New Jersey's efforts shifted north to Tuckerton and Toms River. Whalers at Tuckerton could sail out of the inlet at the southern end of Long Beach Island; whalers from Toms River would use the Cranberry Inlet (which was open from about 1740 to 1812). Both ports were also nearby to shipbuilding operations. In the 1830s, stock companies arose in Newark and Perth Amboy to purchase and equip ships for whaling in the Indian Ocean, the North Sea, and along the coast of South America. These extended voyages could last three years and included facilities on board to render the blubber into oil to avoid the return to shore. The whaling industry came to an end in the early 1900s, however, when kerosene, petroleum, and natural gas replaced whale oil as the major source of lighting.

PIRATES

We associate pirates today with warm seas, tropical beaches, and the sheltered coves of the Caribbean. Swarthy crews, sailing under the flag of the Jolly Roger, swinging aboard merchant ships with a cutlass held between their teeth. This vision captures (or, perhaps, embellishes) the life of pirates in the late 1600s and the early 1700s, the heyday of fearsome buccaneers operating not just in the Caribbean, but along the Atlantic coast as well. Legend and fact have commingled in the past 350 years making specific claims of pirate's buried treasure suspect, but without question the waters and beaches of the New Jersey coast lured pirates, including Blackbeard and Captain Kidd, who sought shelter, water, supplies, and convenient storage for illegal booty. The details of what actually occurred on the Jersey beaches and along its high seas may never be fully known, but we can safely allow our imaginations to get the better of us (especially when we begin digging in the sand on a hot and lazy August day, just trying to occupy the kids, but perhaps hoping to stumble on Kidd's treasure).

Spanish treasure ships carrying gold, silver, and other precious cargo traveled regularly from the New World back to Europe in the 1500s. The temptation of riches and a lust for adventure gave rise to pirates in the Caribbean Sea, men on fast ships looking to board and loot convoy stragglers. Spain dominated the region and wanted to keep other nations out, but once the English and French established footholds in the Caribbean, their governments encouraged marauders on Spanish shipping and provided safe harbors in their ports. War eventually broke out between England and Spain and these daring sailors, willing to risk their lives for wealth, became "privateers" who operated under "letters of marque" from their governments that gave them the cover of patriotism as well as a share of the loot. Then, as hostilities waned after the Treaty of London was signed in 1604, these pirate entrepreneurs found themselves unemployed and restless. Many simply returned to pirating, forgetting national loyalties and preying on ships of all nations. The War of Spanish Succession brought the European powers into conflict again in 1702, and with its conclusion in 1713 the European governments cut back their navies, giving pirates leeway in the open seas. By the early 1700s, the treasure ships were few, but merchant ships carrying commodities, especially luxury goods to the growing populations in the English North American colonies, were easy pickings. Many consider the period from 1690 to 1720 to be the "Golden Age of Piracy."

More often than not, just the threatening appearance of a heavily armed pirate ship was enough to secure a merchant ship's cargo. Occasionally, a boarding party would be added persuasion. As a result, the cost of goods rose for British merchants and insurance premiums soared. The New Jersey coast served as a haven from the hurricanes that threatened pirate ships in the Caribbean from June through September and as a source of water and provisions. The active port in Philadelphia also assured pirates of easy marks, as ships moved regularly into and out of Delaware Bay. The governments in the thirteen English colonies along the Atlantic coast were weak and without resources to deal effectively with piracy. Indeed, more often than not, pirates received help from local residents who enjoyed the advantage of buying looted goods at lower prices from the pirates. British merchants, losing merchandise at an alarming rate, demanded protection, especially for Philadelphia-bound merchant ships passing around Cape May. The British government responded by enacting the Piracy Act of 1698, which empowered British men-of-war to engage pirates and gave local governments the authority to deal harshly, and locally, with those captured. One British official reported that he captured four pirates at Cape May in June 1699 and would have had more if the locals had not "entertained the pyratts, convey'd them from place to place, furnished them with provisions and liquors, and given them intelligence and sheltered them from justice."[12]

In 1717, one of history's most famous pirates, Blackbeard (Edward Teach), took refuge off the Virginia coast and in the Delaware Bay while in command of *Queen Anne's Revenge*, a twelve-gun sloop of some speed. He took advantage of the unguarded merchant shipping in and out of Philadelphia, boarding and looting both the American ship *Robert* and the Irish ship *Good Intent* in October of that year. It is no surprise that some historians—and local tourist promoters—claim that Blackbeard buried some of his loot on the shores of Cape May, perhaps near Higsby's Beach, which is now considerably eroded and federally protected. Blackbeard's escapades in New Jersey included finding safe refuge in its back bays and sedge islands around Brigantine Island (just north of what is now Atlantic City). He may also have had a hideout on an island in the Mullica

River. It is said that he once avoided capture by the Royal Navy by floating underwater among the reeds in the salt marsh. Another story tells of
Blackbeard marauding inland towns, sailing his ship up the Navesink
River to attack Middletown for provisions and loot. (While such an event
did occur, the marauders might not have been Blackbeard and his men.)
This pirate raid was celebrated 250 years later at Christ Church in Middletown (near the site of the fight), in full costume.

Another pirate appearing in Delaware Bay was Captain Stede Bonnet
who sailed with Blackbeard in 1717. Bonnet returned in his own ship,
Revenge, the next year, also with success. Bonnet was known as the "Gentleman Pirate" because he was born to a wealthy family in the Caribbean
and left the good life to take to the seas for the pirating life. He treated his
crew as equals. Several years later, Delaware Bay became the graveyard of
the pirate ship *Royal Fortune*, captained by John "Bartholomew" Roberts
who was moving south down the Atlantic coast from Newfoundland
commanding two ships and several hundred pirates. Roberts had already
taken more than 200 ships in the summer of 1720 when a July storm forced
the *Good Fortune* and the *Royal Fortune* into Delaware Bay. While docked
at Cape May, the Royal Navy arrived and blocked his exit. Roberts's ship,
still laden with the treasures taken earlier, was cannonaded and sunk.
Roberts escaped on the *Good Fortune* and continued to take prizes in the
Caribbean and then along the Gold Coast of Africa.

But the life of a pirate was short (two to three years), dangerous, and
often ended at the end of a rope or on a pike. British authorities caught up
with Blackbeard at Ocracoke Island off of North Carolina in 1718 and
ended his pirating after a fierce fight. As a warning to others, Blackbeard's
head adorned his ship, the *Adventure*, on its return to port. Stede Bonnet
was captured in 1718 as well, was tried and convicted, and hanged in
Charleston. The British *HMS Swallow* caught up with Bartholomew Roberts
in February 1722 off the coast of Africa. The official report details his death,
but legend says that Roberts escaped the British once again. If so, he did
not reappear on the seas.

The real question for New Jerseyans, however, is where is Captain Kidd's treasure buried? William Kidd was, alternately, the commander of a naval ship for the British in the Caribbean, a wealthy businessman in New York married to a New Jersey widow, a privateer for the British licensed to attack French shipping, and a notorious pirate. Pirating cost him his life, although some claim that he was double-crossed when his high-placed and anonymous financial backers in London became frightened that their reputations would be ruined as stories began to circulate that Kidd's privateering turned to piracy. Whatever the truth of the story, the bulk of his treasure was never found and many suspect it is still buried along the New Jersey shore. Indeed, almost every town along the shore seeking summer visitors has generated some tale linking their beach to the treasure.

As the verifiable story goes, after successful adventures as a privateer in the West Indies in the 1690s, William Kidd retired to New York, where he pursued real estate and shipping investments. His privateering had made him a wealthy man, but either the lure of greater riches or the need for adventure sent him to London in 1695. He obtained a license from the British government to capture French ships in the Indian Ocean. Pirate crews, by nature, were a difficult lot to control and Kidd had had some close calls in the past, once being left on a deserted island in the Caribbean by a dissatisfied and mutinous bunch. So, when his exploits in the Indian Ocean proved of little value and his men sought to attack British ships as well as French, it appears that he went along. His richest catch was an Indian ship, the *Quedagh Merchant*, which was loaded with gold and jewels and was owned by an Englishman (albeit under French protection). When word got back to England, Kidd was branded a pirate.

Kidd overstayed the term of his license in the Indian Ocean, perhaps understanding that he no longer had the protection of the British government. When he finally left the Indian Ocean he sailed to the Caribbean, not England, and eventually back to North America. He hoped to clear his name through his connections there and, perhaps, by spreading around some of the enormous treasure he was reputed to be carrying. From the Indian Ocean, to the Caribbean, to the coast of New Jersey and the Raritan Bay, Kidd could have stashed the loot at any one of the dozens of places he landed. In New Jersey the most likely possibilities are along the beaches at Cape May, Five Mile Island, Brigantine Island, and Sandy Hook.[13] The best story tells of two large trees at the entrance of Matawan Creek near Cliffwood Beach (on the western side of Sandy Hook in Raritan Bay) used by Kidd as a guide back to the treasure.[14] Gold coins found on the beach stoked the story considerably, but after investigation they were found to be too recent to be Kidd's treasure. For sure, Kidd stopped at Gardiner's Island at the eastern end of Long Island and buried gold worth at least 10,000 British pounds. But the New York authorities dug it up after Kidd turned himself in at Boston in 1699. Unfortunately, neither Kidd's explanations of his actions nor his claimed treasure kept him from the hangman's noose in London in 1701. In one last turn of the story, the rope used to hang him split and he fell to the ground unharmed. Not so on the second try.

For those adventurous souls continuing the hunt for Kidd's buried treasure or Blackbeard's loot, keep in mind that the Jersey Shore continues to shift with each passing day. The treasure, if it is still there, or ever was there, may be well out to sea by now.

Smugglers, Privateers, and the U.S. Navy

Following pirates on Jersey's shores were smugglers of all sorts, avoiding British tariffs and fees before the American Revolution. This practice arose in the eighteenth century and created havoc for those involved in the transport and sale of taxed or prohibited goods, especially molasses for the making of rum. At that time, the English government sought to raise revenues and support for British goods by taxing luxury items desired by American colonists. The Molasses Act of 1733 protected and taxed British molasses, making it much more expensive than equally available French molasses. The taxes were collected as the goods were offloaded at designated ports, in New Jersey at Cohansey (now Greenwich), Perth Amboy, and Burlington. The resulting high prices encouraged the development of an illicit trade. Today we would refer to this enterprise as "smuggling," but the trade was so widespread and accepted in the colonies that, although discussed in hush tones, it was simply known as "the trade." In some respects, the trade in the mid-1700s sustained some who might otherwise have worked the same waters in prior decades as pirates. Rather than boarding unarmed merchant ships, however, smugglers more often used false or forged papers to move goods through the designated ports without tax or bribed officials charged with collecting the tax. However, if enforcement proved too strict, the desired goods were brought in undetected at secluded landing spots.[15]

The New Jersey coast provided a perfect cover for the trade. Smugglers would slip in and out through the inlets to sail to the French West Indies or to waiting ships at sea to pick up their cargo. If needed, shallow inlets could be easily navigated by local seamen but were treacherous for larger British naval vessels without local pilots. Slipping into "Eyren Haven" (Little Egg Harbor) or other bays and backwaters, the goods could be safely unloaded and carried across New Jersey untaxed, overland and on rivers, to their eventual destination, Philadelphia. Many respectable members of society, including most notably John Hancock, were engaged in financing these efforts. The trade proved profitable and the British authorities could do little to eliminate it even though most people knew of its existence, knew some of the profiteers, and benefited by purchasing untaxed luxury goods.[16]

To some degree, the acceptance of smuggling foreshadowed the American Revolution. The colonists could not tolerate the taxation imposed by Great Britain on the goods they needed and wanted and they demonstrated their disdain by trafficking openly in smuggled goods. The dispute turned violent in Cape May in 1765 when a customs agent (a "Scotch Laddy" as honest customs agents were mockingly called) insisted on payment of the duties; his neighbors were bent on avoiding them. Before it was all over gunshots were exchanged and tar and feathers employed. Royal Governor William Templeton Franklin recognized the anger of his constituents and refused to act. The case then went to the local courts where the judge sided with the locals.[17] The culmination of this contempt for British taxes was the Boston Tea Party in 1773 and the Cohansey (Greenwich) Tea Party along the Delaware River one year later in December 1774. Notably, some of the participants in the Cohansey Tea Party (and the Boston Tea Party as well) may have been the same persons involved in the trade. (We will see later on that this same trade in these same waters was resurrected in the 1920s to thwart enforcement of Prohibition.)

It cannot be surprising, therefore, that with the start of the American Revolution those persons skilled at navigating New Jersey's treacherous backwaters left smuggling to take up privateering and were encouraged by the Continental Congress and individual states. The same difficult inlets that enabled experienced mariners to avoid British tariffs allowed them ingress and egress to attack British shipping, taking goods for their private benefit and to help the revolutionaries' cause. The bays, estuaries, and inland rivers offered protection and safe landings. Congress and the states issued licenses to private citizens to prey on enemy ships and many respectable men financed the sailors willing to risk life and liberty for the cause as well as for the money to be made. British merchant ships were fair game wherever they might be, as far away as the English Channel or as close in as the Jersey Shore. The privateers would sell the contents of the ships taken and split the proceeds with their financial backers. Privateers operated from Boston to the Carolinas along the North American coast and from France and Holland in Europe. Even though it cost considerable amounts of money to outfit and crew a privateer, huge gains were made in this speculative business.

Success depended in equal parts on luck, skill, and daring. A skilled crew in a small boat would sneak up to a merchant ship, board the ship, and threaten the captain and crew with bodily harm. Guile and speed were employed, not overpowering armaments. The men were often in refitted whaleboats and would quietly row toward a merchant ship and board her before an alarm would sound. A strong crew could row faster than a slow merchantman might sail. Actual mayhem could usually be avoided and the ship would be sailed back to the Jersey Shore and into Toms River or Little Egg Harbor where the cargo would be off-loaded and sold at auction. If a British warship was nearby, a chase might ensue and cannon fire exchanged, but more often than not, the privateers would sail the merchant ship back to a shallow inlet and pass through to safety, forcing the warship to call off the chase for lack of depth or the lack of a pilot. If a British ship in chase was able to pass through the inlet, the inland rivers provided a quick escape for low draft boats loaded with captured goods, hiding places, and routes inland. From 1776 to 1783, American privateers brought in more than 700 vessels carrying more than fifteen million dollars-worth of British goods, along with captured Hessians and munitions.[18] New Jersey privateers contributed to this toll. One of the most notable American financiers was Robert Morris of Philadelphia, who served Congress as the de facto secretary of the treasury during the Revolutionary War.

Privateers operated up and down the coast, from New Brunswick on the Raritan River, Toms River, Chestnut Neck on the Mullica River, and Cape May. Captain William Marriner, from New Brunswick, went out in a whaleboat in April 1778 to recapture an American privateer, the *Blacksnake*, taken sometime earlier by the British. Not only did he and his nine men succeed, but they immediately put the *Blacksnake* under sail to fight and capture the British *Morning Star*. Marriner's men sailed them both back to Little Egg Harbor. The raiders operating out of Toms River used the Cranberry Inlet (through what would now be Seaside Heights) for access directly to the Atlantic Ocean, with equally devastating effect.

Captain Sam Bigelow captured the *Betsey* and the *Dove* in 1780, operating
from Toms River. The *Dove* had caught itself on the sandbar outside of
Long Beach Island. Bigelow and his man just rowed out, took the ship,
righted it, and sailed it into Toms River.

Some of the most fascinating tales, however, come from the backwaters near Little Egg Harbor and a long-ago abandoned port on the Mullica River known as Chestnut Neck, near Port Republic in Atlantic County.
The privateers using Chestnut Neck as a base of operations sailed through
the Little Egg Harbor Inlet in search of suitable prey. British command-
ers in New York, New Jersey, and Pennsylvania chafed at the success of
these raids and tried hard to put a stop to them (just as they had tried to
stop pirating and smuggling in the years and decades earlier). Twice they
raided Chestnut Neck, but they could not close down its operations. In
July 1777 four British ships made it through Little Egg Harbor Inlet, with
captured pilots, and into the Mullica River. They were able to capture at
least two privateering vessels and retrieve their cargo before retreating. In
response, the patriots built a fort along the heights for protection. Unfortunately, the fort was not fully armed with cannon when a little more than
one year later, in October 1778, the British sent nine ships plus transports
with 300 Regulars and 100 Loyalists "to clean out that nest of Rebel
Pirates," as British commander Henry Clinton saw it. South Jersey privateers had had a particularly successful run for the preceding twelve
months and the British admiralty wanted to put a stop to the depreda-
tions. Warned of their coming, the patriots removed as many ships and
stores as possible and defended their port from their unfinished works
before disappearing into the Pine Barrens. Time and tide eventually drove
the British out, but not before they burned the captured ships, torched the
village, and destroyed warehouses, stores, and a nearby salt works. No
Americans were killed or captured in the fight at Chestnut Neck, but the
Americans suffered a devastating loss that night. At the first alarm, New
Jersey's governor, William Livingston, ordered a detachment of 333 men

under the command of Count Casimir Pulaski to Chestnut Neck. But they got lost in the Pine Barrens and never arrived. Some of the men ended up on Osborne's Island near Tuckerton. The story has it that an American deserter or a Tory sympathizer signaled the British ships as they were heading back to sea and directed them to the sleeping soldiers. In a silent attack, thirty or forty of Pulaski's men were killed where they slept. In their hurry to flee this awful deed, however, the British flagship, *HMS Zebra*, foundered, and the British had to burn it in the shallow waters. The Battle of Chestnut Neck may have seemed a British success at the time (at least according to the official British report), but the "skulking banditti" who disappeared into the woods before the British troops[19] soon regrouped to continue their efforts on behalf of the revolution. In addition to their usual haul of British cargo, one year later Jersey sailors on the privateer *Mars* captured the British ship *Triton* and brought it, its captured crew, and an entire company of Hessians into Chestnut Neck as a spectacular prize, as if to prove that the British raid had failed its purpose!

In this part of the state, however, Tories could be more dangerous than the British Navy, for they too knew the inlets and the shore. One local, William Dillon of Island Heights, Toms River, worked both sides, or so it seemed until he led Loyalists and a British flotilla in March 1782 through the Cranberry Inlet to capture the Toms River blockhouse and burn the town. The raiders took several privateer ships as well. Later that year, a gruesome event occurred on the dark night of October 25, 1782. Privateer Captain Andrew Steelman, sailing the *Alligator* out of Cape May, came upon a British merchant ship that had beached on the north end of Long Beach Island. His men spent the better part of a day unloading the boat's valuable cargo and fell asleep on the beach. Tory Captain John Bacon heard of the beached ship and quietly rowed his men over to the island from the mainland during the night. Without warning or mercy, Bacon and his men killed twenty of the twenty-five patriots, most while they still slept, finishing their slaughter with bayonets. More than six months later, a posse sent to find Bacon to seek retribution for the Long Beach Island Massacre cornered him near Tuckerton and took revenge after a desperate fight.

In 1910 the Daughters of the American Revolution erected a statue near the location of Chestnut Neck to commemorate the battles fought there and the bravery and skill of the hundreds of New Jersey privateers who so inflamed the British Navy. The statue stands fifty feet high with a Minuteman on top facing the Mullica River. In 1988 the Sons of the American Revolution contributed a monument to the thirty-four privateering captains who served from 1776 to 1783.

Not all the maritime activity along the Jersey Shore was fought by privateers. One of the first naval battles of the Revolutionary War took place at Turtle Gut Inlet in Cape May County before the signing of the Declaration of Independence. A privateer brigantine, the *Nancy*, had sailed to St. Thomas and St. Croix to pick up 386 barrels of gunpowder for George Washington's troops. The ship was making its way back to New Jersey waters when it was spotted by two British warships, the *Orpheus* and the *Kingfisher*, blockading the entrance to Delaware Bay. On the morning of June 29, 1776, the *Nancy* neared the coast and was sailing south trying to reach the inlet before the British ships could catch her, but the brigantine was too slow. The British ships closed in. Nearby, Captain John Barry of the newly created U.S. Navy was in command of three ships that had just days before slipped past the British blockade of the bay. Barry sailed two of his ships, the *Lexington* and the *Wasp*, to the *Nancy* as fast as the light winds could take them and, when close, launched longboats to reach her in the shallow waters. Scrambling aboard, Barry ordered Captain Hugh Montgomery to sail the *Nancy* straight into shore, beaching the ship at the entrance to the inlet in an attempt to save as much of her cargo as possible. The heavy British warships could not maneuver in too close and were trying to find the range for their guns. Barry's crew, in what little time they had, began to off-load the gunpowder as British marines approached in longboats of their own. Locals scurried to aid the American sailors, rolling more than 265 barrels of gunpowder off the *Nancy* and onto the beach. Once the *Orpheus* had the *Nancy* within range, time ran out. Barry, Montgomery, and the crew had to leave the ship, but not before using the mainsail to create a giant fuse to blow the remaining 121 kegs in the cargo hold. They lit the fuse and abandoned the ship. As they left, British marines reached the *Nancy* and climbed aboard from their longboats, believing that the Americans had surrendered the ship and its contents. Minutes later a tremendous explosion killed more than two dozen sailors and the British lost their prize. After the Battle of Turtle Gut, Commodore John Barry went on to be hailed as the "father" of the U.S. Navy.

Further Reading

For background on Native Americans, see Gregory E. Dowd, *The Indians of New Jersey* (NJ Historical Commission, 1994); Herbert Kraft, *The Lenape* (NJ Historical Society, 1994); Mark Stewart, *New Jersey Native Peoples* (Chicago: Heinemann Library, 2003); C. A. Weslager, *The Delaware Indians: A History* (New Brunswick, NJ: Rutgers University Press, 1972); C. A. Weslager, John Swiento-chowski, and L. T. Alexander, *The Delaware's Forgotten Folk* (Philadelphia: University of Pennsylvania Press, 1943); and Edward S. Wheeler, *Scheyichbi and the Strand or Early Days Along the Delaware* (Philadelphia: J.P. Lippincott and Company,1876).

On the English and the Dutch, see Jeffrey M. Dorwart, *Cape May County, New Jersey*, (New Brunswick, NJ: Rutgers University Press, 2002); Sydney G. Fisher, *The Quaker Colonies: A Chronicle of the Proprietors of the Delaware* (New Haven, CT: Yale University Press, 1921); Rufus M. Jones, Isaac Sharpless, and Amelia M. Gummere, *The Quakers in the American Colonies* (London: Macmillan, 1911); Albert Cook Myers, ed., *Narratives of Early Pennsylvania, West New Jersey and Delaware, 1630–1707* (New York: Charles

Scribner's Sons, 1912); John E. Pomfret, *Colonial New Jersey* (New York: Charles Schribner's Sons, 1973).

On whaling, see Barbara Lipton, "Whaling Days in New Jersey," *Newark Museum Quarterly* (Spring/Summer, 1975); James C. Connolly, "Whaling in New Jersey," Proceedings of the New Jersey Historical Society, vol. 8, no. 4. (October 1928); Eric Jay Dolin Leviathan, *The History of Whaling in America* (New York: W. W. Norton, 2007); Richard J. Romm, "America's First Whaling Industry and The Whaler Yeomen of Cape May, 1630–1830," master's thesis, Rutgers, State University of New Jersey, 2010; and Harry B. Weiss, Howard R. Kemble, and Millicent T. Carre, *Whaling in New Jersey* (Trenton: NJ Agricultural Society, 1974).

On pirates, smugglers, and privateers, see Daniel Diehl and Mark P. Donnelly, *Pirates of New Jersey: Plunder and High Adventure on the Garden State Coastline* (Mechanicsburg, PA: Stackhole Books, 2010); Angus Konstam, *History of Pirates* (Lanham, MD: Lyons Press, 1999); Edgar Stanton Maclay, *A History of American Privateers* (New York: D. Appleton, 1899); Robert H. Patton, *Patriot Pirates, The Privateer War for Freedom and Fortune in the American Revolution* (New York: Vintage Books, 2008); Robert A. Peterson, *Patriots, Pirates and Pineys* (Medford, NJ: Plexus Publishing, Inc., 2000); Arthur D. Pierce, *Smugglers' Woods, Jaunts and Journeys in Colonial and Revolutionary New Jersey* (New Brunswick, NJ: Rutgers University Press, 1992); Marcus Rediker, *Villains of All Nations, Atlantic Pirates in the Golden Age* (Boston: Beacon Press, 2004); Edward Rowe Snow, *Pirates and Buccaneers of the Atlantic Coast* (Beverly, MA: Commonwealth Editions, 1944); and several of many online resources that deal in particular with Captain Kidd's treasure: Mary Rizzo, *New Jersey's Whaleboat Privateers*, http://www.gardenstatelegacy.com/files/NJs _Whaleboat_Privateer_Rizzo_GSL62.pdf; *Piracy and Privateering in the Atlantic World: 1500–1800*, http://www3.gettysburg.edu /~tshannon/hist106web/site3/beginnings%20of%20piracy%201 .htm; "Jersey Shore Pirates," http://www.jerseyshorepirates.com /lore.php; "Captain Kidd's Treasure Is in New Jersey," worldpress .com; Michael J. Launay, "Hunting for the Buried Treasure of Captain Kidd," *Weird New Jersey*, vol. 14, http://weirdnj.com /stories/mystery-history/captain-kidd/.

CHAPTER 3

1765–1850

THE RISE OF RESORTS

Instead of the sunburnt leafless sea coast we found a spacious sea shore hotel with all the requisites of ball room, excellent bar, well furnished table and comfortable lodging for over one hundred persons. The company of well dressed persons of every shade of fashion seemed thrown together like cabin passengers on board a ship at sea—in number about enough not to make a throng—and civility and good humor the order of the day.
—Comments of an unknown young woman on a second visit
to the Philadelphia House on Long Beach, 1821

In 1800 few people lived near New Jersey's beaches and few others visited. Settlement of what is now New Jersey began slowly in Bergen County (the Dutch) and along the Delaware Bay (the Swedes, the Finns, and the Dutch). The most populous county in the state at the start of the Revolutionary War in 1776 was the farming county of Hunterdon (now one of the least populated), which borders the Delaware River in the western part of the state. The dangerous shoals up and down the coast made navigation difficult for sailing ships approaching from the sea and led to little more than empty beaches and wild brush. The barrier islands were used, if at all, for the untethered and untended grazing of horses and cattle. The sandy beaches offered little to sustain life year round. Sea bathing was not considered a sport or a past time. The inlets and estuaries may have provided opportunities for pirates, smugglers, and privateers, but few others. By 1800, the villages that arose around the whaling industry in Cape May and on Long Beach remained; merchants at Tuckerton, "Squan," and Toms River took advantage of their easy access to the ocean and the New York markets with industries to serve those markets; the military significance of Sandy Hook had become apparent; and several farming communities like "Deale" welcomed occasional sea bathers. But for the most part, the shore remained relatively deserted for more than a century after 1664. Few Native Americans remained in the state to continue their seasonal migrations to the shore.

The attraction of the shore began to change at about the time of the American Revolution. One early visitor may have seen the future clearly. Carl Magnus Wrangel, a Swedish Lutheran minister, traveled from Philadelphia to Little Egg Harbor in 1764 to preach to a congregation that had settled nearby. His journal provides a glimpse of the shore in its natural state, long before the development of any resorts. It also provides a glimpse of what the shore would become. Wrangel was, literally, on a mission, but he took the time to enjoy the beauty and the benefits of the beach. After five days of travel, stopping at homes of the faithful (and not so faithful) along the way, Wrangel reached Little Egg Harbor. At some point, his hosts ferried him across the bay to the ocean at Long Beach (now Long Beach Island). He noted "the pleasant coolness of the ocean," the abundance of oysters and "clawed crayfish" (lobsters) that his party was able to take out of the bay without difficulty, the "wild geese, wild ducks, [and] sea gulls" for the shooting, and mussels, snails, and coral on the beach. The pastor enjoyed strolling the beach for several hours and eating wild grapes that grew in the sand. He extolled the virtues of saltwater bathing—and drinking: "it is considered healthful and therefore a great many people with illnesses come here in the spring and summer for two or three weeks to bathe in the water and drink it." He considered the locals blessed.[1] It took the next one hundred years, but countless others would come to share his appreciation of the shore.

So how is it that the Jersey Shore transformed itself from a sparsely inhabited wasteland to the premier summer resort in the nation? The beginnings of the Jersey Shore as a tourist attraction came in time and in just a few locations—Tucker's Island, Cape May, and Long Branch. These destinations began to attract small crowds as early as 1800. A few enterprising individuals understood that the beaches could offer solace in the hot and humid summer months and recognized the need for hotels with clean rooms and good food to encourage returnees each summer. Physicians touted the sea air and saltwater as therapeutic for a variety of ailments including ennui. The contrast with the heat, smells, and disease in Philadelphia and New York during the summer quickly became apparent to those lucky or wealthy enough to visit New Jersey's few accessible beaches. Soon boarding houses and hotels supplemented the homes and outbuildings of the farmers at Deale and Squan who had entertained those first tourists. By the 1830s the allure of the shore was obvious and several large hotels near the water boasted elegance as well as the beauty and therapeutic benefits of the beach. Other areas sought to attract guests with fishing and gunning. When a railroad showed the way to the shore in 1854, the slow progress in a few locations gave way to fast-paced progress up and down the coastline. The promise of the shore came to life. The early days of the 1800s led the way.

SANDY HOOK, "SQUAN," DEAL, AND TOMS RIVER

Not all of New Jersey's beaches remained undisturbed prior to 1800. Beginning in 1764 the northern end of the Jersey Shore served a significant purpose. The six-mile spit of beach aptly named Sandy Hook, the entrance way to New York's harbor, was of considerable importance. Richard Hartshorne, brother of Hugh Hartshorne, one of the twelve proprietors of East Jersey, had obtained tracts within the Monmouth Patent from the governor and the proprietors in October 1677, which included Sandy Hook. A leasehold for twenty-one years allowed Hartshorne to "enjoy the whole range and benefitt of Hearbage and feed for hogs and cattle with privilege of fowling, fishing, etc." It also recited his proposal

to establish a "fishery" at his own expense. His rent was set at one pep-
percorn a year, "if demanded."[2] Eventually he gained title to much of the
peninsula. Hartshorne, a Quaker and a lawyer, served as high sheriff of
Monmouth County and speaker of the colonial assembly. Title to his
holdings passed to his heirs and a substantial portion of Sandy Hook was
sold in the early 1800s to the U.S. government for military purposes. But
it was the four acres the Hartshorne family sold earlier that holds our
attention still today. Businessmen in New York wanted a light to help
ships coming into New York Harbor and financed the building with a lottery. The Sandy Hook lighthouse was first lit on June 11, 1764, and remains
the oldest continuously operating lighthouse in the country.[3]

When the British occupied New York City in 1776 during the Revolutionary War, the lighthouse served them well, guiding transport and supply ships into the harbor. As a result, American Patriots tried, in vain, to
destroy the lighthouse. Two years later, thousands of British soldiers
massed on the beaches of Sandy Hook in the heat of June 1778, having
marched from Philadelphia to New York through New Jersey. One day
earlier, on June 28, they had suffered a drubbing at the hands of George
Washington at the Battle of Monmouth. The tired soldiers were eager to
get themselves and their baggage train onto the transports that took them
quickly and safely across Raritan Bay to Manhattan. After the American
Revolution, the Sandy Hook lighthouse continued to help ships coming
and going from New York although it was supplemented over the next
250 years with additional lights.

At the time of the Revolutionary War only few people living in New
York City realized the possibilities of the Jersey Shore, the gently sloping
beaches, tranquil bays, soothing breezes, or natural wonders. Some may
have visited the beaches at Deal and Squan (what is now Manasquan). The
history of Deal goes back to 1670 when Thomas Potter from Deale, England,
settled a stretch of beach adjoining Long Pond (now Deal Lake). In the
following decades, fishermen and farmers living in the area would rent
out rooms to boarders who occasionally stopped in the summer to enjoy

the air and sea. Similarly, the first settlers in what is now Manasquan purchased the land from Native Americans in 1685 and the name "Squan" may be a derivation of a Unami expression for "stream of the island of squaws." Neither of these destinations drew crowds, however, even though an occasional report of people enjoying "sea bathing" appeared in city newspapers prior to 1800. Squan was better known as an industrial town. During the war, the British used the Manasquan Inlet to reach and destroy the Union Salt Works in April 1778 and put nearby homes to the fire as well.[4] Loyalist sailors repeated the destruction two years later in April 1780. Both Deal and Squan were mentioned decades later in Thomas F. Gordon's *Gazetteer of the State of New Jersey* (a contemporary form of Fodor guide), in 1834. Squan is described as a place "much frequented for sea-bathing" where accommodations could be found in comfortable farm-houses.[5] A hotel, the Osborne House, was built at Squan in 1815. Even so, Squan Village served more as a farming and merchant location than a resort, with a wheelwright and working boats carrying goods to New York City. Deal is described as a "small hamlet" with "several boarding houses that could accommodate 50 to 100 people comfortably" quite a distance from the beach.

Toms River also played a role in the Revolutionary War, as a haven for privateers as well as a commercial center. The town boasted an active port for the shipping of pig iron and lumber and a thriving shipbuilding industry. The name, of course, is associated with the broad river that empties into Barnegat Bay and the town on the high ground on the north bank of the river. An earlier name for Toms River was Goose Creek. The Dover beaches and Ortley Beach (which are part of the incorporated township today) were barren at the time. The township of Dover, in which the village of Toms River was located, dated back to a Royal Charter in 1768 and was one of New Jersey's first 104 townships.[6] "Tom's" identity has never been settled, however. Some believe Tom to be Captain William Toms and others have identified him as a Native American. The town fathers (at the 225th anniversary of the town) elected to choose ferryman Tom Luker as the town's namesake. Toms River benefited greatly from its convenient access to the ocean through the Cranberry Inlet and the inlet sustained the commercial trade for decades until a storm in 1812 caused it to shoal and eventually disappear, requiring the pig iron and timber to be transported by wagon at a much slower pace and higher cost.

Despite the early interest in Squan, Deal, and Toms River, these mainland villages close to the shore only attracted a few visitors each summer and their existence depended on commerce and farming. Beach communities, which attract transient tourists, need to be accessible.

"Sea Bathing" at the Jersey Shore

Three locations along the shore led the way to the future of "sea bathing": Tucker's Island, Cape May, and Long Branch. But in 1800, a trip from even the closest city was difficult. A tourist would start the trip in Philadelphia, first on a ferry to reach the Jersey side of the Delaware River and then with a ride in a "Jersey wagon" or "Oyster wagon" over backroads. The wagons journeyed from the ferry station south to Cape Island, east to Tucker's Island (across from Tuckerton at the southern end of Long Beach Island), or northeast to Long Branch. These same wagons were used to haul oysters and hay to the Philadelphia market on the westward side of the trip before turning around to take on beachgoers for the return trip to the shore. The ride was anything but pleasant. Few wagons had cushioning springs and the roads were poor. Surely the aromas associated with the westward journey lingered. Going across the state to Tucker's Island or Long Branch could take two days and the uncomfortable passengers had to deal with mosquitoes and green flies all along the way through inland New Jersey. Few women took to the wagons and if they made the trip to the beach at all they came by stagecoach, which offered a slightly higher level of comfort. In the fifty years from 1800 to 1850, stagecoaches became more commonplace and then steamboats from New York, Philadelphia, and places to the south made at least part of the trip

more accommodating. The enjoyment experienced once the shore destinations were reached must surely have surpassed the difficulties in getting there.

Accommodations in these locations were free-wheeling, especially
before the construction of large hotels. Vacationers usually arrived without notice and the boarding houses close to the water welcomed all who
came. It was not unusual for a boarding house to take in arrivals while
still obliging those leaving the next day, or later, on the same wagons or
ferries. Often a more sedate crowd (ten Quaker ladies by one account, for
example) were lodged with a more fun-loving crowd. Since amusements
were left to the vacationers themselves, the fun lovers would spend the
evenings singing, playing instruments, playing cards, and drinking. The
more sedate would have to grin and bear it. Of course, mutual consterna-
tion grew as the days passed. The walk to the water could be as long as a
half mile and rain would bring out mosquitoes. At some resorts like Cape
Island in the 1830s, men and women could not be in the water or even on
the beach at the same time. White and red flags signaled the times,
because some men preferred to swim *au naturel*. At other beaches, and in
later years, visitors were not as innocent. One group of young men at
the beach in the 1840s reportedly carried some "blushing and screaming
maidens" to the top of a sand hill where they tied their legs together and
rolled them to the water.[7]

Like today, sun, surf, and frivolity were the main attractions of a trip
to the Jersey Shore. Other activities enjoyed by visitors in these early days
seem tame by today's standards. In letters and articles, visitors mentioned
the roar of the ocean, looking for shells on the beach, the chance to see
"porpoises" leaping in the water not far from shore, and moonlight strolls
along the beach in the evening. Among the visitors to the Jersey Shore in
the first half of the nineteenth century was one with a purpose, the famed
naturalist John James Audubon. He traveled to Great Egg Harbor in the
warm months of 1829 "for the purpose of making myself acquainted with
[the] feathered inhabitants" to be found there. He enjoyed oysters "as large

and white as any I have ever eaten" and fish caught by the tide in a seine placed in a channel. Sailing in the bay and investigating the swamps and the creeks, Audubon recorded seeing as many as fifty "Fish Hawk" (osprey) nests in a single day. His description of this wildlife wonderland remains captivating:

> In this manner, I passed several weeks along those delightful and healthful shores, one day going into the woods, to search the swamps in which the Herons bred, passing another amid the joyous cries of the Marsh Hens, and on a third carrying slaughter among the White-breasted Sea-Gulls; by way of amusement sometimes hauling the fish called the Sheep's-head from an eddy along the shore, or watching the gay Terns as they danced in the air, or plunged into the waters to seize the tiny fry. Many a drawing I made at Great Egg Harbor, many a pleasant day I spent along its shores; and much pleasure would it give me once more to visit the good and happy family in whose house I resided there.[8]

As today, each person visiting the Jersey Shore in these early years found his or her own pleasures, whether fishing, gunning, boating, bathing, simple frivolities, or just the beauty of nature. Whatever the attraction, vacationers filled up the few available boarding houses and hotels in the summer months and returned in succeeding summers, demonstrating that the lure of the shore was more than a passing fancy.

TUCKER'S ISLAND AND LONG BEACH

Tucker's Island near the southern tip of Long Beach (now Long Beach Island) had a boarding house for sea bathers well before 1800 but storms and the shifting sands at the southern end of Long Beach kept the island from developing into a permanent resort. The buildings erected on the island over the next 150 years *and the island itself* have disappeared into the sea. The island was six miles long and known as Short Beach (as opposed to the eighteen-mile-long island to the north, Long Beach). The first building was a small boarding house and grocery store that attracted visitors from the counties to the west and south and mariners seeking supplies or a safe haven from storms at sea. The proprietors were Ephraim Morse, his wife, and their five children, but the couple left the island and their business after a devastating winter storm took all of their children. The building deteriorated and soon washed away. Reuben Tucker purchased the island and established a boarding house on high ground in 1765. The island became known as Tucker's Island or Tucker's Beach and welcomed the Quakers who settled Tuckerton (known also as Little Egg Harbor and Clamtown) and their friends from Philadelphia. The Quakers would host retreats on the island where the women would enjoy the beach and relaxation while the men would spend their time fishing and gunning in the bay and creeks that teemed with wildlife. The accommodations were rustic at best. A stage from Philadelphia to Tuckerton began operations in 1816. The overland trip took two days before the vacationers reached the bay for the sail to the island. Tucker's boarding house was taken over by Joseph Horner in 1815 and continued to attract guests until it burned down in 1845. Horner had left Tucker's years earlier to open the Philadelphia Company House across the inlet on Long Beach (near present day Beach Haven). This hotel was financed by Philadelphian businessmen who frequented the two islands. In 1851 Captain Thomas Bond became the proprietor of the Philadelphia Company House and enlarged it, adding a billiard room and a bowling alley. Bond's Long Beach House, as it became known, entertained numerous guests in the mid-1800s. Vacationers dined on clams, oysters, crab, game, and mutton from a herd of sheep kept nearby. The hotel, facing the bay, was a considerable distance from the ocean, requiring a long walk or ride in a cart.[9]

Activity at the southern tip of Long Beach was based on its proximity to Tuckerton, which was an established town with a thriving business community during this period. Nevertheless, several entrepreneurs, including the delightfully named Hudson Buzby, built a grand hotel in

1821 well to the north on Long Beach in what is now Surf City. The hotel was named the Mansion of Health because this area of the island is the furthest east and was believed to have significant health benefits as a result. Unlike the more southerly locations, the Mansion of Health attracted most of its visitors from the New York area, in large part sportsmen, before it closed in the 1850s. This part of Long Beach was known as the Great Swamp at the time (Surf City, North Beach, and the southern end of Harvey Cedars today) and shared a unique terrain with an attractive forest of cedar and oak. (As discussed in chapter 2, whalers came to this spot in the early 1600s.) Within months of the building of the Mansion of Health, however, this forest along the ocean was lost to the ferocious hurricane of 1821, which ripped across the island and flattened the trees.

Nature played a part in denying Tucker's Island long-term viability. At one point Tucker's Island hosted two hotels, a lifesaving station, and the Little Egg Harbor lighthouse. But its location in the inlet between Long Beach and the mainland made its existence tenuous as the contours of the island shifted from decade to decade due to the currents at the tip of Long Beach. A storm in 1800 created a creek that separated the southern end of Tucker's Island from the boarding house. The southern area became known as Little Beach and guests at the boarding house needed to make their way over a narrow inlet to enjoy the beach and the ocean. Over time this creek widened and became Little Egg Harbor Inlet with Little Beach separating from Tucker's Island. After Tucker's hotel burned, a lighthouse was erected on the site in 1848, the highest point on the northern end of the island. The lighthouse lost its usefulness because the Old Inlet that it marked was shoaling and a New Inlet opened several miles to the south. Few vacationers visited the island from this point until the 1870s but two hotels—the Columbia and St. Albans-by-the-Sea—were built to welcome folks once a train reached Tuckerton in 1871. These development efforts stalled and the hotels gradually fell into disrepair. In October 1927, erosion took the lighthouse. Lifesaving station #23, built in

1869, had to be moved several times but was eventually lost to the sea in 1935. A replica of the lighthouse has been built at Tuckerton Seaport. The remaining portion of Tucker's Island was completely lost by the early 1950s.

CAPE MAY

Tucker's Island may have been welcoming guests before 1800, but it was Cape May, the former home of whalers, that showed how a beach could be turned into a resort. A "genteel Stage-coach" made the trip from the ferry landing across from Philadelphia to Cape May "every Thursday" as early as 1772, and an advertisement calling for vacationers appeared in the Philadelphia *Aurora and General Advertiser* on July 1, 1801.[10] Ellis Hughes, the proprietor of a hotel in Cape May seeking guests, was able to sum up the advantages of the shore—then and now—in two short paragraphs:

> The Public are respectfully informed that the Subscriber has prepared himself for entertaining company who use sea-bathing, and he is accommodated with extensive house room, with Fish, Oysters, Crabs, and good Liquor—Care will be taken of Gentlemen's Horses.
>
> The situation is beautiful, just on the confluence of the Delaware Bay with the Ocean, in sight of the Lighthouse, and affords a view of the shipping which enters and leaves the Delaware: Carriages may be driven along the margins of the Ocean for miles, and the wheels scarcely make any impression upon the sand, the slope of the shore is so regular that persons may wade out a distance. It is the most delight-ful spot the citizens can retire to in the hot season.[11]

A smattering of beachgoers had been visiting Cape May for many years before the turn of the nineteenth century, but the 1801 advertisement was the first seeking to draw them to this "most delightful spot" in "the hot season." In these early days, the hardy who made the trip to Cape May came mostly from Philadelphia, Virginia, Maryland, and Delaware.

Beginning in the early 1800s, the beauty of the cape and the amenities of the shore began to lure enough visitors to justify the building of boarding houses and eventually hotels. The tip of the cape was an island, "Cape Island," and the whaling village called Town Bank was located northwest of the tip. Gordon's *Gazetteer* in 1834 identified the boarding houses established for these summer tourists and described "Cape May Island" perfectly: "it is a noted and much frequented watering place, the season at which commences about the first of July, and continues until the middle of August, or 1st September. There are here six boarding houses, three of which are very large; the sea bathing is convenient and excellent, the beach affords pleasant drives, and there is excellent fishing in the adjacent waters."[12] A three-story hotel, the Mansion House, was built in Cape May in 1832 by Richard Ludlam, the owner of a store in Dennis Township and a descendant of one of the yeoman whaling families who had settled Cape May more than a century earlier. It had plaster walls, a first for the county, and was intended to relieve the crowding at the boarding houses and other summer establishments.[13]

Visitors enjoyed bathing in the saltwater, watching the wildlife that surrounded the cape, and taking carriage rides along the beach. One young lady staying at an elegant hotel in the summer of 1850 extolled the fun of sea bathing as well as the social scene. She believed that two to three thousand bathers were enjoying the waves, accompanied by several lifeboats to avoid any tragedies. The women wore "pantaloons and yellow straw hats with broad brims, and adorned with bright red ribbon," to venture out into the sea. Porpoises bobbing in the ocean greeted her each morning and "music and earthly fire-works" entertained her from the beach opposite her hotel at night.[14] Hotels offered fine food and drink, entertainment, and the chance to converse with the elite of Philadelphia and many of the southern gentry. Sailing ships ran regularly from Philadelphia to Cape May beginning in 1815 (a two-day trip) and stopped at Newcastle, Delaware, to pick up passengers from locations south, particularly Maryland and Virginia. By the 1820s, steamboats twice a week replaced the sailing ships from Philadelphia to Cape May. Soon trains were running to Newcastle, Delaware, increasing the number of southerners making the trip.

With each passing year, accommodations improved and the lure of Cape May was enhanced by its society appeal and celebrity vacationers. Without question, those able to make the trip and stay at the hotels were well-heeled and the cream of society. Cape May became a place to see and be seen. In 1847, Henry Clay of Kentucky, several times a candidate for U.S. president, stayed at the Cape May Mansion House at the end of the season. He chose the tranquility of the beach to mourn the loss of his son in the Mexican-American War and was able to enjoy the ocean waters on a daily basis. His presence created quite a sensation. Clay was a well-known and well-admired figure and was persuaded to speak at the music hall, the Kersal, during his two-week visit. He also accommodated vacationers, most especially the women, who implored him for a clip of his hair as a memento, which was a fashion at the time. President Franklin Pierce stayed at the resort in 1855. Cape May boasted a number of large and elegant hotels by that time, including the four-story Mount Vernon Hotel, which had wide porches, baths with hot and cold tap water in each room, and accommodations for hundreds of guests at a time. The ballroom hosted bands for dancing and grand events and gambling could often be found at nearby clubs.

Long Branch

The town of Long Branch, named after a nearby tributary, was first settled about one-and-a-half miles inland in Shrewsbury Township by a few farmers. The farmers were granted the land by the West Jersey Proprietors through the so-called Monmouth Patent and purchased the tract from the natives. The lore associated with this area includes the tale that the Europeans and natives could not agree on the boundaries of the area purchased and resolved the issue by a three-bout wrestling match on the beach between John Slocum and Vow-a-Vapon. Slocum won two out of three rounds and settled on or near the beach. His supporters—Eliakim Wardell, John and Joseph Parker, and a man named Hulett—got the land to the north and west.[15] Whatever the truth, these men turned to farming. The sea-bathing trade came later.[16] In the 1800s, Long Branch had the geological distinction among New Jersey beaches of a bluff, a high cliff that stood about twenty feet above the sandy beaches that reached out to the ocean below. Buildings on the ridge of the bluff had a magnificent view and over time hotels were built, which prompted some to call the resort the "American Brighton" as the bluff recalled the cliffs that characterized the fashionable British seashore resort of that name. The Long Branch we know today, with its five miles of beachfront, is an amalgamation of several beachfront destinations including Branchport and Elberon. Unfortunately, the ocean has steadily eroded the bluff, taking the sand north to Monmouth Beach, Sea Bright, and Sandy Hook, significantly deteriorating this natural advantage. Early hotels built on the bluff disappeared over time due to storms, fires, and erosion.

Long Branch farmers accommodated boarders well before 1800, but offered little more than a dry place to rest your head at night. Visitors at the farmhouses and at taverns in town would be transported to the beach for a day in the sun. Philadelphian Ellison Perot spent several days at Long Branch in 1788 and so enjoyed his stay that he asked to return the next summer with family and friends. His host readily agreed, albeit on the condition that Perot bring his own beds and bedding the next year for himself and his group.[17] Those choosing to label Long Branch as the original seaside resort (to the exclusion of Cape May and Tucker's Island) point to an advertisement by Herbert and Chandler in the Philadelphia newspaper *Dunlap's American Advertiser*, that offered "good waiters," "a good stock of liquors," and "houses under the bank for the convenience of bathing" in May 1792.[18] By the turn of the century, Long Branch had become somewhat more sophisticated as can be seen from the observations of a reporter for the *New York Herald* in 1809. He was dismayed that

Long Branch attracted more Philadelphians than New Yorkers in these early years. The New Yorkers were missing out on "riding, walking, reading [and] social converse" as well as "a cheerful cigar and a half pint of wine after dinner." The "young and gay" could enjoy dancing and tea parties. The reporter's only concern was the introduction of horse-race gambling, which, if betting were allowed, might adversely impact the morals of those otherwise enjoying the comforts of the shore.[19] Like Cape May, Long Branch was a place to see and be seen for the Philadelphia elite. By 1834, however, Long Branch was attracting crowds from both cities:

> [It is a] well known and much frequented sea-bathing place, on the Atlantic ocean, 75 miles from Philadelphia, and 45 from New York. . . . The inducements to the invalid, the idle, and the hunters of pleasure, to spend a portion of the hot season here, are many. Good accommodations, obliging hosts, a clean and high shore, with a gently shelving beach, a fine prospect seaward, enlivened by the countless vessels passing to and from New York, excellent fishing on the banks, 3 or 4 miles at sea, good gunning, and the great attraction of all watering places, much, and changing and fashionable company. During the season, a regular line of stages runs from Philadelphia, and a steam boat from New York, to the boarding houses here, of which there are several; Wardell's, Renshaw's, and Sear's are the most frequented. Many respectable farmers also receive boarders, who, in the quiet of rural life, enjoy in comfort and ease, their season of relaxation, perhaps more fully than those at the public hotels.[20]

At first, sailboats and steamships from New York dropped passengers at Red Bank or Sandy Hook for a difficult overland trip to Long Branch, but direct service was running regularly by 1828, which increased the number of visitors from New York.

The large boarding houses, some of which were renovated farmhouses, served hundreds of guests in the 1840s and gave way to large hotels by the 1850s. The Conover House for 175 guests was built in 1839 and an even bigger hotel, the Allegheny House, was built in 1846. The Mansion House (formerly the Morris House), the Monmouth House, the Pavilion Hotel, and the Pitman House were built in the next ten years. Guests at the hotels enjoyed an elegant vacation experience noting the improving fare offered at dinner, including fresh fish, oysters, clams, seasonal vegetables, and fine wines. During its heyday, from after the Civil War to the 1890s, Long Branch reigned as the preeminent summer resort in the country. One New York reporter with a flowery pen who took the steamboat from New York City in 1857 "to escape the burning streets" and "furnace-like atmosphere" of "Gotham" extolled the virtues of the resort. The boat approached from the west, past Sandy Hook, and onto the Shrewsbury River before docking several miles from Long Branch. The passengers on the crowded boat were "full of mirth and gaiety." They spotted a "porpoise" from the boat and then "Fish Hawks" during a moonlit carriage ride along the beach to the hotel. The reporter declared Long Branch the place to be: "Long Branch, now-a-days, seems to be quite a fashionable watering place. People flock here to breathe in the delicious sea breezes, and stroll along the shore, and bathe in the salt waves; and latterly the great influx of stragglers from the beau monde has brought Long Branch before the public in the decided position of a highly popular resort."[21] By 1861, when Mary Lincoln stayed at the Mansion House in the early days of the Civil War, Long Branch could accommodate more than 5,000 guests.

After the Civil War, the title for the leading seashore resort would pass from Cape May to Long Branch. Even though the first railroad to the beach arrived in the newly created Atlantic City in 1854, Long Branch continued to thrive. Town boosters soon arranged for a railroad to Long Branch and the city achieved its fame in the next several decades. In contrast, businessmen and officials in Cape May dallied in an argument over whether a new turnpike should take precedence over a railroad link. As a result, tracks did not reach the town until 1863, during the Civil War, which was not an auspicious time for a resort that depended in large part

on vacationers from south of the Mason-Dixon Line. Tucker's Island had
to deal with its physical and geographical limitations. The only competition for Long Branch along the Jersey Shore from 1854 to the end of the
century would be Atlantic City. This upstart resort, which had a rail link
and little more in 1854, would take several decades to get its infrastructure built and market its advantages before it would challenge Long
Branch. In the meantime Long Branch was able to take immediate advantage of its access to New York and shifted its focused to the northeast.
After the coming of railroads, Long Branch became a summer resort
for the elite in New York City as well as the rich and famous from around
the world.

Further Reading

For background, see Franklin Ellis, *History of Monmouth County,
    New Jersey* (Shrewsbury, NJ: Shrewsbury Historical Society, 1885);
    Thomas F. Gordon, *A Gazetteer of the State of New Jersey* (Daniel
    Fenton, 1834); George H. Moss, Jr., *From Nauvoo to the Hook*
    (Locust, NJ: Jervey Close Press, 1904), and *Another Look at
    Nauvoo to the Hook* (Sea Bright, NJ: Ploughshare Press, 1990);
    Charles Edgar Nash, *The Lure of Long Beach* (Long Beach Board of
    Trade, 1936); George B. Somerville, *The Lure of Long Beach* (Long
    Beach Board of Trade, 1914); Writers Project, Work Projects
    Administration, *Entertaining a Nation, The Career of Long Branch*
    (Long Branch, NJ: American Guide Series, 1940); and U.S.
    National Park Service, *An Historic Theme Study of the New Jersey
    Heritage Trail*, http://www.nps.gov/parkhistory/online_books/nj1/.

CHAPTER 4

1850–1900

RAILROADS, ATLANTIC CITY,
AND LONG BRANCH

The pleasures of surf-bathing carry, of course, a great multitude to Atlantic City, and it is probable that more bathers are to be found every day on its long stretch of beach than at all the other New Jersey coast resorts together. At the fashionable hours of bathing, mile after mile of beach is crowded with thousands of merry bathers, whose shouts and laughter mingle with the roar of the surf, while the popular "ocean promenade," or as it is called the "'board-walk," is lined by a throng of gay promenaders. The scene at this time is as animated as the streets of an old world city on a fete day. The walk, which is smooth, and entirely free from dust, extends along the entire city front, following the beach just above high water-mark. On a moonlight evening, when the beach is filled with equipages, and the promenade vocal from end to end with the murmur of happy laughter and pleasant communion, then, indeed, Atlantic City presents a picture of delightful existence, fairer than any vision of a midsummer night's dream.
—A. L. English, *The History of Atlantic City*, 1884

The railroads gave birth to Atlantic City in 1854.

In 1850 Atlantic City did not exist. Absecon Island was a large and relatively deserted island among dozens of sedge islands, unreachable without considerable effort and discomfort. The Unalatchtigo who traveled to the island each summer had stopped their journeys long before the summers of the 1800s and little activity occurred there until the first train unloaded its passengers across the channel from the island in 1854. The incredible rise of Atlantic City is directly attributable to the arrival of the

Camden and Atlantic Railroad, which supplied the first tracks to the beach. In the decades that followed hundreds of thousands took the journey across the state to get to the beaches of Atlantic City from Philadelphia. A day-tripper could get on a ferry in the early hours of the morning, board a train at Cooper's Ferry in Camden, and arrive on the beach in Atlantic City shortly after noon. Tired and somewhat tanned, the daytripper could be back home by evening. All for only three dollars! Thousands took advantage of this cheap luxury every day, but especially on Sundays. And the rise of Atlantic City changed the destinies of Cape May, Tucker's Island, and Long Branch, as well as dozens of stretches of barren sand all along the coast.

The Coming of Railroads and the Concept of "Vacation"

The story of railroads in New Jersey and the United States begins in the 1830s. It involves financial and real estate speculation, monopolies, fierce competition, overbuilding, bankruptcies, and some short-term and long-term successes. Speculation about railroads began in the early 1800s. Railroads were being built in England and American businessmen saw the potential for a freight line across New Jersey from Philadelphia to New York. Several groups petitioned the New Jersey Legislature for a license to lay rails across the state and permission was granted to the Camden and Amboy Railroad in 1830 for the 61-mile run. Investors quickly raised $1 million. In September 1833 the track was finished and the steam locomotive *John Bull* made its first run from Bordentown to South Amboy. For a short period, the Camden and Amboy had an exclusive license and the state shared in the profits. The monopoly eventually disappeared as demand and technology drove the development of this new and exciting mode of transportation.

Before long, railroad companies realized that passenger traffic could supplement their freight income and they offered cars to eager riders. The first passenger cars, made by wagon makers, had wooden benches and no mechanisms to soften the lurching starts or quell the rocking. Nor did these early cars have windowpanes to keep the noise and soot produced by the engine from entering the passenger cars. Nevertheless, the passengers came and the railroads were soon offering "excursions." One of the first New Jersey excursion trains began service on July 4, 1835, from the docks at Elizabeth (where it picked up New Yorkers) to the Paterson Falls, for fifty cents per person. The investors and their marketers envisioned a rising market for trains to other desirable locations. One man living near the ocean—Dr. Jonathan Pitney—understood that thousands would pay for a convenient train to the beach and worked to make his vision a reality by bringing a train to a new resort in 1854: the beaches of Atlantic City.

At about this same time, a growing middle class in America began to demand time away from their workday lives. Prior to 1850 only the wealthy could enjoy the luxury of summer days or weeks outside of the cities. This began to change around 1850. The growth of railroads paralleled the growing concept of "vacationing," a term that did not become popular in newspapers and magazines until that time. As one social historian put it, the railroads "fed the vacation industry" that was being generated by an enlarged middle class of "self-employed skilled artisans and famers . . . men who worked as professionals and small businessmen," and "male white collar clerks and middle managers."[1] In the next five decades, a vacation was seen as a status symbol and an entitlement for these folks. Easy and inexpensive transportation to New Jersey's beaches made a vacation possible for middle class citizens from Philadelphia and New York City. Tourist guidebooks recognized this change and touted the benefits of destinations at the Jersey Shore and elsewhere in the country. Travel writer John Bachelder put it this way in 1875:

> The custom of setting apart a few weeks of the year as a respite from labor is fast gaining popularity; and each season adds to the number of those who leave their daily cares behind, and seek rest and recuperation for mind and body among the hills and deep green woods of the

country, or at the sea-shore, bathing in surf or sunlight, and cooled by
the invigorating breezes of the sea.

Those who fortune favor can devote the season to travel, visiting
in succession the rare natural wonders with which the country is
stored. . . . A far greater number, however, choose some desirable and
healthful locality where they may secure the desired change and rest,
at cheaper rates even than they could remain at home.[2]

This synergy continued into the twentieth century as working class
men and women also came to expect and enjoy the possibility of one or
more days and weeks away from the factory. Vacationing became a habit
throughout America by the 1930s.[3]

Atlantic City's railroad monopoly only lasted for a short time, but it
fueled the vacation boom by making a trip to the beach available to those
who could not previously afford the luxury. Atlantic City entertained all
comers, anyone who could afford the train fare from Philadelphia. The
businessmen at Long Branch understood that their resort appealed to a
different clientele–high society from New York and Philadelphia—and
they recognized the need to make their resort accessible to trains as
well. The Raritan and Delaware Bay Railroad reached Long Branch in
1860 and the New York and Sea-Shore Railroad arrived in 1865. In either
case, however, passengers from New York City needed to take a steamboat ride to reach the train, emphasizing the more sophisticated crowd
traveling to Long Branch. Cape May initially responded indifferently to
railroading and the first train did not arrive until after the start of the
Civil War. Tucker's Island and Long Beach had to wait even longer, until
1871, when trains arrived across the water at Tuckerton. A short ferry ride
took tourists to either island, but Tucker's Island had to contend with its
eroding geography. Long Beach only flourished after a trestle was built in
1886 to cross Barnegat Bay and tracks were quickly laid all the way down
the island to Beach Haven.

In 1850, the population in Monmouth, Ocean, Atlantic, and Cape May
counties totaled only 55,700, and few people lived by the ocean. No shore

locations are separately listed in the 1850 census. Once Dr. Jonathan Pitney showed the way to tens of thousands of city dwellers, the shore transformed. In the next fifty years, as the shore became more and more accessible for permanent residents and tourists, the population in these counties doubled and continued to increase each decade thereafter at high rates. The fifty years from 1850 to 1900 saw amazing railroad construction that carried the growing populations in and around New York City and Philadelphia to the shore for day trips and longer. Once the success of Atlantic City became evident, a few businessmen could raise enough capital to acquire the right-of-way, lay the tracks, build the bridges, and buy an engine to bring a railroad to their town, or they could persuade nearby railroads to extend lines to their town. Most often, the local real estate developers were also railroad men working hand in hand.

ATLANTIC CITY

The visionary and driving force for a rail line to Absecon Island was Dr. Jonathan Pitney, a medical doctor active in local affairs who believed that a railroad would transform "Further Island" (as the island was also known) into a destination for recreation and healthy living. He believed strongly that sea air and saltwater provided significant health benefits to those able to spend time at the shore. Although many may have agreed with his medical advice, only a few agreed with Pitney's vision for Absecon Island. Pitney needed to persuade several businessmen along the road from the ocean to Camden to back his plan for a beach resort so that they could get cheaper transportation to the Philadelphia market for their manufactured goods. He enlisted Richard Osborne, a civil engineer, and several investors, including Samuel Richards, a local glassmaker and real estate owner, and Joseph Porter, William Cotton, and Andrew Hay, real estate holders and businessmen. Osborne laid out the train route and produced a map of the town and which he labeled "Atlantic City." The island at the end (or the beginning) of the railroad line was a wasteland in 1854 but several factors made the vision possible: first, the terrain

between Cooper's Ferry in Camden and Absecon was flat and un-
obstructed; second, Absecon Island was large enough to sustain a city; and
third, the broad beaches along the ocean were free of dangerous under-
tows. Atlantic City, with its east-west avenues named for the states and its
north-south avenues named for oceans, existed only on surveys when the
first train arrived across the channel. Land on the island, sandy and barren
except for pine trees, holly bushes, and bayberry, was gathered up by the
promoters for as little as ten dollars an acre. The same promoters that organized the Camden and Atlantic Railroad joined together to form the Camden and Atlantic Land Company to engage in real estate development.

The railroad company built a wharf at the end of the line in Absecon
to accommodate a ferry across the channel; a bridge for the train was not
built until 1885. The 600 passengers on the first train on July 1, 1854, were
ferried to the island and then shuttled by carriages to the half-finished
United States Hotel for a lavish reception, still covered in soot after the
harrowing four-hour train ride from Camden. Even so, they were thrilled.
It was an auspicious beginning even if this fabulous "city" had only seven
houses. Three days later, on Independence Day, regular trains started
running and the rush to the Jersey Shore began in earnest. Success was
not immediate, but it came eventually.

A city needed to be built to fulfill Pitney's dream and accommodate
the crowds. Cheap labor was needed to make the vision a reality and itin-
erant workers began showing up on Absecon. The first trains brought
construction workers and tradesmen as well as reporters, investors, and
adventurous tourists. They lived year-round in a tent city that moved from
place to place for several decades as hotels, boarding houses, businesses,
and homes were erected to accommodate and entertain the masses arriving on the trains. Several hotels opened within two years of the first train,
including the Surf House, Congress Hall, and the Mansion House, but in
the first years after 1854, the concept of a cheap and easy trip to the beach
created more of a stir than actual traffic. The trains were slow, noisy, and
filthy; accommodations were works in progress; and, flies and greenheads

buzzed incessantly around those who made it to the beach. A mosquito plague in 1858 drove hundreds from the city.[4] The Civil War also inhibited development.

By 1870, however, Atlantic City had become a phenomenon. A three-hour trip and cheap fares brought enormous crowds—300,000 people in that year. The trains had become more comfortable; hotels, boarding houses, and beach accommodations were in place; and the renowned flies on the beach were reduced. The city attracted day-trippers, newly enfranchised vacationers, eager to escape overcrowded cities for even one day of cool breezes at the beach, which beckoned as they disembarked from the two C&A trains running each day. By 1880 Atlantic City had fifty hotels, dozens of boarding houses, and hundreds of homes. The term "shoebies" was coined to describe the rail passengers carrying their lunches in shoeboxes on a day trip to the shore. The year-round population of Atlantic City reached 14,000.

With such traffic, a second railroad line was built in 1877. The Philadelphia and Atlantic City (narrow gauge) was completed in just ninety days, the fastest rail-per-mile construction to date. And a third line to the city, the West Jersey Railroad, arrived from Newfield (near Vineland) in 1880. The three railroads competed fiercely and fares dropped from $3.00 to $1.50 and occasionally as low as fifty cents for the round trip. The third line, part of the Pennsylvania Railroad with connections throughout the country, brought the reality of visitors from faraway locales. Atlantic City was indeed a railroad town but the three companies could not sustain the competition. In 1883 the Pennsylvania Railroad bought out the original line, the Camden and Atlantic, and that same year the Philadelphia and Atlantic City was sold at a foreclosure auction and became part of the Philadelphia and Reading Railroad. Nevertheless, as the years passed, the trains became faster and faster and the ride became more and more comfortable, making it easier and easier to get to the beach and the fun on the Boardwalk.

Part of the original marketing pitch was Pitney's claim that the sea air and saltwater had a therapeutic effect on the inflicted and invalid.

Physicians would testify to this somewhat miraculous claim and often prescribed such a vacation for certain patients (as we will see later in regard to the beginnings of the Wildwoods). All seashore resorts made the claim, but Atlantic City combined it with the idea that the city was comfortable and inviting in the winter months as well as the summer. An 1881 pamphlet entitled "Atlantic City as a Winter Sanitarium, Its Geology, Climate and Isothermal Relations, and Its Sanitary Effect Upon Disease and Invalids," covers the entire topic, including advertisements for the West Jersey Railroad, the Baltimore and Philadelphia Steamboat Company, Dukehart's Porter ("a tonic and mild stimulant for the debilitated and invalids"), and a list of testimonials from Philadelphia doctors and their cured patients from around the country. The preface, addressed to "Physicians," tells the story: "The extraordinary sanitary benefit to be derived from a Winter's sojourn at Atlantic City is so important to the invalid that the following pamphlet has been compiled for the information of Physicians and the benefit of Invalids." Those said to achieve the most benefit were sufferers of "nervous affections," as well as "chronic bronchitis, laryngitis, incipient tuberculosis, and also scrofula."[5]

The Boardwalk, first built in 1870, became a symbol of the city. It was destroyed by several storms and was rebuilt each time wider, sturdier, and longer. It was officially named "The Boardwalk" by the city council in 1896. An Easter Parade was started in 1876 to lure traffic from the Centennial Exposition held that summer in Philadelphia and the parade became an annual attraction, viewed by 100,000 in 1905. Atlantic City boosters knew how to promote their city and they succeeded in making it a world-renowned resort by the turn of the century.

In 1902, historian William Nelson provided a description of the city dominated by grand hotels, each more spectacular and architecturally alluring than the last:

At the present time the hotels and well kept boarding houses are fully five hundred in number, and represent a value of not less than ten million dollars. The Hotel Windsor, perhaps the most modern hotel on the

Atlantic coast, occupies a ground space of six hundred and eighty by one hundred and fifty feet, and cost $350,000. The ground floor contains a Moorish room and a ballroom and reception room of large dimensions. A portion of the basement is fitted as a cafe, to represent a cabin with port holes, mast tables and other shiplike appurtenances. This hotel has a central French courtyard, the first of the kind in Atlantic City, and it was also the first to provide a regular orchestra for the entertainment of guests.

The Hotel Rudolph has for one of its beautiful adornments a grotto in which are given splendid concerts by a large and well trained orchestra. This cavernlike retreat, when illuminated at night with its myriad variagated incandescent lights, presents a marvelously beautiful spectacle. Many other hotels present special attractions peculiarly their own. Among these having a capacity of two hundred or more guests each are the Traymore, the Waldorf-Astoria, the Dennis, Haddon Hall and the Grand Atlantic, five hundred guests each; the Luray, the Iroquois and the Islesworth, four hundred guests each; and the Shelburne, the Chalfonte, the Pennhurst, the Waverly, the Morton, the Irvington, the Berkeley, the De Ville, the Little Brighton, the Strand, the Runnymede, the Kuehnle, the Cedarcroft and the Richmond, two hundred guests or more each.[6]

Atlantic City never achieved the sophisticated allure that characterized Long Branch in the late 1800s and its boosters did not seem to care. Rather than focus on the wealthy and sophisticated, the businessmen hyped their town and its attractions to the growing middle class who wanted to share in the pleasures of the upper classes. In 1883, a reporter for the *New York Times* described the clientele: "patrons are all Philadelphians, of the small merchant and artisan class, who cannot afford the time or cash to go further away from home" so they rush to Atlantic City on a Saturday night for the "sideshows and attractions for boys."[7] Without question, the luxury hotels built along the Boardwalk entertained the better-heeled; but the small hotels and boarding houses further from the beach housed the not-so-well-off on vacation as well, perhaps for the first time. Atlantic City attracted and welcomed a diverse crowd and, in a strange twist, on the Boardwalk everyone dressed to the nines, making it difficult to tell who was who. For many, the thrill was a simple evening stroll on the Board-walk, from end to end and elbow to elbow, to see and be seen. Some soci-ologists suggest that the city's allure after the turn of the twentieth century depended on the *illusion* of high society. That is, regardless of income sta-tus, all people strolling along the Boardwalk or, better yet, being pushed in a rolling chair, were equals.[8]

Entrepreneurs accommodated the crowds by building piers, the first in 1882, out from the Boardwalk over the sand and over the ocean, with games, amusements, rides, exhibits, and entertainment. The world-famous Steel Pier was built in 1898 and Young's so-called Million Dollar Pier stretched 2,000 feet from the Boardwalk in 1903. By the turn of the twentieth century, Atlantic City was loud, gaudy, and glitzy, offering slightly sinful pleasures all along the Boardwalk and out on its piers. Nelson described the Boardwalk as "entrancingly beautiful," illuminated at night and throughout the year by electric lights. The "Casino" at the Boardwalk offered a swimming pool ("natatorium"), bowling alleys, shuffleboard, reading rooms and sun rooms, a smoking room, and dressing rooms.

As the city matured in the twentieth century, Atlantic City became a place where ordinary folk could go to see the latest automobiles, witness wonders on the piers like the "diving horse," and enjoy the greatest enter-tainers of the day. In the thirties and the forties, Broadway producers and stars could test a show on its way to New York. Mae West, Abbott and Costello, and Jimmy Durante performed, along with the best of the big bands and the best singers. In the following decades, Atlantic City wel-comed Frank Sinatra, Dean Martin and Jerry Lewis (who created their partnership in Atlantic City), Milton Berle, Liberace, Dinah Shore, and Nat King Cole. Frank Sinatra played Atlantic City regularly in the 1950s. At its clubs, including the 500 Club, Club Harlem, Babette's, and the Bath and Turf Club, patrons would be thrilled to share the space with celebrities like Joe DiMaggio, the Gabor sisters, and others who were often on hand to be seen. Those who knew about them could visit gambling tables hidden behind the clubs so that the nightly entertainment could continue.

LONG BRANCH AS THE NATION'S PREMIER RESORT

The legacy of the first train to the beach is more than the birth and rise of Atlantic City. The success of Atlantic City demonstrated the possibilities for beach properties all along the shore, land that had been largely ignored for more than 150 years. The rush to the Jersey Shore after 1854 was transformative as well as exhilarating. Long Branch saw the most immediate effect. Steamships were already transporting those eager to get to Long Branch from New York City but trains promised a shorter and safer trip. Tracks to Hightstown and then Eatontown were used as early as 1848 and 1854, respectively, but the remainder of the trip still had to be made by wagon or stage. The business owners in town realized the need for a direct rail line and they celebrated the 1860 arrival of the Raritan and Delaware Bay Railroad with a dinner and speeches, all on the tab of the boarding house owners. A second line into Long Branch, the Long Branch and Sea-Shore Railroad, was completed in 1865 from Sandy Hook, more convenient because of the quick ferry trip from Manhattan to the train depot, which avoided the roundabout journey by steamboat to Port Monmouth to catch the Raritan and Delaware. The Sea-Shore Railroad ran through federal land used by the military in Sandy Hook and perilously close to the ocean. The tracks were often lapped by waves on stormy days. (These are the tracks that required a seawall for protection that eventually became the seawall for Sea Bright.) Not satisfied, some investors saw a demand for a train that could run from the North Jersey terminals in Jersey City and Newark all the way to Long Branch. In 1875, after building bridges over the Raritan River, the Navesink River, and Matawan Creek, the New York and Long Branch line made the trip in two and a half hours. President Ulysses S. Grant, who enjoyed Long Branch and had a vacation home there, attached his private car to the train for the inaugural trip. Thirty-two years later, residents of New York City could ride the rails all the way to Long Branch with the completion of rail tunnels under the Hudson River in 1908.

Mary Lincoln stayed at Long Branch's Mansion House and entertained and was entertained by the leading ladies there at the beginning of the Civil War in 1861. In the next twenty years, Long Branch would become the most fashionable destination on the Jersey Shore and in the country. Balls, dances, and hops were held regularly at the hotels and many maintained their own brass band to entertain guests and passersby. Beautiful people could be seen every day strolling along Ocean Avenue. Long Branch became irresistible as millionaires and celebrities in all fields chose Long Branch as the place to be while enjoying the sea air. Artist Winslow Homer painted landscapes in Long Branch in 1869; the leading actors of the day, Edwin Booth (who was married in Long Branch), Edwin Forrest, and Maggie Mitchell all vacationed in Long Branch; the Philadelphia elite—Biddles, Astors, Fishes, and the Drexels—all enjoyed fashionable times in Long Branch, as did financier Jay Gould and high-roller "Jubilee Jim" Fisk. Gould built four houses at the resort; Fisk, an ostentatious showman, contributed purses at Monmouth Park.

But it was the selection of Long Branch by President Ulysses Grant after the Civil War that provided the coup de grace. Grant moved the workings of the federal government to the beach for the summer in 1869. Grant returned every summer, as president and then as a private citizen, until 1884, staying in a cottage in Elberon presented to him by several friends. Grant entertained visiting generals, admirals, cabinet officers, and congressmen during his presidency and for years afterwards, including Civil War heroes Philip Sheridan and George Meade and the U.S. Navy's Admiral David Farragut. As one local history puts it: "Everybody flocked there to see the President and the parade of celebrities that his presence inspired. Society leaders, men of wealth and power, and more theatrical stars than ever poured into the hotels. Along with them came thousands of John and Mary Does eager to catch a glimpse of some celebrity, hopeful of at least being able to return to the provinces with the news that 'so-and-so looks exactly like his picture in *Harper's Weekly*.'"[9] Long Branch became the summer resort of presidents for several decades thereafter, as Rutherford B. Hayes, James A. Garfield, Chester A. Arthur, Benjamin Harrison, William McKinley, and Woodrow Wilson all chose to vacation in Long Branch rather than suffer the heat and humidity of Washington, DC. Monmouth County now maintains the Seven Presidents Oceanfront Park, with thirty-eight acres and one mile of beachfront, to commemorate the "Summer Capital."

One of the attractions at Long Branch was gambling. Lounges for card playing were readily available. High rollers were attracted to the gaming houses, which were also frequented by presidents Grant and Chester Arthur. Horse racing at Monmouth Park, just three miles away, arrived on July 4, 1870, with betting pools that promised large winnings. The hotels encouraged the races with purses and stakes. The track closed three years later, but opened again in 1882. President Grant had a box at the track, attended the races regularly, and his expected appearance at a meet was touted to generate greater crowds. Developers and celebrities from New York and Philadelphia bought up the land behind the Long Branch bluff and began building beautiful summer homes to share in the city's magnificence. One of the developers was Lewis B. Brown, whose initials and last name were given to an exclusive section of town, "Elberon." Lots purchased for as little as $500 one year might sell for $5,000 the next. Long Branch had become the premier New Jersey beach resort even if the crowds on the beaches at Atlantic City were larger. The glory of Long Branch extended to the Wild West. The Long Branch Saloon in Dodge City, Kansas—frequented by gamblers, cattlemen, gunslingers, lawmen, and presidents—was named after the resort when it was purchased in 1878 by William Harris, a former resident of Long Branch.[10]

Long Branch's prominence also focused the limelight on a tragic event in 1881. President James A. Garfield was hanging onto life after falling to an assassin's gunshot at a train station in Washington, DC, on July 2. He had spent a previous summer in Long Branch and had left the city just days before the attempted assassination to return to Washington, DC. When his doctors suggested that the salt air of Long Branch would be beneficial to his recovery, Garfield agreed to be moved. The train to transport him was fitted to smooth the journey but the house offered to the president in Elberon was five-eighths of a mile from the station. A special train spur was built in less than two days to bring Garfield to the door of the house as comfortably as possible. The entire town pitched in to help. Unfortunately, President Garfield died several weeks later, on September 19.

The glory days of Long Branch began to fade with the closing of Monmouth Park in 1894. The natural bluff, the horse racing, and the celebrities had made the city the place to be. The bluff continued to erode, horse racing ceased, and the celebrities moved to other venues. One history of Long Branch suggests that by the late 1870s the town had become so "popular" that it was no longer "exclusive" enough for the true aristocrats who were also put off by the "devil-may-care" antics of the gamblers and high-rollers.[11] This is probably an exaggeration, but the increasing competition from Atlantic City and Asbury Park and the rise of numerous other resort destinations (along the Jersey Shore and elsewhere throughout the United States) also had an effect. Even so, Long Branch retained its crowds through the end of the nineteenth century and vacationers continued to return for the next hundred years. But the town's allure declined after 1900 and the elite drifted away. Sometime after the turn of the century, city officials encouraged the rise of industry and Long Branch in the twentieth century no longer had the panache of earlier years. By 1900, Atlantic City eclipsed Long Branch just as Long Branch had eclipsed Cape May decades earlier.

Cape May, Tucker's Island, and Beach Haven

As for Cape May, the years from 1854 to 1863 were spent haggling over whether a new turnpike would be a better investment than a train line. The delay suited the investors and politicians who favored the Atlantic

City monopoly, and a train did not arrive at Cape May until well after the start of the Civil War. The U.S. government had already confiscated for the war effort the steamboats that carried visitors from Philadelphia and, of course, the war suspended resort traffic from the southern states. When the Cape May and Millville Railroad began service in 1863, it had initial success but the trip remained long and somewhat arduous. They optimistic railroad investors built a hotel in 1868. The Sea Breeze Excursion House had a 600-seat dining room, a verandah, and a bar. The track ran right to the hotel for the convenience of the passengers. By the late 1860s Cape May had twenty-two hotels, many of them newly built, including the Congress Hall, Columbia House, Ocean House, Delaware House, La Pierre House, Metropolitan Hotel, Tremont House, Tontine Hotel, Surf House, Ocean Breeze Hotel, Cottage by the Sea, Merchants Hotel, and White Hall. Along with the railroad and its grand hotels, Cape May could boast about its gas streetlights and a refined clientele. The train line may not have appealed to day-trippers, but the resort welcomed these "excursionists," in an effort to maintain its tourist economy.

Even though Cape May flourished for a time after the Civil War, it did not prove resilient. From 1870 to 1900, fires and financial panics ravaged the resort. Major fires occurred in 1868, 1876, and 1878, destroying hotels and businesses, which caused enormous financial loss. All were most likely due to arson. The city's fragile economy suffered and struggled when the overall U.S. economy hit rough times in 1878 and 1893. When a second railroad entered the city in the 1890s, it had to file for receivership before its first year of operation was completed. By 1900, Cape May had become "little more than a quiet country village with a beach" according to one observer; most of its hotels were outdated (as compared to Atlantic City and the Wildwoods) and it faded into the background for the next seventy-five years. That same observer suggested that the reason for the resort's decline was its original dependence on sea-based travel, which made it unable to compete effectively when the masses moved to trains and then automobiles.[12]

In the fifty years from 1850 to 1900, Tucker's Island also declined and was surpassed by its nearby upstart, Beach Haven. The area that became known as Beach Haven at the south end of Long Beach Island can be traced to 1851 when Thomas Bond bought the Philadelphia Company House. Renamed the Long Beach House, the hotel developed a widespread reputation as a sportsmen's resort for decades thereafter. When the Tuckerton Railroad reached the bay in 1871, several Philadelphia businessmen who frequented the Long Beach House saw the opportunity to build a true resort. They chose a spot about two miles to the north and arranged for a paddle-wheeler steamship, first the *Barclay* and then the *Pohatcong*, to ferry guests to that location and into the hotels that were built in succession: the Bay View House, the Parry House, the Baldwin Hotel, and the Engleside Inn, all in the 1870s and 1880s. The developers believed that this spot, and Long Beach Island in general, was free of pollen and would be a boon for hay fever sufferers, like the wife of railroad and land company investor Archelaus R. Pharo. Pharo and others had urged the railroad into Tuckerton, built the dock and some roads, and laid out properties in lots. Pharo's daughter came up with the name "Beach Haven" and, though some later preferred it, the name was never Beach Heaven. The railroad-steamboat connection from Tuckerton was not satisfactory for Beach Haven investors and they pressed the Pennsylvania Railroad to bring a train from the mainland across the Barnegat Bay onto Long Beach. The wooden trestle was completed by 1886 from Manahawkin across a mile of open water and several islands into Ship Bottom. The Manahawkin and Long Beach Railroad quickly developed north and south, covering the entire island. The first train made its way to Beach Haven in July 1886, requiring a number of smaller trestles over ponds and wetlands along the way. The owners of the Columbia Hotel and St. Alban's on Tucker's Island expected that the tracks running south into Beach Haven would be extended just the short distance further to their proposed development at Sea Haven. Plans were drawn for the building of streets and lots were plotted but the dream never became a reality. The tracks stopped at Beach

Haven, perhaps because several investors in the railroad also had an interest in the Beach Haven hotels. Sea Haven languished while Beach Haven grew, and despite its seventy houses Tucker's Island never developed any further. As for Beach Haven, after the turn of the twentieth century, it continued to flourish with modest homes as well as grand hotels. As years passed, in place of gunning and fishing, yacht clubs developed to accommodate those who wanted more refined activities like sneakbox and sailboat racing.

The Jersey Shore as a summer attraction changed dramatically in the years from 1800 to 1900. Its first visitors were boarders or single families lodging in a farmhouse or a barn somewhere near the ocean. The accommodations offered few, if any, amenities. The beaches were difficult to reach and were empty once reached. In the first several decades of the 1800s, Cape May and Long Branch began to offer more to the wealthy and the elite: boarding houses, fine food and drink, and the convivial pleasures of like-situated vacationers. And, by mid-century, the boarding houses gave way to grand hotels alive with entertainment and close to the beach. A week, a month, or the entire summer spent on the beach offered escape from the noisy and foul streets of Philadelphia and New York. Hundreds soaked up the sun on the sand during the day and enjoyed cool breezes in the evening and moonlit walks at night. By 1850, the lure of the Jersey Shore had been established, albeit if only for those who could make their way to Cape May and Long Branch with the time and the money to stay for some period of time. The train to the deserted island between them that became known as Atlantic City transformed the New Jersey coast during the second fifty years of the nineteenth century, from Sandy Hook to Cape May. As Atlantic City built its infrastructure, Long Branch built its reputation as the premier resort in the country. The pleasantries that made Long Branch a lovely place to visit increased in scale and scope, attracting the rich, the famous, and the glamorous and making Long Branch the summer place to see and be seen. Cape May tried to compete,

but its efforts fell short. Its heyday was past and its allure faded from
year to year. Atlantic City, once it got its feet on the ground, became
the darling of the Jersey Shore well into the 1900s, attracting a decidedly
different crowd than Long Branch and Cape May, the working man seeking freedom from the drudgery of a six-day work week and a spot near
the beach where every pleasure could be found. Trains also led to the
development of dozens of new communities in the late 1800s with unique
ideas on how to attract summer tourists. Some of the first of these communities saw the Jersey Shore as a place of religious contemplation and
reflection.

FURTHER READING

For background, see Patricia M. Aron and Michael Aron Rockland,
Working at Play: A History of Vacations in the United States (New
York: Oxford University Press, 1999); Susan Currell, *The March
of Spare Time: The Problem and Promise of Leisure in the Great
Depression* (Philadelphia: University of Pennsylvania Press, 2005);
John Bailey Lloyd, *Eighteen Miles of History on Long Beach Island*
(Harvey Cedars, NJ: Down the Shore Press, 1994).

On the rise of railroads along the shore, see Anthony J. Bianculli,
Iron Rails in the Garden State (Bloomington: Indiana University
Press, 2008); John Cunningham, *Railroads in New Jersey: The
Formative Years* (Andover, NJ: Afton Publishing Company, 1997);
Richard Hyer and John Zec, *Railroads of New Jersey* (1975); and
Frederick A. Kramer, *Pennsylvania-Reading Seashore Lines*
(Ambler, PA: Crusader Press, 1880).

On the rise of Atlantic City, see John Bachelder, *Popular Resorts, and
How to Reach Them, Combining a Brief Description of the Principal
Summer Retreats in the United States and the Routes of Travel
Leading to Them* (Boston, 1875); A. L. English, *History of Atlantic
City* (Philadelphia: Dickson & Gilling, 1884); Randall Gabrielan,

Birth of the Jersey Shore, The Personalities and Politics that Built America's Resort (Charleston, SC: The History Press, 2015); Alfred M. Heston, *Absegami: Annals of Eyren Haven and Atlantic City, 1609 to 1904* (Camden, NJ: Sinnickson Chew & Sons, 1904), *Heston's Hand Book of Atlantic City* (1896), and *South Jersey, A History 1664–1924* (New York: Lewis Historical Publishing, 1924); Nelson Johnson, *Boardwalk Empire* (Medford, NJ: Plexus Publishing, 2002); David G. Schwartz, *Boardwalk Playground: The Making, Unmaking, & Remaking of Atlantic City* (Las Vegas, NV: Winchester Books, 2015); Bryant Simon, *Boardwalk of Dreams* (New York: Oxford University Press, 2004); and, Jonathan Van Meter, *The Last Good Time* (New York: Crown Publishers, 2003).

On Long Branch, see Gabrielan, Randall, *Long Branch, NJ, Reinventing a Resort* (Atglen, PA: Schiffer Books, 2009); Sharon Hazard, *The City Beyond the Bluff, The Life and Times of Long Branch* (Long Branch, 2010); and, Writers Project, Work Projects Administration, *Entertaining a Nation, The Career of Long Branch* (Long Branch, NJ: American Guide Series, 1940).

CHAPTER 5

Religion at the Jersey Shore

Another cause for special gratitude is, that while we commenced this enterprise purely as a religious institution, and for that reason, under regulations and restrictions peculiar to itself, which regulations and restrictions those outside of ourselves failed to understand and appreciate, and consequently much prejudice existed, yet time, that tempers all things, revealing the propriety of these restrictions, prejudices have been removed, a better feeling everywhere exists, and the distinctive religious character of the place still remains. . . . The transformation of this wild and unsightly waste from a barren sand desert to a comely little city by the sea—the gathering together of multiplied thousands for worship and recreation, even when there were no means of transportation but poor stages over poorer roads; the general prevalence of good order; the freedom from contagion and special sickness of all kinds; our healthy financial condition, notwithstanding the general depression of the times—and though there have been many uncharitable criticisms, yet vastly more kind and pleasant things have been generously said but, above and over all, the wonderful spiritual triumphs that have been achieved—these, and thousands of other things, call for expressions of profoundest gratitude to Almighty God.

—Extract from the Tenth Annual Report
of the Ocean Grove Camp Meeting Association, 1879

A connection between the Jersey Shore and religion has existed in one form or another from before 1800 to the present day. Perhaps it is the apparent closeness to nature that one feels on the beach, or the vastness of the ocean, or the insignificance of a single soul in a raging storm, or simply the tranquility that pervaded the shore in the early days and can often be felt yet today at certain times and locations. Whatever the reason, people have visited the shore for solace, meditation, and evangelization even before Carl Magnus Wrangel's 1764 visit.

TRAVELING PREACHERS AND CAMP MEETINGS

The few clusters of people maintaining a subsistence living at or near the ocean before 1800 did not settle in these isolated communities to escape religious persecution or to establish religious communities. They came for the whales. Their subsistence living did not provide them the time or the resources for the building of churches and meeting houses or the maintenance of pastors. East Jersey did not have religious beginnings; the Quintipartite Deed in 1676 gave the West Jersey Proprietorship to a group of Quaker investors, including William Penn. Even so, up and down the coast, religious training and fervor most often came in the person of a traveling preacher. Many of these fervent souls left journals describing their travels and the small congregations of believers they found along the shore.

Decades before Wrangel, Quaker John Fothergill traveled the same territory. He came to America in 1705 and preached throughout the middle and New England colonies and the Caribbean from 1721 to 1736. In 1721, Fothergill made several stops along the shore: "We took our Journey through the Deserts of Little Egg Harbor . . . and had a pretty good time in extending the Love of Truth to the poor people there-away." He then proceeded south to Great Egg Harbor and then to Cohansey, Greenwich, and Cape May to visit congregations there, traveling over "dismal Marshes" and sometimes by canoe. Fothergill visited the Townsends, the Garrisons, and the Smiths in Cape May.[1] Two other Quakers—Samuel Hopwood and John Woodman—covered the same ground in the 1740s with the latter getting as far north as Squan. In the 1800s the best known traveling preacher was the Reverend Bishop Francis Asbury of the Methodist Episcopal Church, who traveled extensively along the east coast from 1771 to 1815. Reading from some of his journals it appears that the people near the shore were found wanting in spirit, despite the visits of his predecessors over the previous one hundred years; so too the weather, the accommodations, and other distractions. In September 1783 Asbury "rode a long, barren way to Little Egg Harbor" only to "get wet" in "poor lodgings, with plenty of mosquitoes."[2] Several years later in 1786, while staying at "Monmouth," Asbury took the time to sail "over the bay to the sea, for the benefit of the air." He then continued on to Cape May but was disappointed to find "a dearth of religion in these parts." Another trip in 1809 took Asbury to "Absecum," Tuckerton, and Long Branch.[3]

Another, quite different, preacher arrived at the northern end of the shore several decades later. The story of Sea Bright as a community begins with the unusually named fishing village of Nauvoo, which came into existence sometime in the early 1830s. Apparently, the founder of the Mormon Church, Joseph Smith, visited this spot on the ocean in 1840 before heading west. Some of the locals who heard him speak chose to name their community Nauvoo, a place name Smith later used for his settlement when he reached Illinois. "Nauvoo" is a Hebrew word that means "beautiful" or "place of beauty."[4] Sea Bright did not build on its Mormon connection. A large hotel was built near the fishing village as early as 1842, other hotels followed in the next several decades, and the town grew into a beautiful vacation spot for New York's elite. A fire in 1890 destroyed the fishing village.

The "camp meeting" phenomenon swept the United States in the early 1800s. These gatherings were a phenomenon of the Second Awakening among Protestant Christians in England, Scotland, and the United States. As the name implies, families would come from miles around and camp out at a designated location to hear preachers and be part of a community of worshippers. The events served as part social gathering and part religious experience. Camp meetings were common on the American frontier in the 1800s where churches and preachers were few and far between.[5] In 1812, some 400 Methodist camp meetings were held in the United States. Bishop Asbury was part of this movement, which continued into the 1830s. As one historian put it, camp meetings "offered [famers and their families] a legitimate reason to take a vacation, and one that involved intense socialization. Within a few years, farm families from all across the nation looked forward to spending a week to ten days at a camp meeting as soon as their spring planting was complete, or later after the fall crops were in. They came seeking not only to renew their faith and ensure their salvation but also to visit old friends and make new acquaintances."[6]

The camp meeting movement waned by the mid-1800s but was revived after the Civil War, perhaps as a reaction to the war's bloodshed and despair. In 1863 more than 10,000 people traveled across several states to get to a camp meeting in Cape May in August that lasted for three days. Years later, in 1875, this meeting would become the South Seaville Camp Association, settled in a parklike area north of Cape May and west of what is now Sea Isle City. The encampment remains today within Dennis Township, with some of the original cottages still intact (it celebrated its 150th anniversary in 2015). A railroad stop was built at Seaville to accommodate its followers.[7] In the same vein, camp meeting associations developed at Island Heights in 1877 and at Atlantic Highlands on the Sandy Hook Bay in 1881. The borough of Island Heights lies due east of Toms River on the river and across the bay from Seaside Heights. The driving force behind its development was the Reverend Jacob McGraw of New Brunswick,[8] and a railroad spur on the Pennsylvania Railroad line running from Camden to Seaside Park was laid down in the 1880s to accommodate this Methodist retreat. A railroad also made its way to Atlantic Highlands in 1892 and by 1900 more than twenty hotels welcomed guests from New York City arriving by railroad and steamboats (three a day) to a pier built out into the bay.[9]

The most successful camp meeting settlement in New Jersey remains, of course, Ocean Grove, which continues to preserve many of its original characteristics. Asbury Park, to its north, was not started as a religious community but its founder and driving force, James Bradley, was one of the faithful from Ocean Grove, and he tried to put his moral stamp on that community. Ocean City and Sea Grove in Cape May County were two more religious communities built on New Jersey's coast.

OCEAN GROVE

The camp meeting revival after the Civil War developed one of its strongest communities among the Methodists in Vineland, New Jersey. The organizers began a search for a suitable permanent location and soon decided that a beach site would serve them well. The first possibility was Seven Mile Beach in Cape May County but that deal fell through, perhaps because of the swarming mosquitoes that welcomed the elders when they visited. Whatever the reason, the search continued and in 1869 the Ocean Grove Camp-Meeting Association purchased 274 acres in Monmouth County bordered by Wesley Lake to the north, Fletcher Lake to the south, and the Atlantic Ocean on the east. Lots were "sold" (actually leased from the Camp Meeting Association) the next year. Ocean Grove did not have a train station, but the Association helped to finance six miles of track from Long Branch to Asbury Park in 1875. By then, the camp was flourishing and the station was close enough.

Most camp meetings created after the Civil War transformed into "respectable middle-class summer resorts with only a tinge of religion" within just a few decades.[10] But not Ocean Grove. This New Jersey phenomenon still retains more than a "tinge of religion" after 150 years. The pious, as well as the secular, enjoying vacations by the 1860s, preferred locations that catered to like-minded folks. Railroad companies encouraged this traffic with advertisements announcing camp meetings. Ocean Grove, with its accessible and affordable lots and tents, drew enormous crowds and potential homeowners with single- and multiple-day events well into the 1900s. The first meeting in 1870 was attended by more than 10,000 followers who stayed for one to two weeks and returned year after year. The association sold its first lots for $100 to $250. Its parklike and forested land was serene and remote. Doubtless, the founders did not anticipate that one day their idyllic setting would find itself squeezed between Asbury Park and Bradley Beach along one of the busiest stretches of beachfront and entertainment on the New Jersey shoreline.

In 1870 the New Jersey Legislature granted the association a charter as the Camp Meeting and Christian Seaside Resort, which established this seaside property as a place of perpetual worship.[11] All the land in Ocean Grove was owned by the Camp Meeting Association. By the fifth season, more than 600 tents, hundreds of cottages, and almost 80 hotels and boarding houses were welcoming the faithful in the summer months. The state charter gave the association the right to govern within the confines of its holdings. As a result, the beach was closed on Sundays (and still today until noon on Sundays) in deference to the religious tenor of the town; streets and bridges were closed and guarded at 10:00 P.M. on Saturday nights and all day on Sunday to prevent horse traffic through the town. Trains stopping at nearby Asbury Park stations could not stop on Sundays. The rules set by the association for its homeowners and visitors, as Gustav Kobbé noted in his 1889 survey of New Jersey's shore communities, were "maintained with unrelaxed severity." Prohibitions included walking to or from the beach in beach attire; taking unseemly poses on the beach; the sale of liquor or tobacco; theatrical performances; the distribution of handbills and the sale of newspapers on Sundays; fireworks; and carriages, cycles, or "velocipedes" on the beach or the "plank walks."[12] The restrictions may appear somewhat over the top today, but the earliest visitors were fervent worshippers and welcomed the resulting tranquility. The association acted in other more practical ways to please its residents by providing for sanitary conditions, freshwater, and electrical needs. Heavy brush and trees inland were cleared to allow for the laying out of wide streets and usable lots and, in an ironic twist to twenty-first-century concepts, the association leveled the natural dunes (12 to 15 feet high) to provide a clear view and easy access to the beach throughout the length of the town. They soon reaped the effects of this last effort as the beaches immediately began to erode from the fierce storms endemic to the shore.

The association then had to build jetties to maintain and preserve the beach. The large crowds appreciated the improvements and most accepted the restrictions, as evidenced by their return each summer and the success of the community. By 1885 the price of an ocean lot reached $1,500.

The limits on personal habits and choices within Ocean Grove have not been without controversy over the years. Some early writers suggested that many who entered Ocean Grove (or who tried but were turned back) were curiosity seekers who wanted to see if the pious truly were so. One of the favored activities in these early years was boating on Wesley Lake where hundreds of boats filled with young people could be seen. Kobbé noted with some cynicism that swearing was prohibited not only throughout the town but on boats as well "where, it is presumed, parties might be inclined to indulge in unseemly speech, out of earshot of the Association."[13] The prohibition against traffic on Sunday caused an embarrassing moment for President Grant, whose first attempt to attend Sunday services in the community brought him face-to-face with the guards at its boundary. He was told that his horse and carriage could not enter the town. Grant defused the awkwardness of the situation by graciously acknowledging the restriction and walking into the camp. The restrictions also impacted Ocean Grove's neighboring town of Asbury Park. James Bradley, an Ocean Grove lot owner and the founder of Asbury Park, agreed to forbid stops at the train station near Ocean Grove on Sundays in deference to the association until the inconvenience of this restriction grew tiresome for the Asbury Park merchants, who protested year after year. In 1910 the Asbury Park Council ginned up the courage to join with their merchants and filed a petition with the newly created New Jersey Public Utilities Authority, which put an end to this neighborly courtesy as of November 1, 1911.[14] Despite the demands on its neighbors, its visitors, and its owners, Ocean Grove continued as a peculiarly different summer resort from all of the others along the Jersey Shore well into the 1900s.

The association built public spaces to advance its purposes. One of the first was an auditorium that sat seventy-five in an open space. A second, larger building was constructed in 1875 and a third in 1880 that could seat 5,000. In July 1894, the association opened the present auditorium, which seats 10,000 with a choir space for 500. Its pipe organ, originally constructed in 1908, is one of the largest in the world. Modern renovations have limited the seating somewhat but the auditorium has been in continuous use for lectures, services, schooling, and concerts. The renowned preacher Billy Sunday gave a series of lectures over nine days in August 1916 to overflow crowds, with many people bused in from Paterson and Philadelphia for the event. Booker T. Washington, William Jennings Bryan, and Norman Vincent Peale all spoke at the auditorium as did a series of U.S. presidents from the late 1800s into the twentieth century: James Garfield, William McKinley, Teddy Roosevelt, and William Howard Taft. Grant made his last public appearance in Ocean Grove, on crutches before a warm and welcoming crowd in the summer of 1884 to speak to a congregation of Civil War Army chaplains. Roosevelt spoke twice, once as the governor of New York and again as president before the National Education Association in 1905.[15] Woodrow Wilson spoke as governor of New Jersey and President Richard Nixon spoke at the auditorium in 1970. In the twentieth century onward, the auditorium has invited more secular celebrities and entertainers, including John Philip Sousa, Enrico Caruso, Tony Bennett, the Lettermen, Seals and Croft, Mel Tormé, Peter, Paul and Mary, Victor Borge, and Ray Charles.[16]

It appears that the twenty-first century may not be as welcoming to Ocean Grove's peculiarities, however. Like some of its neighbors, the housing stock and appeal of Ocean Grove languished in the mid-1900s, in part due to the Depression and World War II. The camp continued along, quietly maintaining its particularities (one hundred or so original tents survive today) until, in the last forty years, Ocean Grove experienced rebirth, establishing itself as a desired location and appealing to those who choose quietude and quaint ways to the honky-tonk of much of the shore nearby. The community's new-found popularity, however, embroiled the association in several lawsuits that threatened its origins. In 1979, the

New Jersey Supreme Court was presented with an appeal of a drunk driving conviction in the Ocean Grove Municipal Court. The court used the opportunity to declare unconstitutional the original charter granted to the association by the legislature as a violation of the separation between church and state:

> The Ocean Grove Camp Meeting Association of The United Methodist Church is first and foremost a religious organization. Such a state of affairs is not only evident from its name, but also from the purposes underlying its formation, its internal governmental structure, and the various activities which it undertakes.
>
> The main goal sought to be achieved by the Association is that of providing and maintaining "for the members and friends of *The United Methodist Church*" a proper, convenient and desirable permanent "*camp meeting ground* and *Christian* seaside resort." Association By-Laws, Art. II. In order that this goal not be frustrated, only *Methodists* in good and regular standing can be selected to sit on the Board of Trustees—the Association's governing body. *Id.,* Art. III, § 1. At least ten of these trustees must be Methodist ministers. *Id.,* Art. III, § 1. Finally, two of the three Board committees responsible for the day-to-day functioning of the community deal exclusively with non-secular matters. The program committee organizes and oversees Ocean Grove's "religious services," *id.,* Art. VIII, § 2, while the development committee is charged with the duty of implementing financial programs necessary to maintain Ocean Grove's character as a "Christian" Seaside Resort. *Id.,* Art. IX, § 2.
>
>   . . .
>
> In effect, the Legislature has decreed that in Ocean Grove the Church shall be the State and the State shall be the Church. Individuals chosen by the followers of a particular faith to safeguard their spiritual and cultural way of life have been accorded the authority to

determine what shall constitute acceptable modes of conduct for Methodists and non-Methodists alike. Government and religion are so inextricably intertwined as to be inseparable from one another. Such a fusion of secular and ecclesiastical power not only violates both the letter and spirit of the First Amendment, it also runs afoul of the "establishment clause" of our own State constitution, *see N.J. Const.* (1947), Art. I, ¶4.[17]

As a result, the elders lost the ability to set rules arbitrarily and the town came under the jurisdiction of Neptune Township. This led to the eventual opening of the streets on Sundays.[18] More recently, challenges arose when the association refused use of its boardwalk pavilion for gay and lesbian civil union ceremonies. The association had long advertised its pavilion as a wedding venue and had never before denied an applicant. The couple filed a complaint with the New Jersey Division of Civil Rights and the matter was decided in January 2012 in their favor. The administrative judge recognized that the association's policy was created well before civil unions were legal in New Jersey, but declared that the association could no longer offer its facility to any couples unless it was also available for civil union ceremonies. After losing its authority, the association discontinued all weddings and civil unions at the pavilion to preserve its religious objections, this notwithstanding the large number of gays and lesbians who have moved into and operate businesses in the quiet town since the turn of the twenty-first century.[19] Surely, this unique shore town will see more changes in the decades ahead.

Asbury Park

Asbury Park's history is inextricably tied to Ocean Grove even though Asbury Park was not organized as a religious community. Shortly after the Camp Meeting Association settled in Ocean Grove, 500 acres to the

north of Wesley Lake became available. Although interested, the association elders could not agree on whether to purchase what was just barren
property. Instead, an owner of one of the Ocean Grove lots bought it.
James Bradley of New York had purchased his lots within Ocean Grove
hoping that the sea air would help cure his poor health. He bought the adjacent acreage for $9,000 in part to protect Ocean Grove from undue influ-
ences. He laid out the land into lots, crossed by wide streets, and named
the town Asbury Park in honor of Bishop Francis Asbury, the Methodist
cleric mentioned earlier who preached throughout the American frontier
until his death in 1816. Asbury Park was not established as a religious
community, however, and Bradley did not limit his advertising or his
welcome to the pious. Nevertheless, Bradley's ties to Ocean Grove and
his personal moral and religious beliefs guided his decisions as the resort
developed. As a result, Asbury Park became a city of contradictions.

Bradley's vision for Asbury Park set the tone. In a gesture of faith, he
included a prohibition against the sale of liquor in the deeds for the lots
sold. In addition, in 1874, the New Jersey Legislature enacted a law to provide a buffer for Ocean Grove by prohibiting the sale of liquor within one
mile of a camp meeting.[20] Bradley envisioned Asbury Park as a healthy
destination to attract families and encouraged wholesome entertainments
in the summers and throughout the year. Bradley avoided the severe personal restrictions preferred in Ocean Grove and sought to enforce his
ideas about appropriate behavior with persuasion and mild efforts such
as posting rules at the beach; for example, "Modesty of apparel is as
becoming to a lady in a bathing suit as it is to a lady dressed in silk and
satin. A word to the wise is sufficient."[21] Nonetheless, Bradley proselytized
over the following decades against two specific vices, gambling and alcohol. Notably, as a state legislator Bradley was one of the strongest oppo-
nents of horse-race gambling and he supported the legislation that led
directly to the closing of Monmouth Park in 1894, eliminating this unique
advantage of his rival town, Long Branch. As to alcohol, however, his prohibitions were side-stepped throughout the city. The law became more

honored in the breach than in enforcement with almost a hundred illegal saloons in operation by 1885.[22]

Bradley's ego drove him to continuously enhance his creation. He built the boardwalk, public parks, piers, and pavilions; he insisted on an open beach front throughout the length of the town and prohibited building on the ocean block to achieve a boardwalk untrammeled by businesses and concessions. Bradley succeeded in bringing a railroad to his city in 1875 and his business acumen propelled his 500 acres to quickly develop into a year-round city. Secular crowds flocked to Asbury Park. By 1883, the Asbury Park railroad stations that served both communities brought more than 600,000 summer visitors, notwithstanding the prohibition against Sunday stops in deference to Ocean Grove's religious sensibilities. Gustav Kobbé, writing less than two decades after Bradley purchased the acreage, was surely impressed. In his 1889 review, he described Asbury Park as

a thriving town with a permanent population of some 4,000 and over 30,000 in the summer, a large printing establishment, three papers, three national banks, an opera house, a handsome library and a lecture hall (Educational Hall), brought from the Centennial grounds at Philadelphia and capable of holding 1,500 people, eight churches, an electric tramway and a system of drainage into the sea unsurpassed on the coast for efficiency. . . . The streets and the beach are also universally lighted by electricity all the year. To crown all, we find as a result of this enterprise nearly 200 hotels and boarding-houses and some 800 private residences.

The place has been laid out with good taste, many natural features of beauty having been skillfully utilized. . . . The opportunity offered by these features has not been neglected. The streets are of ample dimensions, lined with shade trees; those running angles to the sea are from 100 feet to 200 feet broad; the sidewalks and crossings are covered with flagging, asphaltum, cement or planks. In many spots clumps of the

primeval pine and cedar break picturesquely in upon modern formal-
ity. Along the beach there is a well-kept plank walk one mile long, with
seats and pavilions, at intervals joining the esplanade of Ocean Grove
thus giving an unbroken promenade of nearly two miles.[23]

Below the surface, however, Asbury Park struggled with internal issues.
Bradley accommodated the ethnic communities that came to the city—
Jewish merchants, Italian laborers, and southern blacks—all necessary to
keep the hotels and businesses going throughout the summer. But these
"ethnics" were relegated to the west side of the railroad tracks in Neptune
Township and were not welcome to mingle with the tourists. Nor did their
living conditions reflect in the least the houses they built or the lifestyles
they maintained for those living close to the beach. In the 1880s, Bradley
became embroiled in a series of conflicts arising from crowds of locals
hanging around the pavilions and allegedly disturbing the sight and pleasures of the paying visitors.[24] Bradley dealt with the issue by restricting
the movement of the locals and tried to characterize the restrictions that
were put in place as simple business decisions. Nevertheless, tensions ran
high, especially within the black community. Blacks were not allowed on
the tourist beaches and had to bathe at a blacks-only beach at one end of
the beachfront. Although Asbury Park was not the only Jersey Shore
resort that discouraged or prohibited locals (mainly, blacks) from the
hotels, amusements, and beaches, this legacy severely impacted the city
almost one hundred years later. (See chapter 13 for a fuller discussion of
race issues at the shore.)

By 1900, Asbury Park had become renowned as a pleasing seashore
resort. William Nelson described it as "an admirable and well governed
city, possessing all the advantages which science and art have devised."[25]
At the height of its popularity after 1900, Asbury Park rivaled Atlantic
City, Long Branch, and Cape May as the premier beach destination at the
Jersey Shore. The National Education Association held its annual convention in Asbury Park (and Ocean Grove) in 1905. Asbury Park was on the

move and the crowds were significantly different from those visiting Ocean Grove. The next two decades were its heyday. Although it could never supplant Atlantic City as the Jersey Shore's leading resort, Asbury Park competed with its accessibility and family atmosphere. Being so much closer to New York City and populated areas in northern New Jersey gave Asbury Park a geographic advantage. Its year-round population soared to 4,148 in 1900 and then to 12,406 in 1920. The crowds at its Baby Parades and Easter Parades matched those at Atlantic City.[26]

But all was not perfect. A *New York Times* story reporting that Asbury Park competed with Atlantic City for "the supremacy for Summer excursions" (day-trips) also reported that "bunko" men and pickpockets worked the city, requiring Bradley to hire private detectives at his own cost.[27] And political tensions arose. Bradley remained possessive and in control of Asbury Park and would not easily retreat from his vision for the town, his religious principles, or his claims of ownership of the beach, the boardwalk, the piers, and the parks. At the turn of the twentieth century visitors, businessmen, and city officials bristled at Bradley's one-man control over the city. In 1903, the Asbury Park City Council found enough independence to defy Bradley and demanded that he relinquish his claims of ownership, arguing that these amenities belonged to the city. Bradley had ignored these demands in prior years but finally agreed to *sell* his rights for $150,000 ($100,000 for the land and $50,000 for the sewer system), a low enough price to dissuade the council from pursuing litigation. Within a few years the council discovered, to its dismay, that the annual revenues from the boardwalk concessions that they coveted did not cover expenses and when the deficits mounted (which Bradley claimed that he had funded), the council chose to annex the west side ethnic communities from Neptune in 1906 for added tax revenues to make up the difference. Merchants and developers soon demanded that the prohibition against building on the oceanfront and boardwalk be lifted and substantial changes began to be made in the look and feel of the resort. The changes accelerated after Bradley's death in 1921, including construction of the

3,200 seat beaux-arts Convention Hall, a casino and carousel, and the 1,600-seat Paramount Theatre on the beachfront, much of which is now gone.

The glory of Asbury Park began to fade by the 1930s. Prohibition and the Depression had their impact. Even so, Asbury Park was blessed by a disaster, the beaching of the *Morro Castle* on its doorstep in September 1934. The burning wreckage of the ship on the beach by the Convention Hall drew thousands at the end of that summer season. (See chapter 7 for a detailed discussion of this disaster.) The sensational newspaper coverage, with pictures and stories of the inquisition, ran for months and years after the event.

In 1943, the Yankees chose Asbury Park for its war-time restricted spring training. Its family-friendly atmosphere revived Asbury Park to a significant extent in the 1950s with new attractions and thrill rides on the boardwalk: the "Tillie" image was painted on the side of the Palace Amusements building in 1956 as part of its marketing campaign and soon became a symbol of the city, even though the original image appeared in Coney Island years earlier.

Nevertheless, Asbury Park began a decline in the 1960s that it has struggled to overcome. It carries the burdens of a big and diverse city, as well as the legacy of troubled race relations. Its housing stock grew old and tired and many of its hotels closed or burned without any need to rebuild. Its boardwalk, once a fun-filled and exciting place, fell into disrepair and disrepute. In July 1970 Asbury Park suffered a race riot and the decaying housing that was one rationale for the riot has yet to be fully remedied. In the 1970s the city became known for its music venues. In 1973, Bruce Springsteen celebrated the city with his album *Greetings from Asbury Park* and the Stone Pony nightclub opened in 1974 at the corner of Second and Ocean Avenues, with performers like Southside Johnny and the Asbury Jukes. In the 1980s, the Stone Pony featured Elvis Costello, the Ramones, and Blondie, among others.[28]

Numerous attempts have been made by the town fathers since the 1970s to renew the oceanfront, but with limited success. In the last two decades, Asbury Park has become an attraction for the gay and lesbian community like its neighbor Ocean Grove, and music and film festivals in recent years have once again provided hope that Asbury Park can bring back its glory days.

OCEAN CITY

Ocean City, the largest community in Cape May County, is a Jersey Shore community contained within its own barrier island. The northern part of the island begins at Great Egg Harbor Bay and the island is separated from Ludlam's Island at its southern end by Corson's Inlet. Native Americans fished from the island and mainland farmers used it to graze cattle. Originally owed by the Somers family, the island became known as Peck's Beach after whaler John Peck purchased it around 1700 and used it to store and process whales. Little more happened on Peck's Beach until four Methodist ministers—Ezra B. Lake, James E. Lake, S. Wesley Lake, and William Burrell—selected it in 1879 as the location for a year-round camp meeting fashioned along the lines of Ocean Grove. The ministers met under a cedar tree that still stands today at Sixth Street and Asbury Avenue and the camp meeting opened the next year. A tabernacle was built nearby. The founders laid out the town and sold lots to their followers. At one time the city was known as a "moral seaside resort" and bathing was not allowed on Sundays until 1887. The association went about building a vibrant city with wharves and electric lights and industry. Even though religious authority over the island ceased when the island incorporated as a city in 1897, so-called blue laws continued to prohibit shopping on Sundays for almost a hundred years thereafter. Several court cases and a nonbinding 1986 referendum finally repealed all the restrictions (much to the relief of the amusement pier proprietors). Nevertheless, Ocean City remains a "dry" town with no sale or serving of alcoholic beverages, due to its religious beginnings.

One of the most enduring features of Ocean City is its 50-foot-wide boardwalk, which runs two and a half miles from North Street to Twenty-Third Street and is the home of one amusement thrill after another throughout its length. The first boardwalk was built in 1883, and over the decades storms and fires led to the boardwalk being moved and rebuilt several times. A municipal music pavilion was first built at Moorlyn Terrace in 1905 and then rebuilt in 1928 when the boardwalk was moved closer to the ocean. The new Music Pier, famous for its mediterranean revival architecture, juts out over the beach and still hosts concerts on a regular basis in the summer. The first amusement center was the Excursion House on the beach in 1887, which entertained visitors until it burned down in 1900. It was replaced by the Hippodrome which burned in 1927. Today, Gillian's Wonderland Pier on Seventh Street invites revelers to its 144-foot-high giant Ferris wheel, carousel, and much more. The city fathers have long proclaimed Ocean City as "America's Greatest Family Resort" and list a host of awards on the municipal website to prove their point. The action on the boardwalk—rides, games, shops, and food—is lively. Some have described the boardwalk experience in Ocean City as similar to the Wildwoods, only dry (that is, without alcohol).

Like all its neighboring shore communities, Ocean City has seen its share of shipwrecks, beginning with the loss of the Revolutionary War privateer *Fame* in February 1781. All but eight of the crew's twenty-eight men perished. Another notable wreck was the *Perseverance*, a richly laden ship that got stuck on a sandbar in December 1815 near Beasley's Point, strewing its cargo of lace and china all along the beach. The frequency of wrecks led to the building of three lifesaving stations on the island in the 1800s—#30 in the north (Beasley's Point), #31 in the middle of the island (Peck's Beach), and #32 at the south end (Corson's Inlet). In 1901 the two northern units responded to the distress flares from the *Sindia*, a four-masted barque returning from Japan with an unknown cargo. The ill-fated ship had traveled thousands of miles from Asia through the Cape of Good Hope at the bottom of Africa but grounded on a New Jersey sand bar in a fierce storm on December 15, just days short of arriving in New York. Only 150 yards off the beach, lifesaving crews had to wait for the light of morning to launch boats. Twenty-six of the thirty-three members of the crew were rowed to safety, but what makes the *Sindia* wreck compelling is the mystery surrounding her cargo. Water and sand filled the ship quickly and the cargo could not be recovered. Questions arose early on about whether the cargo was mostly magnesium ore as claimed or Buddhist relics looted from temples during the Boxer Rebellion of 1900, ongoing at the time the ship was loaded in Shanghai and Kobe, Japan. The remnants of the ship remained visible from the Ocean City beach for years as the ocean's sands slowly captured the entire vessel, leaving just her mast protruding above the water until an Army Corps of Engineers beach nourishment project finished the work. The cargo at the bottom of the ship has never been extricated despite several efforts, even in recent years, to see if reality matches the legend.

"Sea Grove," Dry Towns, Retreats, and Ethnics

Other locations along the Jersey Shore, in the past and still today, carry the impact of religious beginnings or serve as the home of religious orders. The tip of Cape May, Cape May Point, began as a summer retreat for Presbyterians in 1876. The area had been known for 150 years as Stites Beach but the name was changed to Sea Grove by its founder, the Reverend Alexander Whilldin. Sea Grove boasted a large number of churches and one of the town's earliest structures was a pavilion in its center used by all faiths with room for as many as 2,000 worshippers. Eventually, four substantial hotels were built to cater to summer guests, religious and otherwise, and the town incorporated in 1878 as Cape May Point. The restrictions placed on the residents proved too much (in contrast to the acceptance by Ocean Grove's residents) and the town lost favor. The religious Sea Grove

Association responsible for the development of the town went bankrupt and their lots were sold at auction. In addition, beach erosion was a constant problem. Much of the town—including a substantial portion of the grand pavilion area—was lost over time. Of the four hotels, only the Shoreham Hotel remains today, but it upholds the religious beginnings of the town. The Sisters of Saint Peter from Philadelphia purchased the 150-room hotel in 1909, renamed it St. Mary by-the-Sea, and use it, along with several other buildings, as a retreat house. Ironically, during World War II the house was leased and used by the U.S. military. Over the last one hundred years, the sisters have had to spend considerable sums on jetties and dunes to protect their investment. In the same religious tradition, the Marianist Society of New York now occupies the former Wanamaker mansion as a summer retreat.

Cape May Point remains a "dry town." Mantoloking and Wildwood Crest are also a "dry" towns. The first developers of Mantoloking, Frank Hall, and Frederick Downer, made gifts of title to the Church of St. Simon by-the-Sea (Episcopal) as well as to the Mantoloking Yacht Club and the Mantoloking Water Company. All the deeds contained restrictions against alcohol. Seaside Park began in 1874 as an effort to build a Baptist retreat on the beach similar to Ocean Grove, with a park in the center, and named Park City. The sand did not prove amenable to the trees selected and the park and the retreat never materialized, so subsequent owners divided the land into lots for sale using the name Sea Side Park.

In the twentieth century a number of religious communities continued the tradition of religion-by-the-sea by establishing retreats on the beach. In addition to the St. Mary by-the-Sea retreat in Cape May Point, Villa Maria by-the-Sea in Stone Harbor was purchased during the Depression for the sisters of the Immaculate Heart of Mary; the Sisters of Mercy have a retreat in Sea Isle City; Maris Stella in Harvey Cedars is a summer home for the Sisters of Charity; Stella Maris in Long Branch served until recently as a home for the Sisters of Saint Joseph for Peace; Catholic Redemptionists maintain the San Alfonso Retreat House in Long Branch;

and the Religious Teachers Filippi have a twenty-two-bedroom complex in South Mantoloking. The Villa Maria by-the-Sea three-story convent house in Stone Harbor faces the ocean across Second Avenue and across from the Bird Sanctuary at 111th Street. The sisters moved to Stone Harbor in 1937 after their original retreat house in Cape May Point (the former Carleton Hotel) fell into the sea. When the Stone Harbor convent was built, there were no roads nearby and only twenty bungalows on Seven Mile Island. Stone Harbor built up around the house, which still welcomes almost 600 sisters throughout the summer. One unique Jersey Shore event is the annual Nun's Beach Surf Invitational, inaugurated in 1993 as a thank you from the local surfers to the nuns for allowing them to surf the "Nun's Beach." One of the favorite tee-shirt slogans at the event is "Pray for Surf." Proceeds go to the upkeep of the house. Generous neighbors contribute to maintain the landscaping.

Modern era economics threaten the viability of these communities. Several of these properties were purchased for a song—the sisters bought their Stella Maris site in Long Branch for $14,000 in 1941 and the Sisters of St. Joseph purchased the Shoreham Hotel in Cape May point in 1909 for $9,000—but the modern-day upkeep has become extraordinarily expensive even as the properties have increased significantly in value. The Sisters of Charity of New York sold their retreat in Ventnor in 2002 and the Archdiocese of Philadelphia sold a retirement home for priests in the same town in 2012. The latter had nineteen rooms, 175 feet of boardwalk frontage, and was assessed at $6.5 million. It had been a gift to the church in 1905. The Stella Maris complex in Long Branch was put up for sale in 2014 and closed on December 31, 2015, because of the expense of maintenance, with the sisters hoping to sell it as a nature preserve.[29]

Another religious retreat is the former Harvey Cedars Hotel, which was built in 1841 as a "sportsmen's hotel" to accommodate wealthy vacationers who fished and hunted game. One hundred years later the hotel became an interdenominational vacation bible school after serving purposes other than sport for many years, including a period as a retreat for women (Camp Whelen). The building sits on the bay side of Long Beach Island surrounded now by a complex of fields and newly built dormitories to entertain busloads of children who visit in the summer for one or two weeks. In earlier years, the hotel was separated from the rest of the area by a creek. The Sisters of Charity maintain Maris Stella within easy walking or sailing distance. Despite selling pieces of their property over recent years, the sisters still own a swath of land at this narrow part of Long Beach Island from the ocean to the bay. They maintain summer residences for the sisters, a chapel, and a conference center.

For some shore towns, the tenor of the community has ethnic overtones rather than religious associations. Spring Lake, for example, is known as the Irish Riviera because of the number of Irish-Americans who have moved there over the last fifty years, especially retired policemen and firemen. Bradley Beach has a substantial Jewish community, especially Sephardic Jews from Syria, and many have moved up to the higher-priced houses in Deal where there had long been a community of Ashkenazi Jews. Most of these homeowners and visitors came after the turn of the twentieth century, but wealthy German Jews had vacationed and settled in Long Branch (Elberon), Sea Bright, and Allenhurst decades earlier, in the second half of the 1800s. Jesse Seligman provided his home in Long Branch to President James Garfield's family when the president sought to recover from an assassin's bullet at the shore. Belmar also developed a Jewish community in the 1900s, particularly writers and artists.

Long Branch has had a thriving Italian population dating back to the late 1800s and two communities in Cape May County have Italian connections as well. Sea Isle City came into being in 1880 after its founder, Charles Landis, returned from a trip to Italy smitten with Venice. Landis, who had previously founded Vineland and helped to build Hammonton, purchased Ludlam's Island and began to develop his year-round seashore community modeled on what he had seen in Italy. His original designs included canals, public baths, fountains, and Italian architecture surrounded by statuary. Not all of it came into fruition or lasted for long. A statue of the Roman god Neptune, the only remaining original piece from Landis's collection, now sits in the garden of the town's Historical Society. Landis's Italian dream had the advantage of broad sandy beaches and access to the bay and the ocean for both sport and commercial fishing. Ironically, the city attracted a large number of Italian immigrants and has had a dynamic Italian community ever since. It also attracted German immigrants and at one point there was a German-language newspaper in town. Even Ocean City, originated by Protestant ministers, eventually developed a lively Italian section. Its Little Italy was the home of Gay Talese, a writer who wrote an autobiographical account, *Unto the Sons*, about growing up there and the tension between the Italian and Irish Catholics. One of the leading Irish Catholic families in Ocean City in the mid-1900s was that of John Kelly, a Philadelphia businessman with a beautiful daughter, Grace. He spent summers as a boy in the resort and owned a house that his daughter, Academy Award-winning film star and soon to become Princess of Monaco, Grace Kelly, occasionally visited.

Further Reading

On traveling preachers, see Benjamin Abbott, *Experience and Gospel Labours of the Rev. Benjamin Abbott* (New York, 1830); Francis Asbury, *Journal of the Rev. Francis Asbury* (New York: Lane and Scott, 1852); John Fothergill, *An Account of the Life and Travels in the Work of the Ministry of John Fothergill* (London, 1753); Hopwood, Samuel, "Samuel Hopwood's Travels in America, 1741–44," in *Bulletin of Friends Historical Association* (vol. 39, 1950); and John Woolman, *The Journal of John Woolman* (Philadelphia, 1774).

On Ocean Grove, see Wayne T. Bell, *Ocean Grove* (Charleston, SC: Arcadia Publishing, 2000); Morris S. Daniels, *The Story of Ocean Grove Related in the Year of its Golden Jubilee* (New York: Methodist Book Concern, 1919); Christopher M., Flynn, *Greetings from Ocean Grove* (Atglen, PA: Schiffer Publishing, 2007); and

E. H. Stokes, ed., *Ocean Grove, Its Origins and Progress* (Philadelphia: Haddock and Son, 1874).

On Asbury Park, see Helen-Chantal Pike, *Asbury Park's Glory Days, The Story of an American Resort* (New Brunswick, NJ: Rivergate Books, 2005); Joseph G. Bilby and Harry Ziegler, *Asbury Park Reborn, Lost to Time and Restored to Glory* (Charleston, SC: History Press, 2012); Daniel Wolff, *4th of July, Asbury Park, A History of the Promised Land* (New York: Bloomsbury Publishing, 2005).

On Ocean City, see Frank J. Esposito and Robert J. Esposito, *Ocean City, New Jersey* (Charleston, SC: Arcadia Publishing, 1998); and Fred Miller, *Ocean City, America's Greatest Family Resort* (Charleston, SC: Arcadia Publishing, 2003).

On religious and ethnic communities, see *Patricia M. Ard and Michael Aron Rockland, The Jews in New Jersey, a Pictorial History* (New Brunswick, NJ: Rutgers University Press, 2001); Paul D. Boyd, *Atlantic Highlands, From Lenape Camps to Bayside Town* (Charleston, SC: Arcadia Publishing Co., 2004); Michael J. Eula, *Between Peasant and Urban Villager: Italian-Americans of New Jersey and New York, 1880–1980: The Structures of Counter-Discourse* (New York: Peter Lang, 1993); Roger Finke and Rodney Stark, *The Churching of America, 1776–1990: Winners and Losers in Our Religious Economy* (New Brunswick, NJ: Rutgers University Press, 1992); Charles A. Johnson, *The Frontier Camp Meeting: Religious Harvest Time* (Dallas, TX: Southern Methodist University, 1955); William Warren Sweet, *Methodists in American History* (Nashville, TN: Abington Press, 1953); and Gary Wells, *Head and Heart, American Christianities* (New York: Penguin Press, 2007).

CHAPTER 6

The Rise of Resorts, Monmouth County

Spring Lake . . . is one of the most beautiful localities on this part of the coast. It derives its name from a lake near the beach of limpid water, fed by a thousand springs, which affords a supply for the hotels and cottages; and is used also to some extent for boating and fishing. The ground around belongs to an association, who have improved it, to a considerable extent, by water works, drainage and streets. A depot of the New Jersey Southern Railroad is within half a mile of the beach. The principal hotels are the Monmouth, Carlton and Lake. They are first class. There are besides, some fine boarding houses. The place has not grown as much as it deserves. Still there are fine residences here, and lots, in every variety, await purchasers, at reasonable figures, and on accommodating terms.
—William C. Ulyat, *Life at the Seashore*, 1880

Without question, the Jersey Shore had become a destination by the 1850s, albeit for the well-to-do at a few chosen locations. Middle class vacationers needed the development of railroads. Atlantic City was the only shore resort that could be readily accessed by train in 1854, but it could hardly be called a "resort," with only a few houses dotting the island and one half-finished hotel. Nonetheless, its railroad monopoly lasted long enough for promoters to make Atlantic City a household name throughout the United States. Long Branch could be reached directly by train by 1860 and Cape May by 1863; Ocean Grove developed next, appealing to a different crowd, and soon shared a train depot with its neighbor Asbury Park, by 1875. Most of the remaining beach front developed after 1875, as the

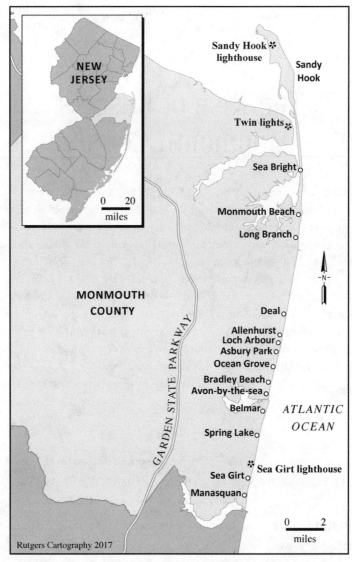

NEW
JERSEY

0   20
miles

Sandy Hook ✵
lighthouse

Sandy
Hook

Twin lights ✵

Sea Bright ○

Monmouth Beach ○

Long Branch ○

-N-

MONMOUTH
COUNTY

Deal ○

Allenhurst ○
Loch Arbour ○
Asbury Park ○
Ocean Grove ○
Bradley Beach ○
Avon-by-the-sea ○
Belmar ○

ATLANTIC
OCEAN

Spring Lake ○

✵ Sea Girt lighthouse
Sea Girt ○
Manasquan ○

0   2
miles

Rutgers Cartography 2017

Map 2. Monmouth County Shore Communities and Lighthouses.
Map designed by Michael Siegel, Rutgers University.

growing acceptance and demand for railroad transportation allowed local businessmen the opportunity to make their own resort visions a reality. Dozens of shore towns incorporated between 1875 and 1900 as the trip to the beach became bearable, inexpensive, and faster.

Railroads and New Resorts

The race to the shore by the railroads in the late 1880s must have been exhilarating. Newly formed railroad companies organized and began laying tracks to sprouting boroughs, crisscrossing the state and running parallel to the ocean along the seashore as each new set of investors saw profits in their lines or in their real estate at the end of those lines. The building of hotels, boarding houses, and individual homes boomed as each municipality promoted its particular virtues for day-trippers, true believers, or potential second home buyers. Tracts of beachfront and inland property were purchased with the goal of subdividing all undeveloped pieces of the shore into lots and selling them at a profit. As Atlantic City was gilding its reputation, every stretch of beach up and down the shore angled for its own railroad stop and, by 1900, most of the shore could be reached by one railroad or another, or more than one. Rail lines were speculative ventures fueled often by the ambitions of local businessmen looking to make a quick profit. Many railroad companies that once had a piece of the shore came and went amid the scramble, the bankruptcies, the mergers, and the competition, including:

New York and Long Branch Railroad
Long Branch and Seashore Railroad
Long Branch and Sea Girt Railroad
Long Branch and Barnegat Bay Railroad
Farmingdale and Squan River Railroad
Squankum Railroad and Marl Company
Monmouth Park Railroad

Tuckerton Railroad

Long Beach Railroad

Manahawkin and Long Beach Transportation Company

Brigantine Beach Railroad

Philadelphia and Brigantine Railroad

Atlantic City Railroad

West Jersey and Seashore Railroad

Pemberton and Seashore Railroad

Philadelphia and Atlantic City Railroad

Philadelphia and Long Branch Railroad

Philadelphia and Beach Haven Railroad

Seacoast Railroad

Stone Harbor Railroad

West Jersey and Atlantic Railroad

Ocean City Railroad

Anglesea Railroad

Wildwood and Delaware Bay Short Line Railroad

Cape May Railroad

Cape May and Millville Railroad

Tuckahoe and Cape May Railroad

The race, which lasted several decades, was on, and not all of the railroad competition was friendly. At one point a work gang of Irishmen and a work gang of Italians from competing lines fought it out at Woodbine (in Cape May County) when a second line sought to cross its tracks over the first. A court injunction preventing the crossing did not stop the construction crew and the scuffle settled this "frog fight" in favor of the new line. (The necessary crossing track was called a "frog.") In another bizarre incident late in the nineteenth century, a crew laid tracks to Ocean City in Cape May County each day for a month only to have the tracks ripped up each night by a rival crew. Finally, a court sided in favor of competition and the tracks went down and stayed down. To add to the frenetic

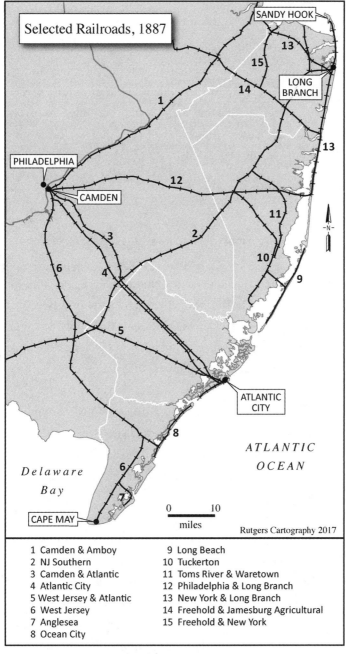

Selected Railroads, 1887

SANDY HOOK

13

15

14

LONG
BRANCH

1

13

PHILADELPHIA

12

11

CAMDEN

3

2

10

6

4

9

5

8

ATLANTIC
CITY

ATLANTIC
OCEAN

Delaware
Bay

6

7

CAPE MAY

0   10
miles

Rutgers Cartography 2017

-N-

1 Camden & Amboy	9 Long Beach
2 NJ Southern	10 Tuckerton
3 Camden & Atlantic	11 Toms River & Waretown
4 Atlantic City	12 Philadelphia & Long Branch
5 West Jersey & Atlantic	13 New York & Long Branch
6 West Jersey	14 Freehold & Jamesburg Agricultural
7 Anglesea	15 Freehold & New York
8 Ocean City	

Map 3. New Jersey Train Routes, Shore Lines, 1881. The main
railroad lines traveling to and along the Jersey Shore are taken from
an 1881 statewide map that can be found at http://mapmaker.rutgers
.edu/HISTORICALMAPS/RAILROADS/RR_of_NJ.jpg. Map
designed by Michael Siegel, Rutgers University.

action and confusion, lines merged, lines went bankrupt, lines were abandoned, and lines were sold at auction, making the game all the more
intriguing. Major railroad lines would also lease or acquire shorter runs
to extend their reach with name changes and corporate maneuvers making the results difficult to follow. As an example, the Raritan Bay and
Delaware Railroad incorporated in 1854, went bankrupt and became
the New Jersey Southern in 1867, and eventually became part of the
New Jersey Central Railroad when the New Jersey Southern went bankrupt in 1869.

Tracks to the beach most often followed the formation of a new municipality at the beach, or vice versa. Creating a new municipality offered
significant advantages. As independent municipalities, seashore communities could be shaped by the local fathers (and investors). New Jersey has
long had the reputation as a "home rule" state that allows small municipalities to exercise extraordinary jurisdiction over their domain. State
laws made incorporation easy, allowing deserted beaches with nothing
more than brush, shrubs, and trees to be carved away from large inland-
oriented townships and converted into newly minted boroughs so that
lots could be easily plotted and sold. One 1878 law, later ruled unconstitutional, applied uniquely to "Seaside Resorts" and allowed the residents to
incorporate if the borough to be created was no more than two square
miles, as long as it had taxable ratables of $100,000 or more. Many of
the referenda taken (to separate from the townships) involved fewer than
one hundred votes. The development of the individual shore towns was,
of course, uneven in terms of timing and quality. Rail and land bridges
were needed to reach most of the beaches and each geographical location
had its own requirements and difficulties. For some resorts, municipal
incorporation followed fast upon initial developer interest and the first
crowds to arrive; for others, the incorporation came several years later.
Development followed no definite pattern, following instead the whim of
railroad executives and local entrepreneurs. Some of the early train lines
combined the possibility of freight with seashore passengers. This was the

case for the Squankum Railroad and Marl Company, which ran from Freehold to Farmingdale. The harvesting and shipping of marl, the shore sediment that has multiple uses, including as a fertilizer, had become a major industry in this area of the state. This railroad, as its name indicates, was organized in part to get the marl to its markets. The end of the line was originally Toms River, to accommodate the considerable commercial interest in that town. An extension to the beach at Squan followed shortly thereafter to accommodate those who had visited the area for decades to enjoy bathing in the ocean and the Manasquan River.

The data in Table 2 reveals that geographic location did not rule development; that is, the northern beaches did not necessarily develop earlier than the southern beaches. Nor did adjacent boroughs always develop or incorporate at the same time: for example, Ocean Grove (1870) and Bradley Beach (1893), Belmar (1873) and Avon-by-the-Sea (1900), and Avalon (1892) and Stone Harbor (1914).[1]

By 1900 the Jersey Shore was no longer just a few resorts with boarding houses or hotels servicing those lucky enough to be able to leave the hot cities in the summer months. In the preceding twenty-five years the Jersey Shore had transformed and was well on its way to providing beach access to all levels of society. In this period, twenty-five boroughs were incorporated, each catering to the different demands of multiple constituencies. Ten new seaside boroughs would follow in the next twenty-six years, from 1900 through 1925. Only a handful of these new communities—notably Manasquan and Point Pleasant, Surf City, and Beach Haven—had a significant resort history prior to their incorporation.

Railroad men understood that the money to be made in fares was only part of what was available. Selling lots and building houses could be just as lucrative and maybe less risky. Their efforts to create "resorts" and sell real estate can be seen in the "booster" books that the railroad companies produced to lure buyers to the shore. In 1876 the New Jersey Southern Railway Company published "for gratuitous distribution" a pamphlet entitled *Homes on the Sea-Shore on the Line of the New Jersey Southern*

TABLE 2

Municipality	1st Incorporation	1st Form	Separated From / Became
Atlantic City	1854	City	Egg Harbor and Galloway Townships
Sandy Hook	1846	Military Reservation	Middletown Township
Cape Island	1848	Borough	Lower Township / Cape May [1851]
Long Branch	1867	Commission	
Ocean Grove	1870	Charter	Ocean Township
Asbury Park	1874	Borough	Ocean Township
Berkeley	1875	Township	Dover Township
Cape May Point	1878	Borough	Lower Township
Sea Isle City	1882	Borough	Dennis Township
North Spring Lake	1884	Borough	Wall Township / Spring Lake [1903]
Ocean City	1884	Borough	Upper Township
Anglesea	1885	Borough	Middle Township / North Wildwood [1906]
Ocean Beach	1885	Borough	Wall Township / Belmar [1889]
Holly Beach	1885	Borough	Lower Township / WildwooD [1912]
South Atlantic City	1885	Borough	Little Egg Harbor Township / Margate [1909]
Manasquan	1887	Borough	Wall Township
Point Pleasant Beach	1886	Borough	Brick Township
Bay Head	1886	Borough	Brick Township
Lavalette	1887	Borough	Dover Township
Sea Bright	1889	Borough	Ocean Township
Beach Haven	1890	Borough	Eagleswood Township
Brigantine	1890	Borough	Galloway Township
Avalon	1892	Borough	Middle Township

(continued)

TABLE 2 MUNICIPAL INCORPORATION *(continued)*

Municipality	1st Incorporation	1st Form	Separated From / Became
Spring Lake	1892	Borough	Wall Township
Bradley Beach	1893	Borough	Neptune Township
Harvey Cedars	1894	Borough	Union Township
Long Beach City	1894	Borough	Stafford Township / Surf City [1899]
Wildwood	1895	Borough	Middle Township
Allenhurst	1897	Borough	Ocean Township
Deal	1898	Borough	Ocean Township
Sea Side Park	1898	Borough	Berkeley Township / Seaside Park [1947]
Longport	1898	Borough	Little Egg Harbor Township
Long Beach Township	1899	Township	Eagleswood, Little Egg Harbor, Ocean, Stafford, and Union Townships
Avon By-The-Sea	1900	Borough	Neptune Township
Ventnor	1903	Borough	Egg Harbor Township
Barnegat City	1904	Borough	Long Beach Township / Barnegat Light [1948]
Monmouth Beach	1906	Borough	Ocean Township
Wildwood Crest	1910	Borough	Lower Township
Mantoloking	1911	Borough	Brick Township
Seaside Heights	1913	Borough	Berkeley and Dover Townships
Stone Harbor	1914	Borough	Middle Township
Sea Girt	1917	Borough	Wall Township
Shipbottom-Arlington	1925	Borough	Long Beach Township / Shipbottom [1943]
Loch Arbour	1957	Village	Ocean Township

Railway, for New York Business Men, which walked its readers through each station stop and the lots available with easy access to each stop. The virtues of each new community were heralded, maps of available lots were included, and advertisements from local developers and builders filled the rest of the pages.[2] The marketing drive continued for decades. The Central Railroad of New Jersey published *Along the Shore and in the Foothills* in 1910 for the same purpose. This pamphlet started with a clear description of its purpose:

> Though from green-topped hills of Atlantic Highlands to the shelving beaches at Point Pleasant [the run of its line] is a stretch of some twenty-five miles, cities and towns and villages follow one another in such close succession that this whole region is more like one great community. There is a railroad station for nearly every one of the twenty-five miles of the shore line, and the splendid transportation facilities afforded for all-rail lines and Sandy Hook Route steamers of the Central Railroad of New Jersey make this whole section from spring to fall a vital throbbing part of the great suburban zone of the Metropolitan district.[3]

Eventually, the railroad author gets around to Atlantic City, "the greatest all-the-year resort of the Western Continent," and proclaims that the Central's "splendid service" can make the run in three hours from New York City "through miles of the famous pine belt of New Jersey, with its ozone-laden air, and the highly cultivated agricultural section which furnishes New York and Philadelphia with so much of their table necessities."[4] Barren seashore land purchased at a small price before the arrival of a railroad line could be sold after its arrival for many times more. Descriptions of the beauty, the amenities, and the health benefits of seashore resorts accompanied the assurance of a safe and smooth ride and embellished each summer destination.[5]

In 1860, vacationers had the choice of just a few large resorts. The oceanfront in between remained mostly barren. Today, beach communities run almost continuously across the 127 miles from the tip of Sandy Hook to Cape May Point. A survey of New Jersey's twenty-first-century beach communities north to south can help understand the pace of development and the haphazard nature of the development once railroads competed to run their tracks to the ocean.

Monmouth County

New Jersey's northernmost beaches along the Atlantic Ocean can be found at Sandy Hook, within Gateway National Recreational Area. The public could not enjoy sea bathing on a regular basis at Sandy Hook until 1881. Its history in the previous 150 years centered on maritime and military considerations.

As mentioned earlier, Sandy Hook was leased to Richard Hartshorne in the 1600s for a "fishery" and the lighthouse was built in 1764. Limited fortifications (Fort Gates) were erected in the early 1800s and may have had some beneficial impact on the security of New York City during the War of 1812. Two lifesaving stations were built in the 1850s. In the 1860s, the Long Branch and Seashore Railroad built a pier at Spermaceti Cove where ferries from New York City shuttled vacationers heading to Long Branch. After the Civil War, politicians began to fear expansionist European powers and in 1874 the U.S. Army established a proving ground at the northeastern tip of the barren peninsula to test heavy weapons and munitions. Tracks were laid for a special train to get the materiel to the site and a permanent facility was established in 1903. The proving ground had a 3,000-yard range to the south for smaller weapons and out to sea for longer-range guns. Fort Hancock was completed in 1899 and its batteries could launch shells twenty miles out to sea with power enough to stop armored ships coming into the harbor. Some of the guns "disappeared" after they fired, folding back into concrete bunkers with the assistance of steam engines and counterweights. These fortifications served their purpose through 1919 but they were large and expensive and repeatedly passed into obsolescence over the next fifty years. During World War II the fort

housed between 7,000 and 12,000 army personnel, including members of
the Women's Auxiliary Army Corps. In the 1950s, when high altitude
bombers became a threat to the country, Nike surface-to-air missiles were
installed on Sandy Hook to intercept incoming planes, one of nineteen
sites protecting New York City and its surroundings. Nike Ajax and Her-
cules missiles could intercept Soviet bombers as far as ninety-four miles
from shore. Soldiers remained at the ready twenty-four hours a day from
1954 until the bomber site was dismantled as part of the Strategic Arms
Limitations Talks with the Soviet Union in 1974. Today, the entrance to
Fort Hancock at Sandy Hook is adorned by two Nike missiles and the
U.S. Coast Guard maintains a post at the tip.

Sandy Hook's other life—as a beach—began in 1881 when the southern end, known then as Wardell Beach, was sold by Anthony and Mary
Reckless to the Highland Beach Association and subdivided into seventy-
four lots for development. The peninsula measured as few as one hundred
yards from the ocean to the Shrewsbury River at some spots, making it a
desirable spot for bathing. Its location was easily accessible for the thousands living nearby. The Sandlass family purchased more than ten lots at
the turn of the twentieth century and was instrumental in bringing attractions to Highland Beach, including a dance hall, a roller-coaster, and a
"Bamboo Bar." The U.S. Army had purchased the lots north of Highland
Beach much earlier as a buffer to its operations and in 1962 took the Sandlass lots by eminent domain.[6] When the army's need for Fort Hancock
diminished, the beach was leased to the state as a park and then incorporated into the Gateway National Recreational Area in 1974 when the fort
was closed. Visitors can enjoy swimming, fishing, biking, hiking, and
more. Bathers can choose one of seven beaches, including New Jersey's
only nude beach (Gunnison Beach); bikers can enjoy a seven-mile path
around the peninsula and around Fort Hancock; fishermen can cast from
the beaches day and night; and birders can try to count all 325 species that
visit Sandy Hook throughout the year. The orderly houses on "Officer's

Row" sit empty facing the bay and provide a splendid facade for visitors to admire.

Sandy Hook offers beautiful views at every point. On the eastern observation decks, a visitor can see the Verrazano-Narrows Bridge, Staten Island, Brooklyn, and Coney Island and Long Island stretching out along the water. To the west, the Navesink and the Shrewsbury Rivers flow gracefully into Sandy Hook Bay. Visitors to Mount Mitchill State Park on the mainland have a spectacular view of Sandy Hook as the narrow spit unfolds into the bay with the fort and the lighthouse at its tip. Mount Mitchill is the highest point on the east coast south of Maine. The shore towns running southeast to northwest from Sandy Hook are on the Raritan Bay: the Highlands, Atlantic Highlands, Belford, Port Monmouth, Keansburg, Middletown, North Middletown, and Union Beach. While technically not along the Jersey Shore (at least for the purposes of this book), these towns share in its lore. Keansburg, for example, remains one of the best shore amusement playgrounds, reachable easily from most spots in northern New Jersey. Belford remains one of New Jersey's six major fishing ports responsible for the huge tonnage of menhaden caught every year in the waters nearby. Atlantic Highlands (originally Portland Point) began as a religious camp meeting location; the Twin Tower lighthouse is located in the Highlands and James Fennimore Cooper used the Highlands as the location of his novel *Water Witch* (1830); Prohibition bootleggers used the waters along Atlantic Highlands and the Highlands to their advantage in the 1920s. Naval Weapons Station Earle has operated from Leonardo (Middletown Township) on the Sandy Hook Bay since 1943. Its nearly three-mile-long pier (one of the longest in the world) is used to safely load and unload munitions.

Sea Bright and Monmouth Beach, located just south of Sandy Hook, developed as seashore resorts before Sandy Hook. These two towns offered views of the Shrewsbury and Navesink Rivers and attracted permanent residents as well as vacationers. The permanent residents adorned their homes with lawns and flower beds. Although Sea Bright did not incorporate until 1889, the locale had a colorful history well before then. The land originally belonged to the Wardell family and its story began with the fishing village called Nauvoo in the early 1800s. The first large hotel was open for business in 1842 and other hotels followed. Developers Paul Mifflin, Samuel B. Dodd, and William W. Shippen saw an opportunity to build a community around the hotels and laid out the town into individual lots. The Long Branch and Seashore Railroad from Sandy Hook brought traffic from New York City after 1865 to aid in the development.

Gustav Kobbé, writing in 1889, found the fishing village "the most picturesque portion of Sea Bright."[7] William Nelson, writing in 1901 after the fire destroyed the fishing huts, preferred the "wealth and culture" of the tourist village and describes "Seabright" as "one of the most delightful villages on the coast" with grand hotels close to the beach. The Octagon Hotel "boasted piazzas its full length on either side," maintained an orchestra for its ballroom, and entertained 350 guests. Nelson mentions three hotels "west of the railroad" as well—the Peninsula Hotel, the Rutherford Arms, and Panacci's. The houses in the town were "of beautiful design, in all styles of architecture, and are surrounded by well-kept lawns adorned with ornamental trees and shrubbery." Beach clubs, especially the Seabright Beach Club, provided "exclusive accommodations for bathing and greater conveniences" than the public bathing houses. The crowd visiting at the turn of the century enjoyed lawn tennis, cricket, and carriage rides.[8]

Neighboring Monmouth Beach, like most of Sea Bright and the southern end of Sandy Hook, was also farmland originally owned by the Wardell family. The Wardell farmhouse, built before the Revolutionary War, was in this section of the farm but Monmouth Beach developed later than Sea Bright because the New York and Seashore Railroad tracks from Sandy Hook that passed through this area were too close to the ocean to allow for beachfront development. The town was developed after the tracks were moved westward at a significant cost to the developers, Edward Q. Keasbey, Daniel Dodd, and John Torrey. As a result, there were no hotels in Monmouth Beach at the turn of the century. Like Sea Bright, the community developed around a beach club culture. One railroad booster book printed in 1873 was over the top about the location even though the area did not incorporate as a borough until 1906: "And at a glance the intelligent traveler will perceive that these attractive dwellings, facing, in one direction, the billowy Atlantic, and in the other, the beautiful landscape stretching away inland, are the homes, not of those who come and go with the ostentatious show and vulgar extravagance of the *nouveaux riches*, but of the better class of society who, while availing themselves of the unequaled attractions of the New Jersey Sea Shore, yet maintain here that exclusiveness to which a high social position entitles them."[9]

Long Branch occupies the next two-mile stretch of beach along the Jersey Shore and its history is covered in chapters 3 and 4.

The historic community of Deal welcomed sea bathers before 1800. They stayed in farmhouses for the most part. William Hathaway purchased a sizable farm in Deal in 1855 that was previously owned by T. Borden, and converted its large house into the Hathaway Inn to entertain visitors. Hathaway worked the farm and ran the inn for years thereafter, but Deal needed the arrival of a railroad to transition from farming community to beach resort. In 1894, Theodore S. Darling opened a boarding house in Deal and two years later persuaded the railroad at Long Branch to lay tracks to "Darlington" Station. Darling soon thereafter sold his property to the Atlantic Coast Realty Company and development moved quickly. The company brought in a landscape architect, Nathan Barnett, to lay out the town. Barnett's work gave the community its original style. William Nelson's description of Deal in 1901 provides a written picture:

The principal feature of the land adornment of Deal Beach is a broad esplanade reaching down to the ocean. The garden at the entrance is hedged with privet. The pathways meander among beds of flowers, and large palms and pieces of statuary occupy convenient intervals. The path opens into a garden with white gravel walks, box hedges, and beds of variegated flowers. Another section is paved with bricks and cement, and is set with shrubbery and adorned with vases of flowers. Farther, the path and driveway come together in an open court, at considerable elevation—a beautiful view point for the ocean lying below. By night the grounds appear to splendid advantage under myriad electric lights.[10]

Nelson also makes note of the Deal Golf Club, incorporated in 1898, as "the finest in the country." The borough of Deal incorporated that same year.

Allenhurst is a tiny but wealthy community south of Deal with large and beautiful homes in a variety of styles, including Victorian and Tudor, all surrounded by well-kept lawns. The town occupies only 0.30 square miles and had a population of only 718 in the year 2000, yet the annual household income was among the highest in New Jersey that same year. The town is named for the Allen family, who owned the land and farmed it for years in the 1800s. The farm was sold to the Coast Land Company in 1896 and the Long Branch and Seashore Railroad built a station on the west side of town in 1889. The borough incorporated the next year. The original rail station, built in Queen Anne style, was listed on the National Register of Historic Places in 1980, but has since been demolished. A historic district was listed in 2010 to recognize the Victorian architecture. An L-shaped jetty at the north end of the Allenhurst beach is renowned for fishing and scuba-diving, with a variety of colorful fish as well as an occasional lobster for dinner. One scuba-diving website claims that the jetty was built after the 1916 shark attacks to protect young bathers.[11] Whatever reason, the jetty has played a part in a long-term tradition. In 1901, William Nelson noted in his book that the residents of Allenhurst celebrated the town's founding on August 10th each year with a parade and an evening ball. That tradition faded into the past, but since 1943 local residents celebrate on the day before Labor Day by dyeing the ocean green. The origins of this tradition may be somewhat sketchy, but in a strange way it recalls the jubilation of the town's nineteenth-century forebears. Unfortunately, the jetty may be eliminated if plans to replenish the beach after Superstorm Sandy are carried out. Dyeing the ocean without the lagoon will be difficult and recent celebrations have become somewhat bittersweet as residents, fishermen, and scuba divers negotiate with the U.S. Army Corps of Engineers to avoid bringing this unique aspect of their town to an end.[12]

Decades later, a small section of Ocean Township south of Allenhurst (just 0.10 square miles) became New Jersey's last incorporated municipality, Loch Arbour. Its beachfront runs only two blocks. Loch Arbour was carved out of Ocean Township and incorporated as a village in 1957 to avoid the building of condominiums. The village has never had more than 400 residents. Deal Lake runs along the southern end of Loch Arbour and separates the village from Asbury Park except for the Ocean Avenue block, which runs along the beach. Kobbé referred to Deal Lake, at the south end of the village, as "Locharbour" in his 1889 discussion of Deal, before Allenhurst and Loch Arbour were incorporated.

Asbury Park and Ocean Grove share the beachfront south of Loch Arbour and north of Bradley Beach. Their histories are covered in chapter 5.

You can blame the officials of Bradley Beach the next time you pay to get on a beach in New Jersey. The first beach badges in the United States were sold at Bradley Beach in 1929. These tin badges were required for anyone who was not a resident or hotel guest. Bradley Beach was started, like Asbury Park, as an extension of the camp meeting grounds at Ocean Grove. In 1871, Asbury Park's James Bradley teamed up with William B. Bradner to buy fifty-four acres south of the camp meeting for development. Despite land donations to three churches—Methodist, Episcopal, and Catholic—Bradley Beach developed as a secular community with hotels and a train station for the New York and Long Branch Railroad in 1880. One of the first and grandest hotels was the LaReine Hotel with one hundred rooms, all with an ocean view, built in 1900. The hotel was lost in a fire in 1974 after it had stood empty for more than a decade. The railroad station was placed on the National Registry of Historic Places in 1984. Of course, Bradley Beach has its own Captain Kidd legend, complete with two pine trees marking the spot where he buried, and never retrieved, his treasure.

After a severe storm in 1992, the borough built substantial sand dunes to protect its beaches and its properties. The dunes were credited for the limited damage that the community suffered in Superstorm Sandy.

One of the last towns in Monmouth County to incorporate was Avon-by-the-Sea, in 1900. Prior to its incorporation, the town was known as Key East and was listed by Kobbé under that name in 1889. It may be that the town's incorporation name came from the Avon Inn, which opened in 1883.[13] Sylvan Lake on the north separates Avon-by-the-Sea from Bradley Beach (except for the ocean block) and the Shark River, which empties into the Atlantic Ocean, separates the town from Belmar to the south. Kobbé provided this lovely description of the town in 1889:

> The greater part of the area of Key East is somewhat higher than most of the Jersey coast, and clumps of oak, pine, maple and cedar still remain. Ample means are afforded for bathing, and a picturesque pavilion is near the bath-houses. Excellent boating and fishing are to be found on

Shark River which, westward of the bridges, becomes a lake of considerable size. The Seaside Assembly occupies a block near the center of Key East, and the American Institute of Christian Philosophy holds its annual summer school in the grove of the Assembly grounds from July 26th to August 12th. A summer home for crippled orphans, called the Home of the Merciful Savior, is maintained at Key East under the auspices of the Episcopal Church.[14]

As can be seen by Kobbé's description, Avon-by-the-Sea had a religious bent from the beginning although it was not established as a religious community. Residential development did not begin in earnest until 1879 when Philadelphia tobacco manufacturer Edward Batchelor purchased the land for $45,000 with the idea of moving his tobacco factory to the shore. Thankfully, Batchelor was persuaded by his engineers to develop the town as a residential resort and today it boasts beautiful homes along broad streets. The noncommercial boardwalk and the wide boulevards provide the town with a graceful and peaceful aura for the thousands who visit each year.

One of the first of the new resorts in Monmouth County (that is, without a history before 1850) is Belmar, between Avon-by-the-Sea and Spring Lake. Belmar ("beautiful sea" in French) was incorporated as Ocean Beach in 1885 but changed its name in 1889 to avoid confusion with Ocean Grove. Its development goes further back, however. In 1872 a group of Philadelphia businessmen purchased the land from Stephen Bennett, John Brown, Isaac Newman, and Peter White. A large hotel, the Ocean Beach Hotel, was built shortly thereafter. The original layout of the town included wide numbered streets that ran from the ocean to the Shark River and were crossed by lettered streets. Perhaps the best known street in Belmar is E Street which gave its name to Bruce Springsteen's E Street Band in 1972. In its early days, the band practiced there in the home of the mother of one of its members. The band was inducted into the Rock and Roll Hall of Fame in 2014.

In its early years, a gated toll bridge controlled entrance at the west end of town over the Shark River. The toll was ten cents. Several of the original hotels in the town came from the Philadelphia Centennial Exposition in 1876, dismantled, carried to the sea, and rebuilt, including the Delaware, Kansas, and Colorado halls from the exposition. By 1890 the town boasted more than seventeen hotels, including the fashionable Columbia and the block-long Atlantic, which was also a Centennial building. Both of these hotels were eventually destroyed by fire, the Columbia in 1939 and the Atlantic in 1972. One of the original attractions of Belmar was the tidal flats of the Shark River just before it empties into the Atlantic Ocean, an advantage to boaters for access close to the ocean. The Belmar Marina, just one-half mile from the ocean, operates today for casual boaters, charter boats, and party boats. Belmar continues to live up to the description given by William Nelson in 1891: "For pleasant and quiet bathing, fishing and driving, its advantages are unsurpassable."

North Spring Lake separated from Wall Township in 1884 and incorporated as a borough. Spring Lake followed its lead in 1892. The two boroughs merged in 1903 into present-day Spring Lake. The resulting borough is defined by three bodies of water, other than the Atlantic Ocean: Spring Lake, a spring-fed lake in the center of town; Lake Como to the north, separating the borough from Belmar; and Wreck Pond to the south, separating it from Sea Girt. Spring Lake was once called Fresh Creek Pond and Wreck Pond got its name from the numerous ships wrecked in the narrow inlet that once led to it from the Atlantic Ocean. Mariners often confused the inlet with the navigable Manasquan Inlet. A lifesaving station situated near Wreck Pond dated back to the 1840s (Station #4), and became the Spring Lake Station when the borough was incorporated. It was abandoned in 1947. Among the stationmasters were members of the original farm families in the area, Newman, Ludlow, and Osborn. Like Belmar, Spring Lake converted buildings from the Philadelphia Centennial Exposition: the Public Comfort Building was modified to become the ninety-two-room Lake House Hotel that operated until it was demolished in 1904; the fair's Agricultural Hall, a vast building, was taken down and its lumber used to build eight homes, a railroad station, and a bridge over Wreck Pond.

Spring Lake developed in four distinct sections, each formed from farmland purchases and defined by a large hotel. Spring Lake Beach (the Osborn farm) was the center of the community and the Monmouth House was its anchor hotel; Villa Park (the Reid farm) had the Villa Park House; Brightens (the Walling and Ludlow tracts) had the Wilburton-by-the-Sea, which became the Breakers Hotel; and to the north, the Como section (the Morton and Curtis farms) was intended to have a hotel but the building was never used as other than a private residence. The Monmouth House, built in 1876 along the ocean road at the center of the town, had frontage of 233 feet and four stories. It was lost to fire in 1900 and rebuilt and expanded as the Monmouth Hotel in 1903. The borough developed around this fabulous hotel, which was demolished in 1975. Its twentieth-century rival, the Essex and Sussex, built in 1914 and also on the ocean road, was built in the colonial revival style with more than 400 rooms. In 2002, it converted into upscale residences for people sixty-two and older.

The residential community of Spring Lake was created in large part by Philadelphia and New York businessmen and quickly became a favored resort for the high society of those cities. They built beautiful homes in the last decade of the nineteenth century and the first decade of the twentieth century, many in the Queen Anne style. In a quaint manner, all residences no matter how grand are referred to as "cottages." Two such cottages are on the National Register of Historic Places: the Audenreid

Cottage on Tuttle Avenue (now the Normandy Inn) and the Martin Maloney Cottage on Morris Avenue. The resort's churches and public buildings matched its residences. Holy Trinity (Episcopal) Church at the corner of Monmouth and Third Avenues is on the National Register as is the Frederic A. Duggan First Aid and Emergency Squad Building which was originally a firehouse. The overall effect led William Nelson to observe as early as 1902 that the "streets, cottages and churches" make Spring Lake "a resort conspicuous for the elegance of its exterior."[15] The resort is considered one of the premier spots along the Jersey Shore and its average house price confirms that assessment.

Sea Girt, which shares Wreck Pond with its northerly neighbor, Spring Lake, did not incorporate until 1917, but its history goes back well before that year. Wreck Pond served as the site of the annual Big Sea Day at the end of the 1800s. Farmers would travel with their families from all over the state to camp under tall cedar trees near the pond in a celebration that included not only sea bathing and a clambake, but also music, dancing, and lively entertainment. Sea Girt's history as a resort goes back to the 1870s when a group of Philadelphia businessmen purchased much of what now makes up the municipality from Commodore Robert F. Stockton, who had owned it from 1853 and built a mansion for a summer estate. The Stockton mansion became the Beach House, expanded by wings on either side, which later became the Stockton Hotel and operated until it was destroyed by fire in 1965. The Philadelphia connection to Sea Girt must have been strong because Gustav Kobbé, writing in 1889, stated it this way: "The great majority of [Sea Girt's] summer visitors are Philadelphians, and it is said that if you shake the genealogical tree of a Sea Girt summer visitor, a Binney or a Biddle is sure to drop off."[16] Although the area was known as Sea Girt from Commodore Stockton's time, it was not separated from Wall Township and incorporated as a borough until 1917.

Before Sea Girt existed as a municipality, the state purchased 120 acres in this area to use as a training and campground for the military. The camp remains active today and includes beachfront originally used as a seacoast battery. In the early years, the New Jersey National Guard would hold a military review at the Sea Girt Camp on Governor's Day, with a formal ball at night. Governor Leon Abbett hosted the ball in 1885 and then used a house on the grounds during the summer to conduct state business. The campgrounds accommodated successive governors each summer thereafter and became known as New Jersey's "summer capital by the sea." Notable guests included President Theodore Roosevelt in 1902, presidential candidate Al Smith in 1928, and President Franklin D. Roosevelt, making the first stop on his election campaign in 1932. New Jersey's Governor Woodrow Wilson learned of his nomination for president in 1912 while staying at the house with his wife. The original retreat house was replaced with New Jersey's Exhibit Hall at the 1904 Louisiana Purchase Exposition in St. Louis. The last governor to use the house as a summer retreat was Charles Edison in 1941. It was demolished thirty years later. The National Guard campgrounds were only annexed to the borough in 1939. Superstorm Sandy destroyed much of the base in 2012, but the National Guard announced a major rebuilding effort in 2014.

The Sea Girt lighthouse, first lit in December 1896, provided a continuous visible light in the forty-five miles between the Navesink Twin Lights to its north and the Barnegat Light to its south. Prior to its construction, mariners could lose sight of both lights, which was not a comfortable position to be in, especially during a storm. At first the light was intended for the Manasquan Inlet and so named, but the location was settled at Sea Girt so that it would also mark the inlet that used to exist to Wreck Pond. The light was attached to the lightkeeper's house and holds the distinction of being the last of its type built on the Atlantic Coast. It served until World War II. An automatic light was installed after the war so the need for a lightkeeper was lost and eventually the light was moved to a freestanding tower. That light continued to help mariners until 1977 and the original lighthouse was eventually sold to the borough to be used as a museum.

The history of Squan, now Manasquan, the most southerly resort in Monmouth County, is told in the earlier chapters of the book.

The Sandy Hook, Twin Lights, and Sea Girt lighthouse described here are just three of the many lighthouses along the Jersey Shore erected to make passage through its waters safer. The lights assisted and saved innumerable ships over the years. Nevertheless, New Jersey's shoreline has taken many others, often within the sight and hearing of those on the shore.

Further Reading

For background, see Appleton's *Illustrated Handbook of American Summer Resorts Illustrated Handbook of American Summer Resorts* (New York: D. Appleton & Co., 1893); George L. Catlin, *Homes of the Sea-Shore on the Line of the New Jersey Southern Railway for New York Business Men* (1873); Central Railroad of New Jersey, *Along the Shore and in the Foothills* (New York: Nature Press, 1910); J. Dristurell (comp.), *Summer Resorts and Watering Places* (New York: John Wiley & Sons, 1877); Franklin Ellis, *History of Monmouth County, New Jersey* (Shrewsbury Historical Society, 1885); Pennsylvania Railroad Company, *Cape May to Atlantic City, A Summer Note Book* (1883).

For the incorporation of municipalities and name changes, see John P. Snyder, *The Story of New Jersey's Civil Boundaries: 1606–1968* (Trenton, NJ: Bureau of Geology and Topography, 1969).

For the histories of individual communities, see Joseph G. Bilby, *Sea Girt, New Jersey: A Brief History* (Charleston, SC: History

Press, 2008); Centennial Journal, *Borough of Deal, 1898–1998* (Deal, NJ: 1998); James Thomas Gagen, *History of Avon-by-the-Sea* (The Avon Journal); William C. Schoettle, *Bay Head, 1879–19111966*); Andrew McCollough, *Highland Beach, New Jersey: A Jersey Shore Destination 1881–1962* (Sandy Hook Gateway National Recreation Area National Park Service, 2005), https://www.nps.gov/gate/learn /historyculture/upload/Copy%20of%20Higland%20beach%20 Research%20Paper.pdf.

CHAPTER 7

Shipwrecks, Lifesaving, and Lighthouses

The waters roared and the winds howled, and in their fury would lift the waves high in the air and then dash them across the vessel. . . . My husband was standing by me, with the child in his arms, holding on to the rigging with one hand . . . when a tremendous wave came leaping and roaring over the bows of the vessel, sweeping whatever stood before it. My husband was knocked down and the child was swept along by me . . . far beyond my reach. I could render it no assistance!—my feelings cannot be described! My husband sprang upon his feet, after the wave had passed over him . . . and the next wave swept him by me and I saw him no more. I was tempted to plunge into the water and follow him, and what prevented me I know not.
—Maria Snethen, 1853

Early in New Jersey's history it became apparent to all who were dependent on the sea that the New Jersey coast could be a frightening and deadly place. The variable tides, the strong currents, especially around the inlets, the sandbars and shoals hundreds of yards from the beaches and just a few feet below the surface, have claimed able and intrepid mariners as well as careless and inadequate captains. Storms have taken ships at sea, smashed others into the shoals near to shore, and washed others onto the beach. A tempestuous sea has no mercy. Fog, so dense that a captain can barely make out the bow of his own ship, contributes to collisions that ultimately sink the more damaged of two suddenly surprised combatants— or both. These factors, combined with the tremendous volume of shipping over the centuries to the ports in Philadelphia and New York, have earned the New Jersey coast the title "graveyard of the Atlantic." New Jersey's beaches have been littered with the remains of ships from many nations in the past 350 years. Passengers as well as crew. The loss of lives on sailing ships without modern navigational tools might be understandable, but the carnage has continued into modern times.

Crew members and passengers on sailing ships torn apart by a raging ocean who make it back to firm ground cannot forget the terror of being at the mercy of the sea in a sinking ship with the wind howling and the cold waves crashing across the decks, clinging to whatever floats and praying that another ship may be nearby to come to their rescue. In the 1800s, as more people came to live and work on the coast, the tragedy of a shipwreck just yards from the beach and within the sight and hearing of onlookers became a common occurrence. A ship caught on the sandbar might hold fast for hours and even days. In calm weather, people on shore could help those in distress, but most shipwrecks occurred in the winter months when high winds, heavy rain, and huge swales combined to make those on shore helpless onlookers. Each new tragedy became a call for the creation of a lifesaving service with men and tools to save as many lives as possible. The U.S. Lifesaving Service began in 1849 and saved thousands over the following decades. It eventually morphed into the U.S. Coast Guard.

One does not need to dive deeply to generate a list of storm-ravaged, shoal-claimed, and collision-lost ships in New Jersey's waters over the last 350 years. The stories in this chapter just skim the surface and provide examples of ships of various sizes and types that met their demise.

EARLY WRECKS

Some of the earliest recorded shipwrecks involved warships. In the Revolutionary War, a British transport ship, the *Mermaid*, was on its way to reinforce New York City in March 1779 when it foundered on the shoals off Brigantine Beach in a snowstorm. The aptly named Captain Snowball was lost along with 144 soldiers, sailors, women, and children. Forty-two others were rescued the next day by small ships launched from shore. Two years later, a heavy gale capsized the American privateer *Fame* at the Great Egg Harbor Inlet, with twenty lost and only three saved. A British warship fighting in the Napoleonic Wars, the *HMS de Braak*, was lost in May 1798 after a successful voyage against French vessels in the Caribbean. This man-o'-war was overloaded when it reached the Delaware Bay and capsized off Cape Henolopen. Thirty-nine men and all its treasure were lost. Numerous salvage attempts from the eighteenth through twentieth centuries proved unsuccessful until divers in 1984 brought up coins and doubloons taken from the French and proved the authenticity of the site by the inscription on Captain James Drew's gold ring, which was salvaged in the dive.[1]

The stormy night of February 14, 1846, offers a frightening lesson for all seamen. A nor'easter raged. Dozens of ships passing across New Jersey were caught in its clutches. Ten ships between Sandy Hook and Mantoloking were wrecked, which resulted in tremendous loss of property and life. The slow death of the *John Minturn* deserves telling. En route to New York from New Orleans, the *John Minturn* carried cargo, passengers, and twenty mariners that had been rescued off the coast of Galveston, Texas. Their ship, the *Cherokee*, had been wrecked on a sandbar several weeks earlier. The *John Minturn* picked up an experienced pilot thirty miles off of the Atlantic Highlands at about 4:00 P.M. to help guide the ship into New York Harbor, only a short distance north. But the steady rain thrashing the ship soon turned to snow and ice as the temperature dropped over the next few hours. The old sails on the three masts could not be managed in winds that reached up to sixty miles per hour. The ship lost its topsails and was being pushed south and closer to shore, which was now only four miles away.

The crew struggled all night, but with daylight and most of the sails gone with the wind, the captain and the pilot agreed to raise the mainsail, which had been reefed the night before, and sail straight into shore rather than risk being rolled sideways into the surf. The beautiful ship struck the bar thirty yards from shore, about one mile south of Mantoloking. The powerful waves and winds quickly broke its back leaving the crew and passengers at the mercy of the elements. The pilot ordered the masts cut to give the crew more time. Word of the shipwreck spread quickly inland and a crowd soon gathered on the beach. The ship could be easily seen and the cries of the passengers and crew heard despite the storm. A few of the braver men on the beach tried to launch a boat to get close enough to throw a line to the ship and bring some people in to shore. But the wind, the waves, and the wreckage prevented their efforts. The storm continued to rage, freezing those who watched helplessly from shore as well as those clinging to the remaining timbers of the *John Minturn*. Several crewmen launched a small boat from the ship and made a harrowing journey to the shore, a few others clung to debris and were plucked from the surf as they neared the beach, but everyone else perished, their frozen bodies eventually washing up onto the beach along with the cargo, timbers, and splinters of the ship. Thirty-eight of the fifty-one people on board died including the captain and his wife and children.

Some New York newspapers ran headlines accusing those on shore of not trying hard enough and looting the bodies that washed ashore. Lost in the controversy, were nine other ships taken in the storm, all but one of which had survivors: The *Mary Ellen* was beached at Sandy Hook and everyone on board was saved; the *Register* beached at Long Branch and only one passenger was lost; the *Pioneer* was broadsided in the surf off of Sandy Hook, with all saved by a line from shore tied to the mast; the *Antares* took on water and sank off of Goose Pond (near Monmouth Beach) but all were saved; the *Arkansas* was beached at Deal with one life lost; the *New Jersey*, beached eight miles north of the Manasquan Inlet, with all lives saved; the *Lotty* was also lost north of the Manasquan Inlet, and the crew was saved by a group of men who made it close enough in a small boat to run a line. In almost all these wrecks, it was the valiant efforts of a few people on shore who fought the elements for hours and saved lives. The *Alabama*, which broke up a quarter mile from the shore just south of the Manasquan Inlet, was not so lucky. All hands were lost.

A frightening ordeal began for the passengers and crew of the *Ayrshire* as the year turned from 1849 to 1850. The passengers were 166 Irish and English immigrants on their way to America. A nor'easter drove their ship onto the bar at Absecon Beach on the December 29. The crash broke the ship's rudders and brought down her masts. Only 200 yards from the beach, the ship could not help herself when released from the bar and she began an agonizing drift at the mercy of the winds and the sea. Even when the ship drifted close to shore, no one was there to see her distress. We may find this difficult to imagine today, but the *Ayrshire* drifted for two weeks past empty beaches without being seen. The passengers huddled in a room on the upper deck. We can only imagine the terror of the women and children on board, wet, freezing, and helpless, as each day passed. Finally, a second nor'easter brought the ship's journey to an end on January 15 as she crashed again on the bar, just off Manasquan. The stationmaster at the newly created lifesaving station on Chadwick beach sighted the wreck at midnight and called for his crew to come to the ship's aid. The wind, snow, and waves prevented the launching of a lifeboat so they used oxen to drag an iron life car across the beach until it was in line with the ship, which was now breaking up on the bar. They fired a rope cannon, but the rope fell short. They reloaded and fired again. This time they hit the ship and the rope was secured. Soon the life car was on its way to the terrified passengers and they climbed in, up to five at a time, for the ride to the beach. Back and forth the life car went over two days, fifteen minutes for each round trip, bouncing on or over the waves, through the night and until noon the next day. When the rescue was finished, only one passenger had been lost. The value of the life stations established just years earlier along the Jersey Shore and the effectiveness of their apparatus were proved by the valiant efforts of the lifesaving crew. The *Ayrshire* rescue is the first recorded use of the life car. This unique device saved many hundreds more in the years to come and is now on display at the National Museum of American History in Washington, DC, a reminder of the efforts from shore to avert a tragedy. The remains of what is believed to be the *Ayrshire* were just recently unearthed, in November 2014, by contractors building a seawall at Brick Township after Superstorm Sandy.[2]

Many ships traveling near the New Jersey coast in the mid-decades of the nineteenth century, like the *Ayrshire*, were packed with immigrants carrying dreams of a new life in a new land. More than two million walked ashore safely, but others landed on the beaches of New Jersey at the end of a difficult journey. Hundreds more washed ashore, ending their lives in the nightmare of a roiling sea. In January 1853, the immigrant ship *Cornelius Grinnell* crashed into the bar at the same location as the *Ayrshire*. Lifeboats and the life car saved 270 people. Just months later, in October 1853, 600 passengers were rescued from the *Western World*, which was entrapped off of Spring Lake. Unfortunately, New Jersey rescuers could not help hundreds more, like those who chose to cross the Atlantic on the *Powhatan* in April or on the *New Era* in November 1854. The *Powhatan* crashed into the bar at the south end of Long Beach Island. The local stationmaster and his small crew spotted the distressed ship from the uninhabited beach at Beach Haven. But they could do little to help. The storm that grounded the ship prevented the station crew from setting up its equipment or launching its boats. They watched helplessly as bodies drifted to the beach, more than one hundred men, women, and children had been swept overboard by the wind and sea along with all their personal belongings. Later that year, the *New Era* crashed onto the bar at Deal, due more likely to the negligence of the captain and crew as to how to manage the storm around them. Despite finally getting a line to the ship from shore and the arrival of two nearby ships, more than 200 German immigrants perished, but not the captain or most of his crew, who saved themselves. An inquiry found the captain negligent, but no charges were filed. The bodies of the victims were buried in the cemetery of the First Methodist Episcopal Church in West Long Branch.

One of the most interesting modern shipwrecks involved Cold War drama in March 1987. A Russian tanker, the *Komsomolets Kirgizii*, carrying foodstuffs from Canada to Cuba, began to list in heavy seas after an engine failure. U.S. Coast Guard helicopters rushed to the scene and airlifted all thirty-seven crew and passengers from the ship in twenty-foot seas. Shortly afterwards, the tanker rolled and sank near Atlantic City. The distress call and the American response created something of an international event at the time as the Russians and the Americans had not yet reached detente. President Ronald Reagan gave the rescued Soviet sailors a tour of the White House.[3]

A MYSTERIOUS DEATH LEADS TO AN ICONIC GROUNDING

In the first decades of the twentieth century, the broad streets, public spaces, and long boardwalk of Asbury Park attracted hundreds of thousands of visitors each summer. In the 1930s, however, its fortunes were sagging and it needed a public relations boost. Providence designed a tragic event that did just that: the grounding of the *Morro Castle* on its beach on the evening of September 8, 1934. The events leading to the wreck remain shrouded in mystery and intrigue. It may have been fate, but the event had been foreshadowed fifty years earlier by a local booster who wrote that all Asbury Park needed to accompany its fabulous summer attractions was the beaching of a ship next to its pier to create a winter attraction that could keep the party going all year round: "We want a first-class shipwreck. Why? To make Asbury Park a famous winter resort . . . She should strike head-on, so that her nose would ram the Baby Parade grandstand, and her tail might hop around even with the end of the pier. . . . We need a spectacular ship." And so it happened.[4]

The *Morro Castle* was a party ship that transported its passengers from their workaday lives to the beaches of Cuba in just fifty hours, and for as little as sixty-five dollars. The Ward Line built two ships at Newport News, Virginia, in 1930—the *Morro Castle* and the *Oriente*. The ships were built

with the latest in ocean safety, carrying sufficient lifeboats, luxury accommodations, an onboard gymnasium, a writing room, a tea room, a library,
and a ballroom. The ships could carry almost 500 passengers and half as
many crew. The restrictions of Prohibition were still in place when the
Morro Castle made her maiden voyage to Havana in August 1930. The
Ward Line offered five-day, seven-day, and longer trips to exotic Cuba and
the liquor started flowing as soon as the boat was sufficiently far from
New York's docks. Passengers ranged from the wealthy to those who had
saved for months to see the nightlife of Havana (even if for just one night)
and enjoy the beaches. But the reality of the adventure was quite different
and more dangerous than the passengers imagined.

Despite the alluring advertisements, by 1934 the *Morro Castle* Havana
cruise was a daily grind for its captain and crew. The party-going life
offered above deck masked intrigue below. The repeal of Prohibition in
1933 and the financial woes of the Great Depression cut down on the
number of passengers eager and able to afford the trip, and cabins routinely remained empty. The *Morro Castle* relied on a $750,000 annual
contract with the U.S. Government to carry the mail between Cuba and
New York and on income from carrying cargo. But the cargo was often
more than fruit. Rumors circulated that the ship carried guns and ammunition from New York to support the Cuban government's fight against
agitators, including communists dissatisfied with conditions in Cuba, and
that the weapons were replaced by cheap liquor going back. Other contraband might have been illegals hidden below or mixed with the passengers above. Cuba, in the early 1930s, was a hotbed of political strife
with union riots on the docks and criminal activity in the city and countryside. The passengers were safely (and unknowingly) escorted to appropriate locales when off the ship to avoid any disturbance of their pleasure
vacation. The ship's crew was a motley lot that turned over frequently.
They were underpaid and overworked. Some members may have supplemented their income by running drugs. Captain Robert Wilmott had no
difficulty entertaining the passengers, but he had trouble keeping order

among the crew. The result was a tragedy that ended on the beach in Asbury Park.

The *Morro Castle* left Havana on its return to New York on September 5 and the trip quickly turned deadly. Out to sea just a few hours, Captain Wilmott took ill complaining of stomach pains. On the evening of September 7 Wilmott was found dead. The ship's doctor determined the cause of death was "acute indigestion" but many people believe the 56-year-old captain was poisoned. Command of the ship went to Williams Warms, a man few thought capable of the task as the ship approached New Jersey in a severe September storm. At 2:45 A.M., a fire was discovered in the writing room, which most investigators believed was arson. Attempts to contain the fire before calling a general alarm failed and it quickly spread throughout the ship and knocked out all power. Acting Captain Warms steered the ship toward shore and into the fierce wind, which accelerated the fire. The 318 passengers had never had a lifesaving drill and neither had most of the 231 crewmen. SOS alarms were sent but investigators disagree about when and to whom. Soon the ship was disabled and the passengers were in a panic. Six lifeboats were put into the water, but most contained the crew, including the first with one passenger and thirty crew members.

The lookout from the Shark River Coast Guard Station could see the fire at 4:15 A.M., as could nearby ships, but the high seas prevented small ships from reaching the *Morro Castle*. The Coast Guard cutter *Tampa* finally got close, out two miles from Sea Girt at about 8:00 A.M., and attached a line to the ship to tow her to port. By this time, many passengers had leapt from the fiery decks and were fighting for their lives in the rough water. The luckier ones were taken aboard Coast Guard ships and other ships nearby. The fishing boat *Paramount*, captained by John Bogan, Jr., pulled sixty-seven passengers and crew from the water and took them to the Manasquan Inlet Yacht Club dock. But it was too late for many others. 138 people died. Six charred bodies were found on the ship. Some of the drowned floated to shore in the next several days and washed up on the beach, like those lost in the wrecks of the 1800s. The *Tampa's* towline line was finally secured to the *Morro Castle* by 11:00 A.M. but the small cutter had difficulties with the massive cruise ship. The line snapped at 6:00 P.M. and the *Morro Castle* was on its own. It drifted at sea until finally coming to rest on the Asbury Park beach, just across from the convention center, a smoldering giant that could be reached by onlookers at low tide. Over the next several days hundreds of thousands rushed to Asbury Park to see the attraction and the crowds kept coming for months, perhaps 10,000 each day, walking the boardwalk and extending the summer season for the resort. Despite numerous investigations, a definitive account of what happened and why has never been determined. The newspaper pictures were fabulous and the inquiries and the intrigue associated with all aspects of the tragedy kept the story alive for years.

Collisions on a Vast Sea

The Atlantic Ocean is vast, but the shipping lanes along the New Jersey coast are narrow. Sometimes too narrow for ships passing in the night.

The night was dark, but the skies clear and the water calm at about 8:30 P.M. on October 30, 1890. The *Vizcaya*, a Spanish steamer, was heading south from New York to Havana, Cuba, with seventy-seven crew and officers and sixteen passengers, including men, women and children. The much larger *Cornelius Hagreaves*, a four-masted schooner carrying coal to Massachusetts, had recently left Philadelphia. By the time the crewmen on the *Vizcaya* saw the ghostly sails of the schooner appear out of the darkness on their starboard side they had no time to react. The *Cornelius Hargeaves* smashed directly into the side of the *Vizcaya* and opened a huge hole in the engine room. Water poured in and the crew knew immediately that the ship could not be saved. The *Cornelius Hargreaves* separated from its victim but could not prevent hitting it again and the *Vizcaya* sank within five minutes. All sixteen passengers and most of its crew were lost. The *Cornelius Hargreaves* followed almost immediately into the sea, with many of her crew in the water clinging to floating debris. A few were able to climb onto the rigging, scrambling as high as possible in hope of rescue. The *Humboldt* was sailing nearby and came upon the wrecks and the desperate men fighting for life, most of whom had already succumbed to the freezing water. About twenty-five men from both boats, encrusted with ice and terrified, were taken from the rigging. A surviving crewman from the *Vizcaya* adamantly declared after reaching land that his ship's lights were shining but the *Cornelius Hargeaves* had no lights. A crewman on the *Cornelius Hargreaves* claimed that he saw the lights of the *Vizcaya* directly ahead and alerted the captain. The captain was unconcerned and, as a result, went down with his ship. Carelessness on All Souls' Eve led to the death of ninety people that night.

Collisions continue right to the present day despite modern communication technology. In January 1935, just months after the *Morro Castle* beached at Asbury Park and while its hulk was still there, its replacement, the *Mohawk*, veered across the bow of a Norwegian steamer, the *Talisman*, on a clear night several miles off of Mantoloking. It may be that freezing temperatures had fouled the steering on the passenger ship *Mohawk*. Whatever the cause, the *Mohawk* was cut in half and quickly sank to the bottom. Forty-five people drowned. Fourteen years later, fog was blamed for the December collision between the oil tanker *Gulfstream* and a Coast Guard icebreaker, the *Eastwind*. Fires flared up on both ships and killed thirteen crew members aboard the *Eastwind*. An inquiry found that the *Eastwind* failed to follow procedures for fog conditions. Allegations flew back and forth when the Israeli cruise ship *Shalom* broadsided the Norwegian tanker *Stolt Dagali* in heavy fog on Thanksgiving Day 1964. The freighter was traveling from Philadelphia to Newark and the liner had just left New York for the Caribbean. They met near the Ambrose Lightship just outside of the New York Harbor. The huge liner cut the freighter completely in half and the stern sank with the loss of nineteen crew members. The wrecks of the *Mohawk* and *Vizcaya* and the stern of the *Stolt Dagali* are all dive sites today.

The mysterious sinking of the *Lady Mary*, a small commercial trawler working off of Cape May in 2009, may have been the result of a collision as well (see a full discussion in chapter 11). Fishing boats are unstable when loaded with a catch and suffer some of the worst losses of life. Six of the seven crew were lost on the *Lady Mary* and her full story will never be known. An award-winning investigation by the *Star Ledger* suggested that the fully loaded scallop trawler was struck in the early morning hours by the much larger German container ship *Beatrice* on her way to Philadelphia. Despite better built ships, better communications, and better navigational tools, collisions still occur and not always on dark and stormy nights.

Shipwrecks as Fact and Fiction

Shipwreck stories in the 1800s enraptured the public much like horror stories do today. Passengers traveling complacently one moment face forces beyond comprehension the next moment and must summon the strength to fight for survival even while friends and family are taken away. More often than not, the protagonist is a young woman engaged in a life-and-death struggle. The treacherous New Jersey seas offered a perfect setting for these horrifying tales, whether they are true or not.

One early story combined the dangers of sea travel with the dangers of the New World. A ship carrying a bride and groom from the Netherlands in 1647 foundered as it neared shore and wrecked close to the beach at Sandy Hook. The surviving passengers and crew chose to walk to the nearest Dutch settlement, but Penelope van Pris Stout stayed on the beach to care for her injured husband. Alone, the two were attacked by hostile natives and her husband was killed. Penelope, severely injured, hid in a hollow tree for days before coming out exhausted and hungry to seek mercy. Friendly natives brought her to their camp and nursed her back to health. After some time she was found by Dutch settlers, married, raised ten children, and lived out her life in Middletown, Monmouth County.

More modern stories made it to print in the 1800s. A fictional account of terror at sea is that of Kate Aylesford, a young woman returning home from school in London. She was awakened by the howling wind and violently rocking ship to realize that she faced a life threatening struggle with the sea. The captain was unable to maintain course in the storm and the ship struck the sandbar outside of Little Egg Harbor. After the masts snapped, the cowardly crew grabbed the only usable lifeboat to save themselves and Kate watched as they were swallowed up in the enormous waves. Kate, her elderly aunt, and the captain clung to the ship through the terrifying night hoping that help would come with the dawn. Indeed, it did, in the person of brave Major Gordon who had heard the ship's distress horn during the night and coaxed a small band of men to the beach to rescue the fair damsel and her companions. Just when it seemed that all was lost for the "Heiress of Sweetwater,"[5] she found herself safely brought to shore. In Charles Peterson's 1855 novel set during the American Revolution, Major Gordon was on a mission in the Pine Barrens for the American forces under General Anthony Wayne. As the novel progresses, it tells in its own way the true story of the privateers working out of Chestnut Neck on the Mullica River and the British raid that burned the small town to the ground in an attempt to put an end to their efforts. The book captivated its readers and ends with Miss Aylesford in the arms of Major Gordon. All's well that ends well, even if most of the first nine chapters are spent at the point of death within sight of the beach and with little hope for rescue.

At about the same time, a "reality" tale came to print, but with a much sadder story. Maria Snethen wrote a true-life account of a shipwreck near "Absecum Island" in 1853. Although Maria survived the wreck, she lost her husband and her baby son, both of whom were washed away from the deck before her eyes as she clung desperately to the ship in a brutal storm. Stripped of family and belongings and shivering on the beach, Maria was taken in by the few people living near the beach and eventually made it to New York City to tell her tale.[6] This story has a chilling counterpart in the

New Era wreck off of Deal mentioned earlier. One of the women saved that night also saw her husband and son washed away but managed to float to shore on some debris. The woman, who was nine months pregnant, gave birth to a healthy baby the next day.

The destruction of ships, identified and unidentified, was such a commonplace occurrence that the littering of the beaches with the waterborne cargo was considered a natural event for locals nearby who gathered up the lost goods. Rum, fine wines, silks, and furniture might be brought in by the tides. Stories of finds date back to the 1600s and prompted the proprietors to claim ownership in 1672 to salvaged goods from all "wrecks at sea" subject to recompense for the finders "as the Governor and Council shall think fit."[7] Owners and insurers wanted to recover as much as possible, even if much of it was waterlogged. The State of New Jersey enacted a law regulating salvage in 1799 and gave county sheriffs authority over wrecks. Any person retrieving goods "cast by the sea on the land or found in any bay or creek" was required to turn over the property within four days. The sheriff was obligated to keep the goods for one year and one day to be reclaimed by the rightful owners.[8] With the passage of time, insurance salvagers would quickly arrive at the littered beaches after a wreck, empowered to take control of all that washed up that could be salvaged. The goods retrieved were often sold at auction right on the beach for the best prices possible. An anonymous vacationer on Long Beach Island in 1828 described the last rites of "a British barque bound from Liverpool to Brazil [that] had so missed its reckoning" as to go quietly ashore at the next island:

> Coming up to the hulk, a sudden notice from Col. Tucker, the wreck-master, caused a quick huddling together of the wreckers around the camboose—old sheathing copper, casks, masts, sails and chair cables, dragged ashore on the sand, and now to be knocked off to the highest bidder.... The flotsam and jetsam, it seems, all went off at fair wreck prices.... At this wreck sale at sea—seven miles from any mainland on

an island and on sand, we observed among the mainland throng no
noise or clamour other than of real business. . . . When all was over,
they separated quietly into groups, discussing their probable loss or
gain. People living near the sea coast are always excited by the stranding of a vessel, especially a large one.[9]

The amount of cargo delivered to the wreckers by the locals, of course,
varied based on its value to those recovering it, and its portability (or
potability). One New York shipowner recovered much of the cargo from
his ship *Three Friends*, mostly shingles, staves, and iron that washed up
on Manasquan beach in 1811. Cargoes of rum, coffee, lace, and edibles
were not as likely to find their rightful owners.[10] An early story tells of the
ship *Perseverance*, which hit the shoals off Peck's Beach near Beasley's
Point on its way to New York from Havre, France, in December 1815. The
ship held a cargo of fine china and glassware estimated at $400,000, which
was strewn along the beaches. But perhaps the best stories detail the fate
of the *Francis*, a merchant ship carrying fine wines and spirits that broke
up near Little Egg Harbor in May 1897. State-authorized "wreckers"
appeared and offered three dollars per barrel for the liquid gold found on
the beach and floating into the bay, and many locals earned a good day's
pay by scavenging. But much of the cargo was consumed during the work
or disappeared into homes and taverns near the shore. Locals had the
chance to enjoy what good fortune brought to their doorstep, so to speak.

Among the shipwreck stories of the 1800s were lurid tales of the Pirates
of Barnegat, supposedly a band of miscreants who would carry lanterns on
the beach during a storm hoping to confuse captains and lure boats
onto the bar to wreck, so to steal their cargoes. Since the goods were just
as often intermingled with the bodies of the poor souls lost in the tragedy, these stories described in detail how the "pirates" fleeced corpses
while waiting for the cargo to wash up. Although no hard evidence confirms this dastardly practice, the 1799 salvage act contains the following
paragraph:

And be it enacted That if a person shall put up false lights in order to bring any vessel into danger or shall prevent the escape of a person who shall endeavor to save his life from any vessel so stranded in danger of being stranded or in distress or shall wound such person with intent to kill him or shall make or assist in making a hole in any vessel in distress or steal her pumps or willfully do any act or thing tending to the immediate loss of such vessel or whereby such vessel shall be lost or destroyed then every person so offending shall be guilty of a misdemeanor and on conviction shall be punished by fine not exceeding one thousand dollars and by imprisonment at hard labor not exceeding three years.[11]

Whatever the truth, stories of such evil-doing made good copy for newspapers, so the legend of the Barnegat Pirates lingered through the decades and helped to keep each wreck's tale on the front pages. Several New York newspapers used the tragedy of the *John Minturn* in 1846 to resurrect these charges, chastising the timidity of those on shore for failing to make more of an effort to save the passengers, for looting the bodies that washed ashore, and for making off with the cargo. The furor became so great that New Jersey's governor appointed a commission to investigate. The commission not only exonerated New Jersey's residents, but also commended them for the assistance given to the survivors making it to the beach in such terrible circumstances.[12] Nevertheless, a ghastly story often overshadows reality and the legend of the Barnegat Pirates lived on for decades thereafter in New York stage shows, dime novels, and short stories, even as the number of wretched wrecks waned over the years.

U.S. LIFESAVING SERVICE

One of the obvious reasons for the long list of wrecks along the Jersey Shore is the great volume of shipping that makes its way to and from the ports of New York and Philadelphia, laden with passengers and cargoes of every variety. After the tragedy of the *John Minturn* in 1846 many people living near the Jersey Shore called for a constant presence to save survivors within sight and those fortunate enough to make it to the beach alive. The turning point came in 1848 when New Jersey Congressman William A. Newell from Manahawkin sponsored legislation to create life-saving stations along the Jersey Shore. Newell witnessed the tragedy of the Austrian ship *Terasto* in 1840 from Long Beach Island. All thirteen crewmen drowned when their ship broke up upon the bar. The legislation, the Newell Act, provided $10,000 for the purchase of lifesaving equipment along the New Jersey coast from Sandy Hook to Little Egg Harbor.[13]

The first eight stations in New Jersey started as volunteer operations in 1849 with no full-time staff and no supervision. If a wreck was sighted an alarm would be sounded for volunteers to rush to the beach to see if they could be of any assistance. More often than not the wreck was occasioned by a violent storm and little could be done. With each passing year, the ability of these life savers increased, their tools improved, and money was allocated to build a reliable force of men who could respond quickly. In 1854, Congress appropriated sufficient funds to provide for a full time "keeper" in each station during the winter months when wrecks were more prevalent. The keeper would patrol the beach, watching for wrecks, and sound the alarm. Even within this haphazard system, New Jersey's "surfmen" performed admirably, as evidenced by the stories of the *Ayrshire* in 1850 and the *Cornelius Grinnell* and the *Western World* in 1853. After the Civil War, Congress answered the call of New Jersey and its neighboring coastal states for more effective support. In 1871, Summer Increase Kimball was appointed the chief of the Treasury Department's Revenue Marine Division and his energy and efforts transformed the lifesaving service into a dynamic force along the coast. By 1872 New Jersey had forty permanent lifesaving stations at intervals of about three miles along its beaches from Sandy Hook (Station #1) to Cape May (Station #40).

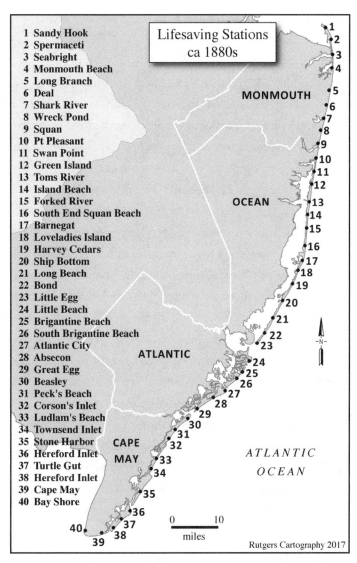

Lifesaving Stations ca 1880s

1 Sandy Hook
2 Spermaceti
3 Seabright
4 Monmouth Beach
5 Long Branch
6 Deal
7 Shark River
8 Wreck Pond
9 Squan
10 Pt Pleasant
11 Swan Point
12 Green Island
13 Toms River
14 Island Beach
15 Forked River
16 South End Squan Beach
17 Barnegat
18 Loveladies Island
19 Harvey Cedars
20 Ship Bottom
21 Long Beach
22 Bond
23 Little Egg
24 Little Beach
25 Brigantine Beach
26 South Brigantine Beach
27 Atlantic City
28 Absecon
29 Great Egg
30 Beasley
31 Peck's Beach
32 Corson's Inlet
33 Ludlam's Beach
34 Townsend Inlet
35 Stone Harbor
36 Hereford Inlet
37 Turtle Gut
38 Hereford Inlet
39 Cape May
40 Bay Shore

MONMOUTH

OCEAN

ATLANTIC

CAPE MAY

ATLANTIC OCEAN

0   10
miles

Rutgers Cartography 2017

Map 4. U.S. Lifesaving Stations in New Jersey. Map designed by Michael Siegel, Rutgers University.

If rescue was possible, the life savers were ready. Their presence on the shore saved thousands of lives.

In 1878 Congress designated the "Life-Saving Service" as a separate agency within the U.S. Treasury Department.[14] With Kimball's leadership and more funding, the stations were manned with crews of six and equipment necessary for quick action, including standardized lifeboats, flags, rockets, and Lyle guns. The men alternated patrols along the beach from station to station to watch for wrecks. If a wreck was spotted, the crew could row out or run a line to the ship, depending on wind and wave conditions. The Lyle gun, essentially a mortar, could shoot a line to the ship up to 600 yards from the beach. The service would then use a breeches buoy, to pull passengers and crew to shore one by one. A life car was invented in the late 1830s by Toms River boat builder Joseph Francis and could be pulled to a ship from the shore along a line and then pulled back with four or five passengers inside. Most of the station buildings have disappeared, but some remain and the U.S. Lifesaving Service Heritage website recently listed the station on Maryland Avenue in Beach Haven for sale to interested buyers and preservers of New Jersey's heritage.[15]

The Lifesaving Service's glory years were the 1870s and 1880s, when its crews came to the aid of hundreds of ships in distress and thousands of seaborne travelers along the east coast. Gas engines, better navigational tools, and the need to help smaller boats further out at sea led to the merger of the Lifesaving Service and the Revenue Cutter Service into the U.S. Coast Guard in 1915.[16]

LIGHTHOUSES

The lifesaving service was created to assist those ships already imperiled by the waves and to rescue passengers and crew from the sea. Lighthouses and lightships represent attempts to prevent shipwrecks by providing guidance to those still afloat and struggling to find their way in the darkness of night or the terrors of a storm. During its history, New Jersey has had forty-nine lights along its coastal waters and boasts the oldest light-house still in operation in the United States, the Sandy Hook lighthouse that guards New York Harbor. Built in 1764, the Sandy Hook light-house remains a beautiful structure with a definitive purpose. Visitors to Fort Hancock in Gateway National Park can get up close to the lighthouse and climb to its tower on guided tours. The light still guides sailors located up to nineteen miles out from shore.

Lights have aided mariners for hundreds of years. They can be strong beacons that range up to twenty-five miles to warn of the approaching coastline or shorter and dimmer lights at inlets to guide sailors into safe harbors. They can be built on terra firma or fastened to a ship anchored at a key location (lightships or light vessels). Lights can be towers, houses, or standalone beams affixed atop a steel structure. New Jersey has employed all types in its efforts to limit the loss of property and life. Modern naviga-tion equipment has made most of these lights obsolete, but their beauty as landmarks has saved many from destruction. Several serve today as muse-ums to educate visitors about the early efforts to accommodate, if not tame, the sea. Others were built close to the coastline for effectiveness and were taken by the sea before the end of their useful lives.

Just before the Revolutionary War, merchants in New York underwrote two lotteries to build a lighthouse at Sandy Hook in 1764. Its continued usefulness to the British occupying New York City during the American Revolution irked some ardent American patriots. Early in the war a unit was sent to darken the light and came away with its lens. The British quickly repaired the light, forcing Lieutenant Colonel Benjamin Tupper and some local militiamen to maneuver several six-pound cannons close enough to the tower to put out the light permanently. Their cannonballs hit but could not topple the well-built structure. A nearby British warship hastened the retreat of the American patriots.[17] Thankfully, the lighthouse survived the war to help the growth of the United States. Eventually, how-ever, the light began to lose some of its effectiveness as the land in front of it expanded with the littoral action of the waves coming from south of

Sandy Hook and the lighthouse moved away from the dangerous shoals it was built to expose. As a result, two additional lights were built in 1817, one close to the ocean to the east and one close to the bay to the west, the East Beacon and the West Beacon. The East Beacon was replaced in 1867 by a wooden structure that quickly burned down, was rebuilt further south, and then rebuilt further inland (and renamed the North Beacon). Eventually, the building was moved to a site on the Hudson River (Jeffrey's Hook) and replaced by a tower. The West Beacon was undermined by erosion almost immediately after its construction and was moved south (and renamed the South Beacon) until it was dismantled in the 1920s. The original lighthouse was refitted with a more powerful light in 1856. It remains in operation today, not just as a guiding light for mariners but as a beautiful landmark as well.

The first oceanic lightship in the United States was established in 1823 several miles east of the Sandy Hook lighthouse. It was known as the *Sandy Hook Lightship* and served until 1908. A new lightship was then established several miles to the north near the Ambrose Channel and named the *Ambrose Lightship*. The first vessel at this location was built in Camden, New Jersey, and carried a radio beacon as well. Over the next fifty-nine years, three different ships were moored in the spot with tremendous anchors for stability. The only mishap was the ramming of the lighthouse in June 1960 by a cargo ship in dense fog. The lightship (which happened to be a relief vessel in place while the regular ship was in dock for repairs) sunk. Lightships were manned stations and the nine crewmen at Ambrose were fortunately plucked from the sea by the errant cargo ship. In 1967 the last vessel was replaced by a tower, the Ambrose Tower. This structure has legs sunk 170 feet into the ocean floor and sits 90 feet above the water. The last lightship remains in the water nearby.

Perhaps the best-known lighthouse in New Jersey is Old Barney, located at the northern tip of Long Beach Island. Thousands visit it each year and climb its tower while on vacation on the island. Its location was perfect for a light: it marked the 40 degree parallel, an important navigational feature, and was equidistant (60 miles) from New York Harbor and the entrance to the Delaware Bay. In addition, it identified the entrance to the dangerous Barnegat Inlet. The original light at this location was built in 1835 but could not do the job. The tower was short and the light too dim. Some mariners complained that the light was dangerous because they often misidentified it as another ship. A stronger light installed in 1854 helped but did not fulfill the purpose of the lighthouse. The federal government commissioned a new lighthouse to be built slightly inland and the job for its design and construction went to Army Lieutenant George Meade, later to serve in the Civil War as commander of the Union forces at Gettysburg in 1863. Completed in 1859, Old Barney served for eighty-five years until it was decommissioned in 1944. The original lighthouse was taken by the sea shortly after it ceased operation and Old Barney was saved from the same fate when the government shored up the land underneath it with jetties and a bulkhead in the 1930s.

Meade's tower stands 171 feet high and utilized a "first order" Fresnel lens, the most powerful available at the time. The Fresnel technology was developed by Augustin-Jean Fresnel and was first used in a lighthouse in France in 1823. These powerful lights were constructed of hundreds of small lenses mounted on a frame and eventually replaced conventional lenses. The Barnegat light was visible thirty miles out to sea. When the lighthouse was decommissioned, the Fresnel light was removed to the Barnegat Lighthouse Historical Society Museum just a short walk from the lighthouse. The Friends of Barnegat Lighthouse State Park arranged for a new lens to mark the 150th anniversary of the beacon's first light, and it was lit on January 1, 2009. The light continues to mark the tip of Long Beach Island today, and is visible up to twenty-two nautical miles.

Cousins to the Barnegat lighthouse are the Absecon lighthouse and the Cape May lighthouse, both also designed and built by Lieutenant George Meade and fitted with first order Fresnel lenses. The Absecon lighthouse reaches to 165 feet and the Cape May lighthouse to 159 feet. The three lighthouses were built within three years of each other. Absecon lighthouse identified the dangerous waters near Atlantic City; the Cape May lighthouse marks the entrance to the Delaware Bay. The Absecon lighthouse was the only lighthouse built at its location and was decommissioned in 1933. The Cape May lighthouse was the third built at its location; the first two (1823 and 1847) were considerably shorter (68 feet and 88 feet) and had inferior lights. Meade's Cape May lighthouse remains in operation; the original Fresnel lens in the Cape May lighthouse has been replaced and can be found in the nearby Cape May Historical Society Museum. The Absecon lighthouse is now part of a park and open to visitors.

Three good examples of low lights marking nearby inlets are the Hereford Inlet lighthouse in North Wildwood (built in 1874), the Ludlam lighthouse (built in 1885) and the Sea Girt lighthouse (built in 1897). They resemble small houses with a tower attached, about 40 feet high. The Sea Girt lighthouse is made of red brick and was restored by the Borough of Sea Girt after it ceased operating in 1945. The Hereford Inlet Light was also restored after it ceased operation in 1964. The Ludlam lighthouse, which once stood between the Hereford lighthouse (11 miles south) and the Absecon beacon (17 miles north), marked the Townsend Inlet. The building was moved to Sea Isle City after it was decommissioned in 1924 and is used now as a private home.

A lighthouse twice marked the southern end of Long Beach Island on Tucker's Island. The first in 1849 had a dim light and was discontinued in 1859 after the completion of the Absecon lighthouse. The second lighthouse was built nearby in 1867 with a better light. Despite improvements and additions over the years, this lighthouse was lost in 1927 as was the ground under it, Tucker's Island, which eventually disappeared in its entirety.

Although technically not on the Jersey Shore, the Twin Lights at Navesink, first built in 1828 and rebuilt (as we now see them) in 1862, bear mentioning because they served as an ocean beacon and utilized the first

Fresnel lens in America in 1841. The double design distinguished the light from the nearby Sandy Hook lighthouse, but the towers are not perfect twins: the south tower is square and the north tower is octagonal; the south tower's light rotated while the north tower's remained fixed. The Twin Lights were decommissioned in 1949 and the building now serves as a museum. Today we admire these buildings for their beauty, but they all served an important lifesaving purpose for mariners at sea.

Further Reading

For a comprehensive list of shipwrecks, visit the Shipwreck Database, New Jersey Maritime Museum, http://newjerseyshipwrecks.com /shipwreckdatabase.html. For background on shipwrecks, see Margaret Thomas Buchholz, *New Jersey Shipwrecks, 350 Years in the Graveyard of the Atlantic* (Harvey Cedars, NJ: Down the Shore Publishing, 2004); Walter Krotee, *Shipwrecks off the New Jersey Coast* (Published by Author, 1966); David J. Siebold and Charles J. Adams III, *Shipwrecks Near Barnegat Inlet* (Reading, PA: Exeter Books, 1995); and, Alan A. Siegel, *Disaster! Stories of Death and Destruction in Nineteenth Century New Jersey* (New Brunswick, NJ: Rutgers University Press, 2014).

On the *Morro Castle*, see Gretchen F. Coyle and Deborah C. Whit-craft, *Inferno at Sea, Stories of Death and Survival Aboard the Morro Castle* (West Creek, NJ: Down the Shore Publishing, 2012); Rod Redman, "Holocaust at Sea: The Fiery Death of the Morro Castle," *Sea Classics* (Chatsworth, CA, September 2004, 28 and October 2004, 58); and Gordon Thomas and Max Morgan Witts, *Shipwreck, The Strange Fate of the Morro Castle* (New York: Stein and Day, 1972).

On the U.S. Lifesaving Service, see Dennis R. Means, "A Heavy Sea Running: The Formation of the U.S. Life-Saving Service, 1846–1878,"

Prologue 19, no. 4 (1987); Dennis L. Noble, *A Legacy: The United States Life-Saving Service* (U.S. Coast Guard, 1976); and, Robert F. Bennett, *Surfboats, Rockets, and Carronades* (U.S. Coast Guard, 1976).

On lighthouses and light vessels, see Bill Gately, *Sentinels of the Shore, A Guide to Lighthouses and Lightships of New Jersey* (Harvey Cedars: Down the Shore Publishing, 1998); David Veasey, *Guarding New Jersey's Shore, Lighthouses and Life-Saving Stations* (Charleston, SC: Arcadia, 2000); and, the New Jersey Lighthouse Society website at http://www.njlhs.org/njlight/sandy.html.

CHAPTER 8

The Rise of Resorts, Ocean County

Brant Beach is the resort immediately south of Ship Bottom, and today is a tidy, dainty cottaged little resort set out upon the clean white sands beside the boundless sea, and within a gunshot of both the Atlantic Ocean and Manahawkin Bay. . . . Remarkable development has been made at Brant Beach within the last few years, and it possesses all the attributes of a real seashore resort. Next below Brant Beach is Beach Haven Crest, a summer resort partaking of the good things in store for all Long Beach towns. Peahala, the site of the famous clubhouse, is the next station down the beach. The Peahala Club of Long Beach was organized on April 10, 1882. . . . Beach Haven Terrace is an energetic, hustling young municipality on old Long Beach, and boasts of a permanent winter population, two cottage hotels—the "Clearview" and the "Chalfonte"—a bakery, stores, waterworks and post office.

—George B. Somerville, *The Lure of Long Beach*, 1914

Monmouth County ends and Ocean County begins at the boundary line of Manasquan and Point Pleasant Beach. Point Pleasant Beach faces the Atlantic Ocean to the east and the Manasquan River to the west. A barrier peninsula separating the Atlantic Ocean from Barnegat Bay begins at the southern end of Bay Head and stretches twenty-four miles to the Barnegat Inlet. Ocean County's beaches continue an additional eighteen miles along the barrier island of Long Beach Island. The Ocean County beaches attract hundreds of thousands of visitors each summer looking for vastly different experiences. The boardwalks at Point Pleasant, Seaside Heights, and Seaside Park bring thrills, fun, and entertainment; the

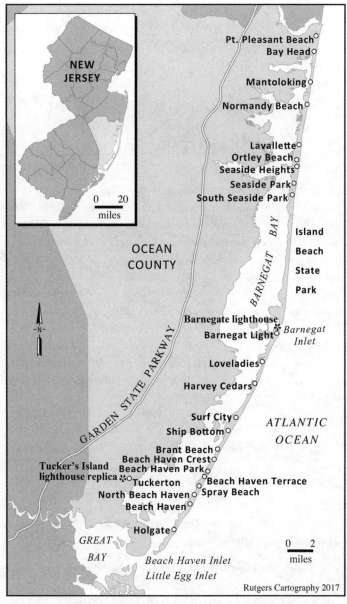

Map 5. Ocean County Shore Communities and Lighthouses. Map designed by Michael Siegel, Rutgers University.

bungalow communities at the beaches in Brick and Toms River townships provide an affordable beach lifestyle for many second-home owners;
the residential communities of Lavallette, Bay Head, and Mantoloking
offer an exclusive, high-end alternative for many more; tens of thousands
of day-trippers enjoy the pristine beaches and environment at Island
Beach State Park; and, thousands more travel to Long Beach Island for
tranquil beach settings.

Point Pleasant to Island Beach State Park

The early history of Point Pleasant Beach at the northern end of Ocean
County intersects with that of Manasquan at the southern end of Mon-
mouth County. This area was purchased from Native Americans in the
late 1660s. The location and territory of the Manasquan Lifesaving Station
overlaps with Point Pleasant Beach, and the salt works destroyed by the
British and Loyalists who sailed through the Manasquan Inlet during the
Revolutionary War were located in what is now Point Pleasant Beach.
Both areas maintained shipbuilding and fishing operations of long standing in addition to attracting summer vacationers, Tourism began in
Point Pleasant Beach in the 1870s when Captain John Arnold purchased
land and built a road to the beach and a bridge over the Manasquan River
connecting the beach resort to Brielle. The northern section of the borough, which Arnold developed, was called Arnold City and was laid out
into 300 50-by-100-feet lots. Another group of developers, the Point Pleasant Land Company, bought 250 acres in 1877 and created lots that stretched
from the ocean almost to the bay. Point Pleasant Beach separated from
Brick Township and became Point Pleasant City in 1886, four years after
the New York and Long Branch Railroad built a station into the town. Several large hotels were built at the turn of the twentieth century, including
the Resort House, the Beacon Hotel, the Leighton, and Zimmerman's.

Today, Point Pleasant Beach is known for its colorful and enjoyable boardwalk with rides and amusements for families throughout the summer.

But the original amusement area was along the Manasquan River amid cedar groves. Clark's Landing, as it was known, featured a merry-go-round, a steam organ, ice cream and other snacks during the 1890s. As the focus of tourists shifted from the river to the ocean, so did the amenities, and by 1915 a permanent boardwalk was built along the entire length of the beach. The southern end of the boardwalk was lost in a 1938 storm and never replaced. Nevertheless, Point Pleasant Beach today boasts one of the liveliest boardwalk attractions in the state. Much of the credit goes to the Jenkinson family that began creating amusement rides and a food pavilion in the 1920s. Starting from a small section of the boardwalk, the Jenkinson Pavilion expanded over the decades, despite storms and fires, providing fun events and rides that changed with the public demand. The early years featured a candy shop and refreshment stand, a swimming pool, a dance hall, and miniature golf. Later on, the boardwalk featured a miniature train, then a games arcade and water slide, and eventually a dinner theater. Ownership changed hands from the Jenkinson's, but the enterprise continued to expand. Today, Jenkinson's Boardwalk includes a 1,200 seat pavilion, an aquarium, and a fun house.

Interestingly, two early writers described Point Pleasant Beach as "wild," though not in regard to the rides on the boardwalk. According to historian Gustav Kobbé in 1889: "The coast at this point possesses remarkable wildness, reminding one of the eastern side of Cape Cod. The sand is heaped up in high, snow-like dunes, overgrown here and there with tufts of salt grass. In stormy weather the drifting sand fills the air like the spray of the surf."[1] Twelve years later, William Nelson suggested the same: "There is an attractiveness about the place that brings thousands to its doors each summer, among them those in search of wild shore and ocean scenery. Marine painters have reproduced it on canvas, and yet come in the hope that the coast storms of the previous winter have produced something new. The scenery at the point is wild and picturesque. On all sides are great piles of sand washed up from the sea and drifted into fantastic shapes by the winds that sweep in mad fury across the peninsula during the heavy storms."[2] Nelson also describes it as one of the "coolest resorts on the coast," not because it keeps with the times, but because of the breezes from the Manasquan River and Barnegat Bay. Nelson goes on to say that the inland area west and south of Point Pleasant Beach is a "sportmen's paradise," plentiful with wild fowl, ducks, and geese that inhabit the bay, and a great place for cycling on well-maintained roads.

Point Pleasant Beach should not be confused with the inland town of Point Pleasant, which lies to the west. Point Pleasant was separated from Brick Township in 1920 and has no ocean frontage. The Point Pleasant Canal is located in this town.

The town of Bay Head was founded by a group of Princeton bankers and remains one of the most exclusive spots along the Jersey Shore. Victorian homes line the oceanfront. The Bay Head Land Company—organized by David H. Mount of Rocky Hill, brothers Edward Howe and Leavitt Howe of Princeton, and William Harris of Princeton—began operations in 1879 with an initial investment of $12,000. In 1890 the town had only seventy-five residents, but new houses were going up quickly. Soon hotels were also built and the town became a desired destination, in part due to its location at the head of Barnegat Bay where summer sojourners could enjoy sailing, fishing, and gunning as well as the sandy beaches. The borough also boasted a shipbuilding industry that specialized in Barnegat skiffs.

Today, Bay Head remains a quiet upper-income community for homeowners and renters. The tree-lined streets are quiet; food and beverages are not allowed on the beach; and there are few hotels and restaurants and little or no night life. A large portion of the borough is included in a historic district designated a National Historic Place in 2006 to preserve the beauty and construction of its homes and its transportation significance. The beaches of Bay Head experienced numerous shipwrecks in the nineteenth century. Kobbé wondered why in 1889 and believed it might be that the Sandy Hook light and the Barnegat light were too far apart to aid mariners (this was before the Sea Girt light was lit in 1896). Kobbé also tells the curious tale that Bay Head has a population of Manx cats "(without tails)" descended from a pair that came ashore after a wreck in 1869.[3]

A protective rock seawall built in the 1880s at the expense of Bay Head homeowners served them well more than 125 years later by limiting the damage from Superstorm Sandy in 2012. However, the seawall has become the center of a controversy with the State of New Jersey over the best way to protect the borough's beaches. (See more on this in chapter 14.)

The beaches along the Barnegat Bay peninsula south of Bay Head are scarcely mentioned in the early histories of the Jersey Shore. They developed in the 1880s, somewhat later than their northern counterparts, and were more difficult to reach until railroad bridges could cross Barnegat Bay. Writing in 1889, Kobbé ran them all together in a single sentence: "Between Bay Head and the point where the Philadelphia and Long Branch Railroad extension of the New York and Long Branch Railroad leaves the beach and crosses the bay to Tom's River are Mantoloking, Chadwicks (a famous old-fashioned gunning resort), Lavallette, Ortley, Berkeley Arms and Seaside Park." Kobbé suggests that they were not developed further because of swarming mosquitoes brought by westerly winds.[4] The southern end of the peninsula to the Barnegat Inlet was referred to generically as Island Beach, and sometimes as Nine-Mile Island in reference to its separation from the peninsula when the Cranberry Inlet existed between the 1740s and 1812.

The beaches of Mantoloking provided excellent winter grazing for cattle for years before the community developed as a beach resort. Mainland farmers could ferry the cattle to the peninsula and let them stay on their own until spring, feeding on the salt hay that grew there. Mantoloking had only two buildings in 1872, a lifesaving station (#12, Swan Point) and a boarding house, yet it soon developed as an exclusive community. Captain John Arnold, who played an important role in the development of Point Pleasant, was also active in Mantoloking and was responsible for securing the construction of the Mantoloking Bridge in 1884. A railroad came into Mantoloking the same year from the west. The north end of town bordering on Bay Head developed last, after World War II.

A centerpiece of the community is the Mantoloking Yacht Club, founded in 1890. The club offers tennis and sailing and has produced ten Olympic sailors, including the 1952 gold medal winners in the 5.5-meter class, skippered by Dr. Britton Chance. The club hosts the annual World Duckboat Regatta, an event for junior sailors that has run for almost fifty years, celebrating not only the wonderful sailing in Barnegat Bay but also the exquisite craftsmanship of Barnegat Bay boat builders.

Mantoloking residents boasted the highest incomes in the state in the 2000 census, confirming its status as one of the most exclusive communities along the shore. According to one real estate website, the median price of a home in Mantoloking in 2013 was more than $3 million. Nonetheless, the wealth of the town could not save the homes from the devastation wrought by Superstorm Sandy in 2012. Every house in Mantoloking (521) was either damaged or destroyed when the ocean breached the bay in three places, including at the base of the Mantoloking Bridge. More than a hundred homes were completely destroyed, as was the Borough Hall. The road at the eastern end of the bridge was washed away and a single home remained, on its own newly formed island, as the waters of the Atlantic Ocean washed around it into Barnegat Bay. The location of this new inlet may have been just south of the Herring Inlet that opened and closed after several storms in the 1700s. The State Department of Transportation moved in immediately to confirm the structural integrity of the bridge, closing the breach and rebuilding Route 35. Crews worked twenty-four hours a day for three days bringing in stone, fill, and sand to reestablish the barrier peninsula. In addition, a 500-foot-long ridge of steel sheeting was driven forty-two feet into the ground. It was eventually extended four more miles to Brick Township. The road—which needed to be cleared of sand hills, cars, boats, and debris—was rebuilt and connected to the bridge within six weeks. At this writing, four years have passed since the storm, but much of the beachfront remains barren and many of the homes spared total destruction remain damaged. The borough had 121 empty lots in late 2014.

The next stretch of the Barnegat peninsula contains beachfront located in two large mainland townships—Brick and Toms River. The three ocean beaches in Brick Township lie just to the south of Mantoloking. The Toms River beaches encompass Dover North (Ocean Beaches 1, 2 and 3, Chadwick Beach, Chadwick Island, Seacrest Beach, Monterey Beach, Silver Beach, Normandy Shores, and half of Normandy Beach) and Dover South, which is known as Ortley Beach. The northern Toms River beaches and Ortley Beach straddle the borough of Lavallette. All of these beaches developed during the seashore building boom in the 1950s. Developers built bungalows at modest prices that middle-income families looking to own a piece of the Jersey Shore could afford. The median home in Ortley Beach, for example, sold for $254,200 in 2010, well below the $3 million price tag for homes in Mantoloking just a few miles north along the same beachfront and less than those in adjacent Lavallette at $482,200.

Even though many units were remodeled and updated over the years, most retained the bungalow facade. At least until Superstorm Sandy. Entire blocks of these tightly packed bungalows were damaged or destroyed, including almost the entirety of the Camp Osborn section of Brick Township in a gas fire that started at the beachfront and raged inland. Firetrucks could not reach the fire because of washed-out roads. Many homeowners repaired or demolished and rebuilt, but the dollar outlays relative to the original cost of the units, and bureaucratic red tape, have slowed their progress. Some of the houses have been elevated to avoid future damage and high flood insurance premiums, changing the look and feel of the communities. The future of these beach communities, unincorporated sections of much larger year-round townships, remains unclear.

Lavallette developed in the 1870s with broad streets, uniform lots, and eight ocean beaches, including a surfing beach and a fishing beach. Commercial activities are confined to the center of the borough and are kept off the boardwalk and away from the bay area. The developer of the town named it "Lavallette-by-the-Sea" in honor of his father, Elie A. F. La Vallette, a real admiral in the U.S. Navy who served aboard the warship *USS Constitution* in 1825. The borough incorporated in 1887, separating from Dover Township, about ten years after the Barnegat Land Improvement Company began its activities. The Lavallette Yacht Club formed in 1904 and became the center of the borough's social life with a clubhouse built on the oceanfront used for dances and other community events.

Seaside Heights and Seaside Park, despite their similar names, developed separately. As discussed in chapter 5, Seaside Park began in 1874 in an effort to build a Baptist retreat on the beach similar to Ocean Grove. When that effort failed, developers purchased the land, divided it into lots, and named it Sea Side Park (a municipal typing error led to the current spelling of Seaside Park). Seaside Park featured grand hotels in its early years. A railroad bridge over the bay brought the Pennsylvania Railroad from Philadelphia right into the Hiawatha Hotel on July 4, 1881. A dedicated station was built several years later and the tracks then turned north (along what is now Central Avenue) to Seaside Heights, Ortley Beach, Bay Head, and Point Pleasant. The track was abandoned after World War II, however, and replaced by roadways for the increasing automobile traffic. A bridge for automobiles had already been built in 1914. An 1880 tourism brochure offers an idealized vision of Seaside Park: "This place is about one mile below Lavallette. It was the pioneer of sea side resorts, on this beach. Two large hotels, Sea Side Park and Franklin, have been erected; which, ever since they have been finished, have been well filled with summer visitors."[5]

Despite the railroad connection to the Barnegat peninsula, Seaside Heights did not develop extensively until after the automobile bridge crossed the bay. This wooden drawbridge, rebuilt in 1927, led to construction of the Freeman Building at Dupont Avenue in Seaside Heights that housed a carousel. Construction of a boardwalk began in 1916 and was completed in 1921.The fortunes of Seaside Heights rose with improved accessibility when the wooden bridge was replaced by the Thomas A. Mathis Bridge in 1950. An additional bridge, the Stanley Tunney Bridge, added three more lanes of traffic in 1972.

Seaside Heights is renowned for its carousels and boardwalk, as well as the disasters that befell them. The boardwalk was wiped away in the 1944 hurricane; the hand-carved Dupont Avenue carousel was destroyed in a spectacular 1955 fire that also took eighty-five buildings along the boardwalk (known as the Freeman's Fire because it destroyed the Freeman Amusement Pier). A new hand-carved carousel replaced the first, only to be sold in the 1980s for the value of its horses and replaced by a much less ornate alternative. Seaside Heights still has a hand-carved carousel the Dentzel Looft Carousel at the Casino Pavilion, which was moved from Burlington, New Jersey, in 1932 after it had been damaged in a fire and repaired. This carousel, with fifty-eight figures including chariots, camels, a lion, and a tiger, was saved from sale in the 1980s by the efforts of a local man, Dr. Floyd Moreland, who remembered it from his childhood. After new owners threatened to dismantle it to make way for newer attractions, the borough purchased it in a land swap in 2017.[6] In 2012, Superstorm Sandy destroyed the boardwalk and the Jetstar roller-coaster at the Casino Pier, creating the iconic image of the coaster under the waters after the storm. In 2013, the newly rebuilt boardwalk caught fire and was destroyed, only to be rebuilt again.

In recent years, the sights and sounds of the boardwalk and the nightlife of Seaside Heights have been made famous by three MTV reality shows based in the beach resort. The last of these, *Jersey Shore*, became a hit in 2009. The show followed eight young adults, including Snooki, Mike Sorrentino (aka the Situation), and JWoww, who shared a beach house in town for the summer. Although some New Jerseyans did not appreciate the representation of the Jersey Shore as a bastion for "guidos" and "guidettes," the show memorialized the term "Jersey Shore."

The ten miles of pristine beach at the southern end of the Barnegat peninsula, now Island Beach State Park, were saved from development by the failure of the railroads to turn south once they reached Seaside Park. The fauna and flora of this undeveloped 3,000 acres appears as the entire Jersey Shore might have looked 200 years ago, with forests of holly, goldenrod, and black cherry and nests of ospreys and falcons. Island Beach State Park is located within Berkeley Township, a large municipality mostly on the mainland that also incorporates South Seaside Park, the few blocks between Seaside Park and the state park. Title to this land was originally granted to the Earl of Stirling in the 1600s. When the earl died without a legitimate heir, William Alexander, a distant New Jersey relative, claimed the title. The island became known as Lord Stirling's Isle even though William Alexander's claim was denied by the House of Lords. Alexander, aka Major General Lord Stirling, served George Washington and the American Cause well during the Revolutionary War. Still, little activity took place at the end of the Barnegat peninsula and it remained uninhabited and undeveloped until the 1850s, when three lifesaving stations (#14, Island Beach, #15, Forked River, and #16, Cedar Creek) were built there. The fishing and gunning attractions of the bay led to the construction of two hunting lodges, the Reed Hotel and the Harding Hotel. Visitors took muskrats, turtles, eels, blue claw crabs, lobsters, striped bass, bluefish, oysters, and clams.

The possibility of developing this area into a glamorous resort led Henry Phipps, a partner of Andrew Carnegie's in the steel business, to buy the land in 1926 and build three homes. But the Great Crash of 1929 forestalled further building. Phipps turned the land over to a caretaker, Francis Parkman Freeman, who arranged for a limited numbers of visitors to lease portions of the land on the promise that they would leave it undisturbed. In 1953, the state purchased the land for $2.7 million (after the federal government tried but could not come up with the funds). The park opened in 1959 and is now managed by the Division of Parks and Forestry within the New Jersey Department of Environmental Protection. This spectacular beach welcomes more than one million visitors every year to bathe in the ocean's waters, to fish from the surf and in the bay, and to enjoy bird-watching in a preserved environment.

Long Beach Island

Long Beach Island (LBI) runs eighteen miles southwest from the Barnegat Inlet to Little Egg Harbor. This barrier island is no wider than one-half mile at best and had been breached by the Atlantic Ocean on many occasions over the centuries before the most recent breach during Superstorm Sandy. The delicate string of sandy ocean beaches and boat-laden bay lagoons provides a variety of summer enclaves "Six Miles Out to Sea," as the island has sometimes been described. Four miles would be more accurate, but early developers also claimed that the island was perfect for hay-fever sufferers because of a decided lack of pollen. Whatever the case, thousands of summer vacationers make the trip to LBI each summer over a single automobile bridge connection from Manahawkin to Ship Bottom. A railroad trestle that linked the mainland to the island was destroyed in a November 1935 nor'easter. The resort towns along the beachfront developed independently. Harvey Cedars attracted whalers as early as the 1600s; the history of Beach Haven is inextricably tied to the history of Tucker's Island; and one of the island's first hotels was the Mansion House in Surf City. Nevertheless, the remoteness of LBI and the difficulty in reaching its beaches from the mainland slowed the development of resorts until train travel made the island more accessible, and even then, most of the resorts familiar to LBI aficionados today needed the nearby passing of the Garden State Parkway after 1950 to make them accessible as well as desirable. There are no boardwalks along the beaches on LBI.

The history of Barnegat Light includes the 1782 Long Beach Massacre described in chapter 2 and the construction of its two lighthouses. Aside from the gruesome Revolutionary War story, the land at the tip of Barnegat Inlet saw little activity other than the occasional passing ship until 1795, when Caleb Parker settled near Barnegat Inlet and a few fishermen and hunters visited. Several decades later Bart and Ruth Straight built a large house that accommodated boarders, which was later sold to Jacob Herring and became known as the Herring House. John Brown purchased fifty-five acres in 1855 and the area became known as Brownsville. When he left several years later (after his son drowned), the name left with him.

The first lighthouse built at this spot in 1835 washed into the sea; the second, Old Barney, replaced it in 1859 and still stands. A lifesaving station (#17) was built in 1872. Two hotels—the Oceanic and the Sunset (originally the Sans Souci)—were built between 1881 and 1883 to lure visitors and the Barnegat Light Improvement Company laid out the town in 1881 as Barnegat City. Sportsmen could take a train to Toms River and then board a ship furnished by the Pennsylvania Railroad to get to Barnegat City. When the Pennsylvania Railroad crossed Barnegat Bay in June 1886, the tracks turned north and ran all the way to Barnegat Light, providing additional incentives for development that never panned out. This part of LBI incorporated as Barnegat City in 1904 and then changed its name in

1948 to Barnegat Light. The tracks from Ship Bottom were abandoned and taken up in 1936.

Today, the Barnegat Light welcomes a substantial residential summer population. One of the attractions, other than the surf, sand, and bay is Viking Village, a commercial marina and tourist marketplace that bears the legacy of Norwegian fishermen who settled here in the early 1900s. They created a lobster cooperative and then moved on to sea bass, scallops, longline fishing, and gill fishing. The Viking Village is now filled with shops and eateries—in renovated fishing shanties—to entertain summer residents.

For the record, the Barnegat Light fishing boat, the *Lindsay L*, was used in the filming of the 2000 movie *The Perfect Storm*, which detailed the lives and struggles of offshore fishermen (albeit from Gloucester, Massachusetts) who were lost at sea in a severe North Atlantic storm.

More than 300 years ago Surf City and Harvey Cedars shared a forest of cedar and oak and a freshwater lake and was home to a whaling operation. It was known as the Great Swamp until storms and erosion in the early 1800s eliminated both the forest and the lake. Hunters and fishermen enjoyed this area in the late 1800s, with many staying at the Harvey Cedars Hotel on the bay after it opened in 1841.

The train tracks that ran north from Ship Bottom to Barnegat Light ran through Surf City and Harvey Cedars, but both towns did not develop as full resorts until the mid-1900s. Harvey Cedars incorporated in 1894 and developers sold lots and constructed homes, especially at the northern end of the borough. Two hotels built shortly thereafter to welcome guests burned down and Harvey Cedars remained a quiet village for decades, except perhaps for Philadelphia politicians who seemed to take a liking to this area around the turn of the twentieth century. The LBI Fishing Club building at the corner of Ocean Boulevard and Cape May Avenue is the former Harvey Cedars lifesaving station (#19) built in 1871.

Upscale development has occurred in the last sixty years with the construction of the Garden State Parkway.

A single hotel, the grand Mansion of Health, was built in the Surf City area around 1821, closed in the 1850s and burned to the ground in 1874. A second hotel, named the Surf City Hotel, was built on the same spot (Seventh Avenue and Central) and eventually moved to a location across from the railroad station. It has since been expanded and remains there today, reclaiming the name Surf City Hotel in the 1920s after several alternate iterations in the prior decades (Mansion House, Long Beach Inn, and Marquette). For many years the bar has been the locale for sing-alongs—to a Wurlitzer organ in the 1950s and rock music today. The borough incorporated in 1894 as Long Beach City and became Surf City in 1899.

Ship Bottom, at the center of LBI, deserves its nickname the Gateway to Long Beach Island, because the Route 72 causeway, the only route onto the island, crosses the bay from Manahawkin into the borough. The bridge opened to much hoopla on June 20, 1914. The train trestle onto the island, in operation from 1886 to 1935, also crossed into Ship Bottom. The train did not prove to be a boon for Ship Bottom, however, and the borough developed slowly around a lifesaving station (#20) before the coming of automobiles made it a truly accessible resort in the second half of the twentieth century. The borough incorporated in 1925 and its name derives, of course, from a shipwreck. As the story goes, the crew on a schooner slowly making its way north close to the beach in a heavy fog in 1821 could hear the distress calls of a ship nearby and suddenly came upon the hull of a ship beached on a shoal. The bodies of crew and passengers appeared in the water. Moving close to the wreck, the frightened crew could hear tapping from inside the hull. A crewman with an axe climbed atop the ship and cut a hole in the bottom. He pulled a woman to safety, the only survivor. History repeated itself in January 1910 when a dense fog forced the three-masted and iron-hulled Italian ship *Fortuna* to run aground just off the Sixteenth Street beach. Just like the ship in the story that gave the borough its name, the *Fortuna* turned over on the sand bar with her hull out of the water. This time photographers were able to capture the image. The crew of Lifesaving Station #20 rescued all on board including a baby, a pig, and a cat. The baby, the captain's daughter, had been born just days earlier while the ship anchored at Barbados on the way from South America to New York. Seventy-three years later, a local resident found the *Fortuna*'s anchor and other artifacts protruding from the sand on the beach. The anchor was moved to the Borough Hall. The former lifesaving station is now a private beach home, which sold in March 2014 for $450,000.

Ship Bottom originally incorporated as Ship Bottom-Arlington. The borough combined a number of beach resorts—Bonnie Beach, Bonnet Beach, Edgewater Beach, and Beach Arlington—the last of which was also the name of the train station.

Beach Haven, near the southern tip of the island, along with Tucker's Beach, was developed with hotels and boarding houses beginning in the 1830s. Today, the borough still boasts several large hotels, restaurants, bungalows, expensive beach houses, and the island's only amusement center. The borough incorporated in 1890.

The remaining area of LBI incorporated in 1899 within the single, fragmented municipality of Long Beach Township. Harvey Cedars and Surf City were already incorporated by 1899 and Barnegat City and Ship Bottom separated from the township in 1904 and 1925, respectively. The result is a four-section disconnected township that includes beaches north and south of the automobile causeway. The various named beaches that are captured within Long Beach Township (north to south) are:

High Bar Harbor	[south of Barnegat Light]
Loveladies	[north of Harvey Cedars]
North Beach	[south of Harvey Cedars and north of Surf City]
Brant Beach	[south of Ship Bottom] (31st to 74th Streets)
Beach Haven Crest	(75th to 85th Streets)
Brighton Beach	(81st to 87th Streets)
Peahala Park	(88th to 98th Streets)
Beach Haven Park	(99th to 108th Streets)
Haven Beach	(108th to 120th Streets)
The Dunes	(121st to 127th Streets)
Beach Haven Terrace	(128th to 133rd Streets)
Beach Haven Gardens	(27th to 34th Streets)
Spray Beach	(20th to 27th Streets)
North Beach Haven	(12th to 20th Streets)
Beach Haven Inlet	[south of Beach Haven]
South Beach Haven	[south of Beach Haven]
Holgate	[south of Beach Haven]

Each is just a few blocks long and a few blocks wide. Some of these small beach communities have histories going back to the 1800s, but most developed after 1950. North of the causeway are High Bar Harbor, Loveladies, and North Beach, all high-end resort communities. High Bar Harbor features homes connected to the bay with lagoons; North Beach is a narrow stretch (one block to the beach and one block to the bay) with expensive modern homes on pilings and no commercial activity.

Loveladies has a unique history. When the Garden State Parkway's close passage brought a building boom to LBI in the 1950s and 1960s the demand for houses in Loveladies was filled by communists. Three people working for the federal government—Nathan Gregory Silvermaster, his wife Helen, and William Ludwig Ullman—were called out as Soviet spies in 1948 by Elizabeth Bentley, a confessed courier for a Soviet spy ring within the U.S. government. Silvermaster refused to testify before the House Un-American Activities Committee, citing his rights under the Fifth Amendment. None of the three were indicted. They left Washington, DC, amid the scandal, moved to Loveladies, and became successful developers and builders. Ullman died with an $8 million estate in 1993 and, ironically, Loveladies today is one of New Jersey's most exclusive shore communities.[7] The homes include large summer residences on the beach and others on the bay with docks and lagoons. The beach has limited public access and no boardwalk, and the main boulevard has no traffic lights from Harvey Cedars to Barnegat Light. The average sale price of a home in January 2014 was more than $2 million.[8] The unusual name was given to this area in 1871 by the Lifesaving Service when it established Station #18 (abandoned in 1922), adopting the name of an adjacent gunning and fishing island owned by Thomas Lovelady.

South of the causeway, the oddly-named Peahala Park covers the ten blocks from Eighty-Eight to Ninety-Eighth Streets. It was named for the Peahala Gunning Club, which opened in 1882 as a resort for hunters and was run by Captain Tommy Jones. Peahala was just one of the several houses on the island that offered lodging and excellent hunting to its guests, high-end clubs that catered to the wealthy who could take the time to travel by boat from Philadelphia before trains and automobiles made the trip convenient. One local observed that the guests "went into a resort hotel, got the finest guides, the finest sneakboxes, and obtained the best birds made by the best carvers in the area."[9] Hunting shanties on LBI or on islands in the bay were anything but luxurious. The hunters would shoot waterfowl by day and spend the night with limited electricity and few amenities, a rustic vacation at best even in the early 1900s. Apparently, part of the appeal for city-dwelling gentlemen was the realization that they could rough it for several days of sport. The Peahala Club burned down in 1940.

Beach Haven Terrace boasted two "cottage hotels" from around 1900, the Clearview and the Chalfonte, and housed Lifesaving Station #21.

The U.S. Lifesaving Service Heritage Association offered this property for sale as late as 2013, and described as follows: "Own an authentic piece of Long Beach Island history!! U.S. Life Saving Station #21 Long Beach. Constructed in 1800's and beautifully renovated into a residence about 12 years ago. The property is located in the ocean block just 6 houses away from the beach, and sits on an approximate 17,000 sq. ft. lot."[10] To the south, Spray Beach was once the home of Philadelphia lawyer John Luther Long, the author of the short story "Madame Butterfly," which became the inspiration for David Belasco's play and Giacomo Puccini's immortal 1904 opera. Long's 1890 house is now the Cranberry Cottage, which can be rented for weddings, reunions, and vacations and offers a shady porch with rocking chairs among other amenities. This is within the Cranberry Hill section of LBI, named, of course, for the abundance of the red fruit.

Holgate is the section of Long Beach Township south of Beach Haven. The history of Holgate is tied to the life and tides of Tucker's Island. LBI Boulevard going south ends at the public beach in Holgate and the three and a half miles beyond the beach to the very tip of the island are part of the Edwin B. Forsythe National Wildlife Refuge. The refuge is not open to the public in the summer in order to protect the nesting habitats of the wildlife, but trails are available after the end of the season. The entire refuge, which protects migratory waterfowl, consists of 47,000 acres of beach, tidelands, wetlands, and bay that encompasses mainland locations as far north as Forked River and as far south as Oceanville. The Holgate property protects the federally protected, state-endangered piping plover.

FURTHER READING

For background, see Charles Edgar Nash, *The Lure of Long Beach* (The Long Beach Board of Trade, 1936); George B. Somerville, *The Lure of Long Beach* (The Long Beach Board of Trade, 1914); and John Bailey Lloyd, *Eighteen Miles of History on Long Beach Island* (Harvey Cedars, NJ: Down the Shore Press, 1994).

CHAPTER 9

Fires, Storms, and War

Nobody lives in Harvey Cedars anymore. There are no roads. There is no drinking water. Wreckage is everywhere and where there is no wreckage there is just sand, in some places four feet deep. Even the houses don't offer evidence of where the roads were. The houses are everywhere, in no order, sometimes piled two or three together. Around them crushed and mangled cars and trucks lie half buried.

—Newspaper account from the 1962 Ash Wednesday Storm[1]

One of the most fascinating aspects of the Jersey Shore is the resiliency of the people who live near and work on the water. Jersey Shore resorts in the 1800s faced constant threats of fire and the seasonal threat of storms. After each fire and each storm, no matter the devastation, the vast majority of those who lost everything returned and rebuilt. So it was with Superstorm Sandy in 2012. The tagline for New Jersey after Sandy was "Stronger Than the Storm."

Fires at the Jersey Shore have destroyed hotels, businesses, homes, piers, amusement rides, and boardwalks from the early 1800s to as recently as the 2013 blaze at the Seaside Heights and Seaside Park boardwalk. Whether started by accident or purposely set, fires bring property damage, terror, and death. Arson destroyed Cape May on several occasions in the second half of the nineteenth century. Fire codes, experienced firefighters, and modern equipment available today limit most fires to single buildings or blocks, but they still occur, often at the height of the season when hotel and boarding homes are filled with tourists. Those lucky enough to find themselves out on the street with just the clothes they are wearing watch helplessly as their vacation and their possessions go up in flames.

Storms, on the other hand, cause destruction across a vast geographic area. Damages are measured in dollars and the number of structures impacted and have increased with each new storm due to the thousands of homes built in the last seventy-five years up and down the coast. Thankfully, the number of deaths and the injuries sustained have dropped; advanced meteorological warnings and effective evacuation measures get people out of harm's way. But no structure is guaranteed to remain untouched by a storm's wrath. Anyone who lived close to the Jersey Shore in October 2012 can attest to the fury of the wind, surf, and sand of an Atlantic Coast storm.

Superstorm Sandy ripped across New Jersey's islands, beaches, and beach towns, accelerated by high tides and a full moon. Modern weather equipment predicted the strength of the storm and allowed authorities to evacuate almost everyone, but no amount of modern technology or equipment could dissuade the storm from hitting the Jersey Shore head-on or could protect the properties left behind by the evacuees. The devastation was enormous. Houses were lifted off their moorings and thrown into the sea; half-million-dollar boats were beached in areas never intended for watercraft; beautiful beaches of fine sand were obliterated; and seawalls that had stood for decades sundered. The ocean breached the bay at Mantoloking and threatened the underpinning of the bridge that carries thousands each summer's day from the mainland to the beach. After the storm passed, the iconic image of the roller-coaster at Seaside Heights submerged in the sea epitomized the fury of the storm and the inability of people to prevent its destruction. At its height, the storm extended 1,000 miles across the entirety of the Atlantic Coast. Ask anyone who lived through Superstorm Sandy and they will tell you that it was a storm for the ages, a storm like no one had ever witnessed. And yet, the Jersey Shore *had* seen such a storm before, in 1962, 1954, 1944, and on earlier occasions when fewer people lived on the lands affected to chronicle nature's fury in enough detail to tell the full tale.

The Jersey Shore also had to face the impact of war in the twentieth century. Shortages and fear threatened the viability of shore communities that relied on the fun and frolic of good times; submarine warfare brought terror and death right to its beaches.

FIRES

In the 1800s all buildings were made of wood and all communities were prone to fires. Few municipalities had sufficient fire-fighting equipment or trained people to stop a blaze once started. Shore communities featured some of the largest wooden structures of the day, huge hotels with multiple stories and vast gathering rooms that were often close together, so embers and intense heat could threaten entire blocks. Ocean breezes, so pleasant on the beach, stoked the flames of even small fires. The history of almost every shore town contains references to this hotel or that boarding house built in the late 1800s that succumbed to fire, whether localized or widespread. As counterintuitive as it may seem, fires would also accompany horrific storms, which occurred in September 1889 when a nor'easter raged through Atlantic City.

Cape May fared the worst, losing large hotels and a major portion of the town in succeeding fires over more than three decades, from 1856 to 1889. Cape May's first major fire was attributed to arson by a disgruntled employee of the huge Mount Vernon Hotel located at Broadway and Beach Avenue. The hotel was designed as a four-story, U-shaped building, 300 feet across the front with wings 500 feet deep. Several towers, at the center front and the corners, rose to five and six stories. The hotel was designed to accommodate almost 300 guests. In the summer of 1856 one wing remained to be completed, but the hotel had opened for the season and had emptied by early September, except for the manager and his family.

Ulysses S. Grant (*left*) and family in Long Branch, New Jersey. Author's collection.

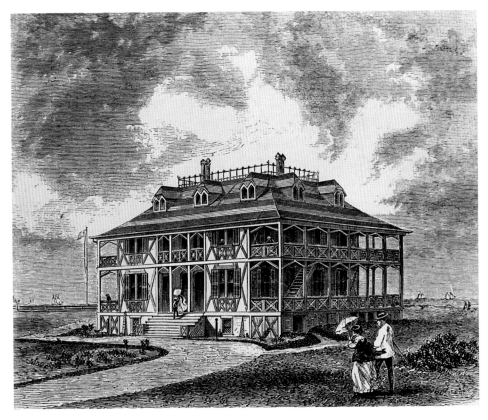

Grant's Cottage in Long Branch, 1870. President Grant and his family spent many summers at this cottage during and after his presidency. The cottage, in this rendering from *Harper's Weekly* in 1870, was donated to the family by friends. Courtesy of the Library of Congress.

Lillian Russell. Courtesy of the Library of Congress.

Diamond Jim Brady and Lillian Russell were among the many personalities vactioning in Long Branch, New Jersey, in the late nineteenth century. They were often seen together in one of several electric cars that Brady frequently drove through the resort.

Diamond Jim Brady. Courtesy of the Everitt Collection.

President James Garfield was shot by an assassin in Washington, DC, in 1881. His doctors thought that the sea air in Long Branch would hasten his recovery. A rail spur was built almost overnight to carry Garfield from the train station to a cottage offered by a local resident for Garfield's recovery. This rendering shows locals as well as railroad engineers working to complete the spur on time. Unfortunately, President Garfield died at the cottage within several weeks of being transported there. Courtesy of the Everett Collection.

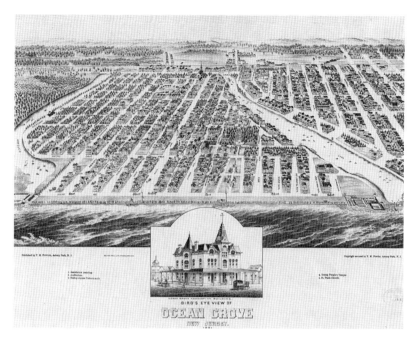

This "bird's eye" view of Ocean Grove from 1881 shows the development of the community in just a few years after its foundation by religious leaders and its advantageous location on the beach and between Fletcher and Wesley Lakes. Courtesy of Library of Congress.

Governor's Mansion at Sea Girt, 1912. New Jersey's governors from the 1880s to the 1940s utilized the cottage depicted here as the state's "summer capital." Courtesy of Library of Congress.

The Sandy Hook lighthouse is the oldest functioning lighthouse in the nation. It was funded in 1764 with the proceeds of two lotteries. The lighthouse withstood attack by patriot forces during the Revolutionary War who tried to darken it because it aided the British forces stationed in New York City. Courtesy of Library of Congress.

Morro Castle, Asbury Park, September 1934. The *Morro Castle*, a cruise ship transporting revelers to Cuba for a few days of fun, caught fire at sea, lost power, and eventually beached at Asbury Park. The tragedy, in which 138 were killed, brought thousands to the boardwalk to see the burning hulk up close. Intrigue aboard the ship fueled months of investigation, but the cause of the fire and the reason for the failure of the crew to handle the fire and the lifeboats was never fully resolved. Courtesy of the Everett Collection.

The Avalon lifesaving station was one of forty stations placed almost every three miles along the New Jersey Shore to watch for shipwrecks and help mariners and passengers in distress close to shore. In 1915 the U.S. Lifesaving Service was incorporated into the U.S. Coast Guard. Courtesy of Library of Congress.

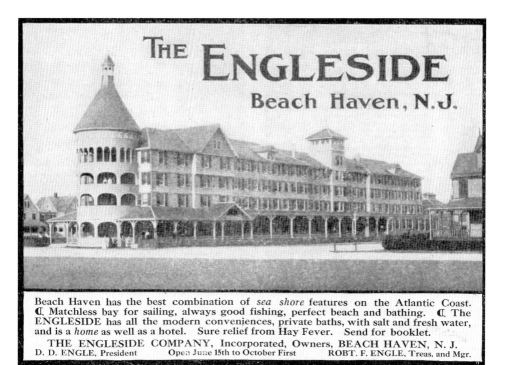

The Engleside Inn in Beach Haven provides a fine example of the grand hotels built along the New Jersey Shore in the late nineteenth century. It was also the scene of a shark attack in 1916. From *Outing Magazine*, author's collection.

USS Monssen, Beach Haven, 1962. This World War II destroyer beached at Beach Haven during the 1962 Ash Wednesday storm. It was being towed to Rhode Island for scrap when the tow broke. Crews worked for weeks to free the ship and move it off of the beach. Courtesy of U.S. Naval Institute.

Lucy the Margate elephant was built in 1881 to lure investors to beach properties south of Atlantic City. It has had a long and colorful history and still receives visitors today. Courtesy of Library of Congress.

The rolling chairs along the Atlantic City Boardwalk were fashioned after similar chairs introduced at the 1876 Philadelphia Exposition and became a phenomemon well into the twentieth century. Courtesy of the Everett Collection.

Bathers in the surf at Atlantic City, 1911. Courtesy of the Everett Collection.

Miss America 1921. Margaret Gorman was crowned the first "Miss Amer-
ica" on the Atlantic City Boardwalk when the contest was known as the
Inter-City Pageant and before it was known as the Miss America Beauty
Pageant. Courtesy of the Everett Collection.

Atlantic City, 1902 "Bathing Beauty" postcard. This is just one of many millions of postcards sent from Atlantic City during its heyday at the turn of the twentieth century. Author's collection.

Baby Parade, Asbury Park, 1915. This event has attracted tens of thousands each year. Courtesy of the Everett Collection.

The 1924 Ku Klux Klan Konclave and parade in Long Branch demonstrated the strength of the Klan in New Jersey during the 1920s and the racial tensions that impacted several Jersey Shore resorts. Courtesy of Getty Images.

Winslow Homer, *Long Branch, New Jersey*, 1869. This painting depicts the Long Branch bluff and the styles worn at the beach in the 1860s. Courtesy of the Museum of Fine Arts, Boston. The Hayden Collection—Charles Henry Hayden Fund, 41.631.

Aerial view of Sandy Hook. Courtesy of Alamy Stock Photo.

James A. Bradley, an early purchaser of lots in
Ocean Grove, was the founder and driving force
behind the development of Asbury Park until his
death in 1921. Courtesy of Shutterstock.

The Dentzel Looff carousel in Seaside Heights. Courtesy of Colleen Kammerer.

The Ferris wheel at the Ocean City boardwalk and music pier. Courtesy of Beth Ferris Sale.

The beaches and boardwalks of the Wildwoods in Cape May County attract daytrippers, weekenders, and more for surf and fun throughout the summer. The beaches are wide and free. The boardwalk rides are thrilling. Wildwoods Convention Center, 2014, photo courtesy of James Godish.

This is one of several posters designed by Edward M. Eggleston for the Pennsylvania Railroad in the 1930s to generate railroad traffic to Atlantic City. Courtesy of Getty Images.

The 24th Street Motel is just one example of Wildwood's doo-wop architecture. Author's collection.

The revival of Cape May in the beginning of the 1970s was built in part on the charm and beauty of its Victorian architecture. Courtesy of Library of Congress.

The revival of Asbury Park has been more of a struggle than similar revivals in Cape May and Long Branch. It came too late to save the Palace Amusements building, but local activists were able to save an image of "Tillie" on its exterior wall. Courtesy of J. Delconzo.

Legalized casino gambling in Atlantic City began a revival of the resort in the late 1970s, but the revival stalled after the turn of the twenty-first century due to competition and over-building. Courtesy of Wikimedia Commons.

Superstorm Sandy in 2012 compromised the bridge from the mainland to Mantoloking and left the house above at sea when the ocean breached the peninsula and reached the bay. Courtesy of Danielle Richards.

Superstorm Sandy destroyed the boardwalk in Seaside Park and cast the roller-coaster into the Atlantic Ocean. Courtesy of Danielle Richards.

The fire began at night, probably set in an interior room, and quickly engulfed the building. The manager, Philip Cain, two of his daughters, and three others perished. The next year the nearby Mansion House burned to the ground. In 1869 an enormous fire took three large hotels—the American House, the United States Hotel, and the Atlantic House. A 27,000-gallon water tank failed to protect the United States Hotel despite extraordinary efforts by employees who could see the fire heading to their building and could do little to prevent its total loss. This fire occurred in late August while these hotels were still entertaining guests who rushed to the streets to save themselves.

The worst Cape May fire occurred in November 1878 and contributed to its decline as the premier resort in New Jersey. Nine hotels burned to the ground along with thirty-three homes in a blaze that swept through thirty acres taking all in its path. The fire was believed to have started in the Ocean House and, like the fires in 1856 and 1869, was blamed on arson. City leaders also decried the lack of effective fire-fighting apparatus. One newspaper report captured the fire's fury:

> The most disastrous fire that has ever visited any seaside resort yesterday laid more than one-half of the principal part of Cape May in ashes. The flames, fanned by a northwest gale, swept through the central portion of the city, and as all of the buildings, from the stateliest to the humblest, are of wood, and the various squares divided by narrow streets, they fell an easy prey. The burned district embraces nearly forty acres of spacious buildings, including ten hotels and nineteen or twenty cottages, representing a total value of over $400,000, and this crisp autumnal morning the black, unshapely ruins mar sadly enough all the associations of last season's pleasures. The hotels in the order of their destruction are as follows: The Ocean House, Congress Hall, Centre House, Merchant's Hotel, Centennial House, Atlantic House, Knickerbocker House, Avenue House, Wyoming House and Columbia House.

. . .

Cape May, though a city of tinder boxes, and liable to be touched off upon the slightest occasions, had only one small fire engine, a truck and a few chemical extinguishers with which to fight a conflagration. With these make-shifts all was done that could be, and buckets of water were passed up from the ocean's edge by a long line of citizens, with all the zeal and determination their energy was capable of, but to practically little or no purpose. The dry frame structures were devoured by the flames one after the other with scarcely a halt in their progress.[2]

The Columbia Hotel was rebuilt of brick in the following years, only to be lost to fire once again in 1889. Devastating fires were not confined to Cape May, or to hotels, or to the nineteenth century, however.

An August fire destroyed the Parry House in Beach Haven in the 1880s. The cause was determined to be a faulty chimney. The hotel accommodated 250 guests and was full when the fire broke out. Thankfully, everyone escaped unharmed. The Berkeley Arms Hotel in Seaside Park was partially burned in 1892 by a fire in the adjacent bath house. A raging fire in April 1902 in Atlantic City took away twelve hotels on the Boardwalk from Illinois to New York Avenues, luckily without any deaths. A southwest wind threatened the entire city for five hours and engines were called from as far away as Camden and Philadelphia. Although early in the season, most of the hotels were filled and the guests poured out onto the streets with whatever belongings they could carry, dumping them in piles on the beach. The militia was called in to keep order and prevent looting. The Tarlton, Stratford, Berkeley, and Rio Grande Hotels were some of the hotels lost in the blaze along with the Academy of Music. In August 1915 a fire raged along the Boardwalk concessions threatening the Steeplechase Pier and in full view of 100,000 vacationers who watched the flames in the middle of the day from the streets and the beach. In 1916 the Overbrook Hotel burned with numerous dead and others injured jumping from windows to escape the heat and flames; in 1919 the Congress Hotel was lost; in November 1924, the Bothwell Hotel burned and several people were killed. Asbury Park lost the Guernsey Hotel in September 1894 and the West End Hotel in January 1911. In October 1925, thirty buildings burned in Ocean City in a fire that took away the largest pier and amusement center—the Hippodrome—as well as three hotels, several movie houses, and dozens of boardwalk stores and concessions. The list of hotels severely damaged or lost to fire continued throughout the twentieth century, including the Atlantic Hotel in Long Branch in August 1925, the North End Hotel in Ocean Grove in 1938 (its namesake had burned in the same spot in 1924), and the Surfside Hotel in Atlantic City in 1963. The Surfside was filled with elderly residents, many of whom were permanent residents at the hotel. Twenty-five people were killed in this tragic event. Four other hotels lost in the fire had already closed for the season.

Hotels were not the only buildings at risk. In August 1897 the Atlantic City Grand Opera House burned to the ground, taking nearby city hall along with it, despite the efforts of firemen and hundreds of volunteers who tried to contain the blaze. The Opera House in Asbury Park went in August 1900 in a fire that started in an oil stove in a nearby cottage and raged for hours. Among the volunteers fighting the blaze was the city's founder, James Bradley. Newspaper accounts lamented the loss of the sets for a new play, *A Stranger in a Strange Land*, which was about to open. Bradley offered other locations for the show to go on. A boardwalk fire in 1987 destroyed most of the amusements at Long Branch, as well as the fishing pier and several stores, and in 2013 the Seaside boardwalk was destroyed just after being rebuilt, adding to the list of fires that have ravaged the wooden promenades.

HURRICANES, TROPICAL STORMS, AND NOR'EASTERS

Storms batter the Jersey Shore from the south and the north. From the south come hurricanes between July and October rising out of the Caribbean and making their way up the Atlantic coast. More often than not, they peter out to just wind and rain. Every now and then, they do not, and devastation ensues. Although most of these storms start as hurricanes, by the time they reach New Jersey their winds decrease and they are officially characterized as tropical storms. The National Weather Service has the authority over such determinations. A hurricane must demonstrate sustained winds of seventy-four miles per hour when it makes landfall to be designated a hurricane. Sandy blew as a hurricane all the way up the East Coast but tempered as it hit New Jersey, and although the state experienced gusts of more than seventy-four miles per hour, the service categorized it as a tropical storm in New Jersey. Notwithstanding its title, Sandy's effects were devastating due to the timing of the high tide and the tidal strength of the full moon. The categories may sound like splitting hairs, but they impact people who own and insure properties at the beach. Clauses in most homeowners' policies apply a deductible for wind damage caused by a hurricane but not by a tropical storm. The designation is not always immediate. Many of Sandy's chroniclers resolved this difficulty by using the sobriquet "Superstorm" to tell their story (as I have in this book).

One company that knows this distinction well is New Jersey Manufacturers (NJM) Insurance Company, the insurer for over 300,000 homeowners in New Jersey. NJM paid out more than $290 million to Sandy victims between 2012 and 2015. The company tracks all significant storms in the state. Their records indicate that only two (unnamed) hurricanes made landfall in New Jersey since 1900, in 1903 and 1904 (see map 6). NJM's experts will tell you that, despite the ferocity of Superstorm Sandy, the most devastating storms in financial terms in New Jersey have been unnamed storms that blow in from the northeast not the southwest, storms known appropriately as nor'easters.

The season for nor'easters runs from October to April and their impact can be as great as southern-born hurricanes. In fact, in the past thirty years it has been nor'easters that have devastated the shore more frequently than hurricanes, bringing inland flooding from raging rivers as

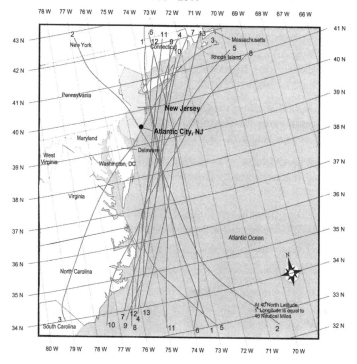

TRACKS OF HURRICANES PASSING WITHIN 75 NAUTICAL MILES OF ATLANTIC CITY, NEW JERSEY
1886 - 2011

Storm Index Number	Storm Name	Year	Month	Day	Maximum Wind Speed at Storm Center (MPH)	*Saffir-Simpson Storm Category
1	Not Named	1893	August	24	98	2
2	Not Named	1903	September	16	77	1
3	Not Named	1904	September	15	75	1
4	Not Named	1934	September	8	74	1
5	Not Named	1936	September	19	95	1
6	Not Named	1938	September	21	104	2
7	Not Named	1944	September	14	113	3
8	Barbara	1953	August	14	83	1
9	Carol	1954	August	31	98	2
10	Donna	1960	September	12	106	2
11	Belle	1976	August	10	89	1
12	Gloria	1985	September	27	95	1
13	Bob	1991	August	19	109	2
14	Irene*	2011	August	28	74	1

* Hurricane Irene had been downgraded to a Tropical Storm when it made landfall in New Jersey on August 28, 2011.

*Saffir-Simpson Storm Category	One Minute Sustained Speed (MPH)
1	74 - 95
2	96 - 110
3	111 - 130
4	131 - 155
5	over 155

New Jersey Manufacturers
Insurance Group, November 2011
Information provided by Science Applications International Corporation

Map 6. Hurricanes and Tropical Storms. New Jersey Manufacturers Insurance Company tracks hurricanes and tropical storms and provides this map to its insureds showing the most damaging storms from 1893 to 2012. Courtesy of New Jersey Manufacturers Insurance Company.

well as battering the coast. In the eighteen years between 1980 and 1998 the shore suffered damage from twelve significant nor'easters. In that same period only two hurricanes, Gloria in 1985 and Floyd in 1999, visited New Jersey with any ferocity. Hurricanes usually move rapidly, causing greater wind damage; nor'easters often linger through several tides along the coast, causing enormous flooding and water damage.

To set a base, let's start with the unnamed storm that hit Atlantic City at summer's end in 1944. The National Weather Service did not start naming hurricanes until 1953. Six unnamed hurricanes had already developed in the Atlantic Ocean in 1944 and at least one drenched the state and its beachgoers with torrential rains. But it was the seventh storm in mid-September that rattled the forecasters as it drove up the Atlantic coastline. It hit the Bahamas and the Outer Banks of North Carolina and then brushed across New Jersey. It was nicknamed the Great Atlantic Hurricane of 1944 *before* it arrived at the Jersey Shore on September 14. When it left New Jersey it ripped through Long Island and Rhode Island. It finally petered out as it passed over Massachusetts and Maine. Even though the Jersey Shore did not receive this storm head-on, its impact was brutal. Rain poured down for two days. Winds destroyed the Cape May boardwalk across its two-mile length in just minutes before moving north to destroy the boardwalks in Sea Isle City, Stone Harbor, and Longport. Large portions of the Atlantic City Boardwalk also disappeared, along with the Heinz Pier and two sections of the bridge that ran to Brigantine Island, which left its unevacuated inhabitants marooned until help could arrive. Whole sections of Long Beach Island were destroyed, including one in every five houses in Harvey Cedars. Some Harvey Cedars residents had to take refuge from the water in attics, and others clung to telephone poles to ride out the storm. Some were not as lucky and did not make it through the storm. Nor were the northern beaches spared. Asbury Park lost its boardwalk, its fishing pier, and all the buildings along the ocean; Ocean Grove lost its boardwalk and pavilions. The ocean broke through Mantoloking in several spots, a paddle-wheeler beached in Keyport, and

New Jersey suffered nine deaths. In all, 390 people died in the northeast, mostly sailors on U.S. Navy and Coast Guard ships caught unaware and close to shore, but also residents who could not find safety in a rage that swept across the beach towns without mercy.

But even the Great Atlantic Storm of 1944 pales in comparison to the Great September Gale of 1821, a hurricane that hit the New Jersey coast and continued inland while still blowing as a hurricane. This storm raged over the Outer Banks of North Carolina and up the coast until the eye sat over Cape Henolopen at the western opening of Delaware Bay. The storm turned east to Cape May and then northeast to wreak havoc on New York City with flooding and destruction. This is the only time that the eye of a hurricane has made land in New Jersey. Reports from the shore were limited, however, because few people lived or worked near the shore at the time. Property damage and the loss of life were limited for the same reason. Nevertheless, Cape May peninsula was breached by the raging waters, trees were flattened, the port at Little Egg Harbor was devastated, and boats were overturned. The storm drove north along the route of today's Garden State Parkway and remnants of the thousands of trees laid down in its path were uncovered when that road was built more than one hundred years later in the 1950s.

Decades after the Great September Gale, a September nor'easter ripped through the state with equal disaster. The nor'easter of 1889 lasted three days, from September 10 to 13, but by this time the Jersey Shore was spotted with beach resorts. The rain and the wind caused damage up and down the coast. A breach occurred at Sandy Hook, opening the Shrewsbury River to the ocean and making the Hook an island once again; mud, sea debris, and seaweed covered streets and railroad tracks at new seaside resorts to the south, at some places three to five feet deep; bulkheads, piers, and berths were destroyed by the ferocious waves and whipping winds. Hundreds of structures were lost. Unprotected, Atlantic City was severely battered and its residents and tourists were frightened beyond reason. When the storm hit, Atlantic City hotels were still accommodating vacationers enjoying the summer's last days. The storm began with just high seas on a Friday, but by Sunday night, the wind howled. Railroads shut down causing a food shortage. Fires started despite the rain and raged with the high winds, taking away houses and hotels and pouring panicked dwellers out into the streets. Stores and a merry-go-round along the boardwalk were swept into the sea. Water filled ocean-side streets to a depth of three feet. Hundreds of terrified tourists and residents desperate to get out of the path of the storm raced to the railroad station early in the morning of Monday, September 23, and boarded trains, even though water overflowed the tracks. The trains started out of the station as the tide rose and the storm still raged. Even with engines in front and back, the trains could not make it out of the city. The rising water threatened to extinguish the engine fires and topple the cars. Rescue engines were brought in to help back the trains to the stations they had left early in the morning, but they did not return until almost 6:00 P.M. The passengers stranded on the tracks while the water and wind threatened were lucky to survive and disembark where they had started.

The terror and devastation of each storm creates a unique story, with different towns and localities affected with property damage, shipwrecks, and lives lost, such that each generation of ocean-goers has its own story to tell. In addition to the 1821 and the 1889 storms, the shore was battered in 1846 by both a hurricane and then a nor'easter. The latter storm sunk ten ships. In 1850 three tropical storms raged up the New Jersey coast; in September 1901 winds blew away the belfry of Holy Innocents' Church in Beach Haven on Long Beach Island just before the church itself was lifted up and placed on nearby trolley tracks; the so-called Vagabond Hurricane in September 1903 took all but six of forty yachts at the Seaside Park Yacht Club; a nor'easter on Christmas 1916 took out the bulkheads in Sea Bright, exposing houses along the beach to a later storm that washed many away; much of Longport was washed away in 1916; and storms in the late 1920s and 1930s overturned dozens of boats, undermined a hotel in Point Pleasant, threatened to take down Barnegat lighthouse on Long Beach

Island, and opened up Island Beach one mile north of the Barnegat Inlet with an inlet 250 feet wide and seven feet deep from the ocean to the bay. The Island Beach breach was closed within weeks by the impact of new storms, along with some man-made help. The survivors of each of these storms surely felt that the storm that threatened their lives and property was a storm for the ages.

With every passing year, the number of homes close to the beach and the value of homes and businesses increases. Also, especially in recent decades, the number of year-round residents in shore communities has increased, exposing more and more people to danger even in the off-season. Fifty years before Superstorm Sandy, the nor'easter of 1962 ravaged the shore with equal fury in the off-season. The 1962 storm hit the Jersey Shore without warning on March 6 and was named the Ash Wednesday Storm. Unlike a hurricane, the devastation it brought came with snow, ice, and cold temperatures. Two weather systems, one from the northwest and the other from the southwest, joined forces and were held in place by a cold front coming down from Canada. The spring equinox and a new moon exacerbated the high tides (one measured almost nine feet) and produced ocean waves as high as twenty-five feet. The storm raged for three days. Those trapped at the shore suffered through five high tides with little or no receding waters during low tides. The waves destroyed dunes, crushed seawalls, and caused massive flooding. Several pertinent facts capture the enormity of this storm: thirty-two people were killed in New Jersey, more than a thousand were injured, 45,000 New Jersey homes were lost, and a navy destroyer was beached at Holgate on Long Beach Island, which was severed in four places.

Most of the residents in the shore towns in mid-March 1962 were either year-round residents or businesspeople preparing for the coming season. They had seen March storms come and go and they expected this surprising spring squall to churn the ocean, batter the beaches, and then pass by after one high tide, maybe two. No one was prepared for the onslaught that came. Thousands were evacuated by army trucks and then by helicopters as the storm worsened. In Sea Isle City, one resident saw bulkheads "smashed . . . like kindling wood" with the Wednesday morning tide, the "granddaddy of them all." He left by helicopter. Houses disappeared in Sea Isle City as did the Windsor Hotel, the Fean Hotel, the Madeline Theater and the convent house of the Sisters of Mercy. Nearby, piers were destroyed and boardwalks ripped from their moorings, including the Steel Pier in Atlantic City that was struck by a 100-foot barge set free and then taken hostage by the high winds. Out at sea, a tanker carrying molasses from Liberia split in two, with its crew divided and seeking safety on the two parts of the 500-foot ship as they drifted apart. Navy destroyers saved the men on the stern; a cruise ship saved the men in the bow. Other large vessels also went adrift during this storm and several trawlers that made their way to sea before the severity of the storm became evident never made it back.

But the strangest story deals with the destroyer *USS Monssen*. This veteran ship was on its way to being decommissioned after a long and storied career that included intense action in the Pacific in World War II. It left Bayonne, ferried on a cable and bound for Newport, Rhode Island. The force of the storm at sea snapped the cable and sent the empty ship adrift in the Atlantic Ocean. Wind and tides carried it to Long Beach Island and drove it onto the beach at Beach Haven. There it sat for six weeks as a tourist attraction, for those choice tourists who enjoyed visiting scenes of mayhem and destruction. The 2,000 tons of metal did not go back to the sea willingly. Seven hundred salvagers worked for weeks, living in tents at Beach Haven and resorting to dynamite to create a viable channel for the ship's release from the beach. One sunny morning on the tide, the ship was dragged back into the water by seven vessels lashed onto her with cables, only to be sold weeks later by the federal government for scrap.[3]

No Jersey Shore town was spared the wrath of this Ash Wednesday Storm, but it seems that Long Beach Island suffered the most. At Seventy-Ninth Street in Harvey Cedars, the narrowest part of the island runs just one block to the ocean and one block to the bay. The force of the huge waves moving inland during the high tide (more than 8.5 feet), destroyed the dunes that protected the town for decades and the breach allowed the ocean's waters to crash onto the streets and cross the boulevard to mix with the rising waters of the bay. Almost fifty people sought refuge in the Harvey Cedars Bible Conference (the former Harvey Cedars Hotel) to ride out the storm, sitting on ground slightly higher than the adjacent land. When the storm finally passed, the Harvey Cedars breach remained, sixty feet wide and twenty feet deep near the bay. Houses in its path were destroyed or simply gone. Indeed, 50 percent of the homes in Harvey Cedars were lost or destroyed. Locals who could not escape the storm began the effort to close the gap as soon as the storm subsided. Using a dredge found on the bay, they pumped sand to the ocean side of the boulevard over three days to seal the breach and coax the waters back into place. Finally, on Saturday, the U.S. Army Corps of Engineers arrived to finish the job with bulldozers. One wonders whether this inlet would have survived were it not for the bulldozers working day and night.

The devastation of the 1962 storm heightened awareness of the vulnerability of people and property at the shore. Within the next two years, more than twelve million cubic feet of sand was pumped onto the beaches of all four coastal counties to ensure the continuing health of the New Jersey tourist economy.[4] The Ash Wednesday Storm proved to be the last storm of consequence until almost 1992. Hurricane Belle in August 1976 and Hurricane Gloria in September 1985 both sent residents and tourists packing from the shore (250,000 in 1976), but their impact did not match the 1962 storm. The storms that had the most significant impact after 1962 were winter storms and their impact was greatest on the beaches, not the structures built behind them. A number of significant nor'easters hit New Jersey, particularly in March 1984 and January 1987; nor'easters on Halloween in 1991 and in December 1992 did the most damage. To some, it appeared that the Jersey Shore entered a period of relative calm after 1962, at least as to hurricanes. One observer of storms over the centuries,

David Ludlum, in his 1983 *New Jersey Weather Book*, reviewed hurricanes and nor'easters and suggested that New Jersey's hurricane activity runs in thirty-year cycles.[5]

Thirty years is just enough time to forget. Building continued apace in the decades after the 1962 Ash Wednesday Storm. More vacationers found affordable lots available and dared to build second homes for investment and enjoyment. More people who loved the shore as a resort moved there permanently as the seasonal communities matured and offered amenities and services for those willing to stay through the winter months. This was seen especially in Monmouth Beach, Sea Girt, Lavallette, Surf City, Avalon, Brigantine, Ocean City, and Sea Isle City. In these towns, the permanent populations doubled from 1960 to 1980.[6] On the other hand, environmentalists raised concerns about the effectiveness of the state's efforts to protect the state's beaches, its endangered animals, and their habitats, and asked that state and national policies be reconsidered to preserve more of the shore in a natural state and discourage further building. Some of these concerns were heeded in the revision of building codes requiring elevated structures, structural innovations, and beach protection. As an example, just months after the 1962 devastation the Borough of Beach Haven acted to preserve its dunes with a restrictive ordinance:

It has been clearly demonstrated that well established and protected sand dunes, together with berms, beaches and underwater slopes of suitable configuration and proper grade and height, are a durable and effective protection against high tides and flooding, and against damage by the ocean under storm conditions, and are the natural protections of coastal areas adjacent thereto, and the State and its subdivisions and their inhabitants have an interest in the continued protection thereof, and the right to restore them in the event of damage or destruction. . . . The best available means of protecting said sand dunes against wind erosion is by preventing indiscriminate trespassing, construction or other acts which might destroy or damage said dunes.

Despite the devastation of the 1962 storm, several homeowners challenged the ordinance as a "taking of their property for public purposes without just compensation." With its memory of the storm still fresh, the New Jersey Supreme Court ruled in favor of the borough declaring that the ordinances were nothing more than "good husbandry" that the homeowners "should themselves impose on the use of their own lands" and that the loss, if any, was "de minimus, and must be suffered in the interest of public good."[7] Superstorm Sandy would have a similar impact on the New Jersey Supreme Court fifty years later.

The state government recognized the risk presented by aggressive building after the 1962 Ash Wednesday Storm but did little, if anything, to stop rebuilding or new construction at the shore. The introduction to the New Jersey Shore Protection Master Plan issued in 1981 simply acknowledged state actions to fund protection efforts: "In recent years, the need for shoreline protection planning has been heightened by the cumulative effect of minor and major storms (particularly the March 1962 storm) and the tremendous boom in oceanfront development. The New Jersey Commission on Capital Budgeting and Planning recognized that the annual one million dollar appropriation for State Aid to municipalities for shore protection purposes was inadequate and in 1977 the voters of the State approved a $30 million Beaches and Harbors Bond Issue, which provided $20 million for State Aid for shore protection purposes and $10 million for harbor cleanup."[8] Perhaps the destruction wrought by Superstorm Sandy will serve as a wake-up call for the current generation of Jersey Shore state officials, municipal officials, and homeowners whose memories do not reach back as far as 1962.

WORLD WAR

Fires and storms were not the only dangers faced by the Jersey Shore and its fun-seekers in the twentieth century. The two world wars brought danger directly to the shore. When the United States entered World War I in

April 1917, the tens of thousands frolicking on New Jersey's beaches did
not immediately fear an impact, reasoning that the vast Atlantic Ocean
protected them from the warring nations in Europe. They did not anticipate that advances in technology and communications had changed the
world dramatically in the decades leading up to the war, which made the
United States vulnerable to attack on its Atlantic coast.

Germany deployed 360 U-boats in World War I, submarines that
destroyed millions of tons of British, French, and American shipping. As
soon as the United States entered the war, the German Naval Command
sent six U-boats across the Atlantic Ocean to threaten shipping from the
Chesapeake Bay to New York. One of these underwater threats had substantial success off the New Jersey coast. The mission of *U-151* was to lay
mines in the harbors, cut undersea communications cables, and interrupt
merchant shipping. Its extraordinary success on June 2, 1918, caused the
day to become known as Black Sunday. It appears that the United States
was asleep to this new danger (with its lights on!). *U-151* laid mines in a
fully lit Baltimore Harbor and then headed for Delaware Bay to do the
same. Before it could lay its mines in Delaware Bay, the U-boat encountered easy pickings along the New Jersey coast. It sighted the *Hattie Dunn*,
a three-masted schooner that was no match for the armed submarine. The
Germans brought their submarine to the surface, threatened the ship,
captured its crew, and torpedoed the *Hattie Dunn*. While in the process
of dispatching the *Hattie Dunn*, *U-151* sighted another schooner, the
Hauppauge, and repeated the process, this time boarding the ship and
sinking it with dynamite. Releasing the passengers and crew to lifeboats
would alert the U.S. Navy of the submarine's presence near to the shore
so they were held in the crowded ship as captives. Next easy target was yet
another schooner, the *Edna*.

The shallow bottom of the Delaware Bay almost did the U-boat in.
Looking to lay its mines in the bay, the U-boat struck bottom and damaged its steering and diving ability. When it surfaced to make repairs
the crew laid down mines in the bay. Repaired, this efficient German

juggernaut went back to work, cutting the transatlantic cable. The next morning, another sailing ship, the *Isabel B. Wiley*, appeared in its path off of Long Beach Island, and then, almost simultaneously, a steamship, the *SS Winneconne* arrived. The U-boat could not accommodate any more prisoners, so the German captain had these ships lower their lifeboats and off-loaded his captives. They rowed to shore with the passengers and crew of his latest victims. Some of the twenty-three captives had spent eight days in the U-boat, mostly underwater. The busy shipping lanes across New Jersey continued, nevertheless, to provide their bounty: two more schooners, the *Jacob M. Haskell* and the *Edward H. Coles*, and two more steamers, the *SS Texel* and the *SS Carolina*. All went to the bottom while their crews and passengers rowed to shore. In all, almost 500 passengers and crew came ashore in twenty-one lifeboats. By now, word of the underwater threat had spread and *U-151* ended its terror and headed back to Germany. Most of the lifeboats made their way to shore, some landing in Atlantic City where the survivors were greeted by a brass band, otherwise employed on the Boardwalk, and the cheers of early summer vacationers. Other lifeboats were intercepted at sea by the Coast Guard and towed safely to New York City. Unfortunately, a few people died on their way to the Jersey beaches when one boat capsized in rough waters. *U-151* arrived home almost one year after its departure having admirably accomplished its mission.[9]

U-151 may have been the most successful, but it was certainly not the only U-boat to threaten the New Jersey coast in 1918. In August, *U-117* torpedoed a tanker, the *Frederick R. Kellogg*, carrying oil eleven miles east of the New Jersey coast and thirty miles south of the Ambrose Channel Lightship. The tanker foundered on a shoal, spilling its 70,000 barrels of crude oil onto the beaches from Long Branch to Ocean City. In all, in just the first months of the war, German U-boats along the eastern coast of the United States sank 91 vessels of 166,907 tons, leaving 435 people dead.[10]

World war came to the Jersey Shore again in the 1940s; and again in the form of German U-boats. This time the U-boats could no longer feast on sailing ships, preferring instead oil tankers to slow down the Allied advance in Europe. More than 200 ships were lost to U-boats along the East Coast in the first months after the United States entered the war in January 1942, before it was prepared for the threat. Some of this shipping was lost within sight of the shore. In February, a U-boat torpedoed the merchant marine vessel *Resor*, which carried oil in a convoy from Houston, Texas, as it passed within twenty miles of the Manasquan Inlet; in March, *U-588* torpedoed the *Gulftrade* twelve miles from the North Monument; in May, *U-593* torpedoed the *Persephone*, just three miles off of the Barnegat Inlet. Schoolchildren watched as the *Persephone* burned and sank. Blimps searched the waters for any traces of the submarine that had risked coming so close to shore for the kill, but without success. Unlike the attacks during World War I, the men on the fallen ships during World War II did not always get the chance to row ashore. Some of the sailors on the *Resor* who fell in the water were so coated in oil they could not stay above water; some on the *Gulftrade* feared German attack if they manned the lifeboats and were lost with the ship. Of thirty-six on board the *Persephone*, only twenty-seven made it to shore where they were tended to by those who had witnessed the disaster from Long Beach Island. To avoid panic along the coast, these losses were not always reported by the government.

A recent discovery has brought this battle along the Jersey Shore close to home. In 1991, divers began looking in deep water sixty-five miles east of Point Pleasant Beach to determine if the reason for the extraordinary fishing at the spot was a sunken wreck. They were surprised to find a World War II German U-boat, 240 deep, bow first and upright in the sandy bottom. Its identity remained a mystery for some time. No records, American or German, placed a U-boat sinking at the spot. The wreckage lay so deep that the dives were dangerous, taking three lives before artifacts from the ship could determine its name: *U-869*, launched in October 1943. The divers confirmed their findings with serial numbers and personal items. German authorities had earlier believed that *U-869* was lost with its crew somewhere off the coast of Africa, the destination of its last orders. U.S. Naval records did not record a sinking at the site of the wreck, but did record that two U.S. destroyers escorting a convoy sent depth charges and hedgehogs after a suspected submarine on February 11, 1945. Sailors on board saw some oil and some air bubbles but not enough evidence to get credit for a hit. The matter was dropped for almost fifty years. PBS ran a NOVA episode titled "Hitler's Lost Sub" in 2000 and a book about the dive was published in 2004: *Shadow Divers* by Robert Kurson.[11]

The resort communities also experienced the impact of the war on their beaches. The Cape May Coast Guard Air Base became a Naval Air Station during the war and a number of Atlantic City hotels, including the Breakers, the Chelsea, the St. Charles and the Dennis, were leased by the United States Army, along with the Convention Hall, to house and train air corps trainees. Once the trainees completed their stay, thirteen Atlantic City hotels were converted to hospitals and convalescent facilities until the war's end with thousands of servicemen moving in and out during the course of the war. At least three hotels in Asbury Park were leased by the British army and navy and another in Bradley Beach by the U.S. Signal Corps. Coming out of the Great Depression, these military leases proved a boon to resort businesses. The Sisters of St. Joseph gave up their retreat house in Cape May Point to the military, to be used as a barracks. Desolate Island Beach was used by the Army to conduct high-secret bombing tests.

The war also brought limitations and restrictions: gas rationing, food shortages, limited train routes, oil-slicked beaches, beach curfews, and military orders to keep lights facing the ocean out or shielded at night. The restrictions faced some local resistance but soon became impediments to be worked around. Summer beach vacations did not stop despite the presence of troops or the threat of submarines and attack. Cape May welcomed thousands of soldiers to its beaches during the war and local commerce boards continued to advertise up and down the shore, assuring those interested that the beaches were safe and accessible. Atlantic City gambling, still illegal, flourished during the war as local incomes rose from war-related work.

FURTHER READING

For background on fires, see Alan A. Siegel, *Disaster! Stories of Death and Destruction in Nineteenth Century New Jersey* (New Brunswick, NJ: Rutgers University Press, 2014); and The Ocean County Compendium of History website at http://ochistory.org/Fires_-_Page_3.php.

On storms, see David M. Ludlum, *Early American Hurricanes, 1492–1870* (Boston, MA: American Meteorological Society, 1963) and *The New Jersey Weather Book* (New Brunswick, NJ: Rutgers University Press, 1983); Norbert P. Psulty and Douglas D. Ofiara, *Coastal Hazard Management, Lessons and Future Directions from New Jersey* (New Brunswick, NJ: Rutgers University Press, 2002); and Larry Savadove and Margaret Thomas Buccholz, *Great Storms of the Jersey Shore* (Harvey Cedars, NJ: Down the Shore Publishing, 1993).

On U-boats, see William Bell Clark, *When the U-Boats Came to America* (Boston, MA: Little Brown & Company, 1929); Robert Kerson, *Shadow Divers: The True Adventure of Two Americans Who Risked Everything to Solve One of the Last Mysteries of World War II* (New York: Random House, 2004); and the website uboat.net.

CHAPTER 10

The Rise of Resorts,
Atlantic County

The principal hotels in 1868 were the Surf House, United States Hotel, Congress Hall and Mansion House. None of these are now in existence. The other hotels, "the second class" houses of that day, numbered eleven. Besides these there were fifteen boarding houses—a total of thirty places of public entertainment. To-day the number is over seven hundred. At that time (1868) there were only three churches—the Methodist, open the year around, and the Presbyterian and Catholic Missions, open only a part of the year. No seaside resort in the world has grown as rapidly as Atlantic City, and none stands on a more secure foundation for future prosperity.
—Alfred M. Heston, *Absegami:*
Annals of Eyren Haven and Atlantic City, 1904

The Atlantic County beaches run from the sedge islands at the southern tip of Long Beach Island to the southern tip of Absecon Island. The development of Atlantic City dominates the history of the Atlantic County beaches. To the north is Brigantine, a city that encompasses its own island, and to the south are Ventnor, Margate, and Longport, three resorts that owe their existence and growth to the development of Atlantic City as a major resort after 1854. These neighboring towns arose from the overflow activity of Atlantic City, but have since developed their own personalities.

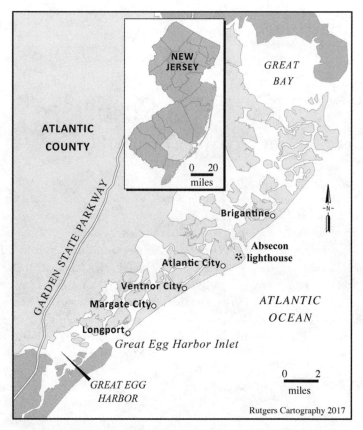

Map 7. Atlantic County Shore Communities and Lighthouses.
Map designed by Michael Siegel, Rutgers University.

ATLANTIC COUNTY

Brigantine is an island city that takes its name from the two-masted,
square-rigged ships of the sixteenth century. The Absecon Inlet separates
Brigantine from Atlantic City. The island developed in fits and starts and
its northern two miles of beach are now part of the Edwin B. Forsythe
National Wildlife Refuge, a natural haven for the barrier island red fox.
The history of Brigantine Island begins with pirates—including Captain
Kidd and Blackbeard—and shipwrecks. Brigantine was supposedly one of

the stops that Captain Kidd made on his last trip carrying the gold and luxury goods he looted in the Indian Ocean. Some say that a local beauty named Amanda captured Kidd's eye and the lovers buried his loot before Kidd was forced to flee (never, of course, to see the beauty or the gold again). Blackbeard allegedly escaped British authorities by floating underwater in the Brigantine sedges breathing through a local reed. Whatever the truth of these colorful stories, the coast, the inlets, and the sedges at Brigantine provided refuge for innumerable pirates traveling along the Jersey Shore in the 1600s and early 1700s. During the Revolutionary War, the *HMS Hastings*, which carried British troops, and the frigate *HMS Roebuck* with forty-four guns both wrecked on Brigantine's shores, and many more ships followed.

The earliest attempts to develop the island into a beach resort occurred in the late 1800s but did not pan out, in most part due to lack of access. At first, steamships carried Brigantine vacationers from Atlantic City and then a railroad bridge was built from Oceanville on the mainland in 1897. Developers saw hope and built hotels, a boardwalk, a golf club, and a (nonfunctional) lighthouse. An electric trolley line was erected from the Absecon Inlet to the Little Egg Harbor Inlet and ran double-decker trolleys along the beach. President Grover Cleveland stayed at one of Brigantine's hotels in the Gay Nineties. Unfortunately, the loss of the railroad bridge in a 1903 storm dashed development hopes and the little-used trolley system was abandoned in 1905. Twenty years later, another development company saw opportunity in Brigantine, laid out streets, and built recreational facilities. Low areas were filled in and millions of cubic feet of sand were trucked in to raise the island eight feet. An automobile bridge crossed the Absecon Inlet to Atlantic City in 1924, but the Great Depression put an end to these grand plans as well, which included a causeway for the improbable crossing of the Great Bay north to the mainland (which was never built).

The population of Brigantine was only 403 in 1940 but the close passage of the Garden State Parkway in the 1950s gave Brigantine another chance at success and the city began to gain population. The opening of hotels for casino gambling in Atlantic City in 1978 contributed to its year-round population, surpassing 12,000 in 2000. More than 2,000 condominiums and 1,700 apartments were built between 1975 and 2000. From 1976 to 1984 one of the most popular attractions in Brigantine was the Brigantine Castle, a fun house and haunted house located on a pier at the north end of the beach. It attracted thousands of visitors each year. (Its historical website claims one million visitors during its height of popularity.) The fun came to an end after a 1982 storm extensively damaged the pier. The castle closed two years later.

Brigantine also serves as the home of the Marine Mammal Stranding Center, a nonprofit organization that has rescued more than 4,500 turtles, whales, dolphins, and seals since 1978. Originally housed at Gardner's Basin in Atlantic City, the center moved to Brigantine in 1983 and operates an Educational Center and Observation Tank that is open to the public.

Three resorts south of Atlantic City—Ventnor, Margate, and Longport—share Absecon Island with the city, which was not always the case. When Atlantic City was first laid out it encompassed all of Absecon Island. The creek that separated Absecon Island from the island to its south filled in after 1854 (at Jackson Avenue today) and the adjacent island was captured. The Camden and Atlantic Land Company, affiliated with the railroad, acquired this land and ran tracks south in 1881. For the northernmost area, the company chose the name Ventnor, the suggestion of the wife of one of its officers, S. Bartram Richards. The couple had recently visited the seashore resort by that name on the British Isle of Wight. The railroad built the 300-bed Carisbrooke Inn in 1891, named after the Carisbrooke Castle at the British resort. Ventnor incorporated in 1903 and developed into a substantial community with many residences around the turn of the century. One of the oldest sections of the city is St. Leonard's, a compact community of about 300 homes built between 1906 and the end of the 1920s. This eight-block planned community contained deed restrictions to preserve its design characteristics and a community association chartered in 1921 still represents the residents before the city. One of its unique aspects is the naming of its streets after English dukes (e.g., Oxford, Cornwall, and Somerset). Another is that some of the homes, built during Prohibition, are alleged to have docks fitted for rum-running to service the illegal trade required by Atlantic City. New Jersey Governor Walter Edge had a home at Oxford Avenue at the beach in St. Leonard's and vice presidential nominee Hubert H. Humphrey stayed in one of the homes as he awaited the results of the 1964 Democratic Convention in Atlantic City.

Today, Ventnor includes condominiums, apartments, hotels, and motels as well. Its boardwalk extends from Atlantic City across the beachfront, but it is free of commercial establishments and amusements.

Lucy the Elephant resides in Margate. Her original purpose was to lure investors in the 1880s to the dunes that were then located in Egg Harbor Township along the railroad tracks. Lucy was one of two elephants built by James Lafferty, Jr., the other being the Light of Asia in Lower Township (Cape May County), which came down in 1900. A third elephant on a beach, built on Coney Island (the Colossus), burned down in 1884. Lucy remains, protected by the Save Lucy Committee created in 1970, and is now owned by the city of Margate. New Jersey's tusked elephant has been used as a hotel, a restaurant, a tavern, a summer home, and simply as an attraction. James Lafferty brought prospective real estate purchasers to Margate in the 1880s to see Lucy and climb her 130 steps to the "howdah" on top for a panoramic view of the beach and its environs. Visitors have included President Woodrow Wilson, John Jacob Astor, Henry Ford, and the Rajah of Bhong. Lucy has survived a lightning strike in 2006 and numerous coastal storms, including the horrific 1944 storm that took out most of the Margate boardwalk and Superstorm Sandy in 2012. She was added to the National Registry of Historic Places in 1971 and designated a National Historic Landmark in 1976.

The first land transaction for what is now Margate can be traced to 1695 when Thomas Bud purchased it for four cents an acre, but little happened on this strip of beach until the railroad and Lucy arrived in the 1880s. Earlier, the land was covered with bayberry, holly, and wild plums, and was known for its snakes and thick brush. Margate began as the borough of Atlantic City South (1885) and then as the city of Atlantic City South (1897). In 1909, like its northern neighbor, the city named itself after an English resort. Margate attracts a substantial summer population and had more than 6,300 year-round residents in 2010. Margate includes, within its city limits, the planned seaside community of Marven Gardens, a real estate development built in accordance with the ideals of the nineteenth-century Cottage Cities movement that encouraged beautifully landscaped second-home communities that captured the contours of their surroundings. This early 1900s community is immortalized in the high-end property Marvin Gardens in the board game Monopoly, which is set in nearby Atlantic City. And, indeed, the original owners were mostly affluent professionals seeking a home near the beach. The name "Marven" (misspelled in Monopoly) is a combination of Margate and Ventnor. The development was once also known as Winchester Gardens and was placed on the National Registry of Historic Places in 1990.

Longport is the southernmost community on Absecon Island and was incorporated in 1898. The borough is named for John Long, who purchased some property in 1857. Its area has ebbed and flowed with the tides, the sea creating and taking dunes and beach. The streets once known as

First through Tenth streets (180 acres) became attached to the island to its southwest after 1900 and are now part of Ocean City. John Long's home on the beach was utilized as a sanatorium around 1900 and Longport hosted several institutions for the care of the disabled thereafter. Peter Widener built the Summer Seashore Home for Handicapped Children along the beach in 1911 for children suffering from infantile paralysis or tuberculosis of the spine. In the early 1940s the Seashore Home was converted to a treatment facility for World War II soldiers. It became a hotel in 1944 and then the Gospel Hall Home for the Aged in 1949. The building was recently demolished. The Betty Bacharach Home for the Afflicted opened in 1924 and also served children with infantile paralysis until it moved in 1975. Eventually this building became the borough hall. A Lifesaving Station (#29, Great Egg/Ocean City) first began operations in 1849 and its successor 1939 building now houses the Longport Historical Society Museum.

Just five miles from Atlantic City, Longport is a fully developed residential community with a mix of permanent residents and seasonal owners. About half of the permanent population is over the age of fifty. Over the past thirty years many of the town's gingerbread cottages, Cape Cods, and bungalows were demolished to build duplexes near the beach. The boardwalk and amusement centers were destroyed by storms in this same period and Longport keeps a watchful eye on the erosion it continually faces from the tidal action and storms that impact its beaches.

ATLANTIC CITY, POLITICS, AND PROHIBITION

Atlantic City was created by a monopoly and gilded its success with powerful promotion. Absecon Island had no history of vacationers attracted to its beaches (other than the Unalatchtigo natives before the 1800s). As described earlier, the Island had the size necessary for a resort city, a somewhat gentler undertow, and promoters with a vision. The city's advantage became access by rail embellished with a sales pitch for the supposed healthful lifestyle year round near the beach. The thousands disembarking from the trains in Absecon bought the dream even though trains soon found their way to Long Branch and Cape May and alternative destinations. Despite competition from newly minted New Jersey resorts, New York beaches, Saratoga Springs, lodges, and lakes, Atlantic City prospered on promotion and glitz. Just like the hawkers on the Boardwalk who drew in strollers with slick talk and colorful gimmicks, Atlantic City lured crowds to its beach. The thrill of being there was enough to satisfy. Indeed, one of the underlying mottos of the local boosters was "Ocean, emotion and plenty of promotion."[1]

To the general public, Atlantic City offered the pleasures described in its marketing brochures: sea, sun, taffy, entertainment, and relatively wholesome fun. The politicians in control of the city made certain that the commercial needs of the city were fulfilled so that the crowds would return every summer and find it as expected. Atlantic City also offered gambling and prostitution. Gambling, legal in the early years of the city's rise, became illegal in New Jersey after the turn of the century; prostitution was always illegal, but its availability in the city was well known, especially to conventioneers. Both gambling and prostitution flourished with the knowing acceptance of those same politicians who carefully guarded the more wholesome public image of the city. Perhaps as a result of this dichotomy, the city's politics developed into one-party rule shortly after the city took shape, then into boss rule, and continued that way for more than a hundred years. For some, this avoided political conflicts and focused the city's efforts on its tourist trade; for others, boss rule bred corruption. Without question, Atlantic City's politicians provided support for legitimate businesses while at the same time providing protection for those offering more tawdry pleasures. The latter operations had the advantage of bringing business into the city in the cold months when business was otherwise slow.

In the last decades of the 1800s, three men—County Clerk Louis Scott, Congressman John Gardner, and Sheriff Smith Johnson—ran the city. The first true boss was Louis Kuehnle, known as the Commodore" who came to the city to manage his father's hotel in 1865 at the age of eighteen. In 1900, after the death of Louis Scott, Kuehnle assumed control of the city with Smith Johnson as his right-hand man. Kuehnle led the Republican Party, which dominated elections in the city. He recognized the importance of those who worked in the hotels and on the Boardwalk during the summer months and made sure that the workers and their families could make it through the winter with generous handouts and benefits. This was particularly true for the residents of the Northside black neighborhood where the jobless winters were tough. This beneficence was rewarded at the ballot box and a strong ward system maintained control. Kuehnle supported civic projects to the same purpose, including a sturdy Boardwalk, utilities, and freshwater. Of course, these projects also provided the mechanism to funnel financial benefits to himself and his supporters.

The inevitable backlash came from aggressive newspaper men, church leaders, and reforming politicians at the state level, especially when evidence of prostitution in the city came to light. Madams driven from Philadelphia at the turn of the century settled in Atlantic City and more than one hundred houses were easily identified in one exposé. As a result, reformer campaigns led to grand jury indictments in 1911 against Kuehnle and more than a hundred city and county officials for election fraud. But the indictments led to few convictions. Eventually, Governor Woodrow Wilson's attorney general obtained a conviction against Kuehnle for taking funds from a water project. He went to prison in 1913 for one year and upon his return to Atlantic City he found Enoch "Nucky" Johnson (Smith Johnson's son) in control of the organization.

Prohibition provided opportunities for Atlantic City. The Eighteenth Amendment ratified in 1919 forbade the sale or consumption of alcoholic beverages throughout the United States. At the shore, the inlets, bays, and inland rivers once again accommodated small boats loaded with illicit cargo. This time instead of smugglers or privateers it was bootleggers and rumrunners avoiding Coast Guard ships to provide alcohol for revelers and thirsty drinkers in Atlantic City, throughout the state, and throughout the nation during the thirteen dry years from 1920 to 1933. Although passed as a noble cause, Prohibition did not take hold in New Jersey and the rise of bootleggers and rumrunners was not discouraged by locals. Just as in the 1700s, everyone, especially in the backwaters of the state, knew of someone in the trade and occasionally enjoyed the illicit cargo brought to shore. Enforcement by state and local police was spotty at best throughout New Jersey; local authorities were reluctant or simply unwilling to enforce the law; the local population, whether in their homes, at speakeasies, or at hotels along the shore, flouted the law, in part because the availability of booze was so widespread. Federal authorities cracked down now and then, but the Coast Guard, especially in the early years of Prohibition, literally could not keep pace with fast New Jersey boats operating from all points up and down the coast, especially from Atlantic City to Cape May.

A line of Canadian vessels sat just outside the legal limit off the Jersey Shore (originally set at three miles and extended to twelve miles in 1924) loaded with alcohol for sale to professional bootleggers or individuals on pleasure boats willing to risk the water and the feds. "Rum Row," as this became known, acted as a wholesale operation for the illegal transport of liquor. The Roaring Twenties were fueled by the engines of Jersey skiffs, faster and more agile than the Coast Guard boats chasing them into the coves and bays. Rumrunners, incentivized by the large profits to be made, would often run without lights at night or in fog to avoid detection. These dangerous activities in New Jersey waters sent many of them to the bottom along with their cargo before reaching shore. Unfortunately, the trade became the livelihood of gangsters and led to violence close to shore. One newspaper account in October 1924 tells of the Coast Guard chasing two darkly painted boats early in the morning through the Little Egg Harbor Inlet and into the Mullica River near Chestnut Neck. The Coast Guard fired a cannon across the bow of the bootleggers' lead boat but they remained at full throttle and returned fire. A Coast Guard machine gun decided the battle, forcing the bootleggers over the side to swim to shore. No wrongdoers were captured, but the boats, including the lead with a hot 300-horsepower motor, were taken along with their cargo: 170 cases of liquor worth more than $24,000 that included a case of Champagne, most likely headed for revelers in nearby Atlantic City. The newspaper reporter filing the account assured the reading public that the hard stuff was distributed to local hospitals after it was tested and found to be pure! (No mention was made about who got the Champagne.[2]) A *New York Times* article earlier in the same year describes a gun battle so close to the Atlantic City shore that bullets sprayed across the Boardwalk. Five cruisers, allegedly laden with booze, escaped in the fog and a few early morning Atlantic City strollers on the Boardwalk complained to authorities about the carelessness of the Coast Guard gunners.[3]

Prohibition proved a boon for Atlantic City. Its reputation as a "wet town" became well known and kept hoteliers and local businesses in the black during the Depression, even in the winter months, as a playground for the connected and licentious in Philadelphia. The city's ruling elite benefited financially from the liquor trade, along with gambling dens and houses of ill repute. Nucky Johnson established an understanding with the mobsters handling the booze that ensured them safe passage, using the police force to make sure that their activities were undisturbed. The extent of the city's mob connections was dramatized by the May 1929 convention of mob bosses hosted in Atlantic City by Johnson that included Lucky Luciano, Frank Costello, Meyer Lansky, and Al Capone, among others. This history provided the basis for the HBO series *Boardwalk Empire*, a recent and colorful recounting of New Jersey's rum running days set in Atlantic City during the Roaring Twenties. The fabulous Convention Hall, 196,000 square feet and able to accommodate more than

20,000 people for an event, was constructed during Prohibition in antici-
pation of a growing convention business at a location that had no qualms
about serving alcohol. Its dedication on May 31, 1929, just days after the
mob convention, demonstrated the lack of concern about enforcement of
the country's liquor laws. The Convention Center boosted the city's claim
as a year-round attraction. The opening ceremonies were attended by the
U.S. vice president and Commodore Kuehnle who was now a city commissioner, having been elected after his one year stint in prison for rack-
eteering and his return to the city. Nucky Johnson maintained one-man
control of the city until his luck ran out in 1941 with a conviction for rack-
eteering. Johnson served four years of a ten-year sentence and returned
to lead a quiet life in the city thereafter.

When Prohibition ended in 1933, table games and card games could
still be found in the back rooms of respectable nightclubs. One of the most
famous was "Skinny" D'Amato's 500 Club. First-class entertainers like
Frank Sinatra, Patti Page, and Liberace would play these clubs and celebrities like Joe DiMaggio and Elizabeth Taylor could be seen there. Those
in the know simply passed through a guarded door after the show to a
back room. Atlantic City immediately embraced legalized horse-race
gambling as well in 1946 when the New Jersey Legislature lifted its
ban. The original stockholders of the Atlantic City Racetrack included
entertainers—Bob Hope, Frank Sinatra, Harry James, Sammy Kaye, and
Xavier Cugat—who understood the importance of attractions to draw
crowds to Atlantic City. Nevertheless, the repeal of Prohibition in 1933
hurt the city's fortunes. Without the unique attraction of alcohol, the age
and disrepair of the hotels and businesses in the city became glaringly
evident and foreshadowed the ultimate decline of a city that had always
had an angle to bring in the crowds.

After Johnson's conviction, control of the Republican Party organization and the city turned over to Frances "Hap" Farley who became a
strong figure in the state as well as the city. He served as president of the

state senate for more than two decades after his election in 1940. At the time, New Jersey's constitution provided that each county had only one senator, regardless of size, which gave the smaller counties and the strong men that ruled them disproportionate power in the state. Farley maintained a hold on the twenty-one New Jersey state senators through his energy and political skills. He required every governor to deal with him directly and other senators sought his support for their county's needs. Farley controlled all legislation that moved in the upper chamber. He used his power to look out for Atlantic City and Atlantic County. Corruption still ran rampant in Atlantic City, however, and exposés, investigations, and indictments continued into the 1970s, naming and capturing officials on a regular basis. Nonetheless, Farley wielded his influence throughout these years without personally running afoul of the newspapers or the prosecutors. His political end came in a lost election in 1971 after the city's and county's demographics changed.

Further Reading

For background, see Jon Blackwell, *Notorious New Jersey: 100 True Tales of Murders and Mobsters, Scandals and Scoundrels* (New Brunswick, NJ: Rutgers University Press, 2008); John T. Cunningham and Kenneth D. Cole, *Atlantic City* (Charleston, SC: Arcadia Publishing, 2000); Charles E. Funnell, *By the Beautiful Sea: The Rise and High Times of That Great American Resort, Atlantic City* (New Brunswick, NJ: Rutgers University Press, 1983); Nelson Johnson, *Boardwalk Empire* (Medford, NJ: Plexus Publishing, 2002) and *The Northside, African-Americans and the Creation of Atlantic City* (Medford, NJ: Plexus Publishing, Inc., 2010); David Nasaw, *Going Out: The Rise and Fall of Public Amusements* (Boston, MA: Harvard University Press, 1993); David G. Schwartz, *Boardwalk Playground: The Making, Unmaking, and Remaking of*

Atlantic City (Las Vegas, NV: Winchester Books, 2015); Jonathan VanMeter, *The Last Good Time, Skinny D'Amato, the 500 Club, and the Rise and Fall of Atlantic City* (New York: Crown Publishers, 2003); and Victoria W. Wolcott, *Race, Riots, and Roller Coasters: The Struggle over Segregated Recreation in America* (Philadelphia: University of Pennsylvania Press, 2012).

CHAPTER 11

Fish, Fish, and Boats

The most picturesque portion of Seabright is the old fishing village of Nauvoo, the largest fishery on the coast. The proximity of the Shrewsbury Rocks, a famous fishing ground, and the easy slope of the strand, making the launching of boats frequently less dangerous than elsewhere south along the coast, attracted fishermen to this spot already some fifty years ago. . . . To anyone with an eye for artistic effects, Nauvoo and the beach in front of it form one of the most picturesque spots on the coast. Against the quaintly-peaked ice-houses nearest the strand winter storms have piled all sorts of flotsam. The beach is a scene of varied activity. A boat is lying with prow seaward and her little white jib and sprit sail hoisted. A fisherman stands at her bow, another near her stern. They shove her through the glistening surf, and, as she rises buoyantly on the incoming billow, leap into her as a rider leaps into the saddle.

—Gustav Kobbé, *The New Jersey Coast and Pines*, 1889

Fishing began at the Jersey Shore well before the coming of Europeans in 1664. Native Americans traveled to the shore to take shellfish from the bays and estuaries for their food value and their shells. The first European settlers along the Jersey Shore came for the whales. Although whales are mammals, not fish, the effort to capture them requires similar skills. European clammers and oystermen followed and the volume of shellfish taken from New Jersey's waters in the twenty-first century remains significant. The fishing industry, which includes commercial fin fishing, shellfish operations and aquaculture, sport fishing, and all the connected activities, contributes more than $4 billion annually to the New Jersey economy.[1]

Sport fishing has a long tradition in New Jersey's ocean waters and bays, as does gunning. In the twentieth century, gunning became less prevalent, but sport fishing has become a significant economic factor. The aggregate catch of sports fishermen rivals that of commercial fishermen in the region. In the peak season, thousands of boats are docked along New Jersey's bays, lagoons, and marinas waiting to take to the water for a one-day fishing trip or an overnight fishing adventure. Sport fishermen often find themselves in conflict with commercial fishermen and, in recent years, environmentalists have joined them in demanding limits on the commercial catch to protect endangered species and sport favorites.

COMMERCIAL FISHING AND NEW JERSEY'S MAJOR PORTS

Early commercial fishing activity at the Jersey Shore centered on clams and oysters, not fin fishing. Before advances in ship propulsion and machinery, New Jersey fin fishermen stayed close to shore in small boats. Markets needed to be close by to reap the benefits of a large catch. Today, six major ports support commercial fishing in New Jersey and highly developed farming techniques, known as "aquaculture," have revitalized the shellfish industry along the coast and the estuaries. In all, New Jersey commercial fishermen take more than a hundred varieties of fin fish and shellfish, providing fresh fish to local restaurants and delicacies to distant consumers around the world. And, like all aspects of the Jersey Shore, the industry differs from town to town and port to port.

The importance of oysters in New Jersey can be traced back to legislation in 1719 that regulated the harvesting of oysters from New Jersey's waters, prohibited out-of-staters from taking the oysters, and established county enforcers for the policy.[2] In the late 1800s, oysters were the dominant seafood on the market, providing a great source of protein. Oysters pulled from ocean sites along the coast, the Delaware Bay, and from beds along the rivers and estuaries, were shipped directly to New York City,

Philadelphia, and Washington, DC, by railroad cars to feed the demand of oyster bars. Port Norris, in Cumberland County, became a thriving seaport in large part due to the oyster beds along the Delaware River. Nearby towns—among them the aptly named Bivalve and Shellpile—were developed for processing and shipping, which attests to the depth of this market. Oyster gathering supported 250 families in Tuckerton in the last decades of the 1800s and more than 1,000 boats of all types were employed in the oyster trade in Atlantic County alone. Oysters were not the only shellfish taken in numbers from New Jersey waters. Tuckerton supplied more than 60,000 clams each day to nearby markets at the end of the nineteenth century.[3] The demand for oysters lessened, however, when a typhoid outbreak in 1927 was blamed erroneously on oysters served in the shell. And the market was devastated in the late 1950s by a parasite that destroyed the valuable oyster beds up and down the eastern seacoast. Only in the 1990s, after considerable work and nurturing, has the New Jersey oyster harvest returned to a robust position in the state's economy. New Jersey's oyster beds are now carefully studied and monitored to ensure that the harvest is safe to eat. As a result, Port Norris remains one of New Jersey's six major ports: 3.4 million pounds of oysters valued at $4.9 million were harvested through Port Norris in 1999.[4]

In the early 1800s, fin fishing along the Jersey Shore depended on small boats launching from its beaches, which meant that commercial fishermen could only reach fish that were close to shore on daily runs. Sailing ships carried just a few men and they did not have the benefit of fish-finding equipment like modern-day sonar. The sleek design of sailing ships limited the capacity for any significant catch at sea; the unavailability of gear needed for hauling fish onboard and preserving them when caught also limited the catch. Most fish were caught using hand lines.

The activity around Nauvoo, the small fishing village in what is now Sea Bright provides a good example of the life of early commercial fishermen. Nauvoo hosted 250 ships during the summer days of the 1880s, and the fishermen lived in small shacks on the beach. Some of the ships had to be carried from the Shrewsbury River to the beach, but the effort was worth the reward. A catch of up to 150 pounds of fish in a single day could be shipped immediately to New York for sale.[5]

By the mid-1800s, some enterprising fishermen developed a new way to take fish from New Jersey's waters, known as pound fishing. The fishermen would establish permanent pounds, or weirs, at regular intervals within two miles of shore using saplings hammered into the ocean floor and wrapped in netting. Fish entering at one end would become trapped and could be taken without lines or long ocean voyages. Scandinavian, Portuguese, and Austrian fishermen perfected this form of fishing in the 1930s with large pounds established up and down the coast at Sandy Hook, Sea Bright, Monmouth Beach, Elberon, Deal, Bradley Beach, Spring Lake, Sea Girt, Manasquan, Point Pleasant, Bay Head, Mantoloking, Chadwick, Seaside, Long Beach Island, Sea Isle City, and Cape May.[6] As many as seventy men would launch boats from the beach to empty the nets once or twice a day. When the boats reached the surf near the beach, they would be hauled ashore by horses. The boats were a Jersey design, Sea Bright skiffs, and the horses were Clydesdales, chosen for their strength. On the beach, the fish were sorted, packed, and iced in buildings erected for the purpose. Like the Nauvoo fishermen, some of these men lived in shacks on the beach during the season.

At its peak, pound fishing brought in 300,000 to 400,000 pounds of fish from April through November, mostly bluefish, but also weakfish, butterfish, and bonita. Nevertheless, pound fishing came to an end in 1962. Severe storms in the 1940s and 1950s destroyed many of the pounds and they were not rebuilt. By the 1950s fishermen could venture far out to sea with the strength and speed of petroleum-based engines and could also trawl the bottom effectively for scallops and clams. Pound catches were becoming smaller and competed with the tourist business for the use of the beaches. As can easily be imagined, pound fishing attracted mosquitoes and flies to the beach and created an awful stench in the summer. Most vacationers were happy to see pound fishing come to an end when the last pound net was taken down.

Today, New Jersey's commercial fishermen use the latest gear and equipment, as well as spot planes, to find large schools of fish far out to sea; motorized dredges and trawlers are utilized to take mollusks from the ocean floor. Breakthroughs in storing and processing the fish on the boats and onshore have increased markets locally and worldwide. For example, refrigerated lockers allow ships to remain at sea for days at a time, especially in the warm summer months; and sea clams dredged from the bottom of the ocean that were once inedible have now become a valuable haul for clam chowder and clam strips with the development of methods for cleaning them of sand and waste. Once brought in to shore, a fresh catch can be served within hours at local seafood restaurants and in New York or Philadelphia. Some fish, such as monkfish, bigeye tuna, butterfish, and eels are marketed in Europe and as far away as Asia.

The commercial fishermen at Cape May epitomize high-tech fin fishing in New Jersey. The port at Cape May ranks among the largest seaports in the United States. Its fishermen venture out on extended sea journeys to capture scallops, mackerel, and squid, as well as shellfish and menhaden, using the most modern techniques for catching, preserving, and processing fish on board. A fishing history that started with thirty-five families chasing whales from the beach now employs thousands of fishermen, fish packers, and fish processors. Moving north, the fishing business changes. In Atlantic County, fishermen depend almost entirely on shellfish, particularly sea clams and quahogs. The latter are hard-shelled clams found on the ocean bottom, not necessarily close to shore. Unlike the smaller and sweeter "little necks" and "cherrystones," these are the shellfish marketed to food companies for use in chowders and strips. The ocean beds have been seeded in the last several decades to ensure continued good harvests. The Atlantic City fishermen stay closer to home than their Cape May counterparts and in smaller boats, not just out in the ocean but in the creeks and estuaries of the sedge islands that make up the coast in Atlantic County.

The commercial fishermen docked at Viking Village in Barnegat Light on Long Beach Island fish in deep water, at the edge of the Continental Shelf, using long lines to bring in a variety of fin fish. In the 1970s, Barnegat Light was considered the "tilefish capital of the world," but the disappearance of tilefish led to increased hauls of swordfish, shark, and tuna. Scallopers from Barnegat Light dredge sea scallops from George's Bank, shallow water located about 100 miles west of Cape Cod. The Viking Village in Barnegat Light has also become a colorful and unique destination at the shore, with shops and restaurants located close to the water and close to the boats and the fishermen. Charter boats and head boats are available during the summer months for vacationers who yearn to feel the ocean spray and the pull of blues and other sport fish on the line. A charter boat takes a group for the day; a head board takes individual tourists at set times for fish or just the ride and usually for just a few hours. Barnegat Light is one spot where commercial fishing activities have been successfully integrated with sport fishing and resort traffic. A trip to the north end of Long Beach Island can include a tour of the lighthouse and majestic views of the inlet as the fishing fleet passes out and back from the Atlantic Ocean.

The Point Pleasant docks have been the home for commercial fisherman since 1810 when Charles Loveland founded a village named Lovelandtown to accommodate clammers and fishermen (mostly family members) looking to take advantage of the abundant fish varieties in the nearby waters.[7] Today, the docks accommodate mostly medium-sized boats taking one or two day trips not too far off the shore looking for mackerel, squid, fluke and silver hake. Clam and scallop dredgers also operate from these docks, which at one point included a large clam processing center. In the 1950s commercial fishermen joined together to form one of only two cooperatives in the state (the other is in Belford), combining resources to operate the docks, sell their fish, and run a seaside restaurant. Many of the fishermen working the seas from Point Pleasant are the third generation; their fathers and grandfathers created the cooperative. In all, the Point Pleasant docks provide an active maritime experience for commercial fishermen, sport fishermen engaging head boats and charter boats, and tourists looking for good seafood.

Fishermen at Belford, on the bay side of Sandy Hook, make their living on menhaden, a fish no one eats. Menhaden is an oily fish used primarily for bait, fertilizer, and animal feed. Most historians believe that the advice given by the Massachusetts Native Americans to the Puritans to place a fish head in each planting refers to menhaden, an abundant species all along the north Atlantic coast. Not very appetizing, but an important fish. The oil is an ingredient in paint, linoleum, cosmetics, and margarine. In recent years, the demand for fish oil as a nutrition supplement has increased the demand for menhaden. These fish are often called mossbunker or bunker and are a staple for sport fishermen as bait and "chum." Commercial fishermen use a method called purse seining to catch menhaden. They surround a large school of fish with netting and then pull it tight at the bottom to trap the fish. The catch is then sucked onto the ship by vacuum and other varieties of fish are separated from the catch. Once the most abundant fish in the ocean, conservationists worry that overfishing, climate change, or both, are responsible for a three-decade-long drop in menhaden volume. In New Jersey, the menhaden take fell from a high of 486,224,400 pounds in 1956 to just 1,581,600 pounds in 1983. In more recent years, the take has rebounded but varies considerably from year to year, hitting a recent high of 85,457,890 pounds in 2012. The overfishing controversy has led to increasingly restrictive bans on purse seining in New Jersey's bays and near the coast. Sport fishermen who use bunker as bait and who fish for bluefish, striped bass, and weakfish find themselves in conflict with commercial fishermen on this issue because the decreasing volume of menhaden impacts the availability of their favorite fish that feed on menhaden.

Recent statistics confirm the strength of New Jersey's commercial fishing industry. More than 187 million pounds of seafood was caught and sold in 2011 at a value of $220 million. Again, like the menhaden take that comprises a significant portion of the catch, the total has varied considerably from a high of 540 million pounds in 1956 to just above 90 million pounds in 1982, but the value of the catch has remained above $100 million since 2000, which illustrates the continued importance of fishing to New Jersey's economy.[8]

THE *LADY MARY* AND THE DANGERS OF COMMERCIAL FISHING

One aspect of commercial fishing that seldom concerns landlubbers but must be at the forefront of thought for every fisherman setting out of port on a rainy day, is the danger. Commercial fishing is a dangerous business and clamming is the deadliest occupation in the United States by a long shot. More than 545 fishermen died at sea in the ten years from 2000 to 2010 and the most hazardous fishing grounds are along the Atlantic coast. The death rate in the United States is 111.8 per 100,000 in the industry (by comparison, the death rate for police is 21.8), and more than one hundred fishermen have been killed on fishing boats off the Jersey Shore since 1931.[9] Dredging for clams is a winter activity when the ocean is freezing and unpredictable. Clam boats, only partially regulated for safety, can become unstable when fully loaded. For a boat miles offshore, a sudden storm can quickly make a profitable two days at sea a life-and-death event. If a fisherman finds himself in the water at the height of the season without a survival suit, his life span can be measured in just minutes. Douglas A. Campbell's 2002 book, *The Sea's Bitter Harvest*, details the life of Jersey clammers and the loss of four clamboats over thirteen days shortly after the first of the year in January 1999.[10] Captains may stay with a boat for years, but most crew come and go looking for a good payday from a one-week gig. They all know the risk and the names of men who did not make it back to shore, but they go out anyway.

The recent loss of the *Lady Mary* underscores the risk. *Star Ledger* reporter Amy Ellis Nutt won a Pulitzer prize for her coverage of the loss of the *Lady Mary* sixty-six miles off of Cape May on March 24, 2009. Six of its seven-man crew died that night when the ship sank suddenly.[11] The lone survivor was plucked from the freezing waters of the Atlantic. The *Lady Mary* was a scalloper, dredging the bottom of the ocean for a lucrative catch over five to seven days. She had left Cape May six days earlier hoping for a valuable harvest that could sustain the owners, the captain, and crew for weeks, up to $15,000 per man. Fishermen on dredgers can only go out a limited number of days each year, but their time on the sea, day and night at work or on alert, totals more hours than the average working man piles up onshore each year. Whatever happened to the *Lady Mary*—and it is still a mystery—happened quickly; so quickly that most of the crew did not have the time or the ability to don lifesaving survivor suits or to access the self-inflating lifeboat required to be on board. The crew had had a successful run for scallops at the Elephant Trunk fishing grounds, south-southwest of Cape May, and were soon to begin the journey home when the *Lady Mary* simply disappeared under the early morning waters. As Ms. Nutt of the *Star Ledger* put it, how could "a sound and stable boat with an experienced crew disappear from the ocean's surface in a matter of minutes and leave so few clues behind?"

The five-part *Star Ledger* story came close to providing an answer. The winds and sea were rough that night, but not so rough that the boat would be so quickly swamped. The reporters suggested that a 722-foot German container ship, the *Cap Beatrice*, traveling at twenty knots through the fishing grounds on its way to the entrance of the Delaware Bay for the trip to Philadelphia, may have clipped the seventy-one-foot *Lady Mary* in the darkness forcing her down to the bottom in seconds. The reporters detail the rescue effort and the subsequent Coast Guard inspection. They present a telling case for a collision including the proximity of the container ship, the quick sinking, and damage found to the stern and the rudder of the *Lady Mary* (laying on the ocean bottom) by divers weeks and months later. Collisions, like furious seas and careless seamanship, take lives every year from commercial fishing fleets. Four and a half years after the sinking, the Coast Guard finally issued a report and attributed the sinking of the *Lady Mary* to an open hatch, rough seas, and poor seamanship. The experts questioned by the reporters and the families of the lost seamen disagree.

Sport Fishing, Gunning, and Recreational Boating

Sport fishing goes hand-in-hand with New Jersey's summer tourism trade as many of the families spending time at the shore spend part of that time in boats, on docks, or at the beach hoping to bring in dinner or just to feel the thrill of pulling in a "big one."

In many ways, sport fishing and tourism compete with commercial fishing for real estate along the coast, for access to the bays and oceans, and for the limited amount of fish available for the taking. Many groups and the state government have worked to eliminate some of the tension that these economic and environmental clashes create and are hoping to create models that create synergies instead. Sport fishing at the Jersey Shore differs from commercial fishing in almost every respect other than its significant economic advantages. Sport fishermen stay relatively close to shore, fish mostly for fin varieties that are not as valuable to the commercial industry, and view their time on the water as fun, not hard work. New Jersey's fleet of charter boats and party boats is the largest on the east coast[12] and the volume and value of the take of sport fishermen rivals that of commercial fishermen. As a result, these two groups often conflict, if not over particular fish (although this sometimes occurs), then over the best ways to maintain the shore's fishing resources and ecology.

If on boats, Jersey sport fishermen can be found in small motorboats in the bays and estuaries, and on larger boats far into the Atlantic Ocean, depending on their preferences and the fish they are seeking. Jersey

fishermen can also be found on the beaches "surf fishing" or "surf cast-
ing" and at the bays and piers with rods, reels, and crab cages. The origin
of surf fishing has been traced to an intrepid couple who waded into the
surf at Beach Haven on Long Beach Island early one morning in 1907
with fishing gear. The woman caught a twenty-pound striped bass, word
spread, and the activity became a sensation once New Jersey's anglers
realized that striped bass could be taken right from the beach if an angler
could get his line out beyond the breakers.[13] Thousands of New Jersey
fishermen enjoy the beauty and solitude of the beach on early mornings,
late afternoons, and evenings angling for the thrill of the catch, albeit only
now and then. The few tourists strolling on the beach pass by and wonder
how the fishermen can derive so much pleasure from so passive an activity. Perhaps the tourists should attend the Governor's Annual Surf Fishing Tournament held each May since 1992 at Island Beach State Park. In
2014, a resident of Atco, New Jersey, caught a thirty-two-inch striped bass
to win the competition. Awards are also given for kingfish, bluefish, and
blackfish.[14]

Charter boats can take large numbers of passengers out to sea for a
half-day trip, all day, or all night. The smaller head boats stay closer to
shore and limit the number of fishermen to just a few. "Blues," a good-
eating fish that also put up a strenuous fight on the line, were once the
mainstay of these boats. But the bluefish have a habit of disappearing
every now and then, so the charter boat captains thrill their charges with
weakfish, blackfish, drum, shark, and striped bass when the blues are not
running. The larger boats go as far as the Continental Shelf with heavy
gear for several varieties of tuna. The tuna ran heavy off the New Jersey
coast in the 1930s, so much so that the Annual US Tuna Fishing Tournament was held from New Jersey docks until the catch fell off in the 1950s.
The season ran from June to September and the catch had been so strong
that six commercial boats calling in to Beach Haven on the same day in
1933 brought home 187 tuna.[15] Today, New Jersey's anglers can still try
to land "the big one" in the annual Manasquan Marlin and Tuna Club

Tournament. The winning fish in the 2015 Bluefin Tuna tournament weighed more than fifty-three pounds.

Except for the equipment, summertime bay fishermen today do not differ much from their predecessors, one or just a few men at most in a small boat using hook and line trying to bring home dinner. In the 1800s, these fishermen used drop lines, then used bamboo for poles and, by the turn of the twentieth century, rods and reels with ever-increasing efficiency. Weakfish are a common game fish for bay fishers along with striped bass, sheepshead, and kingfish. "Gunning" was a winter sport, for teals, broadbills, mallards, and shelldrakes. Hunters came to the Jersey Shore from October to December and the Barnegat Bay offered a veritable playground for these sportsmen who would travel in easy-to-maneuver boats designed for shallow waters or would spend days in shacks on small islands. Boarding houses and small hotels accommodated sportsmen throughout the year, often in rustic settings that were found mostly on the mainland opposite the barrier islands, such as in Forked River, Waretown, Toms River, Manahawkin, West Creek, and Tuckerton. The Harvey Cedar Hotel on Long Beach Island catered to this crowd as did the hotels and clubs further south near Beach Haven and Tucker's Island, including the high-end Peahala Hunting Club.

Boats were designed specifically for fishing and hunting and variations on these designs can still be found along the shore. The classic Barnegat Bay "sneakbox" was designed in 1834 by Hazelton Seaman of West Creek as a functional boat for hunting waterfowl and fishing in the bay. The original sneakbox was about twelve feet long and built for one person. Its low profile and flat bottom allows it to remain stable in shallow or rough water. It has occasionally been described as a "floating duckblind." Sneakboxes were often camouflaged with sea grass and the boats could get their occupants home by sail or oar. Another popular boat from the 1880s was the Sea Bright skiff. The standard skiff was sixteen to thirty-six feet long, with an unstayed mast, rounded sides, and a flat bottom. The Sea Bright skiff was the boat of choice for the original lifesaving crews along New

Jersey's beaches and a practical sailor for pound fishermen. Rumrunners also found them useful in the 1920s equipped then with outboard motors. Lifeguards and recreational sailors still use modified versions of the skiff at the Jersey Shore. The "Cat" boat developed as a functional fishing boat with its mast placed toward the bow, allowing room in the open cockpit and with a wide beam providing storage for the catch. Its shallow draft could handle the shoals but it could navigate the inlets and hold its own in open water. The "Garvey" dates back to the 1700s and may be the oldest boat type in Jersey's waters. It is suitable for dredging for clams and harvesting other shellfish, with a flat bottom and open cockpit.[16]

These boats have been redesigned over the last 150 years to make them faster for the sailing and racing clubs developed just before the turn of the twentieth century. The membership in these clubs was limited—yachting was a wealthy man's sport—but the competitive races and colorful regattas on holidays drew thousands to the shore in the first half of the twentieth century to watch or be part of the show. New Jersey still has dozens of yacht clubs today. In the winter, weather permitting, some of these clubs fostered ice-boating races as well. At one time, the competition within and among the yachts clubs was stiff. The following are among the oldest and still operating, listed with the dates of their founding:

Raritan Yacht Club (originally Perth Amboy, 1865)
Corinthian Yacht Club of Cape May (1870)
Toms River Yacht Club (1871)
Bay Head Yacht Club (1888)
Manasquan River Yacht Club (1899)
Ocean City Yacht Club (1901)
Brant Beach Yacht Club (1900s)
Little Egg Harbor Yacht Club (1912)
Keyport Boat Club (1914)
Yacht Club of Stone Harbor (est. 1930)
Avalon Yacht Club (1941)

Yacht Club of Sea Isle City (1941)

Surf City Yacht Club (1950)

The rise of marinas came later as more and more people gained the ability to own a boat but did not want or need to be a member of a yacht club. The first marina in the state was established at Forked River in 1934. New Jersey now boasts dozens of marinas along the shore. All motorboats and all other boats more than twelve feet long must be registered with the state, just like automobiles. There were more than 145,000 pleasure boats registered in 2016.[17]

Sailboats once served as a means of transportation for those folks living at the shore but today many of the thousands of boats docked along New Jersey's coastline are there simply to provide their owners with the pleasure of being on the water on a hot summer day or evening. The calm and shallow waters behind so many of New Jersey's beaches provide a perfect setting for sailboats and small motorboats. In recent years, kayaks and sailboards have added to the fun, along with water-skis and jet-skis.

THE INTRACOASTAL WATERWAY

For boaters, one of the most practical waterways in the state is the Intracoastal Waterway that begins at the Manasquan Inlet and runs 118 miles along a winding path that takes a boater through the Point Pleasant Canal, behind the barrier beaches and barrier islands, through the sedge islands south of Beach Haven parallel to the Atlantic Ocean, until it reaches the Cape May Canal and then the Delaware Bay. The work necessary to create the Intracoastal Waterway in New Jersey began in 1908 and 111 miles were opened by 1915. At the north, the Point Pleasant Canal, originally proposed in 1833, became a reality in 1926, connecting the Manasquan River with Barnegat Bay. At the south, the U.S. Army Corps of Engineers designed a canal at Cape May to connect the Atlantic Ocean and the Delaware Bay as early as 1935, but the work did not begin until the U.S. Navy funded the project in 1942 to protect shipping along the coast during World War II. The canal made Cape May an island once again. The operation of the waterway was turned over to the federal government in 1954 and provides a safe and protected route that allows small boats (with a draft of less than five feet) to cruise New Jersey's waters without venturing into the Atlantic Ocean. In New Jersey waters, some of the channels are narrow and boaters need to be aware of the heights and the openings for the twenty-six bridges from north to south. A safe trip may take two days. A boater can enjoy herons gracing the bays along the way as well as the beautiful scenery. From the Delaware Bay boats can continue down the East Coast, with little interruption, to Key West, Florida.

"JAWS"

Sharks are one of the many species of fish that visit the Jersey Shore. In 1900, the scientific community generally believed that sharks would never attack humans, despite anecdotal evidence to the contrary from mariners around the world. One such believer proved his point by jumping into a pool of sharks from his yacht *Hildegard* in July 1891, with Teddy Roosevelt on board as a witness. When Hermann Oelrichs returned to his ship after being ignored in the water, he offered a reward of $500 to anyone who could prove him wrong.[18] The thousands of beachgoers enjoying the Jersey Shore after the turn of the twentieth century agreed with Oelrichs or simply did not give the issue a second thought. At least not until July 1916.

At the turn of the twentieth century, heartier beachgoers, especially young men looking to impress young ladies on the beach or the boardwalk, took up long-distance swimming in the ocean. And so, on the afternoon of July 1, those on the beach at Beach Haven on Long Beach Island had no concern when twenty-five-year-old Charles Vansant checked into the Engleside Hotel, quickly entered the water, and swam out past the casual bathers. Suddenly, Vansant was attacked and lifted out of the water by a great white shark more than ten feet long. Those on the beach heard him scream, saw him in the jaws of a large fish, and could see the pool of blood billowing around him. Before friends and lifeguards could reach him and drag his body from the mouth of his attacker, his body was so badly mangled that he died an hour later from the loss of blood.

The witnesses did not fully understand what they had seen. No one had ever heard of a shark attack at the beach and few saw enough of the fish that attacked Vansant to convincingly identify it as a shark (even if they could identify a shark). Over the next several days, scientific experts disputed that the attacker was a shark, suggesting instead a large swordfish or killer whale. The management at the Engleside tried to calm the guests (those that stayed) and quickly put a metal net out in the water to cordon off a "safe" area for bathing. Remarkably, word did not spread quickly up and down the beaches of New Jersey, but slowly by word of mouth, with many wizened beachcombers disputing the claim of a shark attack. When the shark struck a second time just five days later, north at Spring Lake, the claim became harder to dispute. The second victim was Charles Bruder, the bell captain at the Essex & Sussex Hotel, who was taking a long-distance swim late in the afternoon. The attack came just as suddenly and the result was the same: Charles Bruder died on the beach, with one leg completely severed above the knee. After this attack, more nets were built and very few people ventured into the water for days and weeks. Tourists already at the New Jersey beaches to celebrate the Fourth of July were frightened and reservations for the weeks following the two attacks went unfilled. Thousands of dollars were lost up and down the shore.

But the shark that seemed to relish bathers did not go away. A spotter was sent out in a boat to scour the waters off of Asbury Park on July 8 after the news frightened the bathers there. The shark apparently saw the spotter first and attacked the boat which almost capsized. The frightened but intrepid mariner whacked the fish with his oar until it retreated and he then hastily rowed to shore to tell of his adventure. Scientists were now slowly coming around as evidence mounted and panicked businessmen and vacationers demanded that action be taken. But little could be done to assure safety other than staying out of the water. At this point the story took a bizarre turn. For reasons not readily understood, the killer shark continued its trek north and turned into the Raritan Bay, making its way to the Matawan River Inlet, and swimming down the river to the town, in brackish waters.

On July 13, within days of the attack at Spring Lake, the shark came upon a group of boys cooling off at a watering hole on a break from summer work. The boys had no thought of the threat that lurked in the water with them. The shark struck without warning. Twelve-year-old Lester Stillwell screamed as the shark dragged him away. The other boys scrambled out of the water and ran screaming into town only to find that few adults believed their story. Those few adults who returned with them to the watering hole jumped into the water to search for the boy or his body. After almost thirty minutes in the murky water, Stanley Fisher broke the surface and announced that he had found Stillwell's body only to be immediately dragged under when the shark closed its jaws around his legs. His friends went to his rescue and eventually pulled him out of the water. Moments later, moving slowly back toward the bay, the shark came upon another opportunity, more young boys who were in the creek and unaware of the attacks that had occurred just minutes earlier. The shark attacked Joseph Dunn and mangled his leg before his friends and a local man jumped in the water to save his life. By now the town was in an uproar as everyone who heard the story ran home to get rifles and explosives and rushed to the banks of the river to kill the beast. Someone put up netting at the outlet in an attempt to trap the shark in the river, but all in vain. Despite throwing explosives in the river and shooting at every large fish that could be seen, the shark was never taken. While all of this was happening, Stanley Fisher was transported by train to Long Branch and taken to Monmouth Memorial Hospital where he died that evening.

Several days later, two fishermen out in Raritan Bay hoping to catch menhaden realized that their trailing net had hauled in something much bigger. So big in fact that it threatened to drag the boat into the bay at the stern. Within a few minutes they witnessed a great white shark at the back of their boat with its jaws open and attacking. Quick thinking and a broken oar brought the confrontation to an end. The shark died and they trawled its body to shore. One of the two men was a taxidermist who mounted the shark after emptying its stomach to find what appeared to be several human bones. The 1916 summer shark attacks ceased. Nonetheless, not all of the experts agreed that this was the shark responsible for the attacks or whether the attacker was a shark at all. Bathers at the shore were not as skeptical.

The summer passed and by 1917 the newspapers had more explosive stories to tell. The United States entered World War I in April and the much more dangerous underwater menace of German U-Boats arrived just off the Jersey Shore. The memory of the shark attacks faded, at least until 1974. In that year Peter Benchley published his novel *Jaws*, a modern tale of a rogue great white shark terrorizing the small beach town of "Amity" on Long Island. The story had striking similarities to the 1916 attacks. The blockbuster movie hit the theaters in June 1975, just before the start of the summer season. The movie's tagline, "Don't Go in the Water," was as frightening to merchants and businessmen at the Jersey Shore as to those in the theaters who were thinking of a summer vacation at the beach. The scenes of hundreds of beachgoers running from the water screaming had a chilling effect on bathers for several summers but, after forty years and a better understanding of the habits of sharks, *Jaws* has become just one more piece of Jersey Shore lore.

FURTHER READING

For background, on fishing, see Peter J. Guthorn, "Pound Fisheries and Pound Boats," File #49 (New Jersey Maritime Museum, Beach Haven, New Jersey); Glenn R. Piehler, *Exit Here for Fish!* (New Brunswick, NJ: Rutgers University Press, 2000); Merce Ridgway,

The Bayman, A Life on Barnegat Bay (Harvey Cedars, NJ: Down the Shore Publishing, 2000); and the websites for the Garden State Seafood Association, http://www.gardenstateseafood.org/; the State of New Jersey, Department of Agriculture, Jersey Seafood, http://www.jerseyseafood.nj.gov/; State of New Jersey Division of Fish and Wildlife, http://www.state.nj.us/dep/fgw/gsft.htm; the NJ Coast Anglers Association, http://www.jcaa.org/; NJFishing.com, http://www.njfishing.com/Fish_Species.php; the NOAA websites: Report, http://www.nmfs.noaa.gov/mediacenter/2013/03/07_noaa _report_finds_commercial_and_recreational.html; "Community Profiles," http://www.nefsc.noaa.gov/read/socialsci/community Profiles.html; and, the National Marine Fisheries Service, "Commercial Fishing Statistics," https://www.st.nmfs.noaa.gov/st1 /commercial/landings/annual_landings.html.

On boating, see Peter Guthorn, *The Sea Bright Skiff and Other Shore Boats* (Atglen, PA: Schiffer Publishing Co, 1982); Donald Launer, *A Cruising Guide to New Jersey Waters* (New Brunswick, NJ: Rutgers University Press, 1995); and George R. Petty Jr. and Barbara E. Petty, "Ocean County History of Historic Boats" (Ocean County Cultural and Heritage Commission, October 31, 1983).

On the 1916 shark attacks, see Michael Capuzzo, *Close to the Shore, The Terrifying Shark Attacks of 1916* (New York: Crown Publishers, 2003); Richard G. Fernicola, *Twelve Days of Terror* (Guilford, CT: The Lyons Press, 2001); and Angela Serratore, "Terror on the Jersey Shore," *Lapham's Quarterly* (August 9, 2013).

CHAPTER 12

The Rise of Resorts, Cape May County, and the Lore of the Shore

Equidistant—eighteen miles—from Cape May and Atlantic City is Sea Isle City, a new resort that has grown into favor since 1880. It has a very entic- ing beach, of great width, and everywhere evidences of higher ambition than is usually alive in summer cities. At the intersections of the principal avenues there is colossal busts, surrounded with flowers, of Minerva and a dozen other mythological deities, whose white, clear cut, classic features look strangely out of place amid the sand cedars and the modern houses. Their presence suggests that some heathen sacrifice upon the sea-shore is about to be made, some propitiation to Jupiter or the god of storms. The busts are a part of a preconceived plan to effect beauty by example; and the laws of Sea Isle City, to which all its inhabitants subscribe, make it imperative to grow flowers.

—Cape May to Atlantic City, A Summer Note Book, 1883

The beach communities in Cape May County range from the earliest resort at Cape May to some of the last to lure visitors at the end of the nineteenth century. Like the rest of the Jersey Shore, the county offers diverse settings and entertainments: quiet beaches and thrill-filled board-walks, dry towns, neon-lit motels, nightclubs, and nature preserves. The Wildwoods helped usher in the era of motels and rock 'n' roll. Each Jersey Shore resort—from Sandy Hook to Cape May Point—has developed a dis-tinct personality, which allows the Jersey Shore to accommodate all tastes for a summer vacation. Much of what we do and see at the shore today

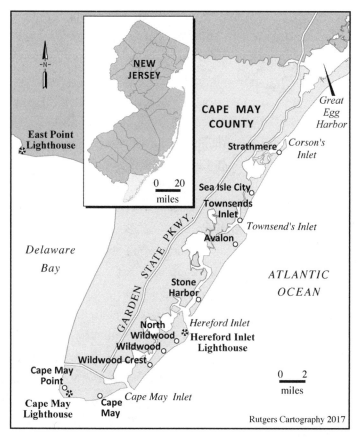

Map 8. Cape May Shore Communities and Lighthouses. Map designed by Michael Siegel, Rutgers University.

relates back to the pleasures originally enjoyed by beachgoers in the late 1800s and early 1900s—the sights, the sounds, the aromas, the food, and the games. We are linked to hundreds of past summers at the shore.

THE PERSONALITIES OF JERSEY SHORE COMMUNITIES

Longtime New Jersey residents interested in the shore communities know that each one is unique in some way. Beaches differ: some are wide, others narrow; some have pounding waves, others gentler; some are great for surfing, others are not; some are always crowded without room for an elbow between blankets and umbrellas, others are wide open with few crowds. Access differs: some towns are long rides from anywhere and others just a hop, skip, and jump for tens of thousands; some welcome day-trippers with amenities like bathrooms, showers, and food concessions, while others would rather that day-trippers not show up, despite state laws that require accommodation. Entertainment differs: some towns are still dry, others have a multiplicity of bars and nightclubs; some offer boardwalks with fun and games and food and rides, some have commercial-free boardwalks, and others have no boardwalks and no commerce along the beach; some towns still bring in shows and entertainers, others have no nightlife at all. Demographics differ: some towns emerged as havens for Irish, Italians, or Jews; some require obvious wealth to live in or visit, and others are easy to enjoy with just a pocketful of change; some welcome college students, whether intentionally or just by tradition, some towns are sleepy cottage communities, and some draw naturalists.

What makes the shore fun and interesting is that these different communities sit side by side, just like vacationers at the original boarding houses in the 1800s—Quakers next to fun-lovers. The Jersey Shore is all things to all people and at the same time each person's individual preference for a summer vacation. Jersey Shore visitors, especially those few who do not return to the same beach each year, can easily recognize the differences in the shore communities, even in bordering towns along the ocean. That's the beauty and the mystery of the shore. Interestingly, visitors who wander from beach to beach each summer as young people eventually settle into a close relationship with just one town and, after a few summers of repeated visits, declare it to be the most desirable of all locations at the shore!

For day-trippers looking to spend a portion of a day on the beach, the state and federal beaches—Sandy Hook at Gateway National Recreation Area in the north and Island Beach State Park further south—often become the choice. In the south, the free beaches of the Wildwoods serve the same purpose. These beaches may get crowded on the hottest days of the year, but they are convenient to millions and are well-maintained and inexpensive. Thousands of day-trippers also lie on the sand of accommodating municipal beaches north and south. Other beaches do not attract many day-trippers, in large part to geography. The Long Beach Island beaches, for example, are a long ride from the heavily populated parts of New Jersey, New York, and Pennsylvania (at least for a day trip), and can only be reached by getting across the one bridge onto the island and then dealing with local traffic. Other, high-end, communities along the shore are just not that welcoming to day-trippers even though all beach towns are subject to the public interest doctrine and must provide changing stations, restroom facilities, and beach access. Frequent day-trippers know which are which and are generally found at the more accessible beach communities.

Some beach towns cater to weekenders, folks living sufficiently nearby who can travel to the beach on a Friday evening and stay until Sunday night (or, perhaps, even Monday morning). Again, these towns need to be near enough to large populations to encourage the two- or three-day sojourn. Many people own or rent a bungalow or apartment for the summer but only use it for weekends when being with friends on the beach during the day and at hotspots at night are the drill. The Dover and Ocean beaches in Brick and Toms River townships, Seaside Heights, and Seaside Park are good examples. Some bungalows, rented by college students or large extended families, accommodate twelve or more on a single weekend. Some of these towns cater to young adult populations and offer a party nightlife that lasts longer than the wakeful (or not) hours spent on the beach during the day. It is no coincidence that "Jersey Shore," the reality show that aired on MTV from 2009 to 2012, was filmed in Seaside Heights.

A large number of beach towns have developed into locations for second-home ownership by in-state and out-of-state families who can afford to purchase a home and have the time to use it. Each has its own style and culture, creating boutique residential resorts up and down the shore. Some take pride in well-manicured lawns and gardens, as in Monmouth Beach; some enjoy the amenities of a vibrant town center with shops, movie theaters, and fine restaurants, as in Beach Haven; and other towns simply offer a rustic seashore environment, as in Stone Harbor. Some are elegant communities with high-priced homes, no boardwalks or amusements, and few rental properties to attract partiers, as in Mantoloking; some are affordable as a family summertime retreat, with activities that appeal to children and adults, as in Ocean City. Many of these properties are rented for all or part of the summer. There once was a time when at least part of a family (mother and children) could spend the entire summer at the beach to be joined on the weekends by a diligently working father and husband. That societal construct may no longer be a norm, but a second home at the beach remains a prize—and a status symbol—for many. And this remains the case even though the summer season has shrunk over the past fifty years. Primary and secondary schools now have later end dates in June, colleges require attendance (especially for freshmen) in August, and many schoolchildren attend camps in the summer or have sports and music commitments before Labor Day.

The Look, Lure, and Lore of the Shore

The lure of the Jersey Shore lies in the opportunity to leave a hot city to enjoy sea breezes at a comfortable spot on a sandy beach and a refreshing few moments in the ocean water. With each passing year, vacationers demanded more, however, and entrepreneurs have accommodated them. Almost all present-day activities at the shore are remnants, reminiscences, and adaptations of late nineteenth- and early twentieth-century summers.

We start with the simple pleasure of running into the water with friends. At first, societal mores at Cape May discouraged men and women from enjoying the saltwater together. This went by the boards early on, replaced by politely wading into the ocean side by side in full dress. Local ordinances adopted in the 1800s by some beach communities specified the length of skirts and the amount of coverage. Swimsuits became skimpier and skimpier with each passing decade and today sea-goers prefer either suits designed for bodysurfing or whatever style will impress the neighbors. Many vacationers still enjoy strolling along the sand in the evenings, but cruising the boardwalks became the chosen pastime by 1900 and continues full throttle into the twenty-first century. At one time John Philip Sousa's band entertained on the boardwalks.[1] Today, rock and jazz concerts continue the March King's legacy of live music, especially in places like Asbury Park, the Wildwoods, and the casinos of Atlantic City, even if Sousa would not recognize the similarity. The practicality of a sneakbox for fishing and gaming and skiffs for sailing led to regattas and racing clubs in Barnegat Bay and that boating tradition continues as thousands of fishing boats, sailboats, and motorboats line the bays and marinas up and down the coast, along with kayaks and jet skis.

The beach towns can argue about where the first boardwalk was laid down, but all agree that the first significant walk along the beach made of wood was constructed in Atlantic City in 1870. The purpose was to keep sand out of the lobbies and rooms of the fancy hotels that were strung along the beach. The original walks in Atlantic City and elsewhere were narrow (ten to twelve feet), were not very safe nor very sturdy, and had a hard time standing up to fierce New Jersey gales. Storms have ripped up boardwalks on a regular basis right up through Superstorm Sandy, but with each passing year more and more miles of boardwalk were laid down, the walks grew wider and safer, and more uses were found to accommodate beachgoers and tourists. As evening strolls along the beach became less strenuous and less untidy, food concessions, amusements, and pavilions filled the walkways along with hawkers of all shapes and sizes. Piers with concert halls, theaters, swimming pools, aquariums, restaurants, clubs, and rides reached out from the boardwalks into the ocean.

The original resorts advertised carriage rides along the beach to attract crowds. By 1900, vacationers could enjoy the luxury of a ride along the boardwalk in "rolling chairs," a phenomenon that started at the 1876 Centennial Exposition in Philadelphia and was brought to Atlantic City where it flourished all year round. Well-dressed tourists paid a small fee to be wheeled up and down the Boardwalk by a "pusher" (a local black resident of the city) and traffic became so great that the chairs overwhelmed the Boardwalk. In 1905 ten patrolmen were assigned to conduct Sunday traffic. One observer in Atlantic City called the chair "a kind of glorified perambulator" that allowed "brisk young girls" and middle-aged men "to play the fool in the proper place." This practice continued well into the twentieth century, coming to an end for a number of years in the early 1970s, only to be picked up again with the advent of casino gambling and the return of crowds. By 2014, the pushers were protesting the introduction of a motorized tram on the Boardwalk as a faster and cheaper alternative. The turn of the century observer who saw the rolling chair as a fool's place also pondered the ability of hawkers on the boardwalk to sell "useless things" like picture postcards, and the willingness of vacationers to buy them. Of course, he then admitted to buying some postcards and "several instruments for cutting up potatoes" which he surely did not need.[2] Those of us who frequent the boardwalks on the Jersey Shore know that at one time or another we have all "played the fool" and have fallen prey to the pitch of a hawker of obscure and useless items.

Picture postcards are a turn-of-the-century phenomenon. Vacationers would send them home to those not fortunate enough to make the trip and see the sights that they were seeing. Many of the postcards featured young women in bathing suits, forcing the postal authorities occasionally to seize the most offensive when prompted by prudish local editors. The numbers were staggering. In just the month of August 1906 1.5 million one-penny postcards were sent from the Atlantic City Post Office.[3] Another Jersey Shore phenomenon is saltwater taffy, a sweet delight synonymous with the Jersey Shore. According to the legend, taffy being sold on the steps of the Boardwalk in Atlantic City by David Bradley in 1883 was left out and washed over by higher than usual nighttime waves. Bradley simply labeled the soaked taffy "salt water taffy" and sold it as a novelty. The name stuck. It soon became the treat to bring back from the shore for those left at home. Again, the numbers tell the tale: 300 million pounds of saltwater taffy were sold in just one 1940s' summer.[4]

Resort entrepreneurs were forever keen to find new ways to attract guests to their hotels and concessions, and babies and beautiful women are always a draw. The seaside boardwalks became famous for their parades. The fashionable Easter Parade in Atlantic City began in 1876 as a way to draw crowds from the Philadelphia Centennial Exposition to the resort before the start of that summer season. This display of color and style became enormously popular and continued every year thereafter, drawing 500,000 to the city as late as 1941. In 1902, the *New York Times* compared it favorably to the New York City Easter Parade: "it is even more charming and grand, as there are no streets to cross, carriages to dodge, or other inconveniences incident to promenade on any city street."[5] The first baby parade was on July 22, 1890, in Asbury Park. City founder James Bradley led 165 babies and their parents down the boardwalk to music. The winner took home a brand new carriage. By the turn of the twentieth century, the Baby Parade had become a regular August date in Asbury Park with hundreds of participants in elaborately decorated carriages and hundreds walking in costumes. In 1901, the *New York Times* devoted considerable coverage to the parade (as it did for years thereafter) proclaiming "the babies were in fine fettle, and the spectators in good humor."[6] In 1910, more than 100,000 people gathered at the boardwalk to witness the parade. Other shore resorts followed suit and the babies paraded right through the twentieth century. You can still find long-running baby parades in Cape May, Ocean City, Stone Harbor, Sea Isle City, and the Wildwoods.

Of course, the most spectacular event devised was the Miss America Pageant, which traces its beginnings to an "Inter-City" pageant first held in 1921. The title of "Miss America" was given to the 1921 winner when she returned for the contest the next year. The pageant ran for several years thereafter, disappeared for several years, and quickly reappeared. Over the years, the pageant became a culmination of state pageants, required a display of talent, and offered scholarships. But it began as just another attraction at the shore to extend the summer season into September. Its promoters realized that combining the most beautiful woman in America in bathing suits with sun and sand could draw an enormous crowd. The Pageant has had its ups and downs over the years and for eight years moved to Las Vegas (2005–2012), only to return to Atlantic City. But it still ranks as the foremost beauty, and now talent, contest in the country even though bathing beauties have been crowned at competing locations (including the more family-friendly "Mrs. America" in Asbury Park) to share in some of the glamour and attention that Miss America brought to Atlantic City.

Another aspect of the Jersey Shore that we take for granted is the work of lifeguards. In early years, bathers entered the ocean at their own risk. Some resorts hung ropes into the surf to assist bathers, to keep them from wandering out too far from the beach, and to help them handle the breakers. Others might have a small boat just outside the bathers to prevent disaster. Volunteer rescuers appeared on Atlantic City's beaches as early as 1855. Even so, in 1865 thirteen people drowned.[7] The early lifeguards relied on gratuities for their work, from beachgoers and from the victims dragged back gasping onto the beach. By 1872, the Camden and Atlantic Railroad needed to assure the public using its trains that ocean bathing was safe. They funded an organized lifesaving service for the purpose. Hotels were soon advertising their efforts to do the same. An 1882 Atlantic City Directory listed two sets of brothers, the Bradfords and the Rutters, who were available to protect the public. Lifesaving teams were organized in Asbury Park, Ocean Grove, and Cape May shortly thereafter.[8] In 1900 the New York Times reported that a law student who saved an "elderly maiden" on the Atlantic City beach in an earlier summer had inherited $7,000 when she died of natural causes some time later.[9] In recent decades, much more attention has been given to the dangers of rip tides, strong beach currents that can suddenly drag a swimmer from shallow water to perilous depths, but unfortunately New Jersey beaches still lose lives to the dangerous surf.[10] 2017 proved to be a particularly deadly year as rip tides took a more than a dozen bathers, most times in the surf after the lifeguards had departed for the day or the season. State regulations in modern times require communities to provide lifeguards to protect bathers and save them when they run into trouble. We expect to find a lifeguard each time we approach a public beach, and we do. They rescue thousands of bathers each year.

CAPE MAY COUNTY

Cape May County beaches run along a series of islands beginning with the island resort of Ocean City; then Ludlam's Island, the home of Strathmere (a part of Upper Township) and Sea Isle City; then Seven Mile Island, the home of Avalon and Stone Harbor; then Five Mile Island, home of North Wildwood, Wildwood, and Wildwood Crest; and, finally, Cape May. Cape May County history began with the whaling settlement of Cape May at the southern tip of the state long before Cape Island beach became a beach resort at the start of the 1800s. Development at the north end of the county began in the late 1800s; development just north of the cape, in the colorful Wildwoods, did not fully blossom until the construction of the Garden State Parkway in the 1950s. Today, Cape May's beaches continue to attract hundreds of thousands in summer. And in the off-season, many more make the trip to view hundreds of thousands of birds that use the county's beaches, wetlands, and forests as a stopping point on their annual migrations.

Ocean City is the northernmost beach in Cape May and its development began in 1884 as a Methodist retreat. In 1897 the borough converted to a city and by 1900 it had a year-round population of more than 1,300. The city continued to grow, reaching 6,040 in 1950, and swelling to more than 15,000 in 2000 as the building boom along the Jersey Shore generated by the Garden State Parkway brought more and more residents.

Ludlam's Island, to the south of Ocean City, is divided between Strathmere at the north end and Sea Isle City to the south. The history of the island can be traced back to the seventeenth century when it was purchased from the West Jersey Proprietors in 1695 by Joseph Ludlam. The southern section was quickly parceled off to John Townsend and referred to as Townsend's Inlet. Despite its early history, however, very little of consequence impacted the island for more than 150 years aside from the grazing of cattle and sheep and an occasional pirate pursuing supplies or a safe haven. The cattle would swim across the salt meadows; the sheep would be transported. The pirates may have now and then filched one or two of these stocks to feed their crews. One story that epitomizes the desolation of the island tells of a shipwrecked crew in 1846 that was able to make its way to shore after two days on the water only to find no one there to help them.[11] Eventually, well before the coming of vacationers, two lifesaving stations were built on the island (#33, Sea Isle City, and #34, Townsend Inlet). A third (#32, Corson's Inlet) was originally built on the Ocean City side of the inlet in 1849 (rebuilt in 1872), but was moved to Strathmere after a storm in 1924.

Strathmere designates the beach section of Upper Township. Who was the winner? Apparently, the Pennsylvania Railroad ran ads in newspapers in 1912 soliciting a name for that "Wonderland of Sun and Sea" where "Corson's Inlet meets the Combers" to encourage real estate investors. Up to that time the area was simply referred to as Corson's Inlet. Everyone knows the winning entry, of course, but no one knows who proposed it. In any event, Strathmere became a substantial seaside resort even though it is only 1.5 miles long and two blocks wide. One of the first buildings was the Whelan Hotel, located at the tip of the island on the bay. This

building, constructed around 1871, is now known as the Deauville Inn
and still operates as a restaurant and sports bar. Its website suggests that
it was once a speakeasy, a gambling casino, and a regular stop for rumrunners in the 1920s and 1930s. Its stage has featured Jimmy Durante,
Eddie Cantor, and Sophie Tucker. President Teddy Roosevelt was among
its many guests.[12]

Sea Isle City came into being in 1880 at the southern end of Ludlam's
Island after Charles Landis returned from a trip to Italy smitten with Venice. Landis purchased Ludlam's Island and began the development of a
year-round seashore community modeled on what he had seen in Italy.
In 1883, Landis persuaded the West Jersey and Seashore Railroad to build
tracks from South Seaville (Sea Isle Junction) east to a station in Sea Isle
City and in 1893 the Pennsylvania Reading Seashore Railroad came into
town by way of Corson's Inlet. Charles Landis also persuaded the U.S.
Congress to fund the building of a lighthouse to help guide mariners passing along the shores of Ludlam's Island. Congress saw the need for a light
between the Absecon lighthouse to the north and the Hereford's Inlet
lighthouse to the south and the Ludlam Beach lighthouse was built in 1885
as an L-shaped building with a light in a thirty-five-foot tower that could
be seen from more than ten miles out at sea. The lighthouse served its
purpose until 1924 when, after suffering damage from recurring storms
and a fire, the building was sold for residential use. Despite efforts to save
the building, it was demolished in 2010.

Sea Isle City incorporated as a borough in 1882 and then converted its
charter to a city in 1907. The railroads made travel to Sea Isle City from
Philadelphia quick and easy, and by the turn of the twentieth century Sea
Isle City was a thriving seaside resort with thirty hotels, including the
Excursion House, the Bellevue, the Continental, the Tivoli, and the Fritz-
Cronecker Depot Hotel. The five-story Continental Hotel featured a steam-
driven elevator. Like so many other seashore resorts, the trains were

eventually overcome by the popularity of automobiles and the building of roads and access ways. The trolley that served the island was decommissioned in 1916 and the railroad tracks were pulled up during World War II to supply steel to the war effort.

The island southwest of Ludlam's Island is the aptly named Seven Mile Island. Its beach communities are Avalon on the north end and Stone Harbor on the south. Seven Mile Island was the site originally selected by the Methodist Camp Meeting Association for its seashore community when it decided to leave Vineland in 1868. A price was fixed, $50,000, but the deal fell through and the Methodists found Ocean Grove. Whether the price was too dear or mosquitoes dissuaded the Methodists is not known. In any event, Seven Mile Island was difficult to reach over the wide salt marshes to the west and over Townsend Inlet at the north and was the last barrier island in New Jersey to develop. The island was owned by Henry Tatham of Philadelphia and used for the grazing of sheep and cattle and hogs amid the junipers, red cedars, and bayberry bushes. Tatham's farmhouse was the only building on the southern end of the island when a lifesaving station (#35, Tatham) was built in 1872. Several Philadelphia businessmen joined together to purchase the island for development in 1887, but it was not until 1891 that the West Jersey Railroad's iron bridge crossed the northern Inlet and proved sustainable. Three earlier attempts had been washed away. Avalon separated from Middle Township the next year as a beach resort offering second homes for Philadelphian families. This area was originally known as Leaming's Beach. "Avalon" was the mythical resting place of Britain's legendary King Arthur.

Avalon and its neighbor Stone Harbor are renowned for their high dunes, wide beaches, and preserved natural vegetation. An automobile bridge at the center of the island provided access to the west in 1911, and a second train line crossed the marsh alongside the road in 1912. Stone Harbor separated from Middle Township two years later. One difference between Avalon and Stone Harbor is the Stone Harbor Bird Sanctuary located at the southern end of the island and other accessible nature spots emphasizing the island and marshland habitats that remain today much as they were 200 years ago. The bird sanctuary began with the efforts of the Stone Harbor Bird Club, organized in 1941, and its successor, the Witner Stone Club, to preserve the bird habitats so unique to the area. The borough council set aside municipal land for this purpose in 1961 and the twenty-one-acre bird sanctuary was designated a National Nature Landmark just several years later in 1965. Walking unguided on its four paths or as a participant in one of the tours offered every summer, a visitor might see several varieties of herons, egrets, and thrush, a glossy ibis or an osprey. Turtles, frogs, and butterflies can also be found within the maritime forest of sassafras and pine and the freshwater and saltwater wetlands. Nearby, just across the salt marsh to the west in Middle Township are 5,000 acres of preserved salt marsh. The Wetlands Institute is within the preserve: thirty-two acres dedicated to the research and conservation of coastal environments. The institute was organized in the 1960s by Herbert Mills, a businessman and executive director of the World Wildlife Fund, which purchased the land. For vacationers just looking for a stroll on an untouched beach, Stone Harbor Point offers just that. Located at the southern tip of Seven Mile Island, the southernmost beach can only be accessed on foot or by bike and offers the opportunity to walk along the beach to Hereford's Inlet, across which the Wildwoods are visible, and around to the channel that is part of the Intracoastal Waterway. Across the channel to the west is Nummy Island, 350 acres of undeveloped salt marsh.

Many species of shorebirds, including terns, plovers, and red knot, make their spring and the fall transitional stop in Stone Harbor as they travel north and south between the northern forest and Central and South

America. The entirety of the Cape May Peninsula has become a destination for birders anxious to join the Audubon Society each year to count the number of species, at least seventy-five, and the number of birds, more than 800,000, stopping to rest and feed at this welcoming midpoint on their journey. The Audubon Society holds its annual Seawatch in Avalon and its website lists "loons, grebes, cormorants, gannets, pelicans, ducks, geese, herons, egrets, swans, gulls, terns, jaegers, and alcids" as regular transients, but also an "Atlantic Puffin, Long-billed Curlew, Wood Stork, [and] Pacific Loon" every now and then. Butterflies use the peninsula for the same purpose. The society maintains an observatory in Cape May Point for viewing the birds and the butterflies.[13]

Development of the Wildwoods on Five Mile Island—North Wildwood, Wildwood, Wildwood Crest, and West Wildwood (not a beach community)—started in the 1880s. The Wildwoods are now generally referred to as a group, known for wide and beautiful beaches, two miles of boardwalk filled with rides and amusements, and one of the finest locations to find so-called doo-wop architecture. Five Mile Island was originally purchased in 1717 by Aaron Leaming, Humphrey Hughes, David Wells, and Jonathan Swain. It was mostly desolate land of limited use. North Wildwood developed first with a small settlement in the early 1800s and a lifesaving station in 1849. Frederick Swope purchased this section of the island in 1885 and arranged its incorporation as Anglesea. The Anglesea Railroad reached the resort in 1883 crossing the marsh north of Five Mile Island on a bed of gravel that did not hold firm in foul weather. The "Mud Hen," as the train was dubbed, made its way across the marsh without any major disasters but the ride was often as bad as some of the rollercoasters that have been featured on the Wildwood boardwalks. It was not until 1890, after the West Jersey Railroad bought up the Anglesea Railroad, that a proper foundation was laid to make the treacherous crossing safer. The borough's name changed to North Wildwood in 1906.

The Hereford Inlet lighthouse was completed in 1874 at the southeast edge of Anglesea to mitigate the dangers of the inlet. It was designed by Paul Pelz, who went on to build five sister lighthouses on the West Coast and to design the Library of Congress building in Washington, DC. The six identical lighthouses are in the Victorian style. The Anglesea tower was 49.5 feet high and the light at the top beamed thirteen nautical miles out to sea. A severe storm forty years later eroded the foundation of the house, and the structure was moved 150 feet west. The light was removed from the tower in 1964 and replaced by a light on an iron tower built nearby. The house began to deteriorate but was rescued in 1982 through the efforts of North Wildwood's mayor and his wife, Anthony and Phyllis Canatoso. The borough purchased the building, began work to restore the tower and the house, and had the light placed back into the tower and relit in 1986. It continues to serve its purpose as an aid to mariners at sea and was placed on the National Registry of Historic Places in 1977.

Before the railroad came to Five Mile Island via Anglesea in 1883, vacationers would take a train to Rio Grande to the west of the island and make their way across by boat or by foot over a log bridge. Early tourists and investors eagerly made the trip and the middle of Five Mile Island soon became a desirable resort renowned for its forest, freshwater lake, and parks, as well as its wide beaches. The borough of Holly Beach was incorporated in 1885 and the borough of Wildwood to its north in 1895. The two communities combined in 1912 into the city of Wildwood. Apparently, as the story goes, the development of Holly Beach began with a doctor's prescription for Sarah Andrews of Vineland to spend some time recuperating from an illness at Townsend's Inlet (on Ludlam's Island). This was not unusual given the general belief that the air on the barrier islands was free of pollen and that saltwater had healing effects. When Sarah's condition improved in 1881, she and her husband Aaron visited Five Mile Island and were impressed with the land and the possibilities.

The next year, the Andrews, Joseph Taylor, John Burk, and several others joined together to form the Holly Beach Land Association. They purchased land covered with holly bushes and began to sell lots. Holly Beach is described in Appleton's 1893 *Illustrated Handbook of American Summer Resorts* as "a quiet seaside resort" rivaled by "few places with better claims to patronage." One of its advantages was "dense forest growth" behind the beach "almost to the strand."[14] In 1890, a Cumberland County politician, Philip Pontius Baker, purchased one hundred acres using the name the "Wild-wood Improvement Company" to reflect the unusual twisted shapes acquired by the pine, maple, oak, and magnolia trees in the area, perhaps as a result of constant sea breezes. A temporary boardwalk was built along the beach in 1900 and a permanent, raised boardwalk in 1903. An automobile bridge replaced the footbridge to the mainland that same year.

A controversy arose in 1920 over whether the city should replace its aging boardwalk and, without warning, the old boardwalk disappeared one night, the work of a crew organized by a city's commissioner, Oliver Bright. A new and improved boardwalk was built in time for the summer traffic, but Bright was booted out of office for his unilateral efforts. The first amusement area was Ocean Pier, which connected with the boardwalk. The revitalized boardwalk became the center of attractions over the following years and contributed to the growth of Wildwood between World Wars I and II. Wildwood had 5,330 residents by 1930 and North Wildwood had 2,049.

Wildwood Crest was the last of the Wildwoods to be developed, as promoters continued to expand their successes on Five Mile Island. Although the first house was not built in Wildwood Crest until 1906, the community grew like its neighbors, with the clearing of dunes and brush, the laying of streets and lots, and the introduction of municipal services. To encourage growth and excitement, the developers, Philip and Latimer Baker, built a thirty-foot arch at the northern entrance to their town and lit it each night with a "Pompeian fire" to attract tourists. Many decades later, the fire was replaced with neon lights as Wildwood Crest became the home of doo-wop architecture. In an effort to lure vacationers traveling by car, local motel entrepreneurs developed their properties in unique and colorful styles with themes of space travel and exotic locales, asymmetrical designs, and the glow of neon lights. Three hundred motels were built in this style in the 1950s and 1960s, many of which were created by brothers Will and Lou Morey who are credited with the first, the Ebb Tide Motel, established in 1957. The arrival of doo-wop architecture in the Wildwoods enhanced the allure of motels and television, new phenomena in the 1950s, and glamorized rock 'n' roll culture. The lights, sounds, and accessibility of the Wildwoods captured the country's mood:

> The advantages of the motel over the hotel were numerous, especially for families: easy access, free parking, no reservations required, no clerks to deal with, no tipping, and an informal, home-like ambience. And, for those of a more illicit nature, the motel's privacy was the principle attraction. To attract families, many motels began to allow children below a certain age to stay free, offered playgrounds and recreation areas, washing machines, and electric irons.
>
> While many beaches worked to attract families, the Wildwoods embraced a more adult clientele. Wildwood's amusement piers became surrounded by bars, nightclubs, and supper clubs, all featuring live entertainment, attracting big-name entertainers. By October 1955 a Newark newspaper was able to report that entertainment booking agents had begun to refer to Wildwood as "Little Las Vegas." Indeed, by the end of the 1950s, the Wildwoods ranked second only to Las Vegas in both the quantity and quality of the entertainment it offered.[15]

Rising stars like Bill Haley and the Comets performed live at the Rainbow Room and the Hof Brau in Wildwood, Chubby Checker's "Twist" was introduced in Wildwood, and Dick Clark premiered *American Bandstand* from the Starlight Room on the boardwalk. Although many of the 300 hotels built in the doo-wop architectural style fell into disrepair or were demolished in the 1970s and 1980s, many still remain thanks to the work of the Doo Wop Preservation Society created in the 1990s. The state of New Jersey created a historic district to highlight the significance of these buildings, and two of the motels—the Caribbean and the Chateau Bleu— were added to the National Registry of Historic places in 1984 and 1985, respectively.

A small stretch of beach toward the southern end of Five Mile Island is known as Diamond Beach, an unincorporated section of Lower Township that is otherwise located mostly on the mainland. Basically, it is an extension of the Wildwoods, developed over fifty years as a location for high-end condominiums.

The storied careers of Cape May and Cape May Point as beach resorts have been recounted in earlier chapters and the resurgence of Cape May as a Victorian seashore resort with gingerbread houses and turn-of-the-century allure is described in chapter 14.

FURTHER READING

For background, see Avalon Home and Landowners Association, *The History of Avalon* (1998); George F. Boyer, *Wildwood-Middle of the Island* (Egg Harbor City, NJ: Laureate Press, 1976); Bernard A., Olsen, Edward Olsen, and Michael Fowler, *Lifeguards of the New Jersey Shore* (Atglen, PA: Schiffer Books, 2010); Russell Roberts, *Down the Jersey Shore* (New Brunswick, NJ: Rutgers University Press, 1993); Emil R. Salvini, *Boardwalk Memories* (Guilford, CT: Insiders' Guide, 2005) and *Historic Cape May, NJ: The Summer*

City by the Sea (Charleston, SC: History Press, 2012); Karen L. Schnitzspahn, *Stars of the Jersey Shore* (Atglen, PA: Schiffer Publishing Company, 2007); and, George E. Thomas, and Carl E. Doebley, *Cape May, Queen of the Seaside Resorts, Its History and Architecture* (The Knossus Project, Mid-Atlantic Center for the Arts, 1976).

CHAPTER 13

The Twentieth Century

TRANSFORMATION

There is an urgent need for additional parkways, freeways and turnpikes to carry the commerce of our State and nation, to permit our citizens more easily to travel back and forth between their homes and businesses, for recreation and equally important, to achieve greater highway safety. . . . I recommend that there is created within the State Highway Department, as an integral part thereof, an Authority to finish the Garden State Parkway promptly as a revenue-financed facility.
—Governor Alfred E. Driscoll, *Fifth Annual Message to the Legislature*, 1953

The last twenty-five years of the nineteenth century set the stage for changes to come in the twentieth. The masses surrounding the Jersey Shore rushed to the beaches every summer in growing numbers for a day, a week, or the season. Atlantic City grew steadily and developed a worldwide reputation, Long Branch and Cape May attracted steady crowds, Asbury Park provided a family-friendly northern beach challenge to Atlantic City, and new boroughs established themselves up and down the coast. By 1900 the term "Boardwalk" was officially applied to the plank walk at Atlantic City and the sights, sounds, and images associated with the Jersey Shore had taken hold of society. More than one million passengers rode the rails to Atlantic City in 1904 on the Pennsylvania Railroad alone. The first half of the twentieth century started with optimism, economic development, and the belief that the Jersey Shore would continue as it was. But the twentieth century brought significant change in transportation, race relations, competition, and where and how visitors would enjoy the pleasures of the Jersey Shore.

TRANSPORTATION AGAIN TRANSFORMS THE SHORE

Just as trains transformed the Jersey Shore after 1854, automobiles would transform the Jersey Shore in the twentieth century, but not before trolleys and bicycles had their day, albeit short-lived. In the 1880s, trolleys made transportation more convenient at the shore and expanded the area that could be used for lodging and entertainment. The first trolleys were cars on tracks pulled by horses. Atlantic City had a horse-drawn trolley as early as the 1860s and Long Branch 's was constructed in 1870. One of Asbury Park's "firsts" was the first electric trolley, or "street railway," in the state in 1887. The original tracks ran from the local train station east to the beach, then were laid north to Deal Lake (1892) and south to Avon-by-the-Sea (1893). Trolleys connected adjacent resorts and encouraged the rise of amusement parks and amenities in areas off the beach that might otherwise be difficult to reach. Most of the horse-drawn trolleys were eventually electrified, and by 1890 Atlantic City's line ran to Margate, Ventnor, and Longport. The Long Branch line ran to Eatontown and Red Bank. Other lines ran in Cape May County (the Five Mile Beach Electric Railroad) and in Bay Head (the Point Pleasant Traction Company). The trolley serving the Wildwoods ran from 1903 to 1945, long after most of its counterparts. But the convenience of automobiles led to the elimination of these lines one by one until they were all gone by 1950.

Another transportation boom that prospered at the shore around turn of the twentieth century was the bicycle. Bicycles came on the scene just before automobiles and, at first, were considered a viable mode of everyday transportation. Both bicycles and cars needed smooth and well-maintained roads and ardent bicyclists worked with budding automobile enthusiasts to convince local governments to build better roadways. The shore towns, with level grades, were a boon to bike riders. Long-distance and competitive bicycling became staples at the shore. In 1893, Asbury Park welcomed the convention of the National League of American Wheelmen. Races were run at a local stadium. Women riders in the city organized the Ariel Club in 1895 and the organization eventually became the Asbury Park Woman's Club. Clubs and magazine articles encouraged trips from Atlantic City to Cape May and even from Atlantic City to Philadelphia. Soon ordinances were enacted to slow down the bikers to keep nonbikers safe. Of course, a parade was organized in Long Branch in August 1895 for this crowd. Eventually, the bicycle craze also gave way to the speed, convenience, and versatility of automobiles.

Automobiles began showing up at the shore by the end of the nineteenth century, first as novelties for the most fashionable and the most daring and then, as roads became better, as an alternative way of getting to the beach. The earliest automobiles, many of them electric models, always drew a crowd of gawkers and locals interested in learning how the machines worked. Automobiles arriving at the shore often came from as far away as Philadelphia and New York and at first the newspapers in Atlantic City, Asbury Park, and Long Branch described each car and driver coming into town. Soon "touring" the seashore towns became a pastime, for some in their own cars and for others in groups in vehicles for hire. In 1905, one driver made the trip from Philadelphia to Atlantic City in less than two and a half hours over local roads. One of the most outlandish purveyors of the automobile craze was "Diamond Jim" Brady who brought six electric cars to Long Branch for his summer visits in the early 1900s (including a custom made Brougham) and toured the town with actress Lillian Russell on board.[1] Apparently, Brady needed six cars because electric cars had notoriously short range.

Shore communities almost immediately saw the advantages of automobiles to attract crowds and carry them to the shore. Cape May, for example, sponsored races to the shore and hosted automobile races on the beach, one featuring both a young Henry Ford and Louis Chevrolet. Ford finished last and had to sell his car to pay his hotel bill. Long Branch was hosting automobile races at Elkwood Park by 1908. Soon newspaper editors, local boosters, and state legislators began lobbying for better automobile roads and for bridges. The state created the Motor Vehicle Department in 1906 and registered 13,759 automobiles that year; in the next ten years the number multiplied tenfold. The early regulation of automobiles (and their drivers) conflicted in at least one unique way with the needs of the seashore: the registration of out-of-state vehicles struck at the heart of the tourist trade. In 1911 Pennsylvania and Delaware, the home of many vehicles showing up at the shore, would not grant reciprocal registration. New Jersey responded by charging its own license fee. The hotel owners in Cape May, Wildwood, Atlantic City, Asbury Park, and Long Branch screamed in protest that the charge would undermine their out-of-state tourist trade. Reciprocity was soon negotiated, but some New Jersey taxpayers living away from the shore, especially frugal farmers, felt overtaxed by maintaining roads for out-of-state tourists.

More passengers boarded trains traveling to the Jersey Shore in 1920 than any year before or since.[2] Even so, the writing was already on the wall and in the next thirty years the automobile would become the preferred means of travel to the shore—on a timetable chosen by each family of vacationers (notwithstanding horrific traffic jams). The transition from rail to road made every stretch of beach accessible to everyone and significantly impacted the look and allure of the shore. By the midpoint of the twentieth century it was clear to average citizens and politicians that something needed to be done to make motoring even more convenient for the hundreds of thousands driving to the state's beaches each summer. When the state began planning through roads in the 1940s one of the routes on the short list ran close to the shore from Sandy Hook to Cape May. That route eventually became the Garden State Parkway in the 1950s. After 1950 and the completion of the Parkway, the smaller communities thrived, but some of the larger ones struggled. Atlantic City had been built for trains and was inconvenient for automobiles and had difficulty accommodating them in the city. Some historians attribute Atlantic City's fading popularity by the second half of the twentieth century to its inability to find the right approach. Even after the completion of the Atlantic City Expressway in 1964, which traversed the state from Camden County to Pleasantville, Atlantic City did not revive.

ECONOMIC DEVELOPMENT AND THE GREAT DEPRESSION

By 1900, the Jersey Shore could boast more than twenty-five summer beachfront destination communities stretched out along the coast. Some of these towns were not much more than one square mile in total area and had no more than a few thousand feet of beachfront. Hotels, motels, bungalows, and mansions were filling in spaces directly west of the beach. Beach vacations were no longer limited to the fashionable or the wealthy, as middle-class families had enough money and could take the time for leisure. Some businessmen saw an opportunity to build luxurious vacation homes at the turn of the twentieth century in new resorts like Allenhurst, Spring Lake, Bay Head, Margate, and Sea Isle City; others focused on modest second homes for the less wealthy. Local officials built boardwalks and music halls and welcomed amusements and rides to attract crowds. In the years from 1900 to 1950, Atlantic City, Asbury Park, and Long Branch also grew, becoming year-round communities as well as seasonal attractions.

By 1900, Atlantic City had more than 27,000 residents and made the list of 161 cities in the United States with a population of more than 25,000! The city reached this number in less than fifty years, with a 50 percent burst of growth from 1890 to 1900. These were not the hundreds of thousands coming to enjoy the sun and sand, but the hoteliers, entrepreneurs, businessmen, and wait staff servicing the crowds and living in the city all year. The city's growth continued into the twentieth century and peaked in 1940 at 66,198, followed by a steady decline thereafter. Long Branch also grew after 1900 as it slowly transitioned from a city solely dependent on seasonal tourism to a year-round community with a significant manufacturing base. Upstart Asbury Park, already the third largest shore community by 1900 with more than 4,000, saw its population quadruple by 1950 to more than 17,000, just a shade below its peak ten years later. Notably, the city of Cape May, no longer effectively competing for summer crowds, experienced up-and-down growth, going from 2,257 in 1900 to 3,607 in 1950.

Despite the incorporation of dozens of beach communities before 1900, the list of incorporated "cities, towns, villages and boroughs" from the 1900 census names only twenty-seven beach communities recognizable today. Atlantic City, Long Branch, Asbury Park, and Cape May had sizable populations. Almost all the remaining towns (20 of 23) had fewer than 1,000 permanent residents in 1900; seven had fewer than 100; and twenty had not been listed in 1890. Only Manasquan (an older town with an industrial base dating back to the 1700s), Sea Bright (incorporated in 1889), and Ocean City (organized as a religious community) had more than 1,000 full time residents in 1900. Several more of the newly incorporated boroughs made the census list in 1910 (Monmouth Beach, Avon-by-the-Sea, Ventnor, and Wildwood Crest); still more in 1920 (Sea Girt, Mantoloking, Seaside Park, and Barnegat Light); and, in 1930, three more (Ship Bottom, Stone Harbor, and North Wildwood). Notably, Ocean Grove does not appear on these census tables because its population was captured within Neptune Township.

In the fifty years from 1900 to 1950, all the shore communities that had incorporated by 1900, other than Cape May, Cape May Point and Sea Bright, more than doubled their year-round population. Most communities in Monmouth County registered more than 1,000 full time residents by 1950 including Belmar (4,636), Bradley Beach (3,911), Manasquan (3,178), Spring Lake (2,008), and Sea Girt (1,178); only two missed the mark, Sea Bright (999) and Monmouth Beach (806). On the other hand, only two communities in Ocean County—Point Pleasant Beach (2,900) and Beach Haven (1,050)—topped 1,000 by 1950, demonstrating the continued

TABLE 3
POPULATION BY MUNICIPALITY, 1900–2000

		1900	1910	1920	1930	1940	1950	2000
Allenhurst	Monmouth	165	306	343	573	520	758	718
Asbury Park	Monmouth	4,148	10,150	12,406	14,981	14,617	17,094	16,930
Belmar	Monmouth	902	1,433	1,987	3,491	3,435	4,636	6,045
Bradley Beach	Monmouth	982	1,807	2,307	3,306	3,468	3,911	4,793
Deal	Monmouth	70	273	420	800	917	1,064	1,070
Long Branch	Monmouth	8,872	13,298	13,521	18,399	17,408	23,090	31,340
Manasquan	Monmouth	1,500	1,582	1,705	2,320	2,340	3,178	6,310
Monmouth Beach	Monmouth		485	410	457	584	806	3,595
Sea Bright	Monmouth	1,198	1,220	856	899	779	999	1,818
Sea Girt	Monmouth			110	386	599	1,178	2,148
Spring Lake	Monmouth	526	853	1,009	1,745	1,650	2,008	3,567
Avon-by-the-Sea	Monmouth		426	647	1,220	1,211	1,650	2,244
Bay Head	Ocean	247	281	273	429	499	808	1,238
Barnegat Light	Ocean			70	69	144	227	764
Beach Haven	Ocean	239	272	329	715	746	1,050	1,278
Harvey Cedars	Ocean	39	33	65	53	74	106	359
Lavallette	Ocean	21	42	117	287	315	567	2,665

Long Beach Twp	Ocean	152	107	106	355	425	840	3,329
Mantoloking	Ocean			37	37	58	72	423
Pt Pleasant Beach	Ocean	746	1,003	1,575	1,844	2,059	2,900	5,314
Seaside Heights	Ocean			154	399	549	862	3,155
Seaside Park	Ocean	73	101	179	571	653	987	2,263
Ship Bottom	Ocean				277	396	533	1,384
Surf City	Ocean	9	40	43	76	129	291	1,442
Atlantic City	Atlantic	27,838	46,150	50,707	66,198	64,094	61,657	40,517
Brigantine	Atlantic	99	67	12	357	403	1,267	12,594
Longport	Atlantic	80	118	100	228	303	618	1,054
Margate	Atlantic	69	129	249	2,913	3,266	4,715	8,193
Ventnor	Atlantic		491	2,193	6,674	7,905	8,158	12,910
Avalon	Ocean	93	230	197	343	313	428	2,143
Cape May	Cape May	2,257	2,471	2,999	2,637	2,583	3,607	4,034
Cape May Point	Cape May	153	162	121	104	126	198	241
North Wildwood	Cape May				2,049	1,921	3,158	4,935
Ocean City	Cape May	1,307	1,950	2,512	5,525	4,672	6,040	15,378
Sea Isle City	Cape May	340	551	564	850	773	993	2,835
Stone Harbor	Cape May				363	383	670	1128
Wildwood	Cape May	150	898	2,790	5,330	5,150	5,475	5,436
Wildwood Crest	Cape May		103	161	738	661	1,772	3,980

TABLE 4

POPULATION GROWTH BY MUNICIPALITY, 1900–2000

		1900/1930 (%)	1930/1950 (%)	1950/2000 (%)
Allenhurst	Monmouth	247	32	−5
Asbury Park	Monmouth	261	14	−1
Belmar	Monmouth	287	33	30
Bradley Beach	Monmouth	237	18	23
Deal	Monmouth	1043	33	1
Long Branch	Monmouth	107	25	36
Manasquan	Monmouth	55	37	99
Monmouth Beach	Monmouth		76	346
Sea Bright	Monmouth	−25	11	82
Sea Girt	Monmouth		205	82
Spring Lake	Monmouth	232	15	78
Avon-by-the-Sea	Monmouth		35	36
Bay Head	Ocean	74	88	53
Barnegat Light	Ocean		226	200
Beach Haven	Ocean	199	47	22
Harvey Cedars	Ocean	36	100	239
Lavallette	Ocean	1267	98	370
Long Beach Twp	Ocean	134	137	296
Mantoloking	Ocean		95	488
Point Pleasant	Ocean	147	57	83
Seaside Heights	Ocean		116	266
Seaside Park	Ocean	682	73	129
Ship Bottom	Ocean		92	160
Surf City	Ocean	744	283	396
Atlantic City	Atlantic	138	−7	−34
Brigantine	Atlantic	261	255	894
Longport	Atlantic	185	171	71
Margate	Atlantic	4122	62	74

(continued)

TABLE 4 POPULATION GROWTH BY MUNICIPALITY, 1900–2000 *(continued)*

		1900/1930 (%)	1930/1950 (%)	1950/2000 (%)
Ventnor	Atlantic		22	58
Avalon	Cape May	269	25	401
Cape May	Cape May	17	37	12
Cape May Point	Cape May	−32	90	22
North Wildwood	Cape May		54	56
Ocean City	Cape May	323	9	155
Sea Isle City	Cape May	150	17	185
Stone Harbor	Cape May		85	68
Wildwood	Cape May	3453	3	−1
Wildwood Crest	Cape May		140	125

difficulty of reaching the Ocean County beaches before the building of the Garden State Parkway. The four communities in Atlantic County other than Atlantic City piggybacked on Atlantic City's popularity and grew their populations in high multiples: Brigantine (13x), Margate (68x), and Ventnor. Ventnor was not listed in 1900, but had more than 8,000 full-time residents by 1950. Cape May County, more easily reached from Philadelphia, saw substantial growth: Wildwood grew from 150 in 1900 to 5,475 in 1950 (37x) and Ocean City continued its growth, reaching 6,040 (5x).

Looking closer at the census numbers, however, it can be seen that much of the growth occurred, especially in Monmouth County, between 1900 and 1930, before the disastrous consequences of the Great Depression and the impact of World War II. The population of the communities listed in 1900 totaled 52,275 with more than one-half of that number in Atlantic City alone. By 1930, the population had almost tripled to 147,998 and, although Atlantic City, Asbury Park, and Long Branch accounted for 58,720 of the increase, the remaining 37,003 new year-round residents were scattered up and down the coast. With a few exceptions, most of the communities had lower percentage increases in the twenty years after 1930 than in the thirty years before and well more than a majority had fewer actual number increases. Total growth from 1930 to 1950 in these communities (including Atlantic City, Asbury Park, and Long Branch) amounted to only 20,371. The Great Depression and World War II put development projects on hold (some were never completed) and lowered revenues up and down the shore.

Not all economic development stalled, however. Local boosters in the smaller communities continued to work on boardwalks, concessions, and rides as well as jetties, seawalls, and groins. Atlantic City used its good fortune from the Prohibition Era to develop more fully into a convention destination, building its vast convention center just as Prohibition ended and the Great Depression took hold. Building along the boardwalk and oceanfront in Asbury Park late in the 1920s (after the death of the resort's founder, James Bradley, in 1921) continued through the early years of the Depression, including the Paramount Amusements building, Convention Hall, the casino complex, and the Monte Carlo Pool, which opened in June 1942 amid hype that it was the world's largest saltwater pool. The Point Pleasant Canal (1925) and the Cape May Canal (1942) were dug to complete the Intracoastal Waterway, which was thought to be a wartime necessity, and hundreds of miles of state roads were paved to the shore in this period. But further development in the smaller communities had to wait for the Garden State Parkway and better economic times. Luckily, by 1929 many Americans had become accustomed to an annual vacation and continued to spend some time each summer at their favorite resorts.[3]

The Garden State Parkway

The Jersey Shore owes its contemporary feel to the completion and acceptance of the Garden State Parkway from its inception in the late 1940s to its present-day configuration. The Parkway enabled small beachfront communities incorporated in the late 1800s and early 1900s to mature into independent resorts with distinct personalities. The Parkway also made the shore accessible to every level of society.

After 1920, as rail passenger traffic diminished, the number of trains to each Jersey Shore station fell and the rail companies struggled to keep the lines running. Tracks laid down to shore communities in earlier decades were pulled up in many communities and the beds often used for roads to accommodate automobiles. Resort communities moved from encouraging hotels and boarding houses to motels and single-family homes and, more recently, condominiums, as each vacationing family chose its own personal destination and no longer needed to rely on train schedules or accommodations close to a railroad station. The railroads tried in vain to maintain their traffic. The Jersey Central created the *Blue Comet* in February 1929, a deluxe train with specialty dining (the Blue Comet Special Plate Dinner) for its two daily trips at lunch- and dinner-time. The hoopla surrounding this specially painted train from New York to Atlantic City included a race with an airplane piloted by an aviatrix (which the train won) and brought it significant ridership at first (62,000 in its first year); but the Depression dampened its chances and it lost passengers continually for the next twelve years until its last run in September 1941.[4] By then, the race with automobiles was lost.

To handle the increasing automobile traffic, state planners envisioned a north-south road. The need was clear: traffic in northern New Jersey at times was at a standstill for local drivers on local roads; travel to the shore depended on just a few roads, such as Routes 1 and 9, which could not handle the summer demand. In August 1950, 75,000 cars were counted coming into Atlantic City in one weekend. Shore roads passed through town after town along the way and drivers needed to stop at every traffic light in those towns. The beach-going public from the north and inland needed a direct and safe road to the shore and relief from a trip that could take three to four hours on local roads to reach even the North Jersey beaches. The state authorized the road in 1946 and tried to build it within

its regular road program. A constitutional budgeting change in 1947, however, hampered the ability of the state to build the shore road and to build
it at the pace necessary. The state's constitution in 1947 eliminated the
dedicated petroleum tax used for financing state roads, making all revenues equal and subject to legislative allocations.[5] By 1953 only three small
sections of the north-south road (in Union, Middlesex, and Cape May
counties) had been built, twenty miles in all. The prior year, Governor
Alfred E. Driscoll proposed that the road be separately funded through
tolls and managed by an independent agency, the New Jersey Highway
Authority. The public concurred by passing a $285 million bond issue in
1952 to pay for its immediate construction. A movie made to help the bond
effort showed a mother and children enjoying the Jersey surf while the
husband/father remained stuck in traffic trying to reach them on the
weekend. Construction of the Garden State Parkway was soon underway.
By September 1954, the southern portion of the road was opened from
Telegraph Hill in Holmdel to Cape May, passing through and over the
state's marshes, creeks, and pine barrens and providing a modern route
to all the beaches along the way. The through trip was only interrupted by
the need to complete the one-and-a-half-mile bridge (the Parkway's longest) over Great Egg Harbor Bay between Atlantic and Cape May counties, which was not finished until May 1956. All 173 miles of paved road
were completed from Cape May to Bergen County's northern boundary
by mid-1957.

The Parkway was unique in a number of ways. The designers wanted a
paved road without horizontal intersections, without steep inclines, and
without stops (except for tolls). They built the road into the contours of
the land it passed through and avoided long stretches of straightaway to
eliminate monotony. They also sought to prevent head-on collisions by
separating the north lanes from the south lanes; wooded medians eliminated the distraction of oncoming headlights. The road was built with
aesthetics and safety clearly in mind throughout and the finished project
achieved its goals. Whether New Jerseyans appreciate the safety and

aesthetic efforts remains unclear, but their acceptance of the road was never in doubt, especially for those rushing to the shore. By 2010 more than 433 million automobiles had traveled on the Parkway.

The governor and the legislature, along with the businessmen in the shore communities, understood from the beginning that the Garden State Parkway was the road to economic growth for the state's substantial tourist industry along its beachfront. The Depression and then World War II slowed the economies in these communities; the Parkway helped to revive them. Faster times getting to the shore brought more people on day trips and made second homes accessible. Owning a cottage or bungalow near the ocean became more of a reality, especially for middle-income families. Construction increased up and down the shore. Tax ratables in towns along the Parkway (including the northern counties) jumped $300 million within twelve months of its completion and retail sales in all the shore counties boomed. In the decades since its opening, the Garden State Parkway has been widened, expanded, modernized, and improved to handle the ever-increasing traffic of people living, working, and vacationing along its shore route.

BUILDING BOOMS

If the development at the shore slowed due to the Depression and World War II, the Garden State Parkway and improved economic conditions after 1950 revived interest in the shore, especially in the residential communities. Real estate developers encouraged the rise of seasonal homes to middle-income buyers and more people moved to the shore to live year-round, no longer feeling isolated. The census numbers from 1950 and 1960 demonstrate the impact. Of the thirty-eight seashore municipalities, all but three grew in year-round population, twenty by more than 25 percent and ten by more than 50 percent. Every beach resort in Cape May County, with the exception of Wildwood and North Wildwood, grew by more than 25 percent, with Avalon at 62 percent and Wildwood Crest at 70 percent.

Although Atlantic City lost population in this decade (−3%), its neighbors grew substantially: Margate doubled, Brigantine more than doubled, and Longport's population grew by 74 percent. Seven of the twelve resorts in Ocean County grew more than 25 percent. The Monmouth County communities, stronger prior to 1950 due to their accessibility, grew as well, but only five of the twelve grew by 25 percent or more.

In the next twenty years, 1960 to 1980, ten communities grew by more than 25 percent, nine by more than 50 percent, and eight communities more than doubled. Clearly, automobile accessibility played a role in this growth and continued to have an impact despite the devastating Ash Wednesday storm of 1962 (described in chapter 9). Interestingly, the geography shifted. Every community in Ocean County grew by more than 50 percent except for Point Pleasant Beach, which grew by 40 percent. The public obviously found Long Beach Island easier to get to: Barnegat Light (+144%), Long Beach Township (+123%), Harvey Cedars (+171%), Ship Bottom (+99%), Surf City (+275%), and Beach Haven (+65%). In Cape May County, Avalon continued to add year-round population (+211%), as did Ocean City (+83%) and Sea Isle City (+90%). Every community in Monmouth County gained residents, except Asbury Park (−2%), with the neighboring towns of Monmouth Beach and Sea Bright topping 50 percent.

Using year-round population figures does not tell the entire story, however, because so many homeowners are not permanent residents. In New Jersey, the ratio of people to the number of housing units ran about 2.5 people to a structure in 2010. But not at the shore. Overall, the ratio runs about 1 to 1, and in most of the small seashore municipalities at a significantly higher number of houses to people. Second homes remain vacant in the winter months and their owners are counted elsewhere in the census. The ratio in Ocean County shore communities is extraordinary. In 2010, Harvey Cedars on Long Beach Island had 3.60 housing units for every person residing in the borough; Long Beach Township had 3.02 and Beach Haven had 2.28. The picture is similar in Cape May County: Stone

Harbor had 3.75 times the number of houses to people and Sea Isle City had 3.26. The Dover beaches in Toms River and Brick townships, where bungalows abound, were above 2 to 1. The Monmouth County beach communities are all above the state norm as well, but are the lowest for the shore, demonstrating the increasing number of people making a shore house their *primary* residence in these accessible communities.

Each beach community has its own tale of development after 1950, but one community's present-day circumstance reflects the building boom of the 1950s and 1960s and the unexpected consequences of Superstorm Sandy in 2012. Sometime around 1950, a local family with acreage along the beachfront in Toms River Township (then Dover Township) saw an opportunity to market their property as small building lots for seasonal homes. The Osborns divided the land into individual lots before the existence of local zoning ordinances and encouraged purchasers to build cottages. Hundreds of families eagerly sought these lots and others offered by property owners nearby, all at affordable prices. Bungalows were built close together in what are now the Dover and Ocean Beach sections of Brick and Toms River Townships. Some of the original units were less than 600 square feet, just enough for a family to bed down for the night. Some of the purchasers of the Osborn properties did not buy the land, however. The Osborns chose to lease some lots (much like the elders in Ocean Grove had done a hundred years earlier), originally for five years and renewable year-by-year thereafter. Just before the turn of the twenty-first century, the lots were offered for sale to the occupants as part of an overall condominium development, the Osborn Sea-Bay Condominium Association. By that time, the bungalows on these lots and in the adjacent communities had become significant financial assets as well as an affordable place to crash within walking distance to the beach, increasing in value each year. Many of these homes brought in rents during the summer weeks when not used by the owners.

Unfortunately, the Osborn section of Toms River took a beating in Superstorm Sandy in October 2012 when a gas line fire close to the beach raged westward throughout the community, destroying almost all the homes. The owners, like the majority of Sandy victims, chose to rebuild— but their grit ran into a snag that has exacerbated their personal and financial losses. Seventy-eight houses were part of the Osborn Sea-Bay Association, which governed the common acreage. The density was twenty-two houses per acre. Once the houses were destroyed, the land became subject to the township's current zoning and safety codes that, among other restrictions, limit construction to five houses per acre. The 1950s bungalows had been categorized as "nonconforming use" and, now destroyed, were required to conform. Despite months and years of effort, as late as 2017 the association has failed to come up with a workable solution to this conundrum and most of the families have been stymied in their efforts to rebuild and once again enjoy the benefits of a beach house.[6] Other homeowners nearby with houses on fee-simple lots that survived the storm were similarly obstructed in their attempts to repair or rebuild by bureaucratic and financial difficulties. State and federal relief are not available for second homes; the cost of flood insurance has increased; new building codes require extensive and expensive repairs; and, for some, the need or desire to raise the house above flood level makes the cost prohibitive. We can expect a reshaping of the look and feel of the shore in these communities in the years ahead.

Gambling at the Shore

Gambling at the Jersey Shore revived in the twentieth century. State residents and state voters have always been of two minds on the subject. Horse-race gambling and legal parlor games enhanced the attraction of both Long Branch and Atlantic City in the second half of the nineteenth century. The racetrack at Monmouth Park in Oceanport, just three miles from Long Branch, was opened in 1870 specifically to lure vacationers, and although closed several years later, reopened in 1882. Its success encouraged Cape May to open its own track in 1888. The Cape May track closed after only the one season, but Monmouth Park drew large crowds for more than a decade. Parlor games and card games were openly available in both Long Branch and Atlantic City and enjoyed by presidents and high-rollers. Nevertheless, in 1894 antigambling forces succeeded in adopting a statewide prohibition of parimutuel betting and a ban on parlor games shortly thereafter. Horse racing and legal parlor games came to an end throughout the state. Some observers mark the ban as the beginning of Long Branch's decline as a premier resort. In contrast, the ban enhanced Atlantic City's appeal, as local authorities looked the other way for the next seven decades.

Race-horse gambling returned to New Jersey in 1946. The legislature lifted its ban and Monmouth Park reopened immediately thereafter, on June 19, as the Monmouth Park Jockey Club. Today, the track is managed by the New Jersey Sports and Exposition Authority and draws crowds from those visiting the shore and those who simply like the sport. Triple Crown winner American Pharoah was welcomed at Monmouth just weeks after capturing the title at Belmont in 2015 and thrilled the New Jersey crowd (a record at 60,983) with a runaway victory in the $1.6 million Haskell Stakes. A track at Atlantic City also opened quickly after 1946 and ran successfully for the rest of the century. That track struggled after 2000, however, and in 2015 its owners announced its permanent closure, after a decade of limited race days and simulcast betting.

Of course, Atlantic City has had legalized casino gambling since May 1978 with the opening of the Resorts International Casino. The formula for the birth of Atlantic City—a monopoly fueled by promotion—worked for its rebirth as well. Its original monopoly was railroad access and, after 1900 gambling, albeit illegal, and during Prohibition, booze. By the 1960s, however, Atlantic City's monopolies were gone and its misfortunes exposed. A confluence of factors revealed a city without any distinction and so down and out that no amount of promotion could revive it. The 1964 Democratic Convention, brought to the city to revive its fortunes, instead highlighted its despair. Public appetites had changed.

Large hotels were no longer in fashion and Atlantic City's hotels were old and in disrepair. Families shifted to the convenience of bungalows and motels where appearances were less important and costs more reasonable. Automobiles replaced railroads as the way to the shore and Atlantic City never successfully accommodated automobiles, with its narrow streets and limited parking. Motels were discouraged for years and when they were finally allowed it was too little, too late.

In addition, competition with non-New Jersey resorts overwhelmed the city. The advance of inexpensive airplane transportation to sunnier and exotic locations (especially in the winter months) like Miami and the Caribbean islands drew off many vacationers. The rise and the draw of Las Vegas (with legal gambling) took others. The opening of Disneyland in California in 1955 and Disney World in Florida in 1971 also had an impact. Race relations hurt the city. Even though Atlantic City was able to avoid the riots that plagued other New Jersey cities in the 1960s, it could no longer sustain the facade of exclusivity. Atlantic City had been an exclusive playground for middle-class white society. The white neighborhoods emptied in the 1960s and 1970s, and the appearance of blacks on the Boardwalk, in the shops and hotels, and on the beach frightened the city's patrons. Blacks had always been present to serve vacationers in the hotels and on the Boardwalk but were not accepted as equals.

The overall effect was the notion—reinforced by the reality—that Atlantic City was a dying resort with old and stodgy accommodations and little to offer other than the beach. Local boosters desperately sought one more promotion: casino gambling. This time the locals were joined by state politicians who yearned for the recovery of the city and its accompanying tax revenues. The idea was floated by a few influential South Jersey politicians and gained traction in the 1970s. Gambling in any form requires an amendment to the state constitution and change did not come quickly for a state with such an inconsistent history with legalized games of chance. First came a statewide referendum that approved the New Jersey Lottery in 1970. Working from that success, a broad referendum allowing casino gambling throughout the state was proposed four years later, but failed. On a second try, in 1976, a more limited referendum passed, this time restricting gaming to just Atlantic City.[7] Voters apparently did not want casino gambling next door but also held the hope that casino gambling could be the catalyst to revive Atlantic City's fading fortunes.

Once again, Atlantic City could boast a monopoly: East Coast casinos. Crowds poured into the city, including vacationers, high-rollers, and day-trippers. Seniors on buses hurtling down the Parkway every day with buckets of quarters in their laps became a standing joke in the state, just like the thousands of "shoebies" who came in the 1850s and 1860s on the trains when Atlantic City had a transportation monopoly. Monopoly™, the fantastic board game built around Atlantic City's streets and railroads, helped to continue Atlantic City's fame in the 1930s and 1940s but also presaged its fate. Over the next thirty-five years, the number of casinos multiplied, with twelve at the peak in 2006. Construction soared and employment rose. Tax revenues from gambling reached $413 million in 2006, direct employment totaled more than 38,000, and all agreed that the experiment and Atlantic City's newest promotion was, indeed, a success. But perhaps too much of a success. Nearby states watched with envy as development money poured into Atlantic City and tax revenues grew for New Jersey. The success of Atlantic City, within easy reach of millions in Philadelphia and New York City, lessened the resistance toward gaming within and outside of New Jersey. In 1992, the Native American Foxwoods Resort Casino opened in Connecticut, less than 300 miles from Atlantic City and, more important, just as close to North Jersey and New York populations. Since 2000, ten more so-called racinos (racetrack and casino combined) have opened in New York State and Pennsylvania. Most of these hotels/casinos offer a more pleasant winter location for gambling and a more secure location as well, outside of an urban setting with its attendant dangers and fears. For those who prefer the urban setting, New York City has joined and Philadelphia soon will join the crowd.

Ironically, Atlantic City became the victim of its history and its lore. In 2014, four Atlantic City casinos closed or went bankrupt and almost 10,000 jobs were lost. Tax receipts dropped to a low of $201 million in 2013. The marketplace for vacation dollars has become highly sophisticated and families seeking a beach vacation do not necessarily need casino gambling or the distractions that come with it. Gamblers, on the other hand, do not need the beach. By 2016, the city, as well as a number of its casino/hotels, was bankrupt and about to be taken over by the state.

RACE RELATIONS

The first half of the twentieth century brought yet another change to the Jersey Shore, the beginning recognition that the treatment of minorities, who helped to develop the shore and served its patrons, was less than admirable. The success and popularity of the major beach resorts at the Jersey Shore could never have been achieved without a large pool of construction workers to build the structures and the railroads, tradesmen, a merchant class, and a large pool of servants to work the hotels, boarding houses, restaurants, and attractions, all for low wages. Immigrant labor from Ireland, Italy, Greece, and other countries provided much of the manpower in the construction trades; many Jews operated businesses in the resorts; southern blacks escaping from the "Jim Crow" South in the late 1800s and early 1900s provided the servants—cooks, waiters, maids, porters, and more. These workers were required to live near the beaches. In the heyday of the grand hotels, the summers brought steady work, but their employers preferred that the service help otherwise remain unseen. When not performing their jobs, the help was not welcomed or allowed in the hotels, at the events, on the boardwalks and the beaches, or in the surf next to the paying customers; when the crowds left, the winters were grim, particularly for the black families who had few resources to hold on from one summer to the next. This legacy at the larger resorts—Cape May, Long Branch, Atlantic City, and Asbury Park—created two societies in those towns. Over time, many of the immigrant laborers were able to assimilate into white society. One commentator reviewing the statistics points out that the demographics in the barrier islands in Cape May County did not reflect the demographics in the rest of the county from 1900 because many of the workers from Ireland, Italy, Germany, Scandinavia, and other countries who came to the islands stayed by the ocean when their initial jobs came to an end, making these areas more diverse. This was particularly true in Stone Harbor and Ocean City.[8] But the indignities suffered by blacks in the major resorts festered and caused serious issues in the 1960s and 1970s.

Perhaps the first public acknowledgment of this issue arose in Asbury Park in 1885. The appearance of local blacks on the boardwalks and near the hotels after work hours caused a stir among vacationers and prompted a heavy-handed response from the city's founder. Over the course of succeeding summers, James Bradley sought to reassure the city's visitors that they could come to Asbury Park and enjoy all of its treasures without having to share it with those who worked and lived there. He made it clear to the locals through newspaper editorials and open letters that they should accept their place in the city. Blacks were relegated to a separate part of the beach. A story in the *New York Times* at the time entitled "Drawing the Color Line" noted that complaints had risen about the locals "overstepping all bounds, intruding into places where common sense should tell them not to go, and monopolizing public privileges to the exclusion of whites." As the *Times* saw it, the "majority of white people, although professedly astonished at the blunt notification in cold type to the colored folk that it would be wise to make themselves scarce, do not conceal the fact that they are pleased."[9] In 1885, Asbury Park had a year-round population of about 3,000. Its immigrants, merchants, and serving class (Italians, Greeks, Jews, and blacks) all lived across the tracks, not in the city proper, and were not counted in its population despite their proximity to the beach. Cape May County had a substantial black community as well and similar issues came to a head shortly after the turn of the twentieth century when a local newspaper, the *Cape May Herald*, called for all blacks to be removed from the confines of the city to a community of their own elsewhere in the county so that Cape May, it was argued, could once again become a premier resort.[10] The agitation prompted black leaders to develop Whitesboro, an all-black community inland from the resort. An all-Jewish community, Woodbine, had already been established nearby in Cape May County in 1903.

The Ku Klux Klan, revived in the first twenty-five years of the twentieth century and active in many northern states, had strong chapters in Monmouth and Cape May counties. The Klan organized rallies, including one on the Wildwood boardwalk in 1924. But it was a three-day Konklave of the Klan in Long Branch at Elkwood Park (which the Klan had earlier purchased) that focused the attention of immigrants, merchants, and tourists on the ugly reality of race relations in this venerable seashore community. The tristate Konklave culminated in a July 4 parade, when 4,000 white-sheeted and hooded Klan members marched in a line that ran four hours long. Without question, the Klan in this area of the state had blossomed. The parade drew an enormous crowd (estimated at 25,000) despite the large numbers of Jews, Italian Catholics, and blacks who lived, worked, and vacationed in the city. The impact was immediate. All of the Jews left the next day; frightened Catholics hunkered down; and blacks stayed inside for days. The businessmen in the city felt the backlash and the Klan disintegrated thereafter. But it was too late for Long Branch. Its glitter was irreparably tarnished and it never regained its place as a premier resort. The beaches continued to draw beachgoers but the community could not recover.

In Atlantic City, the race issue may not have received as public an airing as in Asbury Park and Long Branch, but the tension reached a peak after 1920. The welfare of the black serving class in Atlantic City was not much different than in Asbury Park. The demand for servile labor was so great that the black population soared in Atlantic City by 1900 to 6,518 out of a total population of 27,888, 23 percent of the city. In the 1920s, 27 percent of the city's population was black, more than five times greater than any other large community in the northeastern United States. The ruling politicians recognized the value of the serving class to the tourist trade, its main source of revenue, and were careful to ensure that the black population had enough to get by, especially in the winter. Blacks were not prohibited but were seldom seen on the Boardwalk or in the shops or on the beaches, except as workers. Atlantic City catered to a middle-class white crowd and was able to project exclusivity in its public places. The irony of its success can be seen in its noted image of a well-dressed white couple being pushed along the Boardwalk in a rolling chair by a young black porter. The city's approach to race interaction changed after 1920, however, with the influx of blacks from the South into northern cities. At that point, segregation became official. Blacks were segregated in the movie theaters and relegated to "Chicken Bone Beach." Ushers handled violators in the theaters and the local police evicted any blacks attempting to use the white beaches. The history of black exclusion from amusement parks, swimming pools, and beaches throughout America is a broader subject covered in Victoria Wolcott's *Race, Riots and Roller Coasters*, but it is a sad history shared by the Jersey Shore. The Atlantic City version of this story can be found in Bryant Simon's *Boardwalk of Dreams*.[11] Both Wolcott and Simon point out that the issue was dealt with by control of the geography; that is, by erecting geographic, economic, and physical barriers to make sure that blacks and whites remained segregated while, in fact, sharing the same space. In addition, black families were relegated to the aging buildings and poor facilities in the north side of Atlantic City and did not share in the limelight or the benefits found closer to the ocean.

All of this was notwithstanding the fact that whites vacationing in Atlantic City frequented the nightlife at the fringe of the black neighborhoods not otherwise available closer to the Boardwalk. For many on vacation, the jazz clubs and nightclubs in the black neighborhoods could be visited without guilt, to hear more rhythmic music and to see more exotic shows than those found at home or on the Boardwalk. With the advent of the Civil Rights movement, many of the artists who got their start in these clubs in the 1930s and 1940s rose to fame years later. Dinah Washington, Aretha Franklin, Cab Calloway, and Leslie Uggams are among the many black entertainers who performed at Club Harlem on Atlantic City's North Kentucky Avenue to delight mixed-race audiences. Similarly, Count Basie spent his early years in Asbury Park's black clubs. The political bosses in Atlantic City maintained the peace in their city for decades with handouts and benefits, especially in the off-season. They proved more successful than the leaders in Asbury Park where the power was more diffused and confused. When racial tensions exploded throughout the nation during the 1960s, Atlantic City was spared but Asbury Park was not. A race riot erupted on the night of July 4, 1970, and lasted for seven days. Although the riot brought the issues to the surface, little was done immediately and not enough long term to calm the situation.

These cities along the shore bear the scars of the resort heydays when the thousands who helped build these entertainment meccas and contributed to their growth and success could not partake in the fun or the economic benefits, only to be left without support when the good times ended. When the cities began to decline after World War II, their neighborhoods took the brunt of the lost jobs and incomes. The reality of race relations throughout the United States was exposed and the aftermath would bring change to the Jersey Shore in the second half of the twentieth century.

FURTHER READING

For background, see John E. Bebout and Joseph Harrison, "The Working of the New Jersey Constitution of 1947," *William & Mary Law Review* 10, no. 2 (1968); Susan Curell, *The March of Spare Time, The Problem and Promise of Leisure in the Great Depression* (Philadelphia: University of Pennsylvania Press, 2010); and

Charles A. Stansfield, Jr., *A Geography of New Jersey* (New Brunswick, NJ: Rutgers University Press, 1998).

On the Garden State Parkway, see New Jersey Turnpike Authority, *Garden State Parkway* (Charleston, SC: Arcadia Press, 2013); and the Garden State Parkway websites, http://gsphistory.com/home.htm; http://www.nycroads.com/roads/garden-state/.

On race relations, see Bryant Simon, *Boardwalk of Dreams* (New York: Oxford University Press, 2004); Donna Troppoli, "The Invisible Boardwalk Empire," *Garden State Legacy* 28 (June 2015) at http://gardenstatelegacy.com/files/The_Invisible_Boardwalk_Empire_Troppoli_GSL28.pdf; Jonathan Van Meter, *The Last Good Time* (New York: Crown Publishers, 2003); Victoria W. Wolcott, *Race, Riots, and Roller Coasters: The Struggle over Segregated Recreation in America* (Philadelphia: University of Pennsylvania Press, 2012); and Daniel Wolff, *4th of July, Asbury Park, A History of the Promised Land* (New York: Bloomsbury Publishing, 2005).

CHAPTER 14

The Twenty-First-Century Shore

*Interest in owning barrier island properties began in earnest in the 1940s
following World War II. However, development of the shore boomed after
the 1962 Ash Wednesday storm when barrier properties became affordable
for the middle class. Initially, coastal municipalities managed the shoreline and the development on the barrier islands. To mitigate erosion, locals
installed groin fields and bulkheads but, these were installed without consideration of the coastal processes and sediment transport patterns of the
area. In 1994, the New Jersey State Shore Protection Fund . . . was established which allows 75% (state) / 25% (local) cost sharing for shore protection projects. Beach nourishment gained momentum as offshore sediment
supplies became accessible . . . in the mid-1980s. . . . Though beach nourishment projects are constructed for shore protection, New Jersey reaps
the benefits from additional land for recreational use. Tourism is a multi-
billion dollar industry contributing $38 billion annually to the state's gen-
eral fund and eventually the Shore Protection. Spending for shore
protection projects helped save money in storm damage repairs and recovery costs. This was clearly displayed within the communities of Long Beach
Island where the federally-designed beach nourishment projects (including a dune) protected landward structures and infrastructure from Hurricane Sandy's ocean waves and storm surge.*
—Stockton University Coastal Research Center report, 2014[1]

Transportation and development changed the look and feel of the Jersey
Shore after 1950, but the focus began to shift as the twentieth century came
to a close. Municipal boundaries and community identities were fully
drawn, transportation issues faded, and development focused on revivals

in Atlantic City, Cape May, Long Branch, and Asbury Park. The focus by 2000 shifted to ideas and ideals: increased attention and emphasis on environmental issues, recognition that the beaches are fragile resources requiring continued and expensive maintenance, court-driven declarations that beaches are a *public* resource available to all citizens of the state, and the growing perception that private property rights do not trump public access. The competing interests now vying for dominance involve the reluctance of local governments and homeowners to relinquish home rule, the state's interest in guaranteeing public access to its beaches, state and federal efforts to protect the coastline and the citizens living near the coastline from storms and erosion, the state's economic interest in a vibrant tourism economy, the continued viability of the fishing industry, the private property rights of landowners living and working near the shore, and the call of environmentalists to limit construction and rebuilding to preserve as much open space as possible and to reclaim more.

The future of the Jersey Shore will be shaped by the interaction of these competing interests amid storms of varying intensity, politics, and changing attitudes about land use and the environment. Contests will be fought at the local level, in the statehouse, and in Washington, DC, over who will control beach access and pay for beach projects. "Home rule" may still affect the debate, but the state's role has expanded over the last fifty years as has the influence of the federal government, which provides funding for beach nourishment and storm relief.

The Public Trust Doctrine and Eminent Domain

The development of the Jersey Shore over the last 200 years has been tied inextricably with the concepts of private property rights and public access. Like the shoreline itself, these are evolving concepts that change imperceptibly at times and in stormy torrents at others. Perhaps surprisingly, these issues seldom involved the New Jersey courts or the State Legislature until second half of the twentieth century.

A legal doctrine known as the "public trust doctrine" dates back to
Roman law and proclaims that the "air, running water, the sea, and consequently the shores of the sea" belong to all of mankind and cannot be
expropriated by any private citizen. This Justinian concept was first applied
in New Jersey in 1821 in a court case dealing with the harvesting of
oysters under the tidal waters of the Raritan River in Perth Amboy. The
state's highest court determined that the farmer who had seeded the
waters could not prevent another man from harvesting the oysters
because the waters were public. The court declared that the water, the
land under the water, and all lands covered by tidal flows along the state's
rivers and the coast, exist for the common good. This included the "wet
sand" area of the beaches (that is, the area from the mean high water
mark to the ocean's waters) and, under this legal theory, a citizen could
walk parallel to the ocean the length of the beach regardless of county or
municipal boundaries or the private ownership of adjacent land because
this strip of wet sand is held in trust for the common good.[2]

The question then becomes, how does that citizen get to the wet sand
and the water from a spot landward of the high water mark? Despite the
tremendous activity along the Jersey Shore for the next 150 years, the
Supreme Court of New Jersey was not asked to rule on this issue until
1972 in the case of Neptune City v. Avon-by-the-Sea.[3] This case reviewed
the practice of charging nonresidents more than residents for access to a
public beach. The Court held that the public beaches of Avon-by-the-Sea
must be open to all citizens equally and that the right to bathe and fish at
the ocean's edge includes the right to enjoy the "foreshore" area (that is, the
wet sand) for recreational and other beach purposes. In 1981, the right
to enjoy the foreshore was expanded to include the right to utilize the
"upper sand" or "dry sand" as well because of the impracticality of allowing access to the foreshore without access to the upper sand.[4] Then came
the most significant case dealing with the public trust doctrine. The 1984
decision in Mathews v. Bay Head Improvement Association[5] dealt squarely
with the interaction between one citizen's right to use the common area

of the beach and the private property rights of the citizens who owned land adjacent to the foreshore.

The facts of the Mathews case are simple. Bay Head had seventy-six oceanfront properties. Seventy lots were in private hands and six lots were owned by the Bay Head Improvement Association. The association also owned that portion of the beach that extended from the end of seven streets to the high water mark so that its members could access the beach. The association had been formed in 1910 to clean, police, and lifeguard the beach owned by its members. Membership was limited to residents and vacationers in Bay Head. Persons coming onto the Bay Head beach from public access to the north (in Point Pleasant) and from the south (Mantoloking) could use the Bay Head beach. But they could not enter from any place in Bay Head, as Bay Head had no public beaches and no public access to the beaches. The association's rules, in place since 1932, effectively limited beach access in Bay Head to its residents, lessees, and guests.

The Supreme Court determined that the association acted in ways and for purposes that paralleled a government entity and declared that neither the municipality nor the association could deny beach access to nonmembers:

> Exercise of the public's right to swim and bathe below the mean high water mark may depend upon a right to pass across the upland beach. Without some means of access the public right to use the foreshore would be meaningless. To say that the public trust doctrine entitles the public to swim in the ocean and to use the foreshore in connection therewith without assuring the public of a feasible access route would seriously impinge on, if not effectively eliminate, the rights of the public trust doctrine. This does not mean the public has an unrestricted right to cross at will over any and all property bordering on the common property. The public interest is satisfied so long as there is reasonable access to the sea.[6]

The Court went even further in theory. It declared that the public trust doctrine's mandate that all citizens have "reasonable access to the sea" could be extended over *privately held* property if the public was blocked from access to the beach except by going through private property. It refused to make this determination in the Bay Head case and recognized that public access needed to be tempered in some cases by reasonable restrictions, but the ruling was clear: the public's right to access and enjoyment of the state's beaches cannot be denied even if it means that private property rights have to be curtailed. Only if beach communities and private property owners refused to recognize this doctrine would the courts or the state government need to act:

> We have decided that the [Bay Head] Association's membership and thereby its beach must be open to the public. That area [owned by the Association] might reasonably satisfy the public need at this time. . . . We believe that the Association and property owners will act in good faith and to the satisfaction of the Public Advocate. Indeed, we are of the opinion that all parties will benefit by our terminating this prolonged litigation at this time.
>
> The record in this case makes it clear that a right of access to the beach is available over the quasi-public lands owned by the Association, as well as the right to use the Association's upland dry sand. It is not necessary for us to determine under what circumstances and to what extent there will be a need to use the dry sand of private owners who either now or in the future may have no leases with the Association. Resolution of the competing interests, private ownership and the public trust, may in some cases be simple, but in many it may be most complex. In any event, resolution would depend upon the specific facts in controversy.[7]

The Court clearly understood the competing property rights that had been developed over time in New Jersey. Owners of beachfront properties (and their neighbors nearby the beach) who had paid a price for their access and their view, and continued to pay for the maintenance of their beaches, expected privacy and exclusive access. But all the other citizens in the state expect the right to enjoy the state's beaches without unreasonable restrictions. A declaration that all beaches were open to all comers would have turned the shore economy upside-down and created a firestorm of protest. The Court's approach allowed for municipalities, property owners, and the public to develop reasonable access rights over time and established a process. Each case would be reviewed using four criteria: the location of the dry sand area in relation to the foreshore, the extent and availability of publicly owned upland sand areas, the nature and extent of the public demand, and usage of the upland sand land by the owner. Towns that had no public beaches and no public access would have to accommodate reasonable access over private lands; private rights would be upheld where public beaches and public access were available and sizable enough to accommodate those coming to the beach.

The Supreme Court had the chance to apply these factors to a beach access case in 2005 involving Diamond Beach in Lower Township, Cape May County. The municipality had no public beaches, the private owner (Atlantis Beach Club) had allowed public access for the previous ten years (but had discontinued the privilege), and an adjacent condominium complex was required to provide beach access as part of its zoning approvals. The Court required the beach club to provide public access to the beach subject only to reasonable charges for beach maintenance and safety.[8]

This issue arose again in 2008 in the context of regulations enacted by the Department of Environmental Protection (DEP) under Governor Jon Corzine to codify these judicial decisions. To add bite to its rules, the DEP declared that failure to comply would preclude a municipality from receiving matching state funds for beach nourishment. The rules required parking and restrooms every one-half mile and elicited strong opposition from a number of municipalities as burdensome and unnecessary. The Borough of Avalon challenged the rules and an appellate court determined in 2008 that the DEP had exceeded its authority.[9] The DEP under the succeeding Governor, Chris Christie, revised the rules to pass judicial scrutiny and to give local municipalities greater latitude. A challenge to these revisions led a lower court to throw out the rules in their entirety on the theory that the legislature never gave any such authority to the DEP. The governor then had to rush a measure through the legislature to ensure the state's rights to regulate this issue before having the rules reinstated.

The conflict between private property rights to the beach and public access arose in yet another context just before Superstorm Sandy. Some beach towns actively sought to protect their beaches by the construction and maintenance of dunes directly in front of oceanfront houses. The U.S. Army Corps of Engineers facilitated this effort and federal monies had been available on and off for several decades. A property rights issue arises because the dunes must be created above the high water mark and, therefore, on private property. Before work can begin a municipality must obtain an easement from *every* oceanfront homeowner. This was the case in Harvey Cedars in 2008 as the deadline to get federal funds was looming. Several homeowners refused because they were concerned that their view would be impacted, their value would be impaired, or that public money might bring greater public access rights encouraging out-of-towners to use the beach in front of their homes. The dunes would be twenty-two feet high and would cost $25 million, with all but $1 million provided by the state and federal governments. In order to obtain the easements of the remaining few holdouts, the Borough of Harvey Cedars exercised its right of eminent domain as to that portion of the property rights necessary to build and maintain the dunes. The project went forward and was completed while the borough and one homeowner litigated the value taken by the easement. The homeowner had the right to receive a fair value for the "property" taken (that is, the view and access) and the matter went to court. Appraisers testified that the beachfront home was worth almost $2 million before the taking. A jury determined the value of the easement to be $375,000. The homeowner felt justified, but

Harvey Cedars and other municipalities, watching the case as a precedent for their own actions, were appalled by the enormity of the judgment. The trial court had refused to let the jury consider as an offset the added value gained by the homeowners from the protection of the newly constructed dunes. The value was upheld by the appellate division in in 2012.[10] The decisions effectively eliminated the use of eminent domain to obtain dune-building property rights and signaled that one or two homeowners could stop a beachfront dune project even if every other owner in a town agreed to go forward.

Just months later, while an appeal was pending before the New Jersey Supreme Court, Superstorm Sandy struck the Jersey Shore. Just south of Harvey Cedars on Long Beach Island, in Beach Haven and Holgate, the ocean ravaged hundreds of properties and caused enormous damage. In Harvey Cedars, with its newly constructed dunes, the storm had a limited impact with few properties damaged. The houses of the holdouts had been spared substantial damage. Perhaps the impact of the storm on these various properties was due to the direction and strength of the storm; perhaps it was the dunes; perhaps it was just luck or divine providence. Whatever the reason, it appeared to some that the storm had an impact on the pending case. The Supreme Court heard oral arguments *after* the storm passed and reversed the courts below, stating that the value of the protection gained must be netted against the loss of view and other amenities sacrificed by the property owners:

> A jury evidently concluded that the Karans' property decreased in value as a result of the loss of their panoramic view of the seashore due to the height of the dune. A willing purchaser of beachfront property would obviously value the view and proximity to the ocean. But it is also likely that a rational purchaser would place a value on a protective barrier that shielded his property from partial or total destruction. Whatever weight might be given that consideration, surely, it would be one part of the equation in determining fair market value. Although,

in determining the fair market value of the Karans' property, the jury
was instructed to consider all features that enhanced and diminished
the property's value, the jury also was told to disregard "general benefits produced by the dune project which [the Karans] may enjoy in
common with other property owners in the area to reduce the value."
This charge distorted the fair-market valuation of the property by arti-
ficially withholding a key component of the analysis.[11]

The effect of the decision was to give Harvey Cedars (and other watching municipal governments) a stronger position in negotiations for the
value of the property rights lost. The re-hearing on value yielded one
dollar for the homeowner after factoring in the enhanced protection
the property received.

The building and maintenance of dunes continues to be an issue. In the
aftermath of Sandy, Governor Christie declared that the state would pursue dunes up and down the coast as the preferred method of beach protection and instructed the state and municipalities to employ the eminent
domain tool, if necessary. Of the 2,850 easements needed for this $128 mil-
lion project, all but about 330 were quickly and easily obtained. But not
all citizens agree that this is the best approach and a legal and political
battle has arisen. The oceanfront homeowners in Bay Head contend that
their stone seawall provides better and more sustainable protection than
dunes, and most refused to sign the easement deeds. The stone seawall
across the center of the town, built in 1888 with private monies, successfully protected the houses behind it from Sandy's fiercest winds and tides.
In 2013 Bay Head homeowners, having sufficient collective resources ($2.2
million), went ahead without state funding to extend the eighteen-foot-
high wall across its entire sea front. The state nevertheless insists that Bay
Head build the dunes as well and declared that it will use eminent domain
to get easements if they are not freely given.

At the time of this writing, the controversy has not been resolved and
has drawn in other municipalities on both sides. Residents and municipal

officials in adjacent Mantoloking contend that the extension of the Bay Head seawall to the south will adversely impact their community in the next severe storm.[12] Margate, in Atlantic County, taking the Bay Head position, also challenged the state's dune-building projects as did business owners (Jenkinson's Amusements) in Point Pleasant Beach. At one point in the controversy, Governor Christie called those withholding easements selfish.[13] One trial court denied Margate's claims in early 2016 and another denied Bay Head's objections to the state's authority in August 2017, but the judge in the Bay Head case questioned the efficacy of the dune project. Most likely, this litigation will not be concluded for several years and will once again require a decision of the New Jersey Supreme Court.[14] In the meantime, the state's dune-building project continues.

We cannot ignore another aspect of this legal and engineering debate as we view it from twenty-first century societal perspectives. In the 150-year period from the first case in 1821 to the landmark decision in 1978, the practicalities of beach access and control changed dramatically. Before the last quarter of the nineteenth century the vast acreage of the state's beachfront was open to anyone who could find his or her way to the sand. The sale of beachfront lots and convenient access changed that dynamic, however, and demands for privacy and exclusive access led to restrictions on who could be on the beach. In many areas, the state's black citizens were effectively denied equal access to the state's beaches despite the public trust doctrine. As we have seen, Asbury Park officially prohibited the mingling of white and black beachgoers from well before 1900 and Atlantic City did the same after 1920. In the newer communities along the shore, people considered to be undesirable were denied access through economic and physical barriers, such as high beach fees for nonresidents (as in the Avon-by-the-Sea case) or the deliberate failure to provide parking, bathhouses, and sanitary facilities near the beach. The homeowners refusing to grant easements to the state claim that the state is overreaching, taking more rights than it needs, and making their property a public beach.[15] It may be that the owners of some beachfront properties fear the

influx of undesirables on their beach more than the pounding their property may sustain in the next superstorm.

Add into this mix the cost of protecting beaches from storms and erosion through the expenditure of state and federal tax resources. Should
the local, state, and federal governments be in the business of building
seawalls, jetties, and groins, and replenishing beaches with transported
sand at an enormous expense for the enjoyment of private property
owners with homes on or near the beach? On the other hand, can the state
ignore the millions of citizens who enjoy its beaches each summer and
isn't much of the expense recaptured through taxes and the economic
benefits of the tourist trade? This debate underlies all discussions of what
the Jersey Shore should look like, in whatever form it takes; for example,
in the debate over whether state-funded dunes should trump privately
built seawalls; in the forum where it arises (in the courts or in the legislature); and in whatever policy is being debated (such as the extent that private property rights should restrict public beach access).[16]

State Action, Federal Funding, and University Support

Prior to the 1940s most efforts to maintain eroding beaches were local;
desired or demanded by local residents or businessmen looking to maintain
the status quo or, in some cases, to further opportunities for their towns
or businesses. And most of the work was done with a particular town's
interests in mind. This goes back to at least the 1870s when the Ocean
Grove elders cleared their beachfront of trees, brush, and dunes and
then had to build jetties to protect their beach, and when James Bradley
made oceanfront improvements to enhance his Asbury Park beachfront
resulting in the silting in of the shallow inlet from the ocean to Deal
Lake.[17] For decades thereafter, seawalls, dunes, jetties, and breakers were
built locally as stopgap measures. The desirability and effectiveness of
each method depended on the actions of adjacent municipalities, contemporary theories about the best solutions, and cost. The state did not

enter into these efforts with any energy until after 1915 when legislation created the Department of Conservation and Development (now the Department of Environmental Protection), which consolidated commissions that dealt with harbors, canals, and riparian rights. Eventually, the department began providing assistance to local governments in maintaining the shoreline. A 1956 report from the department recited the state's limited effort to that date:

> Over thirty years ago the erosion of the beaches of the State had become a problem of such well-recognized importance that the State began giving technical and financial assistance to communities undertaking erosion control and in 1922 the New Jersey Board of Commerce and Navigation . . . published a [Report] which contained recommended criteria for shore protection structures. A supplement to this Report was published in 1924 and in 1930 a final report was published to bring the whole matter up to date. These early attempts to formulate reliable procedures for controlling erosion were not completely successful. A number of rock groins and considerable lengths of seawall were built which undoubtedly benefitted the properties they were intended to protect. Many stand today and are useful but it is unfortunately true that some of the groins, especially those inclined to the southward, accelerated and promoted the erosion of adjacent properties to the north of them. Large sums were furthermore wasted, often by the owners of privately held ocean front property, in the construction of ineffective protective structures many of which were experimental and some worse than useless.[18]

An important issue, of course, was funding, which increased in the following years. More than $13.5 million was expended by the state and local governments (in equal shares) in the three years after the 1962 Ash Wednesday storm, and was matched by the federal government, for groins, bulkheads, nourishment, and dunes.[19] The state effort was aided when the voters passed a Beaches and Harbors Bond Fund in 1977 in the amount of $30 million. Voters also approved a Flood Control Bond Issue of $25 million in 1978 and a Natural Resources Bond Issue of $145 million in 1980, both of which allocated funds for shore areas.

The state enacted the Wetlands Act in 1970 and the Coastal Area Facility Review Act (CAFRA) in 1973 and began allocating about $1 million each year thereafter toward the effort of preserving and maintaining the beaches. Then, in October 1981, the state government released a Shore Protection Master Plan to coordinate efforts up and down the coast and, in part, to detail how state funds would be expended. The report noted the mixed bag of efforts made to date:

> Local governments in New Jersey have taken different approaches towards shore protection, with some allowing dunes to be overtaken by development, while others worked to acquire oceanfront lots and rebuild dunes. The Federal government has also been actively involved in shorefront protection through the Army Corps of Engineers, and in shorefront development through the National Flood Insurance Program. The net result of these State, Federal and Local activities has been an amalgam and somewhat reactive approach to shore protection. This Shore Protection Master Plan is intended to represent a more cohesive and comprehensive approach to the problem of shore protection for use by the State, and hopefully other levels of government as well.[20]

The report categorized the coastal area into eight major regions and subdivided them into more local "reaches." The eight regions include five along the ocean shore—the Northern Barrier Spit, the Northern Headlands, the Northern Barrier Islands Complex, the Southern Barrier Islands Complex, and the Southern Headlands—plus Raritan Bay, Delaware Bay, and the Delaware River. Each region, and each reach within the regions, was measured for erosion and determined to be Critical, Significant, Moderate, or Non-Eroding. Environmentalists and researchers working at the shore have adopted this framework when discussing shore erosion issues. The 1981 report included a detailed discussion of the various efforts utilized over the prior hundred years to hold back the ocean and the tides; that is, jetties, bulkheads, groins, seawalls, and dunes, comparing their effectiveness and cost.

The 1981 Shore Protection Master Plan also recognized the dilemma faced by the state. On the one hand, the report describes sea level rise as a continuing natural effect that causes the erosion of the beaches and concludes that "man-made barriers and attempts at maintaining a static shoreline position, either through impenetrable stabilized dunes . . . or through use of shore protection structures" prevent the *natural* reconstruction of the beaches.[21] The report predicted that these man-made efforts would result in the "eventual loss of the beach." On the other hand, the report acknowledged that New Jersey's "bays and ocean shore areas are extremely important economic assets and constitute coastal environments characterized by their seasonality and dependence on the tourism and resort industry."[22] The report came almost two decades after the devastating 1962 Ash Wednesday storm and its authors noted that that "the devastation of the March 1962 storm was soon forgotten." Development had soared in the intervening twenty years "despite the history of hurricanes, nor'easters, and other storms, the costly damages, and the inevitable risk." The report predicted that "future severe storms will undoubtedly result in far heavier tolls in lives, injuries, and property damage"[23] and suggested (as did subsequent reviews) that dune-building and beach nourishment efforts, though costly and of mid-range (ten years) impact, can serve as effective methods to slow erosion, protect property, and maintain recreational use of the beaches if retreat from the beach is not pursued.[24]

In the years after the 1981 Report, the state ramped up funding for shore projects. Voters passed a Shore Protection Bond Issue in the amount of $50 million in 1983, which specifically included the funding of loans and grants to counties and municipalities. The state tied these funds to matching funds available for the beach nourishment projects of the Army Corps of Engineers to maximize their effect. The federal government picks up 65 percent of the cost and the state and each local municipality share the remaining 35 percent. Indeed, one recent report claimed that New Jersey has benefited more than any other state from federal funding for beach nourishment in recent years.[25] In 1994, the legislature established the Shore Protection Stable Funding Act, which initially provided $15 million annually for the specific purpose of conducting shore protection projects along the coastline. Receipts from the Realty Transfer Tax now provide a constant $25 million source of state money for Shore Protection Fund. Stockton University, which is located in Atlantic County, calculated that the federal government, state government, and local governments spent $500 million in New Jersey on beach nourishment projects from Sandy Hook to Cape May in the fifteen years between 1990 and 2005.[26] Whether federal funds will be available in future years remains to be seen. Recent U.S. presidents have sought to curtail this program and funding requires congressional appropriation each year.

Despite the continuous utilization of federal beach nourishment funds, the program has not been consistently applauded by all observers. Critics believe that repeated nourishment encourages building in environmentally sensitive areas and benefits wealthy property owners. They would prefer less aggressive government action in favor of action that would discourage building along the beachfront and reclaim developed properties and are concerned that the harvesting of sand from the sea floor will bring its own environmental issues. Their efforts have not been very successful. The 1995 $340 million Green Acres Bond Issue endorsed the purchase, for recreation and conservation, of "coastal properties that are prone or have incurred flood or storm damage" but included only $15 million in funding. Critics also fault the federal government's handling of its flood insurance program, enacted as the National Flood Insurance Act of 1978. The program quickly became the primary source of flood insurance for the owners of beach properties and a significant percentage of claims have been for second homes, some reimbursed repeatedly after successive storms. Environmentalist and budget hawks argued that the program made insurance readily available, cheap, and dependable in flood-prone areas. When Hurricane Katrina sapped the fund's reserves in 2005, Congress passed the Biggert-Waters Flood Insurance Reform and Modernization Act of 2012 just months before Superstorm Sandy hit the Jersey Shore. This overhaul required, among other reforms, that premiums for second homes and businesses be set to market rates over a five-year period. This change significantly increased the financial burden for Jersey Shore homeowners seeking to repair damaged properties after Sandy. A howl of protests led to a congressional retreat, postponing the increases to give the distressed homeowners time to absorb the higher premiums.[27]

Other federal legislation has been helpful. The Coastal Zone Management Act of 1972 recognized that the "the increasing and competing demands upon the lands and waters of our coastal zone occasioned by population growth and economic development . . . have resulted in the loss of living marine resources, wildlife, nutrient-rich areas, permanent and adverse changes to ecological systems, decreasing open space for public use, and shoreline erosion." The act encouraged all effected states to develop and implement management plans. New Jersey's plan was approved in 1978, and the DEP's 1981 report recognized the state's obligations under this act, as have subsequent reports. The Disaster Relief Act of 1974 enhanced the federal government's response to storms and other disasters, provided an ongoing source of federal funds for states and local governments to plan for such emergencies, and established financial aid for effected states, municipalities, and individuals. New Jersey benefited greatly from the disaster relief funds available after Superstorm Sandy in repairing its infrastructure as did many individual homeowners. The Federal Coastal Barrier Resources Act of 1982 seeks to preserve undeveloped coastal areas by *denying* federal funding for projects in designated regions. New Jersey has more than 65,000 acres in the John H. Chafee Coastal Barrier Resources System under this act.[28]

Other resources have also become available to the state and local communities still learning to live with the sea. Stockton University created a

Coastal Research Center in 1981 "to assist local municipalities with coastal environmental issues relating to continuing storm damage and shoreline retreat." It website posts annual reports on coastal erosion and assessments of damages after storms.[29] In November 2014, the center issued a report entitled "Hurricane Sandy: Beach-Dune Performance at New Jersey Beach Profile Network Sites," which detailed its findings on which beach dune systems fared well and which did not: "Several shore communities north of landfall suffered extensive damages where dunes were nonexistent or backed a narrow beach. The presence of maintained federally designed beach nourishment projects including engineered dunes played a significant role in protecting landward structures and infrastructure as the projects absorbed the impacts of the storm waters."[30]

Rutgers University has been heavily engaged in coastal and oceanographic research in the last fifty years through its Marine and Coastal Sciences Department, which includes a Center for Ocean Observing Leadership (COOL) at the George H. Cook campus in New Brunswick, a marine field station in Tuckerton that conducts research "from the upper reaches of the Mullica River drainage basin, down through the Great Bay estuary, to the inner continental shelf," and the Haskin Shellfish Research Laboratory, which supports fisheries and aquaculture research with bases in Bivalve, New Jersey, and on the Delaware Bay near Cape May.[31] The marine field station is within the Jacques Cousteau National Estuarine Research Reserve and encompasses 115,000 acres of wetlands and aquatic habitats for research and preservation.[32] The COOL achieved international renown in 2009 when one of its underwater gliders made a successful and unpowered Atlantic Ocean crossing from Tuckerton to Baiona, Spain, transmitting ocean data throughout its journey. Glider RU27 has since been donated to the Smithsonian Institution, other gliders have been deployed throughout the world, and others were used to obtain data during Superstorm Sandy.[33]

In addition to this university support, the National Oceanic and Atmospheric Administration operates the James J. Howard Sciences

Laboratory on Sandy Hook for fifty staffers from the Northeast Fisheries Science Center's Ecosystems Processes Division. This marine research facility seeks to "promote the recovery and long-term sustainability" of living marine resources on the Northeast Shelf; that is, to identify and map fish along the New Jersey and northeast coastline in an effort to maintain their habitats and their continued viability. It is an extension of a laboratory first established in 1961.[34]

REVIVAL: CAPE MAY, LONG BRANCH, ASBURY PARK, AND ATLANTIC CITY

One phenomena that began at the end of the twentieth century and continues today is the effort to revive Cape May, Long Branch, Asbury Park, and Atlantic City.

Cape May became an also-ran in the nineteenth century competition with Atlantic City and Long Branch and in the twentieth-century competition with the new boutique resorts. Devotees continued to visit Cape May but the city lost many of its signature hotels and Victorian homes to fire, storms (including devastation in 1962), and demolition. One commentator described the Cape May of 1975 as "an ugly duckling of a resort of rundown boarding housing on an eroding beach,"[35] an apt but painful description for a town that 150 years earlier had been a sea-bathing community of sophistication and note. What would become of Cape May? Quite a bit, apparently. Sometime in the 1970s, the town's focus shifted away from the typical approach to revival—that is, boardwalk amusement piers and continued demolition of large hotels—to something new— historic preservation of its Victorian buildings and heritage. A combination of political changes at the local level in 1972 and a growing national awareness of preservation saved the resort and many of its historic sites, including the Physick Estate, The Congress, Chalfonte, and Colonial hotels, and eventually the lighthouse. A local nonprofit preservation group played an important role throughout and the business community also bought in. The result has been a revival of Cape May as a colorful Victorian showplace with bed-and-breakfast inns and restored modest-sized hotels. Vacationers have been drawn to the city off-season by tours of historic homes and events like the Victorian Weekend in October, started in 1973. The entire city was placed on the National Register of Historic Places in 1976 and more than 110,000 people visited the restored lighthouse in 1997. The commentator who had little positive to say about the city's prospects in 1975, marveled twenty-five years later at the "elegant swan" the city had become in such a short period of time, "a success story for a new type of heritage tourism . . . that found its pleasures . . . in the charm of restored Victorian cottages along tree-shaded streets."[36]

Long Branch has had a similar revival, coming somewhat later and still in the making. The town lost its luster as the nation's premier resort somewhere around the turn of the twentieth century. The size and glamour of its crowds declined thereafter as the resort fought battles with the sea to prevent erosion of its unique but disappearing bluff. Long Branch left the resort competition quietly, slowly transforming itself into a year-round city with significant industry, particularly the manufacture of clothing, to complement its resort business. Its population grew substantially in the early 1900s as income from its resort business fell below that of its other interests. Town officials tried to revive the city as a desired resort by underwriting the Ocean Park Casino, which opened in 1911 with rides and concerts, but only one hotel—the Hotel Takannassee in 1906—was built in the first twenty years of the new century. Indeed, beachfront properties languished for decades, falling into disrepair and discouraging rather than attracting beach patrons. A 1987 fire at the boardwalk destroyed the Long Branch Pier and all of its amusements. Despite declarations that the pier would be rebuilt and reopened, the burned-out hulk remained unrepaired for seventeen years, emphasizing Long Branch's fall from grace and its inability to share in the economic benefits of being on the Jersey Shore. The *New York Times* described the Long Branch oceanfront as "a

battered array of go-go joints, vacant storefronts, weedy lots, drug deal-
ers, decrepit housing and a defunct water slide."[37]

The turn of the twenty-first century brought revival to Long Branch.
The fire-damaged pier was finally demolished and long-planned urban
renewal projects were executed. Unlike Cape May, which chose to restore
its Victorian past, Long Branch chose to develop as a modern, high-end
community replete with large hotels, luxury stores, and desirable year-
round housing. Pier Village, to be built in three phases, combines stores,
amusements, condominiums, and apartments that have attracted thousands back to the area. Hundreds of residential units sit atop chic shops,
restaurants, and a private beach club on the same oceanfront that sat in
ruins for so many years. The first phase was completed in 2005 to critical
acclaim at a cost of more than $100 million.[38] A second phase was com-
pleted in 2008, the final phase is underway, and the revival has stoked
other projects in the city as well. The high-end stores and luxury apartments that are at the heart of these projects evoke memories of Long
Branch's days of greatness.

The precipitous fall from grace of Asbury Park after the July 1970 race
riot was tragic. The city saw its best years in the initial decades of the
twentieth century, but began a slow decline during the Depression.
The Garden State Parkway allowed tourists to choose smaller beach towns
in Monmouth County and more accessible beach towns in Ocean County.
Even so, Asbury Park continued to attract families in the 1950s and then,
in the 1960s and 1970s, refashioned its music culture by bringing younger
audiences to the resort with rock 'n' rollers like Jon Bon Jovi and Southside Johnnie and the Asbury Jukes featured at the Stone Pony, which
opened in 1974. Unfortunately, a series of woes beset the city. A corrupt
city government allowed the city's structures to deteriorate (even selling
the copper roof off the boardwalk's casino rather than spending the
money to repair it); the rioting in the 1970s damaged the city's buildings
and eliminated its image as a family-friendly resort; in the 1980s a series

of fires of unknown origin destroyed more buildings; and the city had to deal with an influx of homeless as patients were released from deteriorating state mental institutions.

Asbury Park has since sought to restore its glory—several times—but its woes continued to mount. Attempts in the last fifty years to revitalize the city through private-public partnerships have not ended well. In 1986 a developer came to town from Connecticut, secured the development rights for the waterfront, and revealed a grand plan for a city renaissance anchored by a 160-unit condominium project close to the boardwalk. With just the frame of the building finished, Joseph Carabetta ran out of money in 1989, eventually filing for bankruptcy in 1992. The unfinished building languished for fifteen years as a symbol of the city's frustration until 2004. Asbury Partners, LLC had by then picked up the oceanfront development rights, demolished the unfinished structure, and was renovating and rebuilding the boardwalk at a cost of almost $6 million. But the years of neglect impacted the city's glorious past as buildings and artifacts disappeared. The Palace Amusements building was demolished in 2004 and what was remaining of its 1888 carousel was removed in pieces. Intervention by preservationists saved one of two smiling faces of "Tillie" painted on the concrete wall of the building and about 100 other pieces of nostalgia from the building's games and rides. The Tillie images were painted in 1956, copies of a George Tilyou image originally painted in Coney Island years earlier. The saved image, long associated with Asbury Park, was cut out and moved to storage on a truck before the building was demolished. Eventually, Asbury Partners also ran into financial troubles. When the city council declared a default in 2010, the company's parent, iStar Financial, took up the obligations and fulfilled some of the earlier promises. iStar announced in 2016 its intention to build a sixteen-story tower with 128 residences, hotel rooms, and retail space on the Metro/Esperanza site originally abandoned by Carabetta in 1989.

Despite the recent activity, Asbury Park continues its struggles and its future remains more uncertain than its former rivals, Long Branch and Cape May. The city has received some solace from its relationship with rock star Bruce Springsteen, who is famously associated with the city and who elevated the city's image with his 1973 breakout album, *Greetings from Asbury Park*. Springsteen has continued his support with songs that lament the plight of this once-great resort. The music scene that propelled Springsteen in his early days has to some extent come back to the city with concerts and events on the boardwalk. Perhaps the combination of the music scene and new energy will propel Asbury Park back to its glory days.

What will become of Atlantic City? The experiment of bringing casino gambling to Atlantic City may have been well-intentioned and may have been initially successful. But the results, after almost forty years, have been mixed. Despite the casino construction along the Boardwalk and at the marina, the city's housing remains inadequate and its population remains impoverished. The city can no longer support itself financially and has become a ward of the state with the governor and state legislators squabbling as late as 2017 over how best to fix the city. Investment bankers expect that more casinos will close in the coming years. The 2014 bankruptcy of the Revel Casino puts the current environment in perspective. A 2015 story in *New Yorker* magazine detailed the deterioration of this casino project, which may be the city's last.[39] Revel announced its plans to build in 2006, but construction stopped on its half-built tower in 2009 despite the investment of more than $1 billion by businessmen and investment bankers who supposedly knew what they were doing. Multiple players have since sought to revive the property but the difficulties of dealing with the state and local governments, utilities, the bankruptcy court, and its casino neighbors makes the Revel's successful resuscitation highly improbable in the foreseeable future. The fight among bidders over the casino's assets at pennies on the dollar highlights the gloom surrounding Atlantic City's fortunes. Nevertheless, new owners announced a re-opening date in 2017.[40]

SUPERSTORM SANDY

No contemporary discussion of the Jersey Shore can avoid the impact of Superstorm Sandy. This meteorological behemoth slammed head-on into the state's coast in late October 2012 with a ferocity like few other storms. In some ways, Superstorm Sandy recalled the March 1962 Ash Wednesday storm and the September 1944 storm. All three storms were devastating, but in 2012 New Jersey's 127 miles of shoreline from Sandy Hook to Cape May Point was filled with thousands of homes and businesses. Most of these structures were built after the 1944 storm and thousands of people established permanent homes since the 1962 storm in the beach communities and on the barrier islands. The advance warnings from the National Weather Service that heralded the storm's potential ensured that thousands of news cameras and cell phones were available to memorialize Sandy's wrath. The monetary losses were staggering and, despite the warnings, dozens of people were killed.

New Jersey had had a dress rehearsal for Sandy just one year earlier when Hurricane Irene headed up the Atlantic Coast in late August. The National Weather Service issued warnings and Governor Christie ordered a mandatory evacuation of the barrier islands with the elegant phrasing, "Get the hell off the beach." Irene hit New Jersey at the Little Egg Inlet causing $1 billion in damage, much of it inland due to high winds and flooding. Atlantic City casinos were closed for one day. More than 200,000 homes were damaged and almost a million residents lost power. The southern New Jersey beaches were not severely impacted, however. Some who heeded the warnings and left their homes in advance of the storm felt that their initial belief was correct, that weather prognosticators and government officials always exaggerate the risk. Sandy proved them wrong.

More than 300,000 houses in the state were damaged or destroyed by Sandy and $31 billion in losses were sustained. The governor closed the casinos for seven days and canceled Halloween festivities. The state, not just the shore, was in shambles. Thirty-four people were killed in New Jersey and 177 over the vast territory that Sandy traveled as it moved up the Atlantic coast. At one point the storm boasted a diameter of 900 miles.

Sandy began its journey on Sunday, October 21, in the southern Caribbean. It was the eighteenth named storm of the season. Late October seldom produces a hurricane of great magnitude, however, so the early indications that Sandy could wreak havoc as it grew and moved out of the southern Atlantic were viewed with skepticism. Most experts expected that meteorological events would cause this late bloomer to fizzle out somewhere over the Atlantic. But with each passing day, the storm proved more resilient. The experts at the National Weather Service became concerned when Sandy rampaged through Haiti and then Cuba on October 24 and alarm bells rang from Maryland, through New Jersey and New York, up into Connecticut, Massachusetts, Rhode Island, and Maine. Governor Christie announced voluntary evacuations of the barrier islands on Friday, October 26, and then a mandatory evacuation on Saturday. Most shore residents and business people responded and left their homes and businesses. A few stalwarts or foolhardy individuals ignored the warnings, stayed in their homes, or moved to higher ground as the storm approached. Almost all regretted their decision. A full moon appeared on Sunday, October 28, and brought its usual higher tides, just as Sandy made landfall at Brigantine on Monday, October 29. Even though the storm was no longer classified a hurricane, Sandy's tidal surge rose to eight and a half feet at Sandy Hook, pounding the beaches, destroying dunes, ripping up boardwalks, sundering seawalls, and destroying every man-made object in its path, including amusement piers and roller-coasters. Flood waters rose throughout the state and hundreds of thousands were thrown into darkness. Emergency crews could not reach the power lines for repairs and could not keep up with the vast destruction. Almost no one in the state avoided the impact of the storm, and all of those who owned property at or near the beach had to wait days and weeks to see if their businesses or residences withstood the storm or to assess the damage suffered.

New Jersey's northern beaches (from Holgate on Long Beach Island to Sandy Hook) took the brunt of the storm. Steady winds of just under hurricane levels (74 miles per hour) and gusts as high as 91 miles per hour (at Seaside Heights) raked the beach communities. The boardwalk and amusement piers in Seaside Heights and Seaside Park were thrown into the ocean, the roller-coaster left in shallow water; the Barnegat peninsula was breached at Mantoloking and the bridge to the mainland was threatened. More than 1,500 boats were ripped from their moorings later to be found at a distance on land, in marshes, and under bridges. The Raritan Bay communities were especially hard hit. The losses in these communities were even more heartbreaking because primary homes of modest price were washed away. To this day, not everyone has been able to return due to government entanglements and lack of resources, notwithstanding the initial "Restore the Shore" response to the storm. The wrath of Superstorm Sandy left the Jersey Shore devastated from north to south.

Throughout this book we have made references to Sandy and its aftermath: the state's immediate declaration that the shore would be restored and the acceptance of this approach by those affected; the work necessary to repair the Mantoloking Bridge and adjacent roadways as well as filling in the breach at the bridge; the loss of homes in bungalow communities like the Dover and Ocean Beach communities in Toms River and Brick townships, including the fire that engulfed Camp Osborn; the plan to rebuild the seawall at Sea Bright, and the construction of the seawall in Mantoloking and Brick Township; the rebuilding of the Seaside Park amusement pier (and its subsequent loss to fire and re-rebuilding); the governor's decision to adopt dunes and beach nourishment as the standard approach to storms and erosion for all beaches in the state; and, perhaps most significant, the ability of the beach communities, with state and federal help, to be ready for the summer season of 2013 just seven months later. The impact of this storm continues, however, in how we view the Jersey Shore going forward.

As the months and years have passed, the initial public embrace of the state's response to the storm has eroded; lingering issues, like the Camp Osborn conundrum, remain unresolved. Not every homeowner has been able to repair or rebuild. Federal legislation enacted before the storm removed subsidies from the National Flood Insurance Program and federal and state revisions to flood maps after the storm impacted almost every homeowner. Under federal law, a homeowner in a flood zone is not required to purchase flood insurance unless the house has a mortgage loan issued by a bank or mortgage company. Homeowners without mortgage loans before the storm needed loans for reconstruction. As a result, the costs, not just to repair, but to maintain a treasured beach house, rose considerably. Repairing a damaged home in a flood zone without elevating it could have resulted in annual flood insurance premiums more than $10,000![41] Even though the federal government delayed the market adjustments for flood insurance and the state revisited its flood maps and removed some homes from the worst designations,[42] the controversy continues.

A 2014 newspaper article titled "Springsteen Girls Priced Out as Rich Buy N.J. Shore Homes" suggested that the less well-off in the state would be economically banned from the shore as older, more modest, beach homes are abandoned or demolished in favor of new, larger, and more fashionably designed residences.[43] Other commentators after Sandy suggested the same. Could it be that the confluence of environmentalism, concerns about safety, and Superstorm Sandy will once again turn the Jersey Shore into an enclave for the rich? And, at the same time that the state government and the courts are struggling to make sure that all levels of society can share in this resource? In any event, the visual impact can already be seen as communities that featured cookie-cutter bungalows are now spattered with empty lots, low-rise repaired bungalows, and elevated mansion-like structures.

Further Reading

For background, see W. Mack Angas, "Beach Erosion Control on the New Jersey Coast," Report to the Department of Conservation and Economic Development (September 1956); C. F. Wicker, "Problems of the New Jersey Beaches," Report to the New Jersey Department of Conservation and Economic Development (1965); Greg Hanscom, "Flood Pressure: Climate Disasters Drown FEMA's Insurance Plans," January 13, 2014, at the website GRIST, http://grist.org /cities/flood-pressure-how-climate-disasters-put-femas-flood -insurance-program-underwater/; Chris Edwards, "The Federal Emergency Management Agency: Floods, Failures, and Federalism" (December 1, 2014) at http://www.downsizinggovernment.org /dhs/fema#_ednref240; the U.S. Fish and Wildlife Service Coastal Barrier Resources System website at http://www.fws.gov/ecological -services/habitat-conservation/cbra/Maps/index.html; and the FEMA Fact Sheet, "Homeowner Flood Insurance Affordability Act of 2014," at http://www.fema.gov/media-library-data /1414004070850-3e90be61f9762523126c385a1d7fa95a/FEMA _HFIAA_OctoberBulletinFS_100814.pdf.
On Superstorm Sandy, see Diane Bates, *Superstorm Sandy, The Inevitable Destruction and Reconstruction of the Jersey Shore* (New Brunswick, NJ: Rutgers University Press, 2016); Kathryn Miles, *Superstorm: Nine Days Inside Hurricane Sandy* (New York: Penguin, 2014); Karen M. O'Neill and Daniel J. Van Abs, eds., *Taking Chances, The Coast After Hurricane Sandy* (New Brunswick, NJ: Rutgers University Press, 2016); and Adam Sobel, *Storm Surge: Hurricane Sandy, Our Changing Climate, and Extreme Weather of the Past and Future* (New York: Harper Collins, 2014).

The Future of the Jersey Shore

More than thirty miles of the Jersey Shore remains undeveloped today: the northern end of Sandy Hook, Island Beach State Park, the Edwin B. Forsythe National Wildlife Refuge at Holgate, Peck's Beach in Corson's Inlet State Park, the Two Mile Beach Unit in the Wildwoods, Cape May National Wildlife Refuge, and Cape May Meadows. Over the past 350 years the people living and working and vacationing on the Jersey Shore have fashioned the remaining ninety-seven miles to their individual liking, a greater percentage of its coastland than most of its neighboring Atlantic Ocean states.[1] Some people suggest that efforts to protect or replenish beaches are a losing battle, that we should begin a retreat from the ocean, and that we should allow nature to take its course, returning as much of the shore to a natural state as possible. Others prefer the status quo and, as much as we might want to believe that undeveloped beauty surpasses man-made pleasures, hundreds of thousands of visitors still rush to the developed shore communities each year.

Abandoning the beachfront to nature, in the midterm or over decades, has its advocates, but such a policy would impact private property rights, business interests, and the state's economy. The density of construction in place and the state population's emotional attachment to the shore also preclude retreat. People enjoy the boardwalks, the rides, fishing in the bays, riding the waves, and the beauty of an empty beach just footsteps from a summer cottage. Tourists and vacationers would protest the fewer opportunities for their families to enjoy the beaches. Local seashore businessmen would join with them. Just offshore, the state and federal governments cannot move away from continuous efforts to maintain the inlets with jetties and bulwarking to protect fishermen and sportsmen from danger as the inlets and the nearby shoals shift from year to year. Retreat remains a minority view, albeit with strong voices calling for policies to prevent rebuilding of damaged and destroyed properties on or near the water.[2] The debate is complex. A recent study (replete with daunting algebraic formulas) concluded that government efforts to nourish the beaches at the Jersey Shore increase the value of oceanfront properties on an average of 9 percent to 17 percent, with some properties as high as 37 percent. Advocates of retreat see such studies as proof that government programs help the wealthy maintain their properties and encourage rebuilding after storms. Yet the authors of this study suggested in their conclusion that any change in policy needs to take into consideration multiple nonmathematical factors:

> Although our model predicts a sizeable policy-induced inflation in coastal real estate markets, it is neither a call for increasing subsidies nor a call for removing them. Subsidies for breach nourishment are a part of a broader suite of policies that manage coastal hazards. These other policies, including subsidized flood insurance and disaster relief, expose public funds to tremendous risk, and what seem like very costly adaptive measures can be justified by avoided expected storm damage. It may be that subsidies to beach nourishment by reducing demand for disaster relief, constitute a more efficient use of federal dollars relative to other subsidized programs. Whether or not nourishment is an efficient use of public funds, if the subsidies were removed suddenly, it could have drastic consequences, including a crash in coastal property values in regions relying on heavily subsidized nourishment and associated drops in property taxes that fund local public goods such as

schools and infrastructure. As such, we recommend a cautious approach to changing subsidies for beach nourishment. If beach nourishment is not part of a long-run strategy to manage eroding coastlines, a gradual phase-out is more likely to smooth the transition to more climate-resilient coastal communities.[3]

As a society we share a responsibility to maintain the treasure that is the Jersey Shore, in large part because it brings pleasure to millions of people and can continue to do so for millions more in the future. Just as we recognize the impediments to abandoning our shore to nature, we need to recognize the dangers the beaches face from storms, constant erosion, global warming, and continued building at or near the beaches, on barrier islands, and in environmentally sensitive areas. The Jersey Shore is a fragile treasure that needs to be protected and preserved.

How will this debate impact the Jersey Shore as we now know it? Several factors will play a role in the future of the shore. First, we need to recognize that the status quo is an ephemeral notion when it comes to the Jersey Shore, which will continue to change as it has in the past. Second, forces of nature will impact our need and our willingness to make changes, whether as a result of a continued succession of horrendous storms or the chimera of a lull in storm activity. Third, politics will impact the call for solutions and the nature of those solutions. The ability and willingness to fund expensive projects and the rise or disappearance of leadership will have significant impact on the policies pursued. And fourth, our society's growing environmental awareness, locally as well as nationally, will shape the approach to all issues impacting the shore.

The Jersey coast is ever-changing. Geologically, the beaches, inlets, and islands change their contours every day despite human efforts to maintain a constant coastline; culturally, society's perceptions of the shore have changed over the last 200 years with cultural norms; economically, businessmen continuously try new ways to lure vacationers for a visit and to entice potential homeowners to purchase lots. What was once a wasteland, what was once viewed through the prism of just four or five resorts, what was once the permanent home to just a few, what was once the playground of just the elite and those not of color, what was once the dominion of local officials and business entrepreneurs, is no more. Few, if any, of these changes were anticipated. The construction of a railroad to Absecon Island in 1854 coincided with the rising concept of "vacations" for the middle class and led, at first, to the building of grand resort hotels at a limited number of locations. The technology and enterprise that brought railroads to every location along the shore in the following decades encouraged the development of dozens of communities with individual identities. The rise of automobiles in the twentieth century lured more people to the shore for annual vacations, shifted preferences from large hotels to seasonal homes, and made shore communities accessible for year-round living. Change remains a constant at the shore.

Meteorological events will also play a role in the future of the Jersey Shore. Superstorm Sandy may have been a hundred-year storm or it may herald an era of similar storms over the next several decades. Whatever the path, a storm like Sandy precludes a passive response. Already we have seen the state take a more aggressive role in beachfront protection with its embrace of dunes and beach nourishment as a universal approach. We should expect to see continued changes in local building codes and zoning regulations. Surely the look of the shore will change as new homes rise on pilings in communities where there were no raised homes before. We need to take care, however. The 1962 Ash Wednesday storm led to construction codes that made the structures more sustainable and, therefore, more desirable; Hurricane Betsy in 1965 led to the National Flood Insurance program with subsidized federal insurance rates that made those structures more affordable. The building boom at the shore after the 1960s resulted in thousands of more homes in harm's way, only now built on pilings. We should avoid the risk of short-term memory. If few storms of any ferocity visit the Jersey Shore over the next twenty years, will we forget (as we have seemed to do in the past) and simply incorporate Sandy into the lore of the Jersey Shore—until the next devastating storm makes landfall, as it surely will.

Politics will also play a role. Before the twentieth century, local forces dictated the development of each beach community. New Jersey's resilient adherence to "home rule" encouraged municipal splintering and supports resistance to state government mandates. We see the latter trend today in the fight initiated by Bay Head residents over the state's dune-building project. One of the political factors that will impact the future of the shore will be whether the state government can sustain a leadership role in development (or the prevention of development) along the shore or whether state politicians will abdicate that role under local pressures. One example of how this has already unfolded can be seen in the fight after Sandy over the premiums for federal flood insurance and the mapping of flood zones. These rational changes caused a political firestorm at the local level, forcing the state and federal government to backpedal on both issues. Perhaps the reversals were good policy as well as good politics, but the controversy reveals how local pressures in New Jersey continue to impact state and national programs. If we expect that the planning to preserve and protect the New Jersey coastline will be anything other than short-term, the state government needs to take and maintain an active role. Local governments and politicians respond to their homeowners and seldom have the inclination or the resources to look beyond their boundaries. The state needs to recognize its role as the long-range planner, enforce its prerogatives, and demand that local governments review risk/reward analyses for future projects along the shore as they arise.

Politics and funding intertwine. Only the state and the federal governments have the necessary resources to protect and preserve the shore. The federal government has been the major funding source for dune building and beach nourishment over the last fifty years, through the U.S. Army Corps of Engineers. Several administrations (going back to President Clinton) have questioned the wisdom of continuing this program and recent pronouncements suggest that the funding may cease sometime in the next ten years. What will happen at the Jersey Shore if this source of funds dries up? Will state taxpayers pick up the tab going forward? If not, what policy will the state pursue to protect its beaches? The Bay Head homeowners have demonstrated that they have the willingness and the resources to protect their beaches and their properties, but will the public accept as effective public policy a return to local control of beach protection and access rights, a system that may lead to broad, beautiful beaches for the wealthiest and consign middle class and poor citizens to beaches ravaged by every storm?

Property rights and property development have always been part of the story of the Jersey Shore and should be respected. But property owners need to understand that the value of their property depends in large part on state and local efforts to maintain the environment in which it exists. The state has declared its authority over the beaches and access to the beaches. Can the state sustain that authority? The government's role in protecting beaches and beachfront properties, whether at the local or state level, is not an obligation, and all interested parties— property owners, fishermen, sportsmen, vacationers, business owners, and environmentalists—need to be heard as we move forward. As one observer put it before Sandy, in a discussion of how best to live at and with the shore: "The individual who builds or buys a home in a coastal area should fully comprehend the chance of harm to home and family. These risks should be weighed against the benefits to be derived from this location."[4]

Shifting attitudes about the environment and global warming will also impact these discussions. We do not need to settle here the speed of sea level rise or whether it is caused by global warming or whether global warming is the result of human activity. We know already that sea level rise has occurred throughout the 350 years of the state's history, is continuing, and has increased the impact of our most recent coastal storms. After Sandy, the local, state, and federal governments moved quickly to shore up the Mantoloking Bridge by driving a deeper and longer seawall to protect the bridge and its connecting roads. Few could disagree with this response even though most environmental experts believe seawalls to be harmful to the natural evolution of the shore. We can expect that the response of governments to immediate problems will not change significantly, but we should also expect an increased reliance on demands for mid-range and long-range planning efforts as the public awareness of environmental concerns increases. Reasoned environmentalists offer a nuanced approach suggesting that future projects factor in solutions that encompass the impacts of weather-related events and sea rise. They urge long-term strategies such as obtaining and preserving in a natural state as much of the beach as possible over the coming decades and discouraging new projects that will exacerbate flooding and property damage. We can also require builders and property owners to follow common sense proposals to make their projects more environmentally friendly and less vulnerable.

Just as we know that the factors discussed here will impact the future of the Jersey Shore, we should be alert to factors not currently in view. Advances in science and technology will play a role as we become more adept at developing structures to replace jetties, groins, and seawalls; as we find architectural and construction solutions that will better withstand wind and water; and as we monitor carefully the costs, successes, and failures of dune-building and sand nourishment efforts. We can anticipate some of the changes, but others will be unexpected or will have unexpected consequences, as did the railroad in the 1850s and the automobile in the 1900s. And what about offshore windmills? Are they in the Jersey Shore's future? Some advocates are pushing hard for this green technology. Windmill projects will surely pit environmentalists against tourism advocates, homeowners, and, perhaps, fishermen.[5] This prospect is already on the horizon. What consequences and debates can we expect as this industry advances?

Millions still rush to the Jersey Shore each summer to escape the heat and humidity inland and just for the fun of it all. They will not stop coming. The lure of the beach, the sand, the water and the waterways, the breezes, and the attractions are just too great. It would be foolish to try to predict the future of the Jersey Shore over the next fifty or one hundred years. Too many factors are in play. We will find ways to adapt to the changing geology and we will, hopefully, make the shore more available to all and not just for the well-to-do or politically connected. We must. We owe it to our children and grandchildren to preserve this treasure that we have enjoyed all our lives.

Acknowledgments

First and foremost, I want to thank the New Jersey Historical Commission for creating and funding ten volumes for New Jersey's 350th celebration. Any reason for pursuing New Jersey's rich history is worth the effort, even one named a Sesquarcentennial event. The commission's selection of my outline for a history of New Jersey's beach communities provided me with sufficient incentive and their funding made publication possible.

In this same regard, I want to thank Marlie Wasserman, the former Executive Director of Rutgers University Press, for informing me of the commission's request for book ideas and encouraging me to develop this topic for submission. The collaboration between Rutgers University Press and the commission to find, fund, edit, and publish ten new volumes on New Jersey history should be applauded by all of the state's citizens. Micah Kleit, Marlie's successor at the press, continues her encouragement and is bringing the project to fruition.

I want to thank the many reference librarians throughout the state who helped me find obscure laws, pamphlets, books, and other resources. To name any would be to leave out others, including those whose names I never gathered. Particular thanks to the professionals at the New Jersey State Library in Trenton, my home library in Hunterdon County, and to the proprietors of the New Jersey Maritime Museum in Beach Haven with its shipwreck database and extensive collection of materials on the United States Life Saving Service and the wreck of the *Morro Castle*. Director Deborah Whitcraft was as helpful and thorough as the museum's resources. Thanks as well to New Jersey Manufacturers Insurance Company for permission to use its hurricane map and to its officers, Robert Zetterstrom and Scott Markulec, for sharing their knowledge of recent and past storms and the devastating effect on beach communities and other regions throughout the state. I also want to thank the folks at the Garden State Seafood Association for the help provided to someone who knows little about fish and fishing, other than one or two disastrous overnight bluefish adventures.

I spoke with many friends along the way, most of whom have their own Jersey Shore stories and were eager to share them with me. Particularly, I want to thank Nick, Bob, Harvey, Dick, and Ed, each of whom provided a story or insight that made it into the book.

The maps included in this volume can be attributed to the fine work of Michael Siegel, staff cartographer with the Geography Department at Rutgers University. He advised me on where to find maps and what was possible and appropriate for the book. He then created or modified the maps you see in the book. I enjoyed our work together.

Dominick Mazzagetti
Whitehouse Station, NJ

Notes

CHAPTER 1

1. Robert Juet, *Journal* first mate, August 29 and September 3, 1609, from the 1625 edition of *Purchase His Pilgrimes*, transcribed by Brea Barthel for the New Netherland Museum, http://halfmoon.mus.ny.us/Juets-journal.pdf, 590–591. The earliest history of the Jersey Shore begins with the 1524 voyage of Giovanni da Verrazano, a Florentine sailing for France. Verrazano crossed the Atlantic with a single ship and reached the New World at Cape Fear. He sailed north along the Atlantic coast and entered the Raritan Bay at Sandy Hook. He saw the mouth of the Hudson River but did not venture up the river.

2. Norbert P. Psulty and Douglas D. Ofiara, *Coastal Hazard Management, Lessons and Future Directions from New Jersey* (New Brunswick, NJ: Rutgers University Press, 2002), 21.

3. Stockton University Coastal Research Center, "New Jersey Coastal Composition," http://stockton.edu/coastal-research-center/njbpn/geologic-hist.html.

4. Stockton University Coastal Research Center, "New Jersey Coastal Composition."

5. Ibid.

6. NJ Department of Environmental Protection, *The New Jersey Shore Protection Master Plan*, (issued in three volumes in October 1981), I-23–26, which can be found at http://dspace.njstatelib.org:8080/xmlui/handle/10929/21507.

7. Harold F. Wilson, *The Jersey Shore, A Social and Economic History of the Counties of Atlantic, Cape May, Monmouth and Ocean* (New York: Lewis Historical Publishing Co., Inc., 1953), I-20–22.

8. Ibid., I-27–29.

9. Ibid.

10. Stockton University Coastal Research Center, "NJ Shoreline Protection and Vulnerability." Compare this with the *1981 NJ Shore Protection Master Plan*, which includes a chart showing New Jersey's "developed" acreage at 47 percent (about average); its "protected" acreage along the shore at only 20 percent (much lower than its neighboring Atlantic coast states); and its undeveloped and unprotected acreage at 33 percent. See Chart I-C27, I- 59–61.

CHAPTER 2

1. William A. Whitehead, ed., *New Jersey Archives, First Series, Documents Relating to the Colonial History of New Jersey, 1631–1687*, (Newark, NJ: Daily Journal Establishment,1880), 1:205–219.

2. See John E. Pomfret, *Colonial New Jersey* (New York: Charles Schribner's Sons, 1973), for a thorough description of the limited Dutch authority before 1664 and the legal title and land transactions that concerned the English after 1664.

3. Whitehead, *New Jersey Archives*, "Instructions to Deputy Governor Lawrie," July 5, 1683, item 16, 1:431; and see Wilson, *The Jersey Shore*, 1:157–158.

4. William Nelson, ed., *New Jersey Archives, First Series, Documents Relating to the Colonial History of New Jersey: Newspaper Abstracts* (Paterson, NJ: 1894), 11:46, 62–63, 203, 12:125.

5. Wilson, *The Jersey Shore*, 1:163–165.

6. Whitehead, *New Jersey Archives*, 1:1–2. See the June 3, 1631, "Patent" issued by Peter Minuet to Godyn and Samuel Blomaert for sixteen square miles, from the "lawful owners, proprietors and inhabitants on the east side of Godyn's East bay, called Cape de Maye," the sellers being "Sawowouwe, Wynot, Pemhake" and seven other named natives.

7. William Penn to the Free Society of Traders, 1683, reprinted in Albert Cook Myers, ed., *Narratives of Early Pennsylvania, West New Jersey and Delaware, 1630–1707* (New York: Barnes & Noble, 1912), 265.

8. Richard M. Romm, "America's First Whaling Industry and the Whaler Yeoman of Cape May, 1630–1830," master's thesis, Rutgers, State University of New Jersey, 2010, 14–15.

9. Gabriel Thomas, "An Historical and Geographic Account of Pennsylvania and West-New Jersey, 1698," in Myers, *Narratives of Early Pennsylvania*, 352.

10. Jeffrey M. Dorwart, *Cape May County, New Jersey* (New Brunswick, NJ: Rutgers University Press, 2002), 14; and Paul Styrdevant Howe, *Mayflower Pilgrim Descendants in Cape May County, New Jersey, 1620–1920* (Cape May, NJ: Albert R. Hand, 1921).

11. John Bailey LLoyd, *Eighteen Miles of History on Long Beach Island* (Harvey Cedars, NJ: Down the Shore Press, 1994), 11–13.

12. Arthur D. Pierce, *Smugglers' Woods, Jaunts and Journeys in Colonial and Revolutionary New Jersey* (New Brunswick, NJ: Rutgers University Press, 1992), 9; and Col. Quarry to the Lords of Trade, June 6, 1699, in Whitehead, *New Jersey Archives*, 2:280–281. The Lords of Trade had earlier warned the proprietors that aid should not be given to the "many ill-minded persons, Seamen, and others" who had applied themselves to such "wicked and destructive courses," 134–136; and see Aaron Leaming and Jacob Spicer, *The Grants, Concessions and Original Constitutions of the Province of New Jersey, the Acts passed during the Proprietary Governments, and other material Transactions before the Surrender thereof to Queen Anne. The Instrument of Surrender, and her formal Acceptance thereof; Lord Cornbury's Commission and Instructions Consequent thereon,* originally published in 1881 and re-published in 2002 by The Lawbook Exchange, LTD., Union, NJ), 363–366, for "An Act for the Restraining and Punishing Privateers and Pirates," which includes a warning for anyone that would "knowingly entertain, harbor, conceal, trade, or hold any correspondence with any person or persons that shall be deemed or adjudged to be privateers, pirates or other offenders, within the construction of this act, and shall not readily endeavor to the best of his or their power to apprehend or cause to be apprehended such offender or offenders," that they will be prosecuted as well.

13. Governor Basse and others dutifully reported that Captain Kidd had arrived in Delaware Bay with sixty crewmen on June 9, 1699. See Whitehead, *New Jersey Archives*, 2:286–288.

14. See Daniel Diehl and Mark P. Donnelly, *Pirates of New Jersey* (Mechanicsburg, PA: Stackpole Books, 2010).

15. Sydney G. Fisher, *The Quaker Colonies: A Chronicle of the Proprietors of the Delaware* (New Haven, CT: Yale University Press, 1921), 196: "[For] a hundred years Jersey customs officers are said to have issued documents which were ostensibly letters of marque but which really abetted a piratical cruise. Piracy was, however, in those days a semilegitimate offense, winked at by the authorities all through the colonial period; and respectable people and governors and officials of New York and North Carolina, it is said, secretly furnished funds for such expeditions and were interested in the profits."

16. Pierce, *Smugglers' Woods*, 4–26.

17. Wilson, *Social and Economic History*, 1:150–151; and Pierce, *Smugglers' Woods*, 21–25.

18. Edgar Stanton Maclay, *A History of American Privateers* (New York: D. Appleton, 1899), viii–ix.

19. Such is the description of the American patriots given in the Report of Captain Ferguson, of the Seventieth Regiment, Little Egg Harbour, October 10,

1782. This report and a detailed description of the entire event can be found in William S. Stryker, "The Affair at Little Egg Harbor, New Jersey, October 15, 1778," (Trenton, NJ: Naar, Day and Naar, 1894), the reprint of a presentation at the July 3, 1894, dedication of a memorial tablet erected on the field of the massacre of Brigadier General Count Pulaski's men as the British flotilla withdrew.

CHAPTER 3

1. "Pastor Wrangel's Trip to the Shore," *Magazine of New Jersey History* (1969), 87:5–31.

2. The Native Americans at first disputed Hartshorne's claim to the land and continued to take plums, which grew wild along the hook. In August 1868,Hartshorne settled the dispute for the additional payment of thirteen shillings. George H Moss, Jr., *From Nauvoo to the Hook* (Locust, NJ: Jervey Close Press, 1904), 12–13; Price and Rose, *Atlas of the New Jersey Coast*, 16–17; and see the Richard Hartshorne Genealogical website, *Richard Hartshorn (1641–1722) and Six Generations of Descendants*, http://www.hartshorn.us/Family/Fam-B/b8083.htm.

3. *New York Mercury*, June 18, 1764. "On Monday Evening last, the New-York Light-House, erected at Sandy-Hook, was lighted for the first Time. The House is of an Octagon Figure, having eight equal Sides; the Diameter at the Base, 29 Feet; and at the Top of the Wall, 15 Feet; the Lanthorn is 7 Feet high; the Circumference 33 Feet. The whole Construction of the Lanthorn is Iron; the Top covered with Copper. There are 48 Oil Blazes. The Building from the Surface is Nine Stories; the whole from Bottom to Top, 103 Feet. This Structure, was undertaken by Mr. Isaac Conro, of this City, and was carried on with all the Expedition that the Difficulty attending to and fro on the Occasion could possibly admit of and is judged to be masterly finished." See William Nelson (ed.), *New Jersey Archives, First Series, Documents Relating to the Colonial History of the State of New Jersey* (Paterson, NJ: The Call Printing and Publishing Company, 1902), 24:380.

4. "About 135 of the enemy landed on Sunday last about 10 o'clock, on the south side of Squan inlet, burnt all the salt-works, broke the kettles, &c. stripped the beds, &c. of some people there, who I fear, wish'd to serve them—then crossed the river and burnt all excepting Dirrick Longstreet's: after this mischief they embarked. The next day they landed at Shark river and set fire to two small works, they observed fifteen horsemen heave in sight, which occasioned them to retreat with great precipitation, indeed they jumped in their flat-bottomed boats in such confusion that they sank one or two of them." Extract of a letter from Kildare, Monmouth County, April 9, 1778, in Francis B. Lee, ed., *New Jersey Archives, Second Series, Documents Relating to the Revolutionary History of the*

State of New Jersey (Trenton, NJ: The John L. Murphy Publishing Co., 1903), 2:170–171.

5. Thomas F. Gordon, *A Gazetteer of the State of New Jersey* (Daniel Fenton, 1834), 242–243.

6. More than 200 years later, the residents of Dover Township voted to officially change the name to Toms River to avoid confusion with Dover in Morris County and to acknowledge the public's perception of the area as "Toms River."

7. For a description of boarding house accommodations in the early 1800s, see Wilson, *The Jersey Shore*, 423–427.

8. Maria R. Audubon, *Audubon and His Journals* (New York: C. Scribner's Sons, 1897).

9. John Bailey Lloyd, *Eighteen Miles of History on Long Beach Island*, (Harvey Cedars, NJ: Down the Shore Press, 1994), 15–30.

10. See Nelson, *Documents*, 28:108.

11. *Aurora and General Advertiser*, Philadelphia, July 1, 1801.

12. Gordon, *Gazeteer*, 118–119.

13. As years passed, the inlet separating the island from the mainland filled in, but it became an island again in 1942 when a canal was dug at about the same point.

14. Diary of Fredericka Bremer, August 10, 1850, reprinted in Miriam V. Studley, *Historic New Jersey through Visitors' Eyes* (Princeton, NJ: D. Van Nostrand, 1964), 126–135; and, more recently, in Margaret Thomas Buccholz, *Shore Chronicles, Diaries and Travelers' Tales from the Jersey Shore* (Harvey Cedars, NJ: Down the Shore Publishing, 1999), 63–74.

15. See Writers Project, Work Projects Administration, *Entertaining a Nation, The Career of Long Branch* (Long Branch, NJ: American Guide Series, 1940), for a full description of the wrestling bout, at pp. 8–11.

16. A 1768 advertisement for property in Long Branch emphasized its value as farmland but also acknowledged its "cool air" and future possibilities. "It is very conveniently situated for any person that would take lodgers, or keep a tavern; or any gentleman that has an inclination for a summer seat on the seaside, where he will be troubled with no mosquitoes or other vermin, that renders most places, near the salts, disagreeable." See Nelson, *New Jersey Archives* (1916), 28:12–13.

17. Writers Project, *Entertaining a Nation*, 21. See also, Franklin Ellis, *History of Monmouth County, New Jersey* (Shrewsbury, NJ: Shrewsbury Historical Society, 1885), 755.

18. Ellis, *History of Monmouth County*, 757.

19. *New York Herald*, [undated], 1809. See a full rendering of this article in Writers Project, *Entertaining a Nation*, 21–23.

20. Gordon, *Gazeteer*, 170.

21. *Frank Leslie's Illustrated Newspaper*, August 22, 1857, as quoted in George H. Moss, Jr., *Another Look at Nauvoo to the Hook* (Sea Bright, NJ: Ploughshare Press, 1990).

CHAPTER 4

1. Cindy S. Aron, *Working at Play: A History of Vacations in the United States* (New York: Oxford University Press, 1999), 4–5, 32, 49, 54, and 186.

2. John Bachelder, *Popular Resorts, and How to Reach Them, Combining a Brief Description of the Principal Summer Retreats in the United States and the Routes of Travel Leading to Them* (Boston 1875), 13.

3. Susan Currell, *The March of Spare Time: The Problem and Promise of Leisure in the Great Depression* (Philadelphia: University of Pennsylvania Press, 2005), 13.

4. A letter to a Philadelphia newspaper by a visitor in August describes the problem: "In my last letter I said mosquitoes were numerous here. They have since become a plague and there is no peace in the place. Myriads of greenhead flies and clouds of gnats have been added to the mosquito pests since the rain of Friday and the prevailing hot west winds a day or so thereafter. Last week the place was crowded with visitors—now they are escaping the scourge as rapidly as possible. This house is now surrounded with bonfires, in the hope that the smoke therefrom will drive off the enemy. But even the smoke is a nuisance, for it is blinding and dirty." A. L. English, *History of Atlantic City* (Philadelphia, PA: Dickson and Gilling, 1884), 69–72.

5. "Atlantic City as a Winter Sanitarium, Its Geology, Climate and Isothermal Relations, and Its Sanitary Effect Upon Disease and Invalids," (Baltimore, MD: B. H. James and Co., 1881), 7 and 26–27. See also M. D. Boardman Reed, *The Climate of Atlantic City and Its Effects on Pulmonary Diseases* (Atlantic City, NJ), reprinted from *The Philadelphia Medical Times*, December 18, 1880; and B. A. Blundon, Sergeant Signal Service, U. S. A., "Atlantic City as a Winter Resort, Comprising Meteorological Statistics concerning Temperature, Humidity, Amount of Rainfall, etc.; Compiled from Official Reports and Local Observations of the United States Signal Service. Also the Sanitary and Social Features of Atlantic City; its Hotels and Other Attractions; Testimonials of Prominent Physicians as to the Value of the Climate; Suggestions to Invalids regarding Hygiene," (Philadelphia, PA: Lineweaver and Wallace, 1885).

6. William Nelson, *The New Jersey Coast in Three Centuries* (New York: The Lewis Publishing Company, 1902), 117.

7. *New York Times*, August 14, 1883.

8. See Bryant Simon, *Boardwalk of Dreams* (New York: Oxford University Press, 2004).

9. Writers Project, *Entertaining a Nation*, 46.

10. Legends of America, http://www.legendsofamerica.com/ks-facts.html.

11. Writers Project, *Entertaining a Nation*, 72.

12. George E. Thomas and Carl F. Doebley, *Cape May, Queen of the Seaside Resorts, Its History and Architecture* (Philadelphia: The Art Alliance Press, 1976 and Mid-Atlantic Center for the Arts, 1998), 36–39.

CHAPTER 5

1. John Fothergill, *An Account of the Life and Travels in the Work of the Ministry of John Fothergill* (London 1753), 134–135, January 1721.

2. Francis Asbury, *Journal of the Rev. Francis Asbury* (New York: Lane and Scott, 1852), 1:464.

3. Ibid., 2:3–4 (New York: N. Bangs and T. Mason, 1821), 1:3–4, 1786; 3:303–304 (New York: Lane and Scott, 1852).

4. Stanley B. Kimball, "Discovery: 'Nauvoo' Found in Seven States," https://www.lds.org/ensign/1973/04/discovery-nauvoo-found-in-seven-states?lang=eng#footnote2-03030_000_007: "Although direct evidence is thus far lacking, this Nauvoo was most likely the result of a missionary trip by Joseph Smith and Orson Pratt into Monmouth County from Philadelphia during January 1840. Joseph Smith reports succinctly, 'I left Philadelphia with Brother Orson Pratt, and visited a branch of the Church in Monmouth County, New Jersey, where I spent several days, and returned to Philadelphia.' . . . Perhaps they visited the Shrewsbury Branch, which had been organized at least by August 1839. This branch was less than eight miles from the fishing village. Some of the fisherfolk may have joined the Church and given the name to their area, or some may have simply heard the name and its meaning and applied it to their beautiful place by the sea." See also, Moss, *From Nauvoo to the Hook*, 83.

5. William Warren Sweet, *Methodists in American History* (Nashville, TN: Abington Press, 1953), 159–160.

6. Roger Finke and Rodney Stark, *The Churching of America, 1776–1990* (New Brunswick, NJ: Rutgers University Press, 1992), 96.

7. See the community's website, http://southseavillecampmeeting.org/history-of-the-camp/.

8. Edwin Salter, *Salter's History of Monmouth and Ocean Counties*, (1890), 406–409, https://archive.org/details/historyofmonmouoosalt.

9. See the NY/NJ Baykeeper, http://nynjbaykeeper.org/wp-content/uploads/2013/05/AtlanticHighlands_final.pdf; the official Atlantic Highlands website, http://www.ahnj.com/ahnj/About%20Atlantic%20Highlands/History/History%20of%20Atlantic%20Highlands/; and Paul D. Boyd, *Atlantic Highlands, From Lenape Camps to Bayside Town* (Charleston, SC: Arcadia Publishing Co., 2004), which suggests that the Atlantic Highlands Association did little to improve the town, which led, in part, to the collapse of the camp association, 119–121.

10. Sweet, *Methodists in American History*, 333.

11. The charter, as passed by the New Jersey Legislature and dated March 3, 1870, can be found in Morris S. Daniels, *The Story of Ocean Grove Related in the Year of its Golden Jubilee*, (New York: The Methodist Book Concern, 1919), 272–273.

12. Gustave Kobbé, *The New Jersey Coast and Pines* (Short Hills, NJ: DeLeeuw and Oppenheimer, 1889), p. 50.

13. Ibid.

14. City of Asbury Park v. New York & Long Branch Railroad Company and Central Railroad Company of New Jersey, Reports of the Board of Public Utility Commissioners (October 10, 1911); and see Daniels, *Story of Ocean Grove*, 179.

15. Daniels, *Story of Ocean Grove*, 200–201 and 202–207.

16. Wayne T. Bell, *Ocean Grove* (Charleston, SC: Arcadia Publishing, 2000), 58–59; and Christopher M. Flynn, *Greetings from Ocean Grove* (Atglen, PA: Schiffer Publishing, 2007), 22–23.

17. State v. Celmer, 80 N.J. 405, 416–417 (1979); emphasis added.

18. Interestingly, the New Jersey Supreme Court had the opportunity to reach this decision just two years earlier in a case involving the camp meeting's prohibition on delivering newspapers on Sunday and went out of its way to avoid the issue by characterizing the case as a restriction on free speech. Justice Morris Pashman, who wrote an impassioned dissent in Schaad v. Ocean Grove Camp Meeting Association, 72 N.J. 237 (1977), wrote the majority opinion in the *Celmer* case.

19. Bernstein v. Ocean Grove Camp Meeting Association, OAL Dkt. No. CRT 6145-09, Agency Dkt. No. PN34XB-03008 (N.J. Office of Administrative Law 2012).

20. 1874 New Jersey Session Laws, chapter 76, "An act to prevent the sale of intoxicating liquors within one mile of Ocean Grove and Asbury Park, in Monmouth County, New Jersey."

21. Nelson, *The New Jersey Coast*, 59.

22. See Daniel Wolff, *4th of July, Asbury Park: A History of the Promised Land* (New York: Bloomsbury Publishing, 2005), 31.

23. Kobbé, *The New Jersey Coast and Pines*, 46.

24. See *New York Times*, "Drawing the Color Line," July 19, 1885.

25. Nelson, *The New Jersey Coast*, 61

26. See "Asbury Park Baby Parade," *New York Times*, August 21, 1901, describing the "600 Tots" and 50,000 spectators.

27. *New York Times*, July 27, 1890, 10.

28. See Joseph G. Bilby and Harry Ziegler, *Asbury Park Reborn, Lost to Time and Restored to Glory* (Charleston, SC: History Press, 2012). The Tillie image, along with 125 other artifacts, was saved in 2004 by the preservationist group "Save Tillie" (formed for the purpose) when the Palace Amusements building was torn down. The image is on a 16–by-14, ten-ton slab of concrete taken from the wall. See James Lilliefords, *America's Boardwalks, From Coney Island to California* (New Brunswick, NJ: Rutgers University Press, 2006), 52–55.

29. MaryAnn Spoto, "Stella Maris Retreat Property in Long Branch for Sale as a Nature Preserve," *NJ Advance Media*, July 30, 2014, http://www.nj.com/monmouth /index.ssf/2014/07/stella_maris_retreat_property_in_long_branch_for_sale_-- _as_a_nature_preserve.html.

CHAPTER 6

1. John P. Snyder, *The Story of New Jersey's Civil Boundaries: 1606–1968* (Trenton, NJ: Bureau of Geology and Topography, 1969).

2. George Caitlin, *Homes of the Sea-Shore for New York Business Men* (New York: New Jersey Southern Railway Company, 1873).

3. Central Railroad of New Jersey, *Along the Shore and in the Foothills* (New York: Nature Press, 1910), 3.

4. Ibid., 28–32.

5. Kobbé states that lots purchased in Sea Bright in 1865 for $5 an acre were sold a short time later at $100 an acre, and by the time of his writing, 1889, for $7,000 an acre, *New Jersey Coast and Pines*, 17–18.

6. Andrew McCollough, *Highland Beach, New Jersey: A Jersey Shore Destination 1881–1962*, edited by Mary Rasa (Sandy Hook Gateway National Recreation Area National Park Service, 2005).

7. Kobbé, *New Jersey Coast and Pines*, 17–21.

8. Nelson, *The New Jersey Coast*, 46–48.

9. Caitlin, *Homes of the Sea-Shore*, 13.

10. Nelson, *The New Jersey Coast*, 53.

11. See the New Jersey Scuba Diving website: http://njscuba.net/sites/site_allen hurst_jetty.php. See also http://www.aquaexplorers.com/beachdivingallenhurst .htm#.VwFmco-cHIU.

12. See Nelson, *The New Jersey Coast*, 57, for a discussion of the nineteenth-century tradition. For the twentieth-century tradition, see Steven Falk, "Allen-hurst Beach Club Dyes Ocean Green in Annual Tradition," *Asbury Park Press*, August 31, 2014, http://www.app.com/story/news/local/eatontown-asbury-park /allenhurst/2014/08/31/allenhurst-beach-club-dyes-ocean-green/14910945/; and Lisa Rose, "Jersey Shore Town Preps to Dye Ocean Green for Labor Day and Bid Farewell to Historic Lagoon," New Jersey Advance Media, August 31, 2014, http://www.nj.com/monmouth/index.ssf/2014/08/allenhurst_preps_to_dye _the_ocean_green_for_labor_day_and_bid_farewell_to_historic_lagoon.html.

13. An undated town booster book (probably written around 1900) claims that the name "Avone" came from a long-lost Viking village established in 1027. See James Thomas Gagen, *History of Avon-by-the-Sea* (Avon Journal)

14. Kobbé, *New Jersey Coast and Pines*, 53.

15. Nelson, *The New Jersey Coast*, 94–95.

16. Kobbé, *New Jersey Coast and Pines*, 56.

CHAPTER 7

1. William K., Stevens, "188 Years After Sinking, H.M.S. Debraak is Raised," *New York Times*, August 12, 1986; and see New Jersey Maritime Museum, Beach Haven, New Jersey, Shipwreck Archive, Folder #15.

2. Erin O'Neill, "Debris Found at Brick NJ Worksite Believed To Be From 1850 Shipwreck," http://newyork.cbslocal.com/2014/11/03/debris-found-at-brick -n-j-work-site-believed-to-be-from-1850-shipwreck/; Dan Radel, "Shipwreck Uncovered on Brick Beach," *Asbury Park Press*, November 6, 2014; MaryAnn Spoto, "Possible Shipwreck Found on Jersey Shore by Crew Installing Steel Wall," *nj.com*, November 14, 2014, http://www.nj.com/ocean/index.ssf/2014/11 /post_3.html.

3. Robert D. McFadden, "Coast Guard Rescues 37 Russians from a Stricken Ves-sel Off Jersey," *New York Times*, March 15, 1987; and "President Will Greet Res-cued Soviet Crew," *New York Times*, March 16, 1987.

4. See the Prologue to Gordon Thomas and Max Morgan Witts, *Shipwreck: The Strange Fate of the Morro Castle* (New York: Stein & Day, 1972).

5. Charles J. Peterson, *Kate Aylesford: A Story of the Refugees* (T. B. Peterson, 1855); reissued as *The Heiress of Sweetwater: A Love Story* (T.B. Peterson & Brothers, 1873) and most recently as *Kate Aylesford or, The Heiress of Sweetwater* (Medford, NJ: Plexus Publishing, 2001).

6. Maria Snethen, *A Chilling Narrative: Shipwreck and Suffering of Mrs. Maria Snethen, Who Was Wrecked on Absecum Beach* (Boston, 1853). See pages 38–39 for the quote at the beginning of the chapter.

7. Leaming and Spicer, *The Grants, Concessions and Original Constitutions of the Province of New Jersey*, 37–38.

8. "An Act concerning wrecks," passed May 31, 1799, *Laws of the State of New Jersey* (Paterson's Laws, 1800).

9. Anonymous, 1828, reprinted in Buccholz, *Shore Chronicles*, 44–51.

10. Buccholz, *New Jersey Shipwrecks, 350 Years in the Graveyard of the Atlantic* (Harvey Cedars, NJ: Down the Shore Publishing, 2004), 21.

11. "An Act concerning wrecks."

12. Alan A. Siegel, *Disaster! Stories of Death and Destruction in Nineteenth-Century New Jersey* (New Brunswick, NJ: Rutgers University Press, 2014), 96–97.

13. 9 Stat. L. 322.

14. 20 Stat. L. 163–165.

15. See the U.S. Life-Saving Heritage Association website, http://uslife-saving service.org/station/stations-for-sale/.

16. 38 Stat. 800–802 (January 28, 1915).

17. See Price and Rose, *Atlas of the New Jersey Coast*, 17; "The Sandy Hook Lighthouse During the American Revolution," in the Keeper's Log of the U.S. Lighthouse Society (Spring 1995), https://uslhs.org/sites/default/files/articles _pdf/sandy_hook_v11_num03.pdf; and Revolutionary War New Jersey, http:// www.revolutionarywarnewjersey.com/new_jersey_revolutionary_war_sites /towns/sandy_hook_nj_revolutionary_war_sites.htm.

CHAPTER 8

1. Kobbé, *New Jersey Coast and Pines*, 58.

2. Nelson, *New Jersey Coast in Three Centuries*, 97.

3. Kobbé, *New Jersey Coast and Pines*, 59. Curiously, the same story is attributed to Long Beach Island in George B. Somerville's *The Lure of Long Beach*, 73–74: "During the war of the Rebellion an English vessel came ashore at Barnegat, and the only survivor of this wreck was a cat with short front legs, long hind legs and no tail . . . a distinct 'breed of cats' from the Isle of Man, off the English coast. Although frequently crossed with the common and well known variety, several good specimens of these Manx cats, with 'gait like a rabbit and a hopping lope,' are still to be found on Long Beach."

4. Kobbé, *New Jersey Coast and Pines*, 62.

5. William C. Ulyat, *Life at the Sea Shore* (New York: McGuiness and Runyan, 1880), 154.

6. Seaside Heights website, http://www.discoverseasideheights.com/history /seaside-heights-carousel. It is now known as the Dr. Floyd L. Moreland/Dentzel Looft Carousel. See Jean Mikle, "Seaside Heights now owns its historic carousel," *Asbury Park Press*, September 20, 2017.

7. John T. Ward, "The Spies of Loveladies," *New Jersey Monthly*, July 2005, 81.

8. See Buy LBI, http://www.buylbi.com/loveladies-nj-and-the-lbi-nj-real-estate -market.html.

9. Ralph E. Eshelman and Patricia A. Russell, "Historic Context Study of Waterfowl Hunting Camps and Related Properties within Assateague Island National Seashore, Maryland and Virginia" (National Park Service, 2004), 8. Kobbé goes out of his way to extol the virtues of fishing and gunning in Barnegat Bay: "Barnegat Bay is all sport. In summer, hundreds of little vessels scud over its waters to the fishing-grounds near the inlet; and of the early mornings in winter, the figures of gunners may be seen dimly outlined against the gray horizon as they row their sneak-boxes out of the creeks toward some sedgy point or island," *New Jersey Coast and Pines*, 64.

10. U.S. Life-Saving Service Heritage Association website, http://uslife-saving service.org/station/stations-for-sale/.

CHAPTER 9

1. Larry Savadove and Margaret Thomas Buccholz, *Great Storms of the Jersey Shore* (Harvey Cedars, NJ: Down the Shore Publishing, 1993), 137.

2. *Baltimore Sun*, November 11, 1878.

3. This same event occurred again two years later, on a slightly smaller scale. A tug hauling a decommissioned minesweeper ran into a storm and both vessels ended up on the beach at Holgate.

4. Norbert P. Psulty and Douglas D. Ofiara, *Coastal Hazard Management, Lessons and Future Directions from New Jersey* (New Brunswick, NJ: Rutgers University Press, 2002), 178.

5. Ludlum, *The New Jersey Weather Book* (New Brunswick, NJ: Rutgers University Press, 1983), 92.

6. Population growth from 1960 to 1980: Monmouth Beach (1363 to 3318); Sea Girt (1798 to 2650); Spring Lake (2922 to 4215); Lavallette (419 to 2910); Surf City (419 to 1427); Long Beach Township (1561 to 3488); Brigantine (4201 to 8318); Ocean City (7618 to 13,949); Sea Isle City (1393 to 2644); Avalon (695 to 2162). U.S. Census Bureau.

7. Spiegle v. Borough of Beach Haven, 46 NJ 479 (1966).

8. New Jersey Department of Environmental Protection, *New Jersey Shore Protection Master Plan*, I-1.

9. See the website uboat.net for a full listing of the ships hit and sunk by *U-151* during its career, http://uboat.net/wwi/boats/successes/u151.html.

10. See William Bell Clark, *When the U-Boats Came to America* (Boston, MA: Little Brown and Company, 1929), for a full account of the six boats sent to the United States at the beginning of World War I.

11. Robert Kerson, *Shadow Divers: The True Adventure of Two Americans Who Risked Everything to Solve One of the Last Mysteries of World War II* (New York: Random House, 2004).

CHAPTER 10

1. John T. Cunningham and Kenneth D. Cole, *Atlantic City* (Charleston, SC: Arcadia Publishing, 2000),Introduction.

2. "Bootleggers and Rum Runners on the Mullica River," undated newspaper account, http://bassriverhistory.blogspot.com/2010/12/bootleggers-and-rum-runners-on-great.html.

3. *New York Times*, June 17, 1923, 20.

CHAPTER 11

1. See New Jersey Fishing and Aquaculture, "Harvesting the Garden State's Waters," website of the New Jersey Seafood Association, http://www.jerseyseafood.nj.gov/seafoodreport.pdf: "All told, the industry brings in $4.5 billion annually from fisheries, aquaculture and recreational fishing. This is part of a $50 billion-a-year 'Coastal Zone' sector of the state's economy, which employs one out of every six people working in New Jersey. The seafood industry's jobs aren't limited to the nearly 3,000 fishermen on the boats. Thousands of people work in the state's seafood processing plants and wholesalers. Their wages, in turn, keep afloat a variety of businesses from which they buy goods and services." See the NOAA Fisheries, http://www.nmfs.noaa.gov/mediacenter/2013/03/07_noaa_report_finds_commercial_and_recreational.html.

2. Price and Rose, *Atlas of the New Jersey Coast*, 63; Wilson, *The Jersey Shore*, 154–155.

3. Wilson, *The Jersey Shore*, 753–762.

4. NOAA Fisheries, "Community Profiles" for Port Norris, http://www.nefsc.noaa.gov/read/socialsci/communityProfiles.html.

5. Kobbé, *New Jersey Coast and Pines*, 18–21.

6. Peter J. Guthorn, "Pound Fisheries and Pound Boats," File #49 (Beach Haven, NJ: New Jersey Maritime Museum); and Wilson, *The Jersey Shore,* 949–952.

7. Point Pleasant Historical Society, http://pointpleasanthistory.com/time_loveland.htm.

8. National Marine Fisheries Service, "Commercial Fishing Statistics," https://www.st.nmfs.noaa.gov/st1/commercial/landings/annual_landings.html.

9. U.S. Bureau of Labor Statistics, "Fatal Occupational Injuries, Employment, and Rates of Fatal Occupational Injuries by Selected Worker Characteristics, Occupations, and Industries, 2007," http://www.bls.gov/iif/oshwc/cfoi/cfoi_rates_2007.pdf; and Ronnie Greene, "Fishing Deaths Mount, But Government Slow to Cast Safety Net for Deadliest Industry," Center for Public Integrity, August 22, 2012, https://www.publicintegrity.org/2012/08/22/10721/fishing-deaths-mount-government-slow-cast-safety-net-deadliest-industry. Amy Ellis Nutt, "The Wreck of the Lady Mary," *Star Ledger*, November 21–24, chapter 3, http://www.nj.com/news/index.ssf/2010/11/the_wreck_of_the_lady_mary_cha.html.

10. Douglas A. Campbell, *The Sea's Bitter Harvest* (New York, NY: Carroll and Graf Publishers, 2002).

11. Nutt, "The Wreck of the Lady Mary."

12. NOAA Fisheries website, "Community Profile" for Barnegat light, http://www.nefsc.noaa.gov/read/socialsci/pdf/NJ/barnegetlight-nj.pdf.

13. Wilson, 946–947.

14. New Jersey Division of Fish and Wildlife, http://www.state.nj.us/dep/fgw/gsft.htm.

15. Wilson, *The Jersey Shore*, 948.

16. See George R. Petty, Jr., and Barbara E. Petty, "Ocean County History of Historic Boats," Ocean County Cultural and Heritage Commission (October 31, 1983); and, Peter Guthorn, *The Sea Bright Skiff and Other Shore Boats* (Atglen, PA: Schiffer Publishing Company, 1982).

17. New Jersey Motor Vehicle Commission, https://www.dmv.org/nj-new-jersey/boat-registration.php,

18. A story in the *New York Times* at his death in 1914 mentioned that Oelrichs's "reward was never claimed." See Michael Capuzzo, *Close to the Shore, The Terrifying Shark Attacks of 1916* (New York: Crown Publishers, 2003), 4–7; and, The *New York Times*, August 2, 1915.

CHAPTER 12

1. Listen to the "On Jersey Shore March" at the Library of Congress website, written and recorded in 1904 by Arthur Proctor, at http://www.loc.gov/jukebox/recordings/detail/id/566.

2. See the comments of Irish novelist James Hamay, quoted in Buchholz, *Shore Chronicles*, 214–219.

3. Wilson, *Jersey Shore*, 916–917.

4. Ibid., 549.

5. *New York Times*, "Crowds at Atlantic City," March 30, 1902.

6. *New York Times*, "Asbury Park Baby Parade, More than 600 Tots Delight 50,000 Spectators," August 21, 1901. To see a six-minute video of the 1904 Baby Parade shot by Thomas Edison, visit the Library of Congress at https://www.loc .gov/item/mp73003100/.

7. See Harold F. Wilson, *The Story of the Jersey Shore* (Princeton, NJ: D. Van-Nostrand and Co., 1965), 61.

8. See Michael "Skip" Fowler, Bernard A. Olsen, and Edward Olsen, *Lifeguards of the New Jersey Shore* (Atglen, PA: Schiffer Books, 2010), 29–42.

9. "Life Saver Rewarded with a Fortune," *New York Times*, July 27, 1900.

10. New Jersey has averaged about one death by drowning each year. See the American Lifeguard Rescue and Drowning Statistics for Beaches, http://www .usla.org/?page=STATISTICS.

11. See Wilson, I-523, *The Jersey Shore*.

12. For a detailed history of the Deauville Inn, see "History and Memories of Strathmere," http://www.strathmere.net/deauville.html.

13. See the New Jersey Audubon Society website at http://www.njaudubon.org /SectionCapeMayBirdObservatory/CMBOHome.aspx.

14. *Appleton's Illustrated Handbook of American Summer Resorts Illustrated Handbook of American Summer Resorts*,(New York, NY: D. Appleton and Co., 1893), 7.

15. Stephanie M. Hoagland, "The Rise, Fall & Resurrection of Wildwood's Doo Wop Motels," June 2013, http://gardenstatelegacy.com/files/The_Rise_Fall _Resurrection_of_Wildwoods_DooWop_Motels_Hoagland_GSL20.pdf.

CHAPTER 13

1. Writers Project, *Entertaining a Nation*, 119–120.

2. See Charles A. Stansfield, Jr., *Geography of New Jersey* (New Brunswick, NJ: Rutgers University Press, 1998), 166; 1920 was the highest year for passenger rail-road mileage in the United States and the highest year for track mileage in New Jersey.

3. Susan Curell, *The March of Spare Time, The Problem and Promise of Leisure in the Great Depression* (Philadelphia: University of Pennsylvania Press, 2010), 13.

4. Bianculli, *Iron Rails in the Garden State*, 50–52.

5. See John E. Bebout and Joseph Harrison, "The Working of the New Jersey Constitution of 1947," *William & Mary Law Review* 10, no. 4 (1968): 337–354.

6. By Karen Wall, "730 Days Later, It's Still Day Zero for Camp Osborn Man Left Homeless by Sandy," *The Patch*, October 29, 2015, http://patch.com/new -jersey/brick/730-days-later-its-still-day-zero-camp-osborn-man-left-homeless -sandy-o; Amanda Oglesby, "Brick OKs Camp Osborn Redevelopment," *Asbury Park Press*, October 1, 2015, http://www.app.com/story/news/local/brick-point -pleasant/brick/2015/10/01/camp-osborn/73130254/.

7. The 1970 lottery vote was 1,593,239 in favor, 362,947 against; the first casino gambling vote in 1974 was 790,777 in favor and 1,202,638 against; the 1976 restricted casino gambling vote was 1,535,249 in favor and 1,180,799 against. See the New Jersey Secretary of State Election Results, http://www.state.nj.us/state/elections/. In 2016, New Jersey voters overwhelmingly rejected the expansion of casino gambling outside of Atlantic City.

8. See the discussion in Jeffrey M. Dowart, *Cape May County, New Jersey* (New Brunswick, NJ: Rutgers University Press, 2002), 175.

9. "Drawing the Color Line," *New York Times*, July 19, 1885.

10. See Dowart, *Cape May*, 172–175, for a description of the campaign by the *Cape May Herald* "to remove African-American residents from Cape May City" that led to the founding of Whitesboro.

11. Simon, *Boardwalk of Dreams*.

CHAPTER 14

1. *Shore & Beach* 82, no. 3 (Fall 2014): 20–21, available on the Stockton University Coastal Research Center website, http://intraweb.stockton.edu/eyos/page .cfm?siteID=149&pageID=160.

2. Arnold v. Mundy, 6. N.J.L. 53 (E & A 1821).

3. 61 N.J. 296 (1972).

4. Lusardi v. Curtis Point Property Owners, 86 N.J. 217 (1981). See also, Van-Ness v. Borough of Deal, 78 N.J. 174 (1978).

5. Matthews v. Bay Head Improvement Association, 95 N.J. 306, cert. denied, 469 U.S. 821 (1984).

6. Ibid., 323–324.

7. Ibid., 333.

8. Raleigh Avenue Beach Association v. Atlantis Beach Club, Inc., 185 N.J. 40 (2005).

9. Avalon v. New Jersey DEP, 403 N.J.S. 590 (November 19, 2008).

10. Harvey Cedars v. Karan, 425 N.J.S. 155 (App. Div. 2012).

11. Ibid., 156.

12. Mary Ann Spoto, "Two N.J. Shore Towns Stand Divided over New Seawall," March 10, 2013, *NJ Advance Media*, http://www.nj.com/ocean/index.ssf/2013/03

/mantoloking_bay_head_sandy.html; and Laura Poppick, "How Long-Forgotten Seawall Fended Off Sandy," livescience.com, July 18, 2013, http://www.livescience .com/38291-old-seawall-stopped-sandy.html.

13. Wayne Parry, "Battle over Dunes Is Just Getting Started," *Star Ledger*, January 7, 2016, 10; Jenkinson's reached a settlement with the State of New Jersey in July 2017, see MaryAnn Spoto, "Jenkinson's Reaches Settlement with State over Dune Project," *Star Ledger*, July 19, 2017, 3.

14. Josh Dawsy, "Building Dunes at Jersey Shore Stirs New Storm After Sandy, *Wall Street Journal*, December 23, 2014, A15; and, Jean Mikle, "Judge Rules Against Bay Head Homeowners in Dune Case," app.com, August 17, 2017, http:// www.app.com/story/news/local/ocean-county/sandy-recovery/2017/08/17/judge -rules-against-bay-head-homeowners-dune-case/575830001/; Jenkinson's settled its lawsuit just a month earlier by agreeing to build a steel seawall on its beachfront property. See Andrew J. Goudsward, "Jenkinson's Settled Dune Construction Lawsuit; Agrees to Build Seawall," app.com, July 19, 2017, http://www .app.com/story/news/local/brick-point-pleasant/point-pleasant-beach/2017/07 /19/jenkinsons-settles-dune-construction-lawsuit-agrees-build-seawall /489655001/

15. MaryAnn Spoto, "Private Beaches Used for Dunes Would Be Public," *Star Ledger*, February 16, 2016, 15.

16. See a detailed discussion of this debate in Diane Bates, *Superstorm Sandy, The Inevitable Destruction and Reconstruction of the Jersey Shore* (New Brunswick, NJ: Rutgers University Press, 2016), including statistics about the impact of tourism on New Jersey's economy.

17. See Nelson, *New Jersey Coast in Three Centuries*, 55.

18. W. Mack Angas, "Beach Erosion Control on the New Jersey Coast," Report to the Department of Conservation and Economic Development (September 1956), 6.

19. C. F. Wicker, "Problems of the New Jersey Beaches," Report to the New Jersey Department of Conservation and Economic Development (1965), 12. The quote at the beginning of the chapter from this report can be found on page 7.

20. *New Jersey Shore Protection Master Plan*, I-1.

21. Ibid., I-54.

22. "The economic and social importance of the coast is shown by the fact that in 1978 the Atlantic coast communities contained only 5.65 percent of the State's estimated population, but accounted for 8.4 percent of the State equalized value of real property. The population density for the oceanfront communities from Sandy Hook to Cape May Point (Reaches 2-14) was estimated at 1,480 persons per square mile, as compared to the State average of 980 persons per square mile.

The impact and importance of tourism on the coastal communities is reflected in the presence of several significant seasonally-based socio-economic indicators. These include significant seasonal population and seasonal employment fluctuations, and a sizeable seasonal housing component." Ibid., I-59.

23. Ibid., II-41.

24. See Psulty and Ofiara, *Coastal Hazard Management*, 158–161.

25. "Coast with the Most: N.J. Leads U.S. in Beach Projects," *Press of Atlantic City*, January 2, 2015, http://www.pressofatlanticcity.com/communities/atlantic -city_pleasantville_brigantine/coast-with-the-most-n-j-leads-u-s-in/article _0f9c63fa-91f6-11e4-9dca-af7bed3d3659.html.

26. See "New Jersey Shoreline Protection and Vulnerability," http://intraweb .stockton.edu/eyos/page.cfm?siteID=149&pageID=4; Realty Transfer Fee allocation is codified as N.J.S.A 46:15–18.

27. See the National Association of Insurance Commissioners (NOAC) summary of the act, file:///C:/Users/Owner/Documents/NEW%20JERSEY%20SHORE /Biggert-Waters%20Flood%20Ins%202012.pdf. See Greg Hanscom, "Flood pressure: Climate Disasters Drown FEMA's Insurance Plans," January 13, 2014, GRIST, http://grist.org/cities/flood-pressure-how-climate-disasters-put-femas-flood -insurance-program-underwater/; and Jennifer Ludden, "Debate Over Rebuilding Beaches Post-Sandy Creates Waves," on National Public Radio Morning Edition (January 30, 2013, 8:01 AM ET), http://www.npr.org/2013/01/30/170301306 /debate-over-rebuilding-beaches-post-sandy-creates-waves. For a detailed deconstruction of government policies in this arena, see Chris Edwards, "The Federal Emergency Management Agency: Floods, Failures, and Federalism," December 1, 2014, http://www.downsizinggovernment.org/dhs/fema#_ednref240.

28. U.S. Fish and Wildlife Service Coastal Barrier Resources System, http:// www.fws.gov/ecological-services/habitat-conservation/cbra/Maps/index .html, and the New Jersey map, http://www.fws.gov/ecological-services/habitat -conservation/cbra/maps/Locator/NJ.pdf.

29. Stockton University Coastal Research Center, http://intraweb.stockton.edu /eyos/page.cfm?siteID=149&pageID=1.

30. Daniel A. Barone, Kimberly K. McKenna, and Stewart C. Farrell, "Hurricane Sandy: Beach-Dune Performance at New Jersey Beach Profile Network sites," November 2, 2014, 22, http://intraweb.stockton.edu/eyos/extaffairs/content /docs/CoastalResearchCenterArticle.pdf.

31. See http://rucool.marine.rutgers.edu/, http://marine.rutgers.edu/rumfs/, http://hsrl.rutgers.edu/.

32. Jacques Cousteau National Estuarine Research Reserve, http://jcnerr.org /index.html.

33. See "How Rutgers Oceanographers Got Data from Below Superstorm Sandy," Autonomous Undersea Vehicle Applications Center, http://auvac.org /community-information/community-news/view/1853.

34. NOAA Fisheries, http://www.nefsc.noaa.gov/nefsc/SandyHook.

35. George E. Thomas and Carl E. Doebley, *Cape May, Queen of the Seaside Resorts*, 207.

36. Ibid., 207–223.

37. Charles V. Bagli, "Reviving a Seaside Resort," *New York Times*, September 30, 2007, http://www.nytimes.com/2007/09/30/nyregion/nyregionspecial2 /30njlong.html?pagewanted=print&_r=0.

38. Ibid., and Antoinette Martin, "Where Leasing Beats Selling," *New York Times*, March 16, 2008. As to awards, Pier Village received the 2006 Project of the Year Award and designation as a "Great Neighborhood" in 2012 by the Urban Land Institute, http://nnj.uli.org/wp-content/uploads/sites/37/2012/07/Recipients -2006.pdf, and http://nnj.uli.org/uncategorized/pier-village-recognized-as-a-great -neighborhood-in-new-jersey/.

39. Nick Paumgarten, "The Death and Life of Atlantic City," *New Yorker*, September 7, 2015, 56–67.

40. Jeff Goldman, "Shuttered Revel could reopen by May," *The Star Ledger*, December 12, 2017.

41. One newspaper article tells of flood insurance premiums going from $598 annually to $33,000 even though the homeowner raised the house three feet, all due to a flood zone designation: Erin O'Neill, "Union Beach Couple Gets $33K Flood Insurance Bill after Raising Home Above New Federal Standards," *NJ Advance Media*, July 27, 2014, http://www.nj.com/monmouth/index.ssf/2014/07 /union_beach_homeowners_get_33k_flood_insurance_bill_after_raising _home_above_new_federal_requirement.html.

42. FEMA Fact Sheet, "Homeowner Flood Insurance Affordability Act of 2014," http://www.fema.gov/media-library-data/1414004070850-3e90be61f97625 23126c385a1d7fa95a/FEMA_HFIAA_OctoberBulletinFS_100814.pdf.

43. Romy Varghese, "Springsteen Girls Priced Out as Rich Buy N.J. Shore Homes," BloombergBusiness, November 10, 2014, http://www.bloomberg.com /news/articles/2014-11-10/springsteen-girls-priced-out-as-rich-buy-n-j-shore -homes; Josh Daniels, "Sandy's Legacy: Higher Home Prices," *Wall Street Journal*, October 28, 2013; and see Bates, *Superstorm Sandy*, 69–75, and Karen M. O'Neill and Daniel J. Van Abs, eds., *Taking Chances: The Coast After Hurricane Sandy* (New Brunswick, NJ: Rutgers University Press, 2016), 205–217.

THE FUTURE OF THE JERSEY SHORE

1. Stockton University Coastal Research Center, "Shoreline Protection and Vulnerability." See the chart from J. G. Titus, D. E. Hudgens, and D. L. Trescott, et al., "State and Local Governments Plan for Development of Most Land Vulnerable to Rising Sea Level along the US Atlantic Coast," at IOP Publishing (Environ. Res. Lett. 4 (2009) 044008), http://risingsea.net/ERL/plans-for-developing-land-vulnerable-to-sea-level-rise.pdf.

2. Orrin H. Pilkey, "We Need to Retreat from the Beach," posted in *Articles & Dossiers, Sandy Storm, Sea Level Rise*, November 15, 2012, http://coastalcare.org/2012/11/we-need-to-retreat-from-the-beach/; Joe Romm, "How Your Taxes Help Inflate the Value of Coastal Properties Threatened By Climate Change," June 4, 2015, ThinkProgress, http://thinkprogress.org/climate/2015/06/04/3655491/peak-sand-coastal-property-bubble/; and O'Neill and Van Abs, *Taking Chances*, 6–8.

3. Dylan E. McNamara, Sathya Gopalakrishnan, Martin D. Smith, and A. Brad Murray, "Climate Adaptation and Policy-Induced Inflation of Coastal Property Value," *PLOS*, March 25, 2015, http://journals.plos.org/plosone/article?id=10.1371%2Fjournal.pone.0121278.

4. K. F. Nordstrom, P. A. Garès, N. P. Psulty, O. H. Pilkey, Jr., W. J. Neal, and O. H. Pilkey, Sr., *Living with the New Jersey Shore* (Durham, NC: Duke University Press, 1986).

5. Eltman, Frank, "Fishing Groups in Four States Seek Atlantic Wind Farm Delay," *Star-Ledger*, December 9, 2016, 2.

Index

DOMINICK MAZZAGETTI is the author of *Charles Lee: Self Before Country* (Rutgers University Press), which received an Honorable Mention for the American Revolution Round Table of Richmond's 2014 Book Award. Mazzagetti is a lawyer and banker with a fervent interest in American history. He has served as law secretary to the chief justice of the New Jersey Supreme Court, and was Deputy and Acting Commissioner of Banking in the administration of New Jersey Governor Tom Kean.